THE NONPROFIT ALMANAC

THE NONPROFIT ALMANAC

NINTH EDITION

The Essential Facts and Figures for Managers, Researchers, and Volunteers

Brice S. McKeever
Nathan E. Dietz
Saunji D. Fyffe

Copublished with
THE URBAN INSTITUTE PRESS
ROWMAN & LITTLEFIELD
Lanham • Boulder • New York • London

Copublished with the Urban Institute Press

Published by Rowman & Littlefield
A wholly owned subsidiary of The Rowman & Littlefield Publishing Group, Inc.
4501 Forbes Boulevard, Suite 200, Lanham, Maryland 20706
www.rowman.com

Unit A, Whitacre Mews, 26-34 Stannary Street, London SE11 4AB

ISBN: 978-1-4422-7592-8 (cloth : alk. paper)
ISBN: 978-1-4422-7593-5 (pbk. : alk. paper)
ISBN: 978-1-4422-7594-2 (electronic)
ISSN: 1949-8187

∞™ The paper used in this publication meets the minimum requirements of American National Standard for Information Sciences—Permanence of Paper for Printed Library Materials, ANSI/NISO Z39.48-1992.

Printed in the United States of America

Contents

Figures

Tables

Foreword

The year 2016 marks the twentieth anniversary of the Center on Nonprofits and Philanthropy's efforts to define and advance high-quality research and analyses to inform decision-making by nonprofit organizations, foundations and government. With this commemorative publication of *The Nonprofit Almanac*, we would like to acknowledge and express our gratitude to the visionaries who made major investments of time, energy, financial resources, and intellectual expertise to establish the Center and support its development.

The Center's success over these past two decades is the result of the contributions of the extraordinary researchers, advisors, funders, interns, emerging scholars, and collaborators who have worked with and through the Center and the many academics who use our National Center for Charitable Statistics (NCCS) data in their scholarship.

The prime movers were Joel Fleishman, then president of Atlantic Philanthropic Service Company, Inc., and Harvey Dale, then president and CEO of the Atlantic Philanthropies. Joel had the foresight to understand the importance of constructing a data infrastructure for the nonprofit sector, the courage to provide long-term developmental funding, and the stamina to help us make the case for matching funds to sustain it over the long term. Harvey tirelessly supported the Center's efforts and served on the Center's advisory committee for ten years, sharing his deep knowledge and expertise. Under their leadership, the Atlantic Philanthropies provided the initial five-year operating grant in 1996 and a $10 million challenge grant in 2001 to develop and maintain a robust, widely accessible, and sustainable research data system.

Many funders, too many to mention here, provided resources to enable the Center to match the Atlantic Philanthropies challenge grants. We are grateful for their investment in our work and for those who provided project and ongoing operating funds over the years, especially long-term supporters of our data efforts, the Charles Stewart Mott Foundation, and the Bill and Melinda Gates Foundation.

Senior Fellow C. Eugene Steuerle was instrumental in the formation of the Center and has been a creative force and a valued colleague through the years. Virginia Hodgkinson, former vice president for research at Independent Sector, helped move NCCS from the Independent Sector to join the Center at the Urban Institute, generously providing her good counsel throughout the transition and as a member of the advisory committee for ten years. *The Nonprofit Almanac* was initiated when NCCS was at Independent Sector and was copublished with Independent Sector in 2002. Tom Pollak, who came from Independent Sector with NCCS, led its activities and oversaw its growth for many years. In addition, the Center benefited from the efforts of Bill Levis, founder of NCCS, who worked tirelessly on a variety of data projects with the Center for most of its 20 years.

During its first 20 years, the Center has demonstrated that data and research along with dialogue and sustained communications can play a central role in promoting better practices and policies in the nonprofit sector. As a credible, nonpartisan, and accessible source of information, the Center helps to elevate the debate around issues related to nonprofit and philanthropic activity in society. Today, the media cite the Center's data and analysis almost daily; other nonprofit and philanthropy infrastructure groups use the Center's data and research in support of their recommendations; and researchers across a broad range of disciplines use NCCS data to build a knowledge base for the sector.

It has been my pleasure to serve as the founding director of the Center on Nonprofits and Philanthropy. I am delighted that Shena Ashley, the new director, is bringing vision and energy to the Center's research and engagement activities. Under her leadership, the Center and NCCS will move in innovative directions while continuing to provide reliable data and expert analysis to foster better public understanding of the evolving dynamics in the nonprofit and philanthropic sectors.

Finally, I know that preparing *The Nonprofit Almanac* is a large and very demanding undertaking. Data must be pieced together from a variety of sources, verified and often estimated because there is no central source of information on the sector. I am grateful that Brice McKeever took on the task and, with Nathan Dietz and Saunji Fyffe, produced this excellent resource for the field. It is a unique and valuable contribution.

Elizabeth T. Boris
Urban Institute Fellow
August 2016

1

The Nonprofit Sector and Its Place in the National Economy

As of 2016, the nonprofit sector has largely completed its adjustment to the jarring financial crisis brought about by the Great Recession of 2007–09. The recession caused several disruptions in the nonprofit sector, including declines in endowments and investment income, increased demands for social services, and diminished contributions. However, even amid these challenges, the nonprofit sector as a whole showed its resiliency: only 5 percent of nonprofit organizations with $50,000 or more in gross receipts in 2008 had closed their doors by 2012, a percentage only slightly higher than the one between 2004 and 2008, before the recession's effects took hold.[1]

While most nonprofits managed to continue operating through the recession, many still suffered the effects of the economic downturn. The smallest organizations—those with gross receipts between $50,000 and $100,000—saw the largest increases in closure rates and incidence of significant revenue loss between 2008 and 2012, compared with the pre-recession period of 2004–08.[2] By contrast, larger organizations (revenues of $1 million or more) saw no increase in closure rates between these two time periods. However, even many larger organizations—especially those that relied heavily on one type of funding—needed to cut staff, wages, or program activities to make ends meet. All told, while the nonprofit sector has continued to grow over the last few years—not only in numbers, but in employees, wages, and assets—the Great Recession's impact hit some organizations harder than others.

This edition of *The Nonprofit Almanac* presents detailed information from before, during, and after the recession to provide nonprofit managers, researchers, and volunteers with the most current data available about the nonprofit sector. This ninth edition of the *Almanac* adds context to the recovery of the nonprofit sector in the post-recession

---

1. Brown, Melissa S., Brice McKeever, Nathan Dietz, Jeremy Koulish, and Tom Pollak. "The Impact of the Great Recession on the Number of Charities." Washington, DC: Urban Institute (2013).
2. Dietz, Nathan, Brice McKeever, Melissa Brown, Jeremy Koulish, and Tom Pollak. "The Impact of the Great Recession on the Number of Charities by Subsector and Revenue Range." Washington, DC: Urban Institute (2014).

period and illuminates how much the influence and impact of the sector have grown over the last several years and decades.

The nonprofit sector is large and diverse. Nonprofit organizations encourage civic participation; allow for expression of religious, social, and artistic values; provide basic social services; and strengthen communities. These organizations have different board and management styles. Some organizations use professional staff while others use all volunteer labor. Organizations rely on different streams of funding as well, with some organizations depending more heavily on individual contributions and others relying on government funds or fees for services.

The differences between organizations in the nonprofit sector make it easier to define the sector by what it is not. It is not part of government, nor is it a part of the business sector. More descriptively, it is also referred to as the charitable, voluntary, tax-exempt, independent, third, social, or philanthropic sector. These additional names suggest the importance of the nonprofit sector in our society: it is a resource for those in need as well as the voluntary foundation of civil society.

This book explores the nonprofit sector, its finances, and its role in the national economy. Specifically, *The Nonprofit Almanac* examines wages and employment trends, financial trends, giving and volunteering, and the size, scope, and finances of public charities. Chapters 1–4 present statistics on the entire nonprofit sector, while chapter 5 focuses exclusively on the finances of 501(c)(3) public charities.

This first chapter describes the size, scope, and distinctive characteristics of the nonprofit sector, especially as compared with other sectors. Here and throughout the *Almanac*, we rely on two primary sources of data—Internal Revenue Service (IRS) records and Bureau of Economic Analysis (BEA) estimates—for most of our analyses.

The Nonprofit Landscape

In 2015, more than 1.5 million nonprofit organizations were registered with the IRS, meaning they had applied for and received tax-exempt recognition. Nonprofit groups that generate more than $50,000 in gross receipts are required to file a tax return with the IRS known as the Form 990 or Form 990-EZ; these organizations are referred to as reporting nonprofits or filers. Not included in the 1.5 million registered nonprofits are religious congregations or their auxiliary groups, or smaller organizations that are not registered with the IRS. If all religious congregations and smaller organizations were taken into account, the number of nonprofits would be closer to 2.2 million.[3]

The nonprofit sector includes many diverse organizations. Under the Internal Revenue Code, more than 30 types of legal entities are classified as 501(c) organizations; all are exempt from corporate income tax but not all are charitable. Table 1.1

3. The 1.5 million registered nonprofits in table 1.1 does include organizations with gross receipts less than $50,000, which have been required to file IRS Form 990-N (the "e-Postcard") since 2008. The 2.2 million count is based on estimated totals for congregations and nonprofits that are not tax exempt. There are more than 312,000 religious congregations, based on data from the American Church List, and an estimated 400,000 smaller organizations based on data extrapolated from select state registers.

Table 1.1. Types of Tax-Exempt Organizations and Number, Expenses, and Assets by Type

Section of 1986 IRS code	Description of organization	Entities registered with the IRS, 2015	Entities reporting to the IRS, 2013	Expenses of reporting entities, 2013 ($ millions)	Assets of reporting entities, 2013 ($ millions)
501(c)(1)	Corporations organized under acts of Congress	638	24	25	536
501(c)(2)	Title-holding corporations for exempt organizations	4,480	2,932	1,339	13,653
501(c)(3)	Religious, charitable, and similar organizations	1,179,739	389,103	1,696,762	3,953,262
	501(c)(3) Public charities	1,076,309	293,265	1,624,079	3,225,702
	501(c)(3) Private foundations	103,430	95,838	72,683	727,560
501(c)(4)	Civic leagues and social welfare organizations	83,768	27,771	78,513	89,529
501(c)(5)	Labor, agriculture, and horticulture organizations	46,348	19,702	22,377	35,995
501(c)(6)	Business leagues, chambers of commerce, real estate boards, and trade boards	63,468	35,342	42,461	77,898
501(c)(7)	Social and recreational clubs	47,594	18,620	13,220	26,606
501(c)(8)	Fraternal beneficiary societies and associations	45,898	8,842	17,020	132,137
501(c)(9)	Voluntary employee-beneficiary associations	6,426	6,290	145,084	226,378
501(c)(10)	Domestic fraternal societies and associations	16,258	2,077	382	2,757
501(c)(11)	Teachers' retirement fund associations	8	6	147	1,625
501(c)(12)	Benevolent life insurance associations, mutual ditch or irrigation companies, mutual or cooperative telephone companies, etc.	5,293	3,797	60,533	142,671
501(c)(13)	Cemetery companies	8,972	3,040	969	11,255
501(c)(14)	State-chartered credit unions and mutual reserve funds	1,842	2,203	16,083	415,863
501(c)(15)	Mutual insurance companies or associations	694	249	62	310
501(c)(16)	Cooperative organizations to finance crop operations	14	8	10	404
501(c)(17)	Supplemental unemployment benefit trusts	99	98	264	299
501(c)(18)	Employee-funded pension trusts created before June 25, 1959	2	1	150	1,091

(continued)

Table 1.1. Types of Tax-Exempt Organizations and Number, Expenses, and Assets by Type *(continued)*

Section of 1986 IRS code	Description of organization	Entities registered with the IRS, 2015	Entities reporting to the IRS, 2013	Expenses of reporting entities, 2013 ($ millions)	Assets of reporting entities, 2013 ($ millions)
501(c)(19)	War veterans organizations	29,588	8,338	1,265	2,985
501(c)(20)	Legal service organizations	3	4	1	1
501(c)(21)	Black lung benefits trusts	0	0	0	0
501(c)(22)	Withdrawal liability payment funds	0	0	0	0
501(c)(23)	Veterans organizations created before 1880	3	3	333	3,883
501(c)(24)	Trusts described in section 4049 of the Employment Retirement Security Act of 1974	0	0	1	2
501(c)(25)	Title-holding corporations or trusts with multiple parents	784	666	1,107	25,290
501(c)(26)	State-sponsored organizations providing health coverage for high-risk individuals	11	11	609	160
501(c)(27)	State-sponsored workers' compensation reinsurance organizations	15	3	1,167	9,643
501(c)(29)	Qualified nonprofit health insurance issuers	22	17	96	326
501(c)(40)	Religious and apostolic organizations	216	0	0	0
501(c)(50)	Cooperative hospital service organizations	9	0	0	0
501(c)(60)	Cooperative service organizations or operating educational organizations	0	0	0	0
501(C)(71)	Charitable risk pool	1			
501(C)(81)	Qualified state-sponsored tuition program	1			
501(C)(82)	527 political organizations	13			
501(C)(91)	4947(a)(1) Public charity (Files 990/990-EZ)	840	1	1	15
501(C)(92)	4947(a)(1) Private foundations	6,217	2	1	3
	Total	**1,549,264**	**529,150**	**2,099,982**	**5,174,577**

Sources: Urban Institute, National Center for Charitable Statistics, Core Files (2013); and Internal Revenue Service, Exempt Organizations Business Master Files (2015).
Notes: Not all Internal Revenue Code Section 501(c)(3) organizations are included because certain organizations, such as churches (and their integrated auxiliaries or subordinate units) and conventions or associations of churches, need not apply for recognition of tax exemption unless they specifically request a ruling. Organizations that had their tax-exempt status revoked for failing to file a financial return for three consecutive years are excluded. Private foundations are included among 501(c)(3) organizations.

displays the number, expenses, and assets by type of tax exemption. Organizations in the 501(c)(3) category, which can receive tax-deductible contributions, include public charities and private foundations. This category accounts for the largest share of the nonprofit sector in number of organizations, expenses, and assets. Because the range of organizations classified as tax exempt under section 501(c) is quite large, we also categorize nonprofits by the type of services they provide or the types of activities they conduct. These organization types, or subsectors, are explained further below.

Nonprofit Sector Classification Systems

The Nonprofit Almanac uses two major classification systems to identify important components of the nonprofit sector. The first is the National Taxonomy of Exempt Entities (NTEE), a definitive classification system for nonprofit organizations recognized as tax exempt under the Internal Revenue Code. NTEE codes group tax-exempt entities by similarity of mission or primary purpose, activity, type, and major function. The 26 major categories of the NTEE are shown in table 1.2, along with the number of

Table 1.2. Organizations, Expenses, and Assets in the Nonprofit Sector by Type of Organization

Nonprofit category	Number of organizations reporting to the IRS, 2013	Percent of organizations reporting to the IRS, 2013	Reported expenses, 2013 ($ millions)	Percent of total expenses, 2013	Reported assets, 2013 ($ millions)	Percent of total assets, 2013
Arts, culture, and humanities	35,813	6.77	33,497	1.60	130,191	2.52
Education	67,879	12.83	278,167	13.25	1,012,361	19.56
Environmental quality, protection, and beautification	9,054	1.71	10,508	0.50	31,734	0.61
Animal-related	8,740	1.65	7,315	0.35	19,092	0.37
Health	25,643	4.85	1,002,401	47.73	1,426,678	27.57
Mental health and crisis intervention	8,481	1.60	30,766	1.47	26,068	0.50
Diseases, disorders, and medical disciplines	10,697	2.02	19,291	0.92	29,104	0.56
Medical research	2,203	0.42	10,399	0.50	41,443	0.80
Crime and legal-related	8,687	1.64	9,038	0.43	10,463	0.20
Employment and job-related	15,841	2.99	36,237	1.73	50,035	0.97
Food, agriculture, and nutrition	7,444	1.41	14,225	0.68	11,851	0.23

(continued)

Table 1.2. Organizations, Expenses, and Assets in the Nonprofit Sector by Type of Organization *(continued)*

Nonprofit category	Number of organizations reporting to the IRS, 2013	Percent of organizations reporting to the IRS, 2013	Reported expenses, 2013 ($ millions)	Percent of total expenses, 2013	Reported assets, 2013 ($ millions)	Percent of total assets, 2013
Housing and shelter	20,428	3.86	25,941	1.24	90,517	1.75
Public safety, disaster preparedness, and relief	10,857	2.05	3,637	0.17	12,280	0.24
Recreation, sports, leisure, and athletics	43,987	8.31	33,943	1.62	58,650	1.13
Youth development	7,878	1.49	7,484	0.36	16,242	0.31
Human services—multipurpose and other	40,880	7.73	129,873	6.18	189,916	3.67
International, foreign affairs, and national security	7,288	1.38	31,446	1.50	41,863	0.81
Civil rights, social action, and advocacy	2,830	0.53	4,522	0.22	6,228	0.12
Community improvement and capacity building	48,387	9.14	40,629	1.93	117,079	2.26
Philanthropy, voluntarism, and grantmaking foundations	84,338	15.94	90,309	4.30	801,747	15.49
Science and technology research institutions and services	3,039	0.57	20,469	0.97	25,546	0.49
Social science research institutes and services	940	0.18	2,796	0.13	5,481	0.11
Other public and societal benefit	20,862	3.94	91,268	4.35	635,503	12.28
Religion-related	20,699	3.91	14,235	0.68	41,574	0.80
Mutual/membership benefit organizations	15,712	2.97	151,386	7.21	342,608	6.62
Unknown	547	0.10	203	0.01	331	0.01
Total	**529,154**	**100.00**	**2,099,985**	**100.00**	**5,174,585**	**100.00**

Source: Urban Institute, National Center for Charitable Statistics, Core Files (2013).
Notes: Only organizations required to file annually with the IRS (all private foundations, and public charities and 501(c) other organizations that receive at least $25,000 in gross receipts annually) are included in these figures. Expenses include both operating expenses and grants or transfer payments made to individuals and other organizations.

entities that reported to the IRS in each category and the share of reported expenses and assets. In 2013 health organizations, which include hospitals, community health systems, and primary care facilities, accounted for 10 percent of the nonprofit sector expenses and over a quarter of its assets. Education, the second-largest subsector, accounted for 13 percent of expenses and 20 percent of total assets.

The second way of classifying nonprofit activity is with the North American Industry Classification System (NAICS). NAICS is the standard used by federal statistical agencies in classifying for-profit business establishments for the purpose of collecting, analyzing, and publishing official economic statistics. Table 1.3 displays the nonprofit sector according to NAICS, with organizations classified into industries based on similarities in producing goods or services. The first two columns show the numerical NAICS code assigned to the industry and the industry description. To provide a measure of the size of each NAICS industry, the third column reports estimated nonprofit wages (adjusting for unreported wages), and the fourth column shows the percentage of all nonprofit wages that fall under that NAICS code. Again, health care and social assistance organizations, especially hospitals, account for the largest share of wages (57.1 percent).

In addition to wage information about nonprofit organizations whose primary industry can be easily identified, table 1.3 contains estimated wages for nonprofits that are harder to classify using NAICS codes. To estimate wages for this portion of the nonprofit sector, we use definitions that the BEA at the Department of Commerce created to measure the size of the U.S. economy. BEA divides the economy into four sectors: government, business, households, and nonprofit institutions serving households (NPISH). However, unlike the IRS definition, the BEA's NPISH definition does not include all tax-exempt organizations. The BEA definition excludes organizations that serve businesses, such as chambers of commerce, and nonprofits such as credit unions and university presses that are also counted as serving businesses because they sell goods and services in the same ways as for-profit businesses do. Nonprofits that fall under the NPISH definition include those that provide services in one of the following five categories: religious and welfare (social services, grantmaking foundations, political organizations, museums, and libraries), medical care, education and research, recreation (cultural, sports, and civic and fraternal organizations), and personal business (labor unions, legal aid, and professional associations).

The estimated nonprofit wages reported in table 1.3 do not take into account volunteer labor, an important component of nonprofit sector resources. In many nonprofit organizations, volunteers play a crucial role in managing and staffing programs. In 2013 the value of volunteers, calculated using average private wages, was worth $167.2 billion dollars to the sector. The combination of nonprofit wages and volunteer labor exceeded $801 billion in 2013, and volunteers accounted for more than 26 percent of this combined total (table 1.4).

Since 2008, the adult volunteer rate in the U.S. has remained fairly stable, except for occasional year-to-year changes. However, the estimated wage value of the work provided by the entire adult volunteer labor force has increased by 15.5 percent between

Table 1.3. Scope of the Nonprofit Sector as Classified by the North American Industry Classification System, 2013

NAICS code	Industry	Estimated nonprofit wages ($ millions)	Percent of nonprofit wages
11	Agriculture, forestry, fishing, and hunting	411	0.1
22	Utilities	2,884	0.5
48–49	Transportation and warehousing	84	0.0
51	Information	3,023	0.5
52	Finance and insurance	7,517	1.2
53	Real estate and rental and leasing	137	0.0
54	Professional, scientific, and technical services	17,906	2.8
56	Administrative and support and waste management and remediation services	1,041	0.2
61	Educational services	103,366	16.3
62	Health care and social assistance	362,221	57.1
71	Arts, entertainment, and recreation	16,810	2.7
72	Accommodation and food services	413	0.1
81	Other services, except public administration	107,188	16.9
	Industry subtotal	623,000	98.3
	Less nonprofits serving business	*9,580*	*1.5*
	Equals NPISH portion of industry subtotal	613,420	96.8
	Plus other industry wages	10,980	1.7
	BEA NPISH wages	624,400	98.5
	Total nonprofit wages	**633,980**	**100.0**

Sources: Authors' estimates based on U.S. Census Bureau, Economic Census (2002, 2007, 2012); U.S. Department of Commerce, Bureau of Economic Analysis, National Income and Product Accounts (2015); U.S. Department of Labor, Bureau of Labor Statistics, Quarterly Census of Employment and Wages (1998–2015); and Urban Institute, National Center for Charitable Statistics, Core Files (Public Charities, 1998–2013).
BEA = Bureau of Economic Analysis
NPISH = nonprofit institutions serving households
Notes: Industries are listed as classified by the North American Industry Classification System (NAICS). These figures only include actual wages paid; they do not reflect volunteer labor. The industry subtotal is the sum of the industry-by-industry estimates in the rows above it. Because those estimates include nonprofits serving business, but the BEA NPISH estimates do not, we subtract our estimated wages for nonprofits serving business from the industry subtotal, yielding the NPISH portion of our industry subtotal. The difference between that estimate and the BEA's NPISH estimate is the wages of nonprofits whose industry classification is unknown. The total nonprofit wages are the BEA NPISH number plus our estimate for nonprofits serving business. Please see the chapter 2 appendix for a detailed description of the authors' methodology.

Table 1.4. Nonprofit Wages and the Wage Value of Volunteer Work, 2008–13

	2008	2009	2010	2011	2012	2013
Wage value of volunteering ($ billions)[a]	144.7	150.7	154.1	164.8	168.3	167.2
Nonprofit wages ($ billions)[b]	539.9	558.0	571.2	590.1	617.3	634.0
Total ($ billions)	**684.6**	**708.7**	**725.3**	**754.9**	**785.6**	**801.2**
Wage value of volunteers as % of nonprofit wages	26.8	27.0	27.0	27.9	27.3	26.4

Sources:
a. Authors' calculations based on U.S. Department of Labor, Bureau of Labor Statistics, American Time Use Survey (2008–14); Current Employment Statistics (2014); and Current Population Survey, Volunteer Supplement (2008–14).
b. Authors' calculations based on U.S. Census Bureau, Economic Census (2002, 2007, 2012); U.S. Department of Commerce, Bureau of Economic Analysis, National Income and Product Accounts, table 1.13 (2015); private wages from U.S. Department of Labor, Bureau of Labor Statistics, Quarterly Census of Employment and Wages (2015); and wages from Urban Institute, National Center for Charitable Statistics, Core Files (Public Charities, 2008–13).
Notes: See table 3.14, this volume, for the authors' calculations for the wage value of volunteering; see chapter 2 for authors' calculations of nonprofit wages.

2008 and 2013. The value of volunteer work has largely kept pace with increases in the wages paid to nonprofit employees, although in 2013 the value of volunteer work declined slightly, an exception to this trend. Chapter 3 provides more details on trends in giving and volunteering.

The Nonprofit Sector in Comparison with Other Sectors

The BEA's NPISH statistics allow us to compare the economic contribution of the nonprofit sector with the contributions made by other sectors. However, the NPISH statistics underestimate the sector's overall economic impact because the BEA definition of NPISHs excludes nonprofit organizations that serve business, such as chambers of commerce, trade associations, and homeowners associations. In addition, some nonprofits that sell goods and services in the same way as for-profit organizations—such as tax-exempt cooperatives, credit unions, mutual financial institutions, and tax-exempt manufacturers like university presses—are excluded from the BEA definition, but are included in the business sector estimates. Despite these limitations, however, the BEA's estimates of NPISHs are the best data available for comparing the different sectors' economic contributions.

Even looking past the limitations of the BEA definitions, placing a value on the economic product of nonprofits is difficult. First, because the benefits of nonprofit activities are hard to quantify (and because the value of volunteer labor is

Figure 1.1. Nonprofit Organizations' Share of U.S. Gross Domestic Product, 2014 ($ billions)

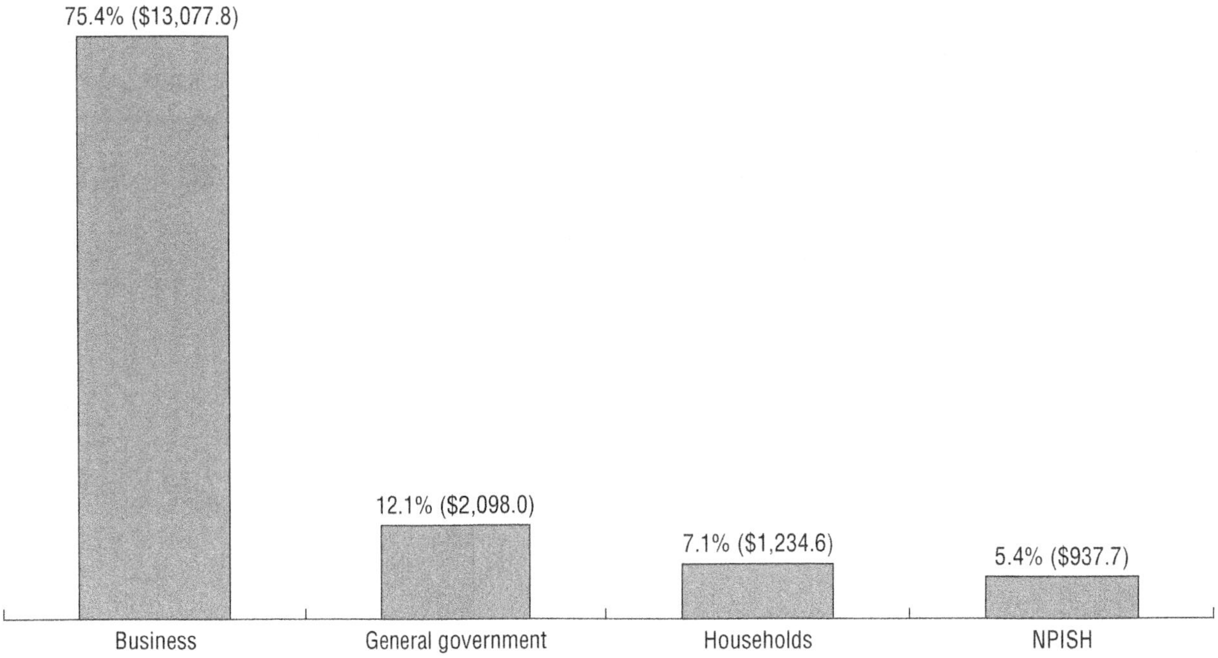

Source: Authors' calculations based on U.S. Department of Commerce, Bureau of Economic Analysis, National Income and Product Accounts, table 1.13 (2015).
NPISH = nonprofit institutions serving households
Note: See table 1.6, this volume, for source data.

not included in the benefit calculations), the value of the nonprofit sector output is typically understated. Furthermore, data on the costs of the resources nonprofits consume are often questionable because cost reporting is not practiced uniformly throughout the sector. Given these constraints, we base our cross-sector comparisons on the amount of wages and salaries paid to employees in each sector. Figure 1.1 shows the relative size of the four sectors as defined by the BEA.[4] In 2014, NPISHs contributed $937.7 billion to the gross domestic product (GDP), which equates to 5.4 percent of GDP.

In general, as seen in table 1.5, the proportion of the GDP attributed to NPISHs has been steadily increasing over the past 60 years. Interestingly, while government and business wages and salaries fell between 2008 and 2009 during the recession, wages and salaries in NPISHs did not. Moreover, NPISH wages and salaries grew by 36.1 percent between 2006 and 2014—faster than in any other sector of the economy.

4. In figure 1.1 (and in table 1.5 that follows), government enterprises—congressionally established private corporations that fulfill a public purpose—are classified as part of the business sector and not general government.

Table 1.5. Gross Value Added to the U.S. Economy by Sector, 1929–2014 ($ billions)

Year	GDP	Business	Households	NPISH	General government
1929	104.6	90.0	7.5	1.6	5.5
1930	92.2	77.9	7.0	1.6	5.7
1931	77.4	63.9	6.2	1.5	5.8
1932	59.5	47.5	5.2	1.4	5.4
1933	57.2	45.6	4.6	1.3	5.7
1934	66.8	54.3	4.5	1.3	6.7
1935	74.3	61.2	4.5	1.4	7.2
1936	84.9	70.0	4.7	1.4	8.7
1937	93.0	78.1	5.1	1.5	8.4
1938	87.4	71.5	5.1	1.6	9.2
1939	93.5	77.4	5.2	1.6	9.3
1940	102.9	86.2	5.4	1.7	9.7
1941	129.4	109.2	5.8	1.8	12.6
1942	166.0	136.4	6.5	2.0	21.2
1943	203.1	159.0	7.1	2.2	34.8
1944	224.6	170.0	7.9	2.4	44.3
1945	228.2	168.3	8.6	2.5	48.7
1946	227.8	179.5	8.9	3.0	36.3
1947	249.9	205.6	9.8	3.6	30.9
1948	274.8	229.5	10.8	4.1	30.4
1949	272.8	224.9	11.7	4.5	31.7
1950	300.2	249.5	13.1	4.9	32.7
1951	347.3	285.8	14.8	5.4	41.3
1952	367.7	298.5	16.6	5.9	46.7
1953	389.7	316.0	18.6	6.4	48.7
1954	391.1	313.8	20.3	6.9	50.2
1955	426.2	343.6	22.4	7.5	52.7
1956	450.1	361.3	24.3	8.2	56.4
1957	474.9	379.2	0.0	9.0	60.5
1958	482.0	379.4	28.3	9.9	64.5
1959	522.5	413.8	30.5	10.8	67.3

(continued)

Table 1.5. Gross Value Added to the U.S. Economy by Sector, 1929–2014 ($ billions) *(continued)*

Year	GDP	Business	Households	NPISH	General government
1960	543.3	426.3	33.1	12.2	71.7
1961	563.3	438.6	35.2	13.0	76.5
1962	605.1	471.5	37.6	14.2	81.8
1963	638.6	496.1	39.7	15.4	87.3
1964	685.8	533.4	41.9	16.8	93.7
1965	743.7	580.4	44.5	18.5	100.4
1966	815.0	635.2	47.3	20.8	111.8
1967	861.7	665.4	50.3	23.1	122.9
1968	942.5	726.5	53.3	26.1	136.6
1969	1,019.9	783.0	57.6	30.0	149.3
1970	1,075.9	816.3	61.8	33.4	164.4
1971	1,167.8	882.9	67.8	37.4	179.6
1972	1,282.4	973.0	73.4	41.4	194.6
1973	1,428.5	1,094.6	79.5	46.1	208.4
1974	1,548.8	1,183.5	86.6	51.7	227.0
1975	1,688.9	1,285.7	95.0	58.0	250.3
1976	1,877.6	1,444.2	103.2	63.2	267.0
1977	2,086.0	1,617.3	112.3	69.2	287.2
1978	2,356.6	1,839.7	127.1	77.3	312.3
1979	2,632.1	2,064.3	142.0	86.9	339.0
1980	2,862.5	2,227.3	161.3	99.4	374.6
1981	3,211.0	2,503.2	181.5	112.5	413.8
1982	3,345.0	2,569.5	199.8	125.7	449.9
1983	3,638.1	2,803.5	216.8	139.0	478.9
1984	4,040.7	3,138.6	234.7	153.0	514.4
1985	4,346.7	3,375.5	252.1	163.7	555.5
1986	4,590.2	3,546.8	272.9	178.7	591.7
1987	4,870.2	3,745.2	295.5	199.9	629.7
1988	5,252.6	4,029.2	322.2	224.6	676.7
1989	5,657.7	4,336.4	346.5	245.9	728.9
1990	5,979.6	4,552.5	372.3	270.2	784.7

(continued)

Table 1.5. Gross Value Added to the U.S. Economy by Sector, 1929–2014 ($ billions) *(continued)*

Year	GDP	Business	Households	NPISH	General government
1991	6,174.0	4,655.1	391.7	292.2	835.0
1992	6,539.3	4,929.9	413.8	314.8	880.7
1993	6,878.7	5,187.9	444.1	337.0	909.8
1994	7,308.8	5,535.9	478.5	354.0	940.5
1995	7,664.1	5,808.8	512.7	373.0	969.6
1996	8,100.2	6,174.7	540.7	390.9	993.9
1997	8,608.5	6,597.2	571.7	412.7	1,027.0
1998	9,089.2	6,972.4	607.8	441.7	1,067.3
1999	9,660.6	7,414.8	651.8	470.3	1,123.7
2000	10,284.8	7,891.5	700.9	501.9	1,190.5
2001	10,621.8	8,082.0	753.1	526.3	1,260.5
2002	10,977.5	8,286.4	790.5	566.7	1,333.9
2003	11,510.7	8,669.9	828.4	598.6	1,413.7
2004	12,274.9	9,268.6	879.5	631.4	1,495.4
2005	13,093.7	9,919.9	944.0	655.5	1,574.3
2006	13,855.9	10,514.0	1,000.6	688.8	1,652.5
2007	14,477.6	10,981.5	1,028.7	720.9	1,746.5
2008	14,718.6	11,019.9	1,086.6	768.7	1,843.5
2009	14,418.7	10,597.5	1,110.1	803.5	1,907.6
2010	14,964.4	11,059.7	1,111.4	817.4	1,975.9
2011	15,517.9	11,536.4	1,130.4	843.9	2,007.1
2012	16,155.3	12,097.2	1,147.6	881.8	2,028.6
2013	16,663.2	12,524.0	1,180.5	905.9	2,052.7
2014	17,348.1	13,077.8	1,234.6	937.7	2,098.0

Source: U.S. Department of Commerce, Bureau of Economic Analysis, National Income and Product Accounts, table 1.3.5 (2015).
GDP = gross domestic product
NPISH = nonprofit institutions serving households
Notes: Value added by the business sector equals gross domestic product excluding gross value added by households, nonprofit institutions serving households, and general government. Government enterprises are classified as part of the business sector, as are nonprofits serving business. Value added by nonprofit institutions serving households equals compensation of employees of nonprofit institutions, the rental value of nonresidential fixed assets owned and used by nonprofit institutions serving households, and rental income of persons for tenant-occupied housing owned by nonprofit institutions. Value added by the general government equals compensation of general government employees plus general government consumption of fixed capital.

Figure 1.2. Nonprofit Organizations' Share of Wage and Salary Accruals in the U.S. Economy, 2014 ($ billions)

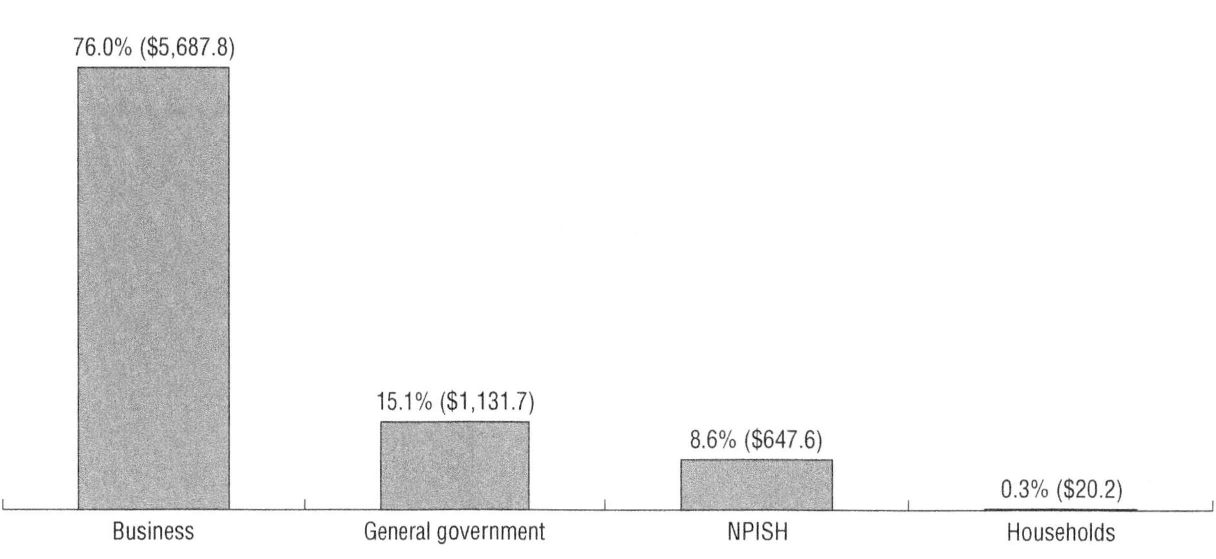

Source: Authors' calculations based on U.S. Department of Commerce, Bureau of Economic Analysis, National Income and Product Accounts, table 1.13 (2015).
NPISH = nonprofit institutions serving households
Note: See table 1.6, this volume, for source data.

Figure 1.2, which shows the 2014 share of wage and salary accruals in the U.S. economy, shows that NPISHs constitute an even larger share of wages and salaries than they do of GDP. In 2014, NPISHs, excluding nonprofits serving business, paid $647.6 billion in wages and salaries. This amounts to 9 percent of all wages and salaries paid to U.S. workers. In comparison, the business sector accounts for the greatest share in the economy at 76 percent (about $5.7 trillion in wages and salaries) followed by government, which accounts for 15 percent (about $1.1 trillion).[5]

Table 1.6 shows the economic contribution of sectors by wages and salaries over time. Historically, wages and salary accruals for both NPISHs and general government have increased as a share of the total. Between 1948 and 2014, wages and salaries for NPISH increased from 2.4 percent to 8.6 percent, and government's increased from 12.4 percent to 15.1 percent. Table 1.6 shows that wages and salaries grew at a faster rate among employees of NPISHs (36.4 percent) between 2006 and 2014 than in any other sector.

As seen in figure 1.3, the share of the national wage bill by sector has seen substantive change since 1948, especially in the nonprofit sector's share. The share of wages and salaries attributed to NPISHs has been increasing steadily over this period, while the shares attributed to business and government have shown greater fluctuation. As figure 1.3

5. The figures in table 1.6 differ from those in table 1.3 because nonprofit organizations serving business are included in the business sector in table 1.6 but are separated from NPISH wages in table 1.3. The breakdown could not be completed for table 1.6 because data are not available prior to 1990.

Table 1.6. Wage and Salary Accruals by Economic Sector, 1948–2014 ($ billions)

Year	Total	Business	Households	NPISH	General government	Government enterprises
1948	135.6	113.2	2.4	3.2	16.8	2.2
1949	134.7	110.5	2.4	3.5	18.3	2.5
1950	147.2	120.8	2.6	3.8	20.0	2.6
1951	171.4	138.4	2.6	4.1	26.3	2.9
1952	185.7	148.6	2.6	4.5	30.0	3.4
1953	199	160.4	2.7	5.0	30.9	3.4
1954	197.4	158.0	2.6	5.4	31.4	3.5
1955	212.2	170.4	3.0	5.9	32.9	3.7
1956	229.1	184.5	3.2	6.4	35.0	3.8
1957	240.0	192.7	3.3	7.0	37.0	4.0
1958	241.4	190.5	3.5	7.7	39.7	4.4
1959	259.8	206.5	3.5	8.4	41.4	4.7
1960	273.1	215.6	3.8	9.6	44.1	5.1
1961	280.7	219.6	3.7	10.2	47.2	5.3
1962	299.5	233.8	3.8	11.2	50.7	5.7
1963	314.9	245.1	3.8	12.1	53.9	6.1
1964	337.9	262.5	3.9	13.1	58.4	6.5
1965	363.8	282.6	3.9	14.4	62.9	7.1
1966	400.3	309.5	4.0	16.1	70.7	7.7
1967	429.1	328.8	4.1	17.9	78.3	8.2
1968	471.9	359.9	4.3	20.3	87.4	9.3
1969	518.2	395.1	4.4	23.3	95.4	10.2
1970	551.5	415.7	4.4	25.9	105.5	11.7
1971	584.6	437.2	4.5	28.6	114.3	12.5
1972	638.8	478.6	4.6	31.3	124.3	13.5
1973	708.7	535.6	4.7	34.5	133.9	14.9
1974	772.2	585.7	4.5	38.3	143.7	16.8
1975	814.9	610.1	4.6	42.5	157.7	18.5
1976	899.7	679.2	5.3	46.1	169.1	19.8
1977	994.2	756.6	5.8	50.1	181.7	20.9
1978	1,120.6	860.9	6.4	56.2	197.1	22.9

(continued)

Table 1.6. Wage and Salary Accruals by Economic Sector, 1948–2014 ($ billions) *(continued)*

Year	Total	Business	Households	NPISH	General government	Government enterprises
1979	1,253.4	972.1	6.3	62.9	212.1	25.0
1980	1,373.5	1,062.5	6.0	71.8	233.2	28.2
1981	1,511.5	1,170.4	6.0	80.9	254.2	31.7
1982	1,587.7	1,217.0	6.1	90.2	274.4	33.1
1983	1,677.6	1,283.4	6.2	98.5	289.5	35.3
1984	1,845.0	1,421.2	7.1	106.7	310.0	38.1
1985	1,982.7	1,527.9	7.2	114.6	333.0	40.8
1986	2,104.2	1,616.8	7.6	125.0	354.8	42.5
1987	2,257.8	1,730.4	7.6	141.6	378.2	45.0
1988	2,440.8	1,867.5	8.2	161.3	403.8	48.3
1989	2,584.3	1,969.1	8.8	175.9	430.5	50.6
1990	2,743.5	2,076.1	9.2	193.8	464.4	54.6
1991	2,817.3	2,107.2	9.0	209.4	491.7	57.1
1992	2,968.5	2,221.9	10.0	224.8	511.8	60.2
1993	3,082.6	2,304.4	10.5	239.7	528.0	61.0
1994	3,240.5	2,430.5	10.9	253.4	545.7	63.8
1995	3,422.0	2,580.2	11.7	266.8	563.3	65.7
1996	3,620.6	2,748.1	11.8	280.6	580.1	68.0
1997	3,881.3	2,971.0	11.9	296.9	601.5	70.4
1998	4,186.3	3,228.2	13.8	316.3	628.0	73.3
1999	4,465.2	3,460.1	12.5	334.8	657.8	76.0
2000	4,832.4	3,762.8	13.4	358.0	698.2	81.6
2001	4,961.7	3,837.1	12.8	374.0	737.8	84.2
2002	5,004.2	3,806.8	12.5	399.6	785.3	87.8
2003	5,146.1	3,890.0	13.9	418.6	823.6	89.7
2004	5,431.2	4,121.2	14.8	437.4	857.8	94.8
2005	5,703.1	4,341.9	15.0	451.2	895.0	96.5
2006	6,068.8	4,642.8	16.1	474.8	935.1	99.9
2007	6,405.7	4,904.7	17.7	498.3	985.0	103.8
2008	6,543.6	4,955.9	18.6	531.3	1,037.8	106.3

(continued)

Table 1.6. Wage and Salary Accruals by Economic Sector, 1948–2014 ($ billions) *(continued)*

Year	Total	Business	Households	NPISH	General government	Government enterprises
2009	6,260.0	4,624.1	16.7	549.4	1,069.8	105.4
2010	6,385.6	4,721.7	14.8	562.6	1,086.5	104.5
2011	6,641.3	4,954.2	15.9	581.2	1,090.0	104.8
2012	6,938.9	5,219.5	16.8	608.0	1,094.6	103.6
2013	7,123.4	5,378.1	17.6	624.4	1,103.3	104.3
2014	7,487.3	5,687.8	20.2	647.6	1,131.7	105.5

Source: U.S. Department of Commerce, Bureau of Economic Analysis, National Income and Product Accounts, table 1.1.13 (2015).
NPISH = nonprofit institutions serving households
Notes: Government enterprises are shown for information only; these are included in the totals for business. The figures in this table do not match those of table 1.3 because the wage and salary accruals for nonprofits serving business are included in the business category, whereas table 1.3 includes an estimate of the number of nonprofits serving business in the NPISH category. The estimates in table 1.3 only go back to 1998 and are therefore not shown here. Business includes domestic business only and excludes wages and salary accruals for the rest of the world, which are not available separately. The business total is the sum of the BEA's wage and salary accruals for corporate business and noncorporate business.

Figure 1.3. Wage and Salary Accruals by Economic Sector, 1948–2014 (percent)

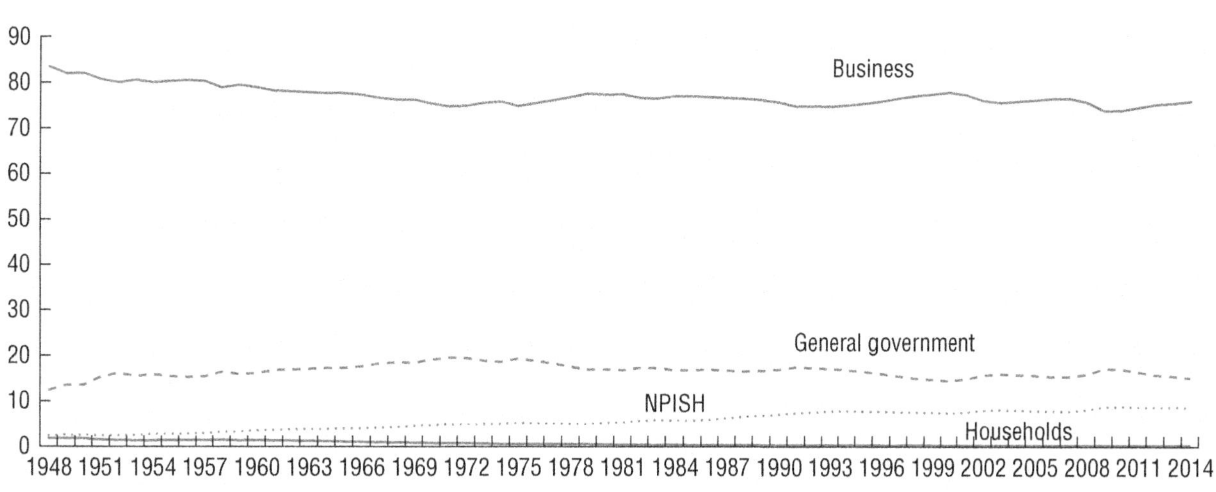

Source: Authors' calculations based on U.S. Department of Commerce, Bureau of Economic Analysis, National Income and Product Accounts, table 1.13 (2015).
NPISH = nonprofit institutions serving households
Note: See table 1.6, this volume, for source data.

shows, the business and government shares of wages have tended to move in the opposite direction from one another. Wages and salaries in the business sector dropped steadily from 1948 to 1975, then rose at a largely steady pace until the recent recession, seeing a sharp dip in 2009. Since then, they have once again risen steadily. The share attributed to government peaked around the mid-1970s, but then declined until around 2000. While they have fluctuated since 2000, general government wages and salaries increased by 21 percent between 2006 and 2014.

Table 1.7 shows that the nonprofit sector's share of the economy changes only very slightly if supplements to salaries are included in the wage estimate. Supplements to salaries consist of employer contributions for employee pension and insurance funds and employer contributions for government social insurance. When these benefits are

Table 1.7. Wage and Salary Accruals and Supplements to Salaries by Economic Sector, 1948–2014 ($ billions)

Year	Total	Business	Households	NPISH	General government	Government enterprises
1948	144.4	118.5	2.4	3.2	20.3	2.5
1949	144.5	116.0	2.4	3.6	22.5	2.8
1950	158.5	127.9	2.6	3.9	24.1	0.0
1951	186.0	147.1	2.7	4.3	31.9	3.3
1952	201.3	157.8	2.6	4.6	36.3	3.9
1953	215.6	170.5	2.7	5.1	37.3	3.9
1954	214.4	168.5	2.6	5.5	37.8	4.0
1955	231.0	182.3	3.1	6.1	39.5	4.2
1956	249.8	198.0	3.3	6.6	41.9	4.4
1957	263.0	207.7	3.3	7.3	44.7	4.7
1958	265.2	205.7	3.5	8.0	48.0	5.1
1959	286.5	224.2	3.6	8.9	49.8	5.4
1960	302.1	235.1	3.8	10.1	53.1	5.9
1961	311.2	239.9	3.7	10.7	56.9	6.2
1962	333.0	256.7	3.8	11.8	60.7	6.6
1963	351.2	269.9	3.8	12.8	64.7	7.1
1964	376.9	289.0	3.9	14.0	70.0	7.7
1965	406.4	311.6	4.0	15.3	75.5	8.3
1966	450.1	343.6	4.0	17.2	85.3	9.0

(continued)

Table 1.7. Wage and Salary Accruals and Supplements to Salaries by Economic Sector, 1948–2014 ($ billions) *(continued)*

Year	Total	Business	Households	NPISH	General government	Government enterprises
1967	482.9	365.0	4.2	19.2	94.5	9.6
1968	532.2	400.2	4.4	21.7	105.9	10.8
1969	586.0	440.5	4.4	25.0	116.1	11.9
1970	625.1	464.4	4.5	27.9	128.3	14.0
1971	667.1	490.3	4.6	31.0	141.2	15.5
1972	733.6	540.4	4.6	34.3	154.3	16.8
1973	815.1	606.8	4.8	38.2	165.3	18.5
1974	890.4	664.9	4.6	42.6	178.3	21.0
1975	950.2	701.7	4.6	47.3	196.6	23.3
1976	1,051.2	784.4	5.4	51.6	209.8	24.9
1977	1,169.0	880.7	5.9	56.4	226.0	26.5
1978	1,320.3	1,004.8	6.5	63.0	246.0	28.9
1979	1,481.1	1,138.0	6.4	70.5	266.2	31.6
1980	1,626.2	1,247.4	6.1	80.4	292.3	35.7
1981	1,795.5	1,377.9	6.2	90.7	320.7	40.1
1982	1,894.5	1,440.3	6.3	101.1	346.8	42.1
1983	2,014.1	1,527.4	6.3	111.8	368.6	45.1
1984	2,217.6	1,692.0	7.3	122.6	395.7	48.7
1985	2,389.1	1,821.5	7.3	132.2	428.1	52.7
1986	2,545.6	1,938.6	7.7	144.4	454.9	54.5
1987	2,725.5	2,071.9	7.7	163.3	482.6	56.9
1988	2,950.9	2,239.6	8.3	184.8	518.2	61.5
1989	3,143.9	2,372.5	9.0	202.8	559.6	65.5
1990	3,344.9	2,506.6	9.4	224.2	604.7	71.7
1991	3,454.7	2,557.3	9.2	243.2	645.0	74.9
1992	3,674.1	2,716.2	10.2	262.8	684.9	80.1
1993	3,824.0	2,825.3	10.8	280.6	707.3	81.1
1994	4,014.1	2,974.9	11.2	296.4	731.6	84.9
1995	4,206.8	3,129.6	12.0	312.2	753.0	87.1
1996	4,426.2	3,313.0	12.2	327.5	773.5	89.9

(continued)

Table 1.7. Wage and Salary Accruals and Supplements to Salaries by Economic Sector, 1948–2014 ($ billions) *(continued)*

Year	Total	Business	Households	NPISH	General government	Government enterprises
1997	4,719.1	3,558.5	12.2	346.0	802.4	93.2
1998	5,082.4	3,859.1	14.1	370.8	838.4	97.1
1999	5,417.5	4,123.1	12.9	394.7	886.8	101.6
2000	5,863.1	4,485.4	13.8	421.1	942.8	109.1
2001	6,053.8	4,594.7	13.1	440.4	1,005.6	113.8
2002	6,149.7	4,587.9	12.8	476.2	1,072.8	118.9
2003	6,372.6	4,711.5	14.2	503.5	1,143.4	123.1
2004	6,748.8	4,992.7	15.2	530.4	1,210.5	132.3
2005	7,098.0	5,265.9	15.4	548.0	1,268.7	135.5
2006	7,513.7	5,596.9	16.5	574.4	1,325.9	140.4
2007	7,908.8	5,897.0	18.1	598.6	1,395.1	145.9
2008	8,089.9	5,963.8	19.2	639.0	1,467.9	149.6
2009	7,795.8	5,591.7	17.6	669.1	1,517.4	148.8
2010	7,969.5	5,700.8	15.5	681.0	1,572.2	151.3
2011	8,277.2	5,968.2	16.5	707.5	1,585.0	152.2
2012	8,618.5	6,266.8	17.7	741.5	1,592.5	150.8
2013	8,848.8	6,459.9	18.3	762.0	1,608.6	152.7
2014	9,258.4	6,803.0	20.8	789.2	1,645.4	154.5

Source: U.S. Department of Commerce, Bureau of Economic Analysis, National Income and Product Accounts, table 1.13 (2015).
NPISH = nonprofit institutions serving households
Notes: Government enterprises are shown for information only; these are included in the totals for business. Wage and salary accruals for nonprofits serving business are also included in business. Business includes domestic business only and excludes wages and salary accruals for the rest of the world, which are not available separately. The business total is the sum of the BEA's wage and salary accruals for corporate business and noncorporate business.

considered, NPISH share declines slightly, by only 0.1 percentage point. In comparison, the 2014 government share of wage and salary accruals increases by almost 3 percentage points (from 15.1 percent to 17.8 percent) and the business share declines by 2.5 percentage points.

Figure 1.4 tracks NPISH wages as a percentage of general government wages over the same time period (1948 to 2014). Looking at wages and salaries only, and not at supplements such as employer contributions to pensions or benefit accounts, NPISH

Figure 1.4. Wages and Salaries of Nonprofit Institutions Serving Households Compared with Government Wages and Salaries, 1948–2014 (percent)

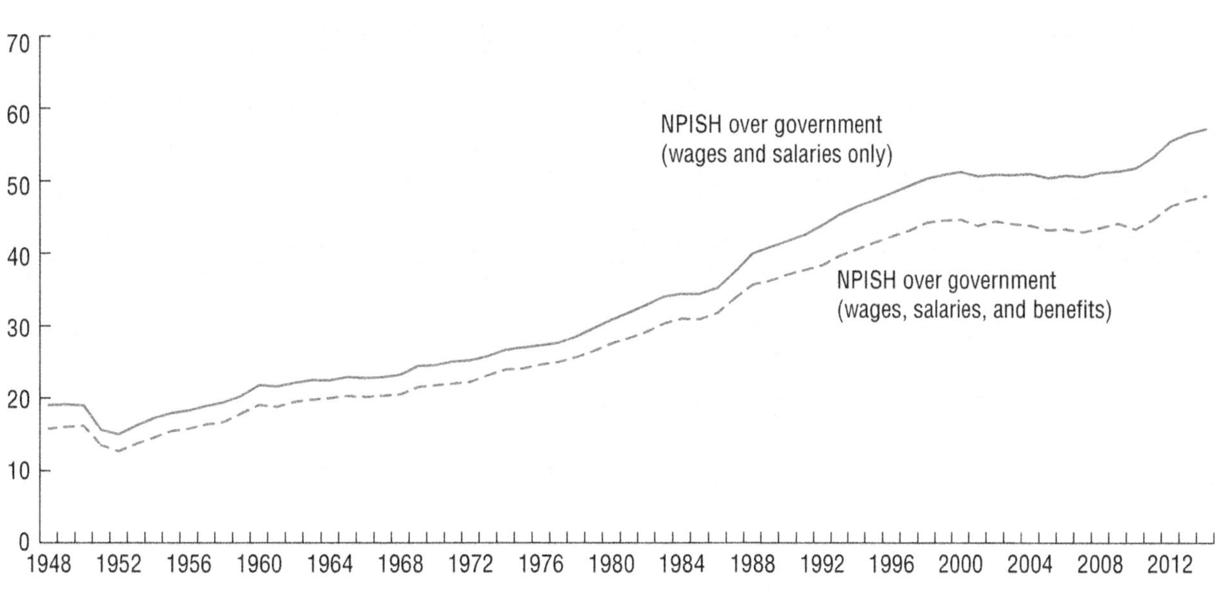

Source: Authors' calculations based on U.S. Department of Commerce, Bureau of Economic Analysis, National Income and Product Accounts, table 1.13 (2015).
NPISH = Nonprofit institutions serving households
Note: See tables 1.6 and 1.7, this volume, for source data.

wages have grown significantly from 1948 to the present. While NPISH wages were only 15 percent of general government wages in 1952, they were 57 percent in 2014. However, if we consider benefits and wages and salaries, the rate of growth is somewhat slower. This indicates that while salaries and wages have been increasing at a faster rate among NPISHs than among government organizations, the benefits and other supplements to income for NPISHs are not at the same level as those of the government sector.

Nonprofit Employment

As table 1.8 shows, in 2013 the nonprofit sector employed more than 14.4 million people. The nonprofit sector has employed steadily more individuals each year over the last decade. Consequently, as seen in figure 1.5, the nonprofit workforce constitutes a larger share of the overall workforce than it did at the turn of the century. Between 2000 and 2013, nonprofit employment grew an estimated 22.6 percent, faster than the overall U.S. workforce. Excluding nonprofits, U.S. nonfarm employment grew by only 1.4 percent between 2000 and 2013. As a result, the share of nonprofit employment to nonfarm employment grew from 8.9 percent in 2000 to

Table 1.8. Number of Employees by U.S. Economic Sector, 2000–13

	2000	2001	2002	2003	2004	2005	2006	2007	2008	2009	2010	2011	2012	2013
Nonprofit employees (thousands)[a]	11,768	12,070	12,423	12,662	12,818	12,929	13,156	13,453	13,757	13,857	13,929	14,033	14,231	14,429
Nonfarm employees (thousands)[b]	132,030	132,080	130,628	130,315	131,732	133,996	136,404	137,935	137,170	131,221	130,269	131,843	134,098	136,394
Nonprofit employees in workforce (%)	8.9	9.1	9.5	9.7	9.7	9.6	9.6	9.8	10.0	10.6	10.7	10.6	10.6	10.6

Sources:
a. Authors' calculations based on U.S. Census Bureau, Economic Census (2002, 2007, 2012); U.S. Department of Labor, Bureau of Labor Statistics; Urban Institute National Center for Charitable Statistics, Core Files (Public Charities, 1998–2013).
b. U.S. Department of Labor, Bureau of Labor Statistics, Current Employment Statistics (2000–13).
Notes: See table 2.2, this volume, for authors' estimate of nonprofit employment. The nonfarm employment figures have been seasonally adjusted.

Figure 1.5. Nonprofit Employees and Nonprofit Employment as a Percentage of U.S. Nonfarm Employment, 2000–13

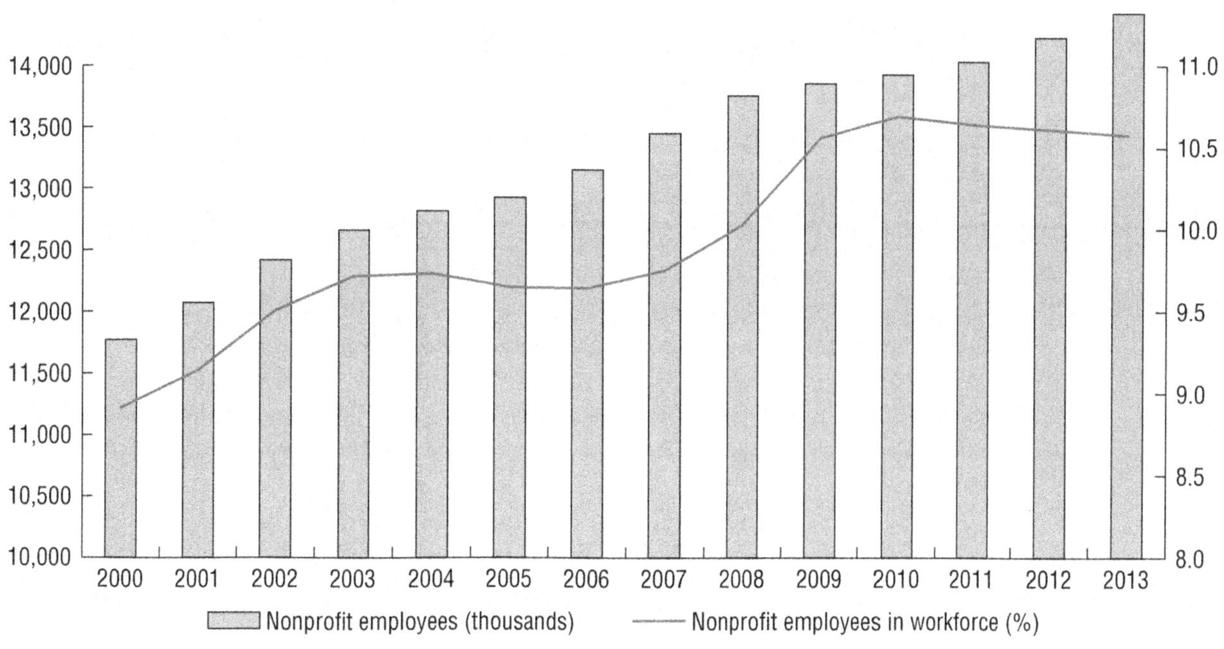

Sources: Authors' calculations based on U.S. Census Bureau, Economic Census (2002, 2007, 2012); U.S. Department of Labor, Bureau of Labor Statistics; Urban Institute National Center for Charitable Statistics, Core Files (Public Charities, 2000–13); and nonfarm employment from U.S. Department of Labor, Bureau of Labor Statistics, Current Employment Statistics (2000–13).
Notes: See table 2.2, this volume, for authors' estimate of nonprofit employment. See table 1.8, this volume, for source data. The nonfarm employment figures have been seasonally adjusted.

10.6 percent in 2013 (see figure 1.5 and table 1.8). See chapter 2 for more details on how the employment estimates and the industry totals were created.

Conclusion

The nonprofit sector plays a vital role in the quality of life in the United States. Its role in the national economy has been increasing in recent years, and its recovery from the Great Recession has been, in many ways, more robust than any other sector's. In 2014, nonprofit institutions serving households, or NPISH—the definition of the nonprofit sector used by the BEA—accounted for an estimated 5.4 percent of GDP and 8.6 percent of the economy's wages. In the remaining chapters of this *Almanac,* we analyze both the financial and human resources of the nonprofit sector. Chapter 2 focuses on wage and employment trends in the overall sector, and chapter 3 discusses the critical role of donors, foundations, and volunteers. Chapter 4 "follows the money" to portray the nonprofit sector's revenues and outlays, and chapter 5 looks in depth at public charities and their finances.

Sources

Mead, Charles Ian, Clinton P. McCully, and Marshall B. Reindorf. "Income and Outlays of Households and of Nonprofit Institutions Serving Households." April 2003.

The Urban Institute, National Center for Charitable Statistics. 1998–2010. "IRS Business Master Files, Exempt Organizations (2010)." Washington, DC: The Urban Institute.

———. 2010. "Core Files." Washington, DC: The Urban Institute.

U.S. Census Bureau, 2002. "2002 Economic Census." http://www.census.gov/econ/census/data/historical_data.html (accessed August 19, 2016).

———. 2007. "2007 Economic Census." http://www.census.gov/econ/census/ (accessed August 19, 2016).

———. 2010. "2010 Census." http://www.census.gov/2010census/ (accessed August 19, 2016).

———. 2012. "2012 Economic Census." http://www.census.gov/econ/census/ (accessed August 19, 2016).

U.S. Department of Commerce, Bureau of Economic Analysis. 2015. "National Income and Product Accounts Tables." http://www.bea.gov/iTable/iTable.cfm?ReqID=9&step=1#reqid=9&step=1&isuri=1 (accessed August 19, 2016).

U.S. Department of Labor, Bureau of Labor Statistics. 1998–2015. "Employment, Hours, and Earnings from the Current Employment Statistics Survey (National)." http://www.bls.gov/ces/ (accessed August 19, 2016).

———. 2008–2014. "American Time Use Survey." http://www.bls.gov/tus/ (accessed August 19, 2016).

———. 2008–2014. "Current Population Survey." http://www.bls.gov/cps/ (accessed August 19, 2016).

2

Wage and Employment Trends

The nonprofit sector contains a wide breadth of paid careers, including doctors, researchers, educators, artists, executives, care providers, counselors, lawyers, and many others. This chapter estimates the total nonprofit wages and employment for the sector and analyzes these findings by the sector's varied industries and subsectors. The chapter goes on to present these findings in comparison to the other pillars of the U.S. economy—the government and business sectors.

Unfortunately, there is no single comprehensive, annual source for nonprofit wage and employment data by industry. The numbers presented in this chapter represent the authors' estimates as compiled from various nonprofit and government sources. Therefore, these estimates are subject to revision as better data and methods become available. For more information on how the estimates were created and how the data in these tables were combined and modified to yield the estimates, please refer to the methodology section of this chapter.

Table 2.1 displays total nonprofit wages for 2000 through 2013 by industry, categorized according to the North American Industry Classification System (NAICS). These figures include religious organizations and other nonprofit groups that may not be registered with the Internal Revenue Service (IRS). Industries not listed have either no nonprofits or too few employees to report separately and are therefore combined in the "other" industry wages category. The wage estimates also include both full-time and part-time employees but exclude such benefits as health insurance and employee contributions to retirement.

In 2003, nonprofit organizations paid an estimated $425.0 billion in wages. Ten years later in 2013, total nonprofit wages had risen to $634.0 billion. This increase in paid wages represents a growth of 49.2 percent (17.8 percent after adjusting for inflation). The growth in the nonprofit sector can be largely credited to the health care and social assistance industry, which includes hospitals, mental health centers, crisis hotlines, blood banks, soup kitchens, senior centers, and similar organizations. In 2013, the majority of all nonprofit wages (57.1 percent) were paid by health care and social

Table 2.1. Nonprofit Wages by Industry, 2000–13 (current $ millions)

NAICS code	Industry	2000	2001	2002	2003	2004
11	Agriculture, forestry, fishing, and hunting	247	295	303	313	310
22	Utilities	1,005	1,122	1,176	1,254	1,379
48–49	Transportation and warehousing	56	38	49	72	72
51	Information	1,798	2,129	2,290	2,402	2,463
52	Finance and insurance	3,374	4,028	4,294	5,516	5,869
53	Real estate and rental and leasing	117	92	108	138	115
54	Professional, scientific, and technical services	9,634	8,526	7,237	8,620	10,186
56	Administrative and support and waste management and remediation services	682	730	765	788	783
61	Educational services	50,052	53,710	58,718	62,259	66,040
	Colleges, universities, professional schools, and junior colleges	*33,786*	*35,814*	*38,608*	*40,893*	*43,561*
	Other education	*16,266*	*17,896*	*20,110*	*21,366*	*22,478*
62	Health care and social assistance	185,384	198,766	214,027	229,690	243,339
	Hospitals, nursing and residential care facilities, and ambulatory health care services	*156,955*	*169,413*	*182,280*	*196,073*	*208,503*
	Social assistance	*28,429*	*29,353*	*31,748*	*33,618*	*34,837*
71	Arts, entertainment, and recreation	9,468	10,624	10,931	11,530	12,110
72	Accommodation and food services	208	234	253	268	283
81	Other services, except public administration	64,054	66,595	72,317	76,011	79,449
	Industry subtotal	326,079	346,889	372,468	398,859	422,396
	Less nonprofit serving business	*5,888*	*6,106*	*6,159*	*6,425*	*6,766*
	Equals NPISH portion of industry subtotal	320,191	340,784	366,310	392,434	415,630
	Plus nonprofit wages not classified by NAICS	37,809	33,216	33,290	26,166	21,770
	BEA NPISH wages	358,000	374,000	399,600	418,600	437,400
	Total nonprofit wages	**363,888**	**380,106**	**405,759**	**425,025**	**444,166**

Sources: Authors' estimates based on U.S. Census Bureau, Economic Census (2002, 2007, 2012); U.S. Department of Commerce, Bureau of Economic Analysis, National Income and Product Accounts (2015); U.S. Department of Labor, Bureau of Labor Statistics, Quarterly Census of Employment and Wages (2000–14); and Urban Institute, National Center for Charitable Statistics, Core Files (Public Charities, 2000–13).

BEA = Bureau of Economic Analysis

NPISH = nonprofit institutions serving households

Notes: Industries are listed as classified by the North American Industry Classification System (NAICS). These figures include only actual wages paid; they do not reflect volunteer labor. The industry subtotal is the sum of the industry-by-industry estimates in the rows above it. Because those estimates include nonprofits serving business but the BEA NPISH estimates do not, the authors subtract estimated wages for nonprofits serving business from the industry subtotal, yielding the NPISH portion of industry subtotal. The difference between that estimate and the BEA's NPISH estimate is the wages of nonprofits whose industry classification is unknown. Total nonprofit wages are the sum of the BEA NPISH number plus the authors' estimate for nonprofits serving business. Please see the methodology section of this chapter for a detailed description of the calculations.

2005	2006	2007	2008	2009	2010	2011	2012	2013
310	329	362	340	332	338	345	381	411
1,448	1,570	1,703	2,252	2,428	2,510	2,680	2,786	2,884
74	80	88	92	89	76	85	84	84
2,607	2,705	2,882	2,976	2,989	2,784	2,870	2,872	3,023
6,260	7,020	7,735	7,603	7,384	7,310	7,132	7,521	7,517
116	128	148	151	139	150	143	143	137
12,120	14,106	16,203	16,743	16,174	16,408	16,838	17,471	17,906
777	801	884	937	948	1,114	1,129	1,042	1,041
69,259	73,955	79,301	84,914	88,780	91,191	95,672	100,265	103,366
46,103	*48,925*	*52,386*	*56,279*	*59,045*	*60,740*	*63,660*	*66,516*	*67,773*
23,157	*25,030*	*26,915*	*28,634*	*29,735*	*30,451*	*32,012*	*33,749*	*35,593*
255,146	271,917	288,423	307,510	320,859	329,451	339,718	353,781	362,221
219,377	*233,871*	*248,355*	*264,949*	*276,958*	*284,058*	*294,360*	*303,859*	*313,168*
35,769	*38,046*	*40,068*	*42,561*	*43,900*	*45,393*	*45,358*	*49,922*	*49,053*
12,596	13,304	14,057	14,959	14,484	14,688	15,260	15,989	16,810
292	310	326	326	319	341	374	400	413
80,936	85,497	90,546	95,083	95,020	94,942	97,186	101,245	107,188
441,941	471,721	502,658	533,886	549,943	561,303	579,431	603,980	623,000
7,222	*7,718*	*8,156*	*8,600*	*8,589*	*8,634*	*8,914*	*9,326*	*9,580*
434,719	464,003	494,501	525,286	541,354	552,669	570,517	594,654	613,420
16,481	10,797	3,799	6,014	8,046	9,931	10,683	13,346	10,980
451,200	474,800	498,300	531,300	549,400	562,600	581,200	608,000	624,400
458,422	**482,518**	**506,456**	**539,900**	**557,989**	**571,234**	**590,114**	**617,326**	**633,980**

Figure 2.1. Distribution of Nonprofit Wages by Industry, 2013 (percent)

Industry	Percent
Health care and social assistance	57.1%
Other services, except public administration	16.9%
Educational services	16.3%
Professional, scientific, and technical services	2.8%
Arts, entertainment, and recreation	2.7%
Nonprofit wages not classified by NAICS	1.7%
All other industries, combined	2.4%

Sources: Authors' estimates based on U.S. Census Bureau, Economic Census (2012); U.S. Department of Commerce, Bureau of Economic Analysis, National Income and Product Accounts (2015); U.S. Department of Labor, Bureau of Labor Statistics, Quarterly Census of Employment and Wages (2014); and Urban Institute, National Center for Charitable Statistics, Core Files (Public Charities, 2013).

assistance organizations (figure 2.1). In particular, hospitals, residential care facilities, and ambulatory health care services account for just under half (49.4 percent) of all nonprofit wages. Wages for hospitals grew from $196.1 billion in 2003 to $313.2 billion in 2013, by far the largest absolute growth of any industry during the same period. If hospitals are removed from the employment trend, nonprofit wages would have grown more slowly from 2003 to 2013, 40.1 percent compared with 49.2 percent.

The "other services" subsector accounts for 17 percent of total nonprofit wages in 2013, making it the second-largest nonprofit industry by wages paid, behind the health care and social assistance industry. This category includes grantmaking foundations, fundraising or other supporting organizations, professional societies or associations, groups promoting or administering religious activities, cemeteries, human rights organizations, advocacy organizations, conservation and wildlife organizations, and others. The educational subsector, which includes organizations such as colleges, elementary, technical schools, exam preparation, hockey camps, and dance instruction, makes up the third-largest segment of wages at 16.3 percent. Higher education accounts for two-thirds of educational services wages and over 10 percent of total nonprofit sector wages.

Proportionally speaking, wages in the utilities industry grew the most over the decade leading up to 2013; wages for this sector more than doubled between 2003 and 2013 (81.7 percent growth after adjusting for inflation). Although it is a small part of the nonprofit sector, the utilities industry includes nonprofits that provide gas, electricity, water, and sanitary services as well as installation, maintenance, and repair of necessary equipment. The professional, scientific, and technical services subsector also saw strong proportional growth during this same period, rising from $8.6 billion in 2003 to $17.9 billion in 2013 (a growth of 64.1 percent after adjusting for inflation). This subsector includes organizations devoted to research and development in the social sciences and humanities; physical, engineering, and biological research services; and offices of lawyers.

The nonprofit sector employed over 14.4 million people in 2013 (table 2.2). The number of employees increased 14.0 percent from the 2003 level of 12.7 million employees. More than half of all nonprofit workers are employed by the health care and social assistance industry (54.8 percent). In 2013, this industry employed over a million more nonprofit workers than it did in 2003, showing the largest absolute growth in number of employees of any nonprofit subsector. The "other services" industry employed the second-largest number of workers in 2013, accounting for a fifth (19.7 percent) of the sector's paid workers. As with wages, the number of employees in the utilities sector grew proportionally more than any other industry between 2003 and 2013, increasing 61.7 percent. The number of workers employed in the real estate and rental and leasing industry declined 29.2 percent between 2003 and 2013, the largest decline in any subsector. Several other industries also saw an overall decline between 2003 and 2013, including agriculture, forestry, fishing, and hunting (9.8 percent); transportation and warehousing (6.4 percent); information (15.8 percent); finance and insurance (5.1 percent); and administrative and support and waste management and remediation services (3.0 percent). The decline shown by these industries represents a very moderate decline in absolute number of employees; in total, each of these declining subsectors employed just over 157,000 employees in 2013, about 1.1 percent of the nonprofit sector total. In general, the larger subsectors showed continued growth while some of the smaller subsectors declined slightly.

Table 2.3 and figure 2.2 show the annual average nonprofit compensation per nonprofit employee by industry. Across all industries, average annual nonprofit compensation increased from $31,501 in 2003 to $43,178 in 2013, a 37.1 percent increase (8.6 percent after adjusting for inflation). These data, however, do not take into account differences in nonprofit wages between staff and executives. Average annual compensation per nonprofit employee varies widely by industry. Both the utilities industry and the finance and insurance industries had average compensations of about $97,000, the highest compensations of any nonprofit industries. Accommodation and food services organizations had the lowest annual average compensation at under $21,000. This industry is also one of the lowest paid in the for-profit sector: the low average pay is in part because the industry includes camp organizations, which hire many seasonal employees. The "social assistance" industry has the next lowest compensation, with annual average compensation of about $26,500. This industry includes child and youth, elderly, disabled, and community food services. Like the accommodation and food services industry, the social assistance industry also tends to be among the lowest paid in the for-profit sector.

From 2000 to 2013, the number of employees in the nonprofit sector increased 22.6 percent while the government sector increased just over 5 percent and the business sector grew less than 1 percent. Wages in the nonprofit sector grew 28.8 percent over the same period, after adjusting for inflation. This growth rate was faster than that of business, which grew 5.6 percent, and government, which increased 16.8 percent.

Table 2.2. Nonprofit Employment by Industry, 2000–13

NAICS code	Industry	2000	2001	2002	2003	2004	2005
11	Agriculture, forestry, fishing, and hunting	11,386	13,107	13,203	13,659	12,724	12,563
22	Utilities	15,748	16,927	17,466	18,331	18,968	19,028
48–49	Transportation and warehousing	1,433	942	1,188	1,696	1,625	1,660
51	Information	30,534	36,023	40,044	40,584	39,272	40,325
52	Finance and insurance	53,670	60,600	65,711	81,656	80,660	82,368
53	Real estate and rental and leasing	3,496	2,679	3,039	3,743	2,949	2,828
54	Professional, scientific, and technical services	178,657	162,710	142,703	162,496	183,674	209,354
56	Administrative and support and waste management and remediation services	28,965	29,241	29,613	29,693	28,190	26,910
61	Educational services	2,016,121	2,058,299	2,140,041	2,186,102	2,251,625	2,249,844
	Colleges, universities, profession schools, and junior colleges	*1,283,408*	*1,293,894*	*1,324,701*	*1,357,244*	*1,414,754*	*1,432,359*
	Other education	*732,714*	*764,404*	*815,340*	*828,858*	*836,871*	*817,485*
62	Health care and social assistance	6,305,850	6,504,403	6,707,611	6,827,773	6,893,517	6,983,509
	Hospitals, nursing and residential care facilities, and ambulatory health care services	*4,930,887*	*5,063,024*	*5,209,350*	*5,314,852*	*5,366,004*	*5,430,728*
	Social assistance	*1,374,963*	*1,441,379*	*1,498,261*	*1,512,920*	*1,527,512*	*1,552,782*
71	Arts, entertainment, and recreation	437,971	452,120	460,296	471,677	488,167	498,306
72	Accommodation and food services	13,716	15,046	15,931	16,475	16,750	16,868
81	Other services, except public administration	2,670,601	2,717,705	2,786,436	2,808,087	2,800,312	2,785,927
	Total	**11,768,149**	**12,069,802**	**12,423,283**	**12,661,970**	**12,818,432**	**12,929,491**

Sources: Authors' estimates based on U.S. Census Bureau, Economic Census (2002, 2007, 2012); U.S. Department of Commerce, Bureau of Economic Analysis, National Income and Product Accounts (2015); U.S. Department of Labor, Bureau of Labor Statistics, Quarterly Census of Employment and Wages (2000–14); and Urban Institute, National Center for Charitable Statistics, Core Files (Public Charities, 2000–13).
Notes: Industries are listed as classified by the North American Industry Classification System (NAICS). Please see the methodology section of this chapter for a detailed description of the authors' calculations.

2006	2007	2008	2009	2010	2011	2012	2013
12,321	12,447	11,407	11,078	11,331	11,759	11,589	12,320
19,681	20,285	26,145	27,899	28,297	28,869	29,072	29,645
1,727	1,837	1,908	1,838	1,541	1,657	1,593	1,587
39,785	40,743	41,560	41,509	36,864	35,905	34,283	34,168
85,919	87,942	85,982	88,989	82,445	76,484	77,943	77,517
2,918	3,281	3,347	3,133	3,274	2,964	2,823	2,652
235,341	256,371	251,331	237,421	230,408	224,246	217,403	216,773
26,727	27,858	28,103	27,969	32,284	32,143	28,879	28,796
2,299,879	2,367,003	2,436,199	2,485,541	2,501,625	2,554,276	2,616,869	2,677,609
1,460,380	*1,502,571*	*1,550,229*	*1,588,303*	*1,603,088*	*1,641,749*	*1,674,273*	*1,690,056*
839,498	*864,432*	*885,970*	*897,238*	*898,537*	*912,527*	*942,596*	*987,553*
7,084,871	7,215,558	7,406,115	7,523,140	7,610,352	7,690,207	7,787,704	7,902,872
5,507,584	*5,606,780*	*5,741,896*	*5,823,315*	*5,871,726*	*5,927,803*	*5,993,736*	*6,052,297*
1,577,287	*1,608,778*	*1,664,219*	*1,699,824*	*1,738,626*	*1,762,404*	*1,793,968*	*1,850,575*
513,879	533,318	545,577	534,374	533,742	543,913	560,724	577,786
17,183	17,463	17,129	16,870	17,669	18,786	19,435	19,947
2,816,093	2,868,929	2,901,733	2,857,227	2,838,722	2,811,853	2,842,760	2,846,923
13,156,323	**13,453,035**	**13,756,535**	**13,856,988**	**13,928,554**	**14,033,062**	**14,231,077**	**14,428,596**

Table 2.3. Average Annual Compensation per Nonprofit Employee by Industry, 2000–13 (current $)

NAICS code	Industry	2000	2001	2002	2003
11	Agriculture, forestry, fishing, and hunting	21,679	22,520	22,943	22,882
22	Utilities	63,816	66,284	67,351	68,400
48–49	Transportation and warehousing	39,296	40,487	41,412	42,275
51	Information	58,884	59,095	57,177	59,195
52	Finance and insurance	62,866	66,471	65,348	67,552
53	Real estate and rental and leasing	33,525	34,517	35,656	36,878
54	Professional, scientific, and technical services	53,927	52,398	50,713	53,045
56	Administrative and support and waste management and remediation services	23,535	24,949	25,829	26,529
61	Educational services	24,826	26,094	27,438	28,479
	Colleges, universities, profession schools, and junior colleges	*26,325*	*27,679*	*29,145*	*30,129*
	Other education	*22,200*	*23,412*	*24,665*	*25,777*
62	Health care and social assistance	29,399	30,559	31,908	33,641
	Hospitals, nursing and residential care facilities, and ambulatory health care services	*31,831*	*33,461*	*34,991*	*36,891*
	Social assistance	*20,676*	*20,364*	*21,190*	*22,220*
71	Arts, entertainment, and recreation	21,617	23,498	23,747	24,444
72	Accommodation and food services	15,129	15,561	15,877	16,274
81	Other services, except public administration	23,985	24,504	25,953	27,068
	Total	**27,709**	**28,740**	**29,981**	**31,501**

Sources: Authors' estimates based on U.S. Census Bureau, Economic Census (2002, 2007, 2012); U.S. Department of Commerce, Bureau of Economic Analysis, National Income and Product Accounts (2015); U.S. Department of Labor, Bureau of Labor Statistics, Quarterly Census of Employment and Wages (2000–14); and Urban Institute, National Center for Charitable Statistics, Core Files (Public Charities, 2000–13).
Notes: Industries are listed as classified by the North American Industry Classification System (NAICS). Please see the methodology section of this chapter for a detailed description of the authors' calculations. Values are not adjusted for inflation.

This long view slightly obscures the fluctuations in the U.S. economy in the new millennium, however. In the first years of the new millennium, the nonprofit sector grew faster than the other sectors. Between 2000 and 2007, employment in the nonprofit sector grew 14.3 percent compared with 6.9 percent in government and 2.8 percent in the business sector (table 2.4). After adjusting for inflation, nonprofit wages grew 15.6 percent during the same period, ahead of the business sector (8.2 percent growth) and just behind wages for the government sector (17.2 percent growth) (table 2.5).

2004	2005	2006	2007	2008	2009	2010	2011	2012	2013
24,357	24,694	26,663	29,060	29,830	29,937	29,831	29,326	32,866	33,365
72,722	76,109	79,776	83,956	86,144	87,027	88,711	92,815	95,826	97,271
44,070	44,825	46,128	47,753	48,436	48,337	49,635	51,147	52,778	53,208
62,704	64,649	67,998	70,747	71,603	72,019	75,522	79,945	83,777	88,463
72,757	76,007	81,702	87,955	88,424	82,981	88,660	93,245	96,492	96,976
39,155	41,021	43,866	45,110	45,103	44,315	45,901	48,347	50,627	51,540
55,455	57,890	59,937	63,200	66,618	68,122	71,212	75,085	80,360	82,601
27,774	28,860	29,958	31,736	33,336	33,885	34,502	35,129	36,088	36,160
29,330	30,784	32,156	33,503	34,855	35,718	36,453	37,455	38,315	38,604
30,791	*32,187*	*33,501*	*34,864*	*36,304*	*37,175*	*37,889*	*38,776*	*39,728*	*40,101*
26,860	*28,327*	*29,816*	*31,136*	*32,320*	*33,141*	*33,889*	*35,080*	*35,804*	*36,042*
35,300	36,535	38,380	39,972	41,521	42,650	43,290	44,175	45,428	45,834
38,856	*40,395*	*42,463*	*44,295*	*46,143*	*47,560*	*48,377*	*49,658*	*50,696*	*51,744*
22,806	*23,035*	*24,121*	*24,906*	*25,574*	*25,826*	*26,109*	*25,737*	*27,828*	*26,507*
24,807	25,278	25,889	26,358	27,418	27,105	27,518	28,056	28,515	29,095
16,878	17,321	18,060	18,663	19,044	18,884	19,318	19,902	20,557	20,699
28,371	29,052	30,360	31,561	32,768	33,256	33,445	34,563	35,615	37,650
32,952	**34,181**	**35,855**	**37,364**	**38,810**	**39,687**	**40,299**	**41,290**	**42,441**	**43,178**

As a result of the 2007–09 economic recession, the unemployment rate reached 10 percent in 2009—the highest unemployment rate since 1982. But even during the recession, employment in the nonprofit sector continued to increase, albeit at a slower rate of increase than during the pre-recession years. From 2007 to 2010 the nonprofit sector grew faster in terms of employees and wages than did business and government (tables 2.4 and 2.5).

With the end of the recession, the U.S. economy has been rebounding. From 2010 to 2013, nonprofit growth in employment (3.6 percent) and wages (4.2 percent, after

Figure 2.2. Average Annual Nonprofit Compensation per Employee by Industry, 2013 ($ thousands)

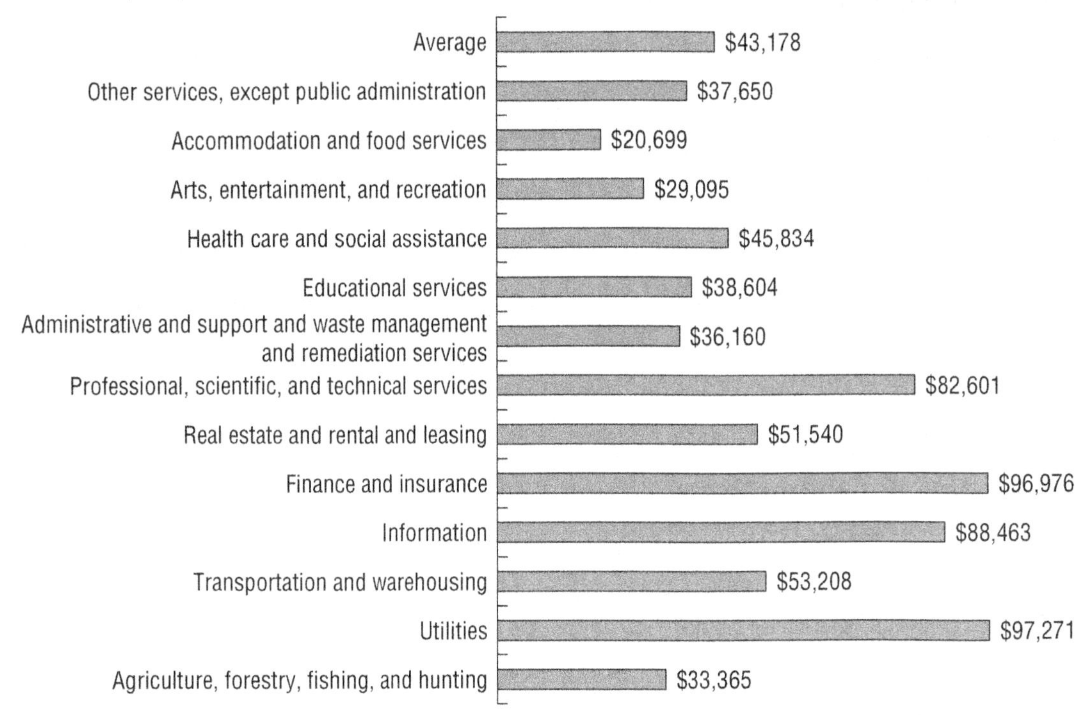

Sources: Authors' estimates based on U.S. Census Bureau, Economic Census (2012); U.S. Department of Commerce, Bureau of Economic Analysis, National Income and Product Accounts (2015); U.S. Department of Labor, Bureau of Labor Statistics, Quarterly Census of Employment and Wages (2014); and Urban Institute, National Center for Charitable Statistics, Core Files (Public Charities, 2013).
Note: Values are not adjusted for inflation.

adjusting for inflation) was surpassed by renewed growth in business (6.7 percent and 7.1 percent, respectively, after inflation adjustments). On the other hand, government employment and wages have both declined slightly in the post-recession years (2.9 percent and 5.3 percent, respectively, after inflation adjustments).

Grouping NAICS industries at the two-digit level masks differences in specific organizations that are not faring well in the current economic climate. When we look at the six-digit NAICS code, a fuller picture emerges of the recession's impact on nonprofit organizations. For example, the classification for musical groups and artists (NAICS code 711130) includes nonprofits that organize, promote, and/or manage concerts for musicians, chamber orchestras, vocalists, and other musical performers. This group saw declines of over 5 percent in wages and salaries between 2007 and 2010. But they have seen renewed growth in the years since the recession, showing almost 20 percent growth in wages from 2010 to 2013. In fact, 2013 wage and salary totals for this group have eclipsed their pre-recession heights, although total employment remains reduced (see supplemental tables 2.12–2.14). Several other types of organizations experienced reduced growth or even decline in wages and employment during the recession period but have seen renewed

Table 2.4. Number of Employees by U.S. Economic Sector, 2000–13 (thousands)

Year	Total U.S. Workers[a]	Business	Nonprofits[b]	Government
2000	132,030	99,471	11,768	20,790
2001	132,080	98,889	12,070	21,120
2002	130,628	96,695	12,423	21,509
2003	130,315	96,073	12,662	21,580
2004	131,732	97,296	12,818	21,618
2005	133,996	99,263	12,929	21,804
2006	136,404	101,272	13,156	21,975
2007	137,935	102,262	13,453	22,219
2008	137,170	100,910	13,757	22,503
2009	131,221	94,811	13,857	22,553
2010	130,269	93,850	13,929	22,490
2011	131,843	95,718	14,033	22,092
2012	134,098	97,950	14,231	21,918
2013	136,394	100,117	14,429	21,849

Sources:
a. U.S. Department of Labor, Bureau of Labor Statistics, Current Employment Statistics (2000–13).
b. Authors' calculations based on U.S. Census Bureau, Economic Census (2002, 2007, 2012); U.S. Department of Labor, Bureau of Labor Statistics; and Urban Institute, National Center for Charitable Statistics, Core Files (Public Charities, 2000–13).
Notes: See table 2.2, this volume, for authors' estimate of nonprofit employment. Nonfarm employment figures have been seasonally adjusted.

growth in the years following, including fitness and recreational sports centers (NAICS 713940), civic and social organizations (NAICS 813410), and museums (NAICS 712110).

Yet not all nonprofit industries have completely recovered following the recession. Some organizations have continued to experience decline in the post-recession era. For example, the offices of nonprofit lawyers (NAICS 541110) saw a slight increase in employment in 2013, but have largely been declining since 2007. Both voluntary health organizations (NAICS 813212) and labor unions (NAICS 813930) have seen general declines in their employment numbers since 2008. At the broader two-digit NAICS level, both the real estate and rental and leasing industry and the finance and insurance industry have largely been declining in number of paid employees over the last several years.

To provide a sense of the relative growth of nonprofits in different industries, figure 2.3 shows the compound annual growth rates in wages and employment from 2003 to 2013. The utilities sector has the highest growth rate in any industry, although it is not a large segment of the nonprofit sector. Growth is also faster than average in professional, scientific, and technical services. However, the real estate and rental and

Table 2.5. Total Annual Wages by U.S. Economic Sector, 2000–13 ($ billions)

Year	Total	Business	NPISH	General government	Households
2000	4,832.4	3,756.9	363.9	698.2	13.4
2001	4,961.7	3,831.0	380.1	737.8	12.8
2002	5,004.2	3,800.6	405.8	785.3	12.5
2003	5,146.1	3,883.6	425.0	823.6	13.9
2004	5,431.2	4,114.4	444.2	857.8	14.8
2005	5,703.1	4,334.7	458.4	895.0	15.0
2006	6,068.8	4,635.1	482.5	935.1	16.1
2007	6,405.7	4,896.5	506.5	985.0	17.7
2008	6,543.6	4,947.3	539.9	1,037.8	18.6
2009	6,260.0	4,615.5	558.0	1,069.8	16.7
2010	6,385.6	4,713.1	571.2	1,086.5	14.8
2011	6,641.3	4,945.3	590.1	1,090.0	15.9
2012	6,938.9	5,210.2	617.3	1,094.6	16.8
2013	7,123.4	5,368.5	634.0	1,103.3	17.6

Sources: Authors' estimates based on U.S. Census Bureau, Economic Census (2002, 2007, 2012); U.S. Department of Commerce, Bureau of Economic Analysis, National Income and Product Accounts (2015); U.S. Department of Labor, Bureau of Labor Statistics, Quarterly Census of Employment and Wages (2000–14); and Urban Institute, National Center for Charitable Statistics, Core Files (Public Charities, 2000–13).
NPISH = nonprofit institutions serving households
Notes: These figures only include actual wages paid; they do not reflect volunteer labor. The NPISH wage includes authors' estimates of nonprofits serving business. Please see the methodology section of this chapter for a detailed description of the authors' calculations. Values are not adjusted for inflation.

leasing industry, the transportation and warehousing industry, and information industry all saw declines in both wages and employment over the same period.

Finally, figure 2.4 shows the compound annual growth rate of average annual nonprofit compensation per employee by industry. Compensation in most industries has been increasing between 3 and 5 percent a year. Arts, entertainment, and recreation; transportation and warehousing; and accommodation and food services have been somewhat below that rate, but still at roughly 2 to 3 percent a year. The professional, scientific, and technical services industry has experienced the highest growth at 4.5 percent a year.

Conclusion

In 2013, nonprofit organizations paid $634.0 billion in wages and employed more than 14.4 million people. Since 2003, wages in the nonprofit sector grew over 17 percent after adjusting for inflation, and employment increased 14 percent. Total nonprofit sec-

Figure 2.3. Annual Growth Rate in Total Nonprofit Wages and Employment by Industry, 2003–13 (percent)

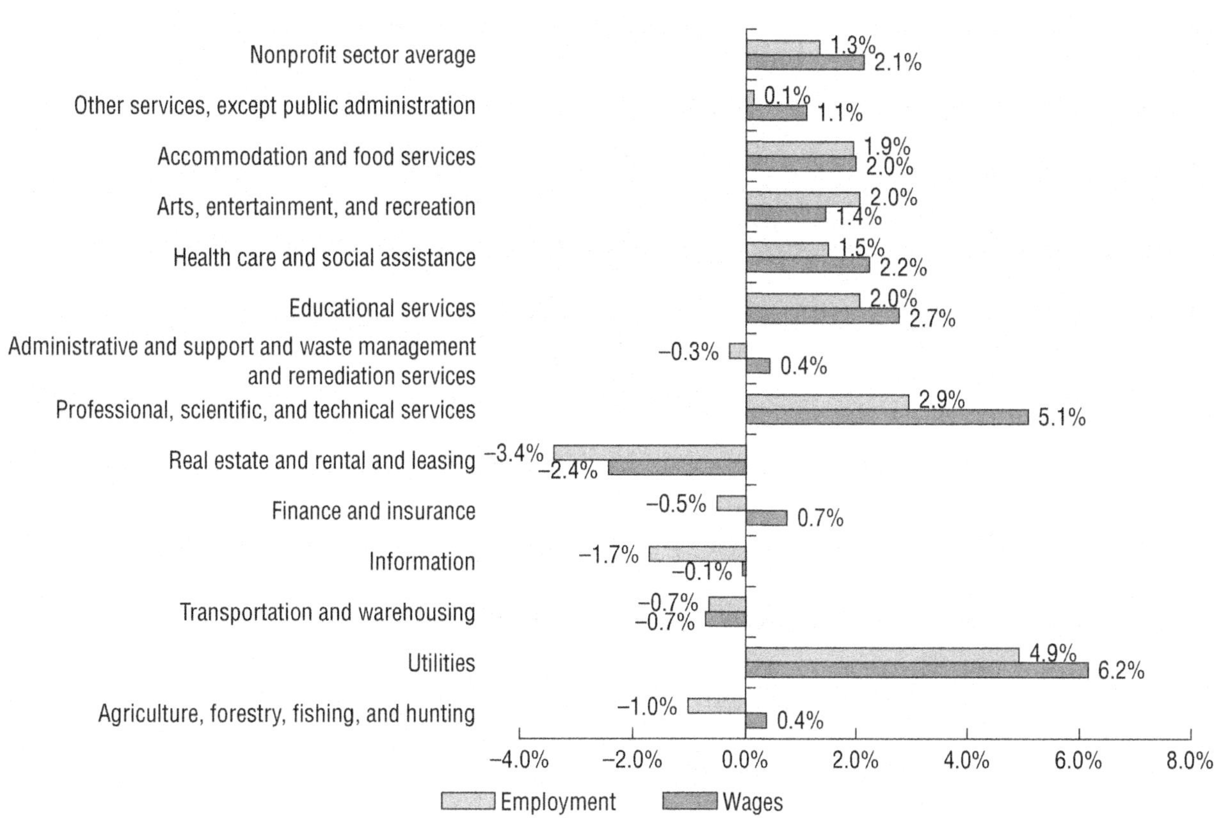

Sources: Authors' estimates based on U.S. Census Bureau, Economic Census (2002, 2007, 2012); U.S. Department of Commerce, Bureau of Economic Analysis, National Income and Product Accounts (2015); U.S. Department of Labor, Bureau of Labor Statistics, Quarterly Census of Employment and Wages (2000–14); and Urban Institute, National Center for Charitable Statistics, Core Files (Public Charities, 2000–13).

tor growth continued during the economic recession (albeit at a slightly slower pace), and the rate of growth has been reinvigorated in the post-recession years. Although the nonprofit hospital wages and employment continue to be the primary drivers behind the growth in the nonprofit sector, most nonprofit industries experienced growth during this time period. Nonprofit-sector growth, in both wages and employees, outpaced both the government and business sectors during the recession, and it has exceeded government growth in the post-recession period (and has been only slightly behind business growth).

This chapter presents the authors' estimates of nonprofit employment and wage data using available data. While these estimates attempt to capture nonprofit-sector employment and wages by combining estimates from both government and nonprofit sources, there is still no single source for nonprofit salary and employment data. Despite recent resources released by the Bureau of Labor Statistics (BLS), comprehensive nonprofit employment data remain among the most significant and largest areas of

Figure 2.4. Annual Growth Rate in Average Annual Nonprofit Compensation per Employee by Industry, 2003–13 (percent)

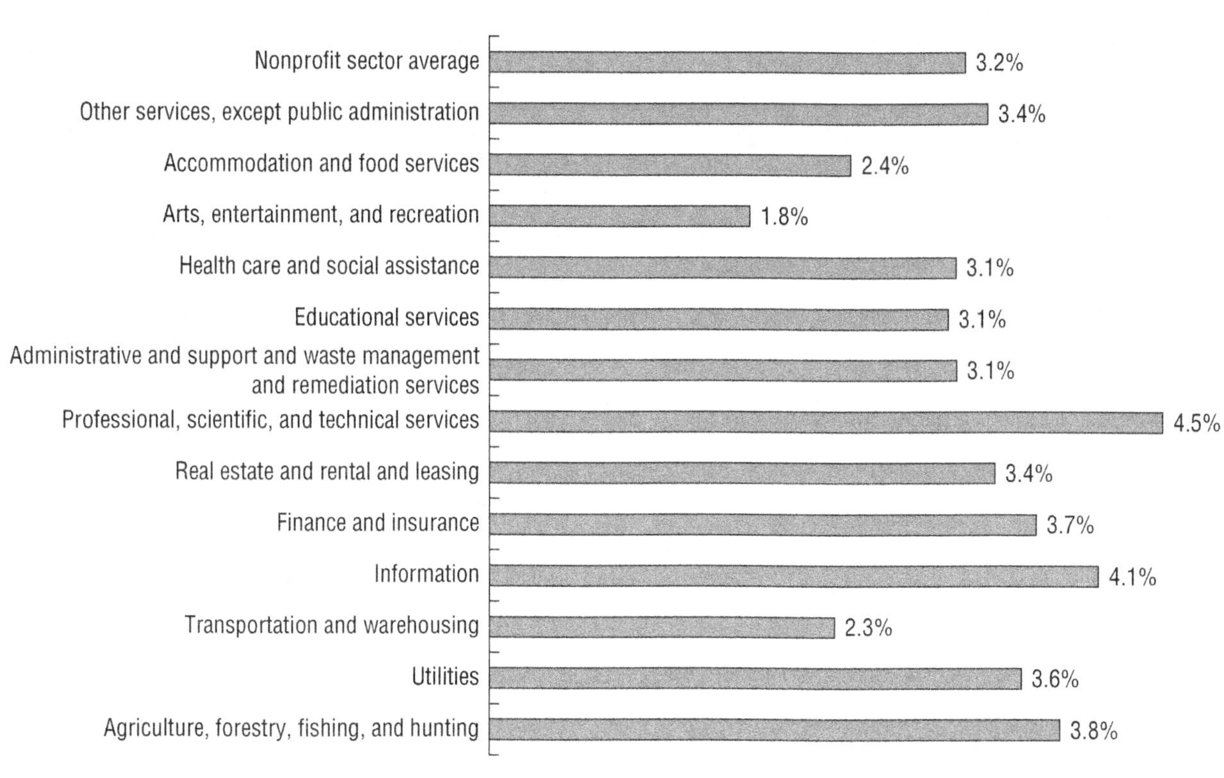

Sources: Authors' estimates based on U.S. Census Bureau, Economic Census (2002, 2007, 2012); U.S. Department of Commerce, Bureau of Economic Analysis, National Income and Product Accounts (2015); U.S. Department of Labor, Bureau of Labor Statistics, Quarterly Census of Employment and Wages (2000–11); and Urban Institute, National Center for Charitable Statistics, Core Files (Public Charities, 2000–13).

missing data on the nonprofit sector. This chapter and its supplementary tables contain the most detailed and comprehensive estimates of nonprofit wages and employment currently available by industry. The authors hope these estimates will form the base for further comparative analysis among industries within the nonprofit sector, and between for-profit and nonprofit organizations in the same industry.

Supplementary Tables

The estimates presented in this chapter attempt to capture nonprofit sector employment and wages by combining estimates from both government and nonprofit sources. The methodology details how nonprofit wages and employment information was compiled. Tables 2.6–2.19 show much of the data behind the estimates presented in this chapter.

- The data for these estimates come from three main sources: Bureau of Economic Analysis (BEA) wage and salary accruals by industry; BLS, Quarterly Census of Employment and Wages (QCEW); and wage and salary data from the National Center for Charitable Statistics based on IRS Form 990 data. The data from the QCEW are based on unemployment insurance data collected from states. Unemployment data are the most comprehensive available on wages and salaries paid by establishments in the United States, including nonprofit organizations. Drawn from reports filed by employers under the Federal Unemployment Insurance Tax Act and the Federal Unemployment Tax Act (FUTA), the data contain the total wages paid during the calendar year for establishments that employ four or more workers. For more information on how the estimates were created and how the data in these tables were combined and modified to yield the estimates in tables 2.1 and 2.2, please refer to the methodology section of this chapter. The supplementary tables include the following: table 2.6 lists the wages of nonprofit employees covered by unemployment insurance in NAICS 61 (educational services), 62 (health care and social associations), 71 (arts, entertainment, and recreation), and 81 (other services, except public administration). These industries have a nonprofit breakdown in the Economic Census. For most industries, wages covered by unemployment insurance are the same as total reported wages.
- Because many nonprofit employees in educational institutions and religious organizations are not covered by unemployment insurance, table 2.7 compares covered wages to total reported wages for those industries.
- For industries not covered in table 2.6, table 2.8 shows the wages reported to the IRS. Two-digit industries missing from both table 2.6 and table 2.8 had zero wages reported to the IRS. This table includes all public charities as well as 501(3) other nonprofits that report to the IRS.
- Tables 2.9, 2.10, and 2.11 are analogous to tables 2.6, 2.7, and 2.8, but for employment rather than wages.
- Tables 2.12–2.14 provide wages covered by unemployment insurance at the six-digit NAICS level for industries making up NAICS 54, 61, 62, 71, and 81.
- Tables 2.15–2.17 list the number of employees covered by unemployment insurance at the six-digit NAICS level for industries making up NAICS 54, 61, 62, 71, and 81.
- Table 2.18 shows the calculation of estimated wages for nonprofits serving business as reported in table 2.1.
- Table 2.19 shows the National Taxonomy of Exempt Entities (NTEE) codes comprising each two-digit NAICS industry reported in tables 2.8 and 2.11.

Methodology

Nonprofit employment data are among the most significant and largest area of missing data on the nonprofit sector. Data on nonprofit wages or employment by industry are not published annually, and what data are available are limited, either by industry or by time periods covered. The estimates presented in this chapter attempt to capture nonprofit sector employment and wages by combining estimates from both government and nonprofit sources, using a consistent methodology applicable to several years' worth of data.

Sources of Nonprofit Wages and Employment

Data for the wage and salary estimates are drawn from five sources: BEA wage and salary accruals by industry, BLS's QCEW, the Census Bureau's Economic Census, the Census Bureau's County Business Patterns, and wage and salary data from the National Center for Charitable Statistics based on IRS Form 990 data.

Estimated nonprofit wages are based on BEA data. The BEA publishes an annual series on wage and salary accruals in its National Income and Product Accounts table 6.3D. The data include a breakdown for nonprofit institutions serving households (NPISH). Unfortunately, NPISHs do not cover the entire nonprofit sector; nonprofits serving business are excluded, but the authors are able to estimate wages and salaries for nonprofits serving business. Nonprofits serving business include portions of NAICS codes 813 (religious, grantmaking, civic, professional, and similar organizations) and 5417 (scientific research and development services). The total nonprofit wages, as reported in table 2.1, are the sum of BEA NPISH wages and the authors' estimates of nonprofit serving business.

The single most comprehensive annual source of wage and employment data by industry is the QCEW, which is produced by the Bureau of Labor Statistics based on state unemployment insurance filings. Data for the QCEW are drawn from reports filed by employers under the Federal Unemployment Insurance Tax Act and FUTA that document the total wages paid during the calendar year for establishments that employ four or more workers. These data include nonprofit organizations. The QCEW is the BEA's major source for wage data and accounts for about 95 percent of BEA wage estimates. Unfortunately, the QCEW published data do not disaggregate the private ownership category into nonprofit and for-profit. In addition, religious organizations and religiously affiliated organizations (mostly schools) are not required to participate in unemployment insurance, although some choose to; as a result, many are missing from BLS data. The BEA's wage and employment estimates are larger because the BEA estimates wages for workers not covered by unemployment insurance and for wages earned but not reported to the government.

Every five years, the Economic Census publishes nonprofit wage and employment estimates for five industries: NAICS 54 (professional, scientific, and technical services), 61 (educational services), 62 (health care and social assistance), 71 (arts, entertainment, and recreation), and 81 (other services, except public administration). Total nonprofit wages in the 2012 Census were $461.0 billion. That was just 76 percent of the BEA NPISH wages for the same year of $608.0 billion. Total nonprofit wages in the 2007 Census were $392.4 billion. That was just 79 percent of the BEA NPISH wages for the same year of

$498.3 billion. Total nonprofit wages in the 2002 Census were $299.4 billion. That was just 75 percent of the BEA NPISH wages for the same year of $399.6 billion. The 1997 Census reported nonprofit wages of $186.7 billion, which was 63 percent of the BEA estimate of $296.9 billion for the same year. The wages missing from the census are understated by these comparisons because the industries that the authors believe make up nonprofits serving business are included in the smaller census estimates but excluded from the larger BEA estimates.

A major reason the census estimates are so low is that the census excludes some important nonprofit industries: elementary and secondary schools (NAICS 6111); junior colleges (NAICS 6112); colleges, universities, and professional schools (NAICS 6113); labor unions and similar labor organizations (NAICS 81393); political organizations (NAICS 81394); and religious organizations (NAICS 8131). Even after these (and other) differences are taken into consideration, however, census wages in 2012 for the five two-digit NAICS industries where nonprofits are tracked are less than private wages from the QCEW for the same industries by over $51 billion. This may be because the Economic Census is not a true census; it only samples smaller organizations.

In addition to the Economic Census, the U.S. Census Bureau releases an annual series of county business data by industry, known as the County Business Patterns (CBP). The CBP series includes data on the number of establishments, employment during the week of March 12, first-quarter payroll, and annual payroll. These data are useful for studying the economic activity of small areas, analyzing changes over time and benchmarking other statistical series to the Economic Census. Data from the CBP are broken down by establishment type (e.g., corporations, sole proprietorships), and include nonprofit organizations. The authors use CBP data for selected industries not covered by unemployment insurance.

Nonprofits that file Form 990 or Form 990-EZ report wages to the IRS. However, small nonprofits and religious organizations are not required to file and are therefore missing from the IRS data. The IRS releases two files containing wage data: the Statistics of Income (SOI) sample files and the Return Transaction File (RTF). The SOI files are carefully reviewed by the IRS for data quality. They contain all large organizations and a sample of small ones, weighted to achieve some totals in the overall population, but not wages. As a result, the sampling results in large year-to-year fluctuations in wages by industry, particularly among smaller industries. Although comprehensive for organizations that file Form 990, the RTF is not checked for accuracy. The authors' review found various errors in which wages from a given Form 990 were off by a factor of 1,000 or more. Both IRS files contain the most recent return filed by an organization. Organizations filing late may be represented in these datasets by a prior year's return. In addition, employment numbers are requested on Form 990 but not Form 990-EZ.

Drawing from both files, which are available from the National Center for Charitable Statistics (NCCS), the authors constructed a dataset consisting of the wages and salaries paid by 501(c)(3) and 501(c) other tax-exempt organizations by NAICS industry code. To construct the file, the authors used the sum of Part IX lines 5A (officers' compensation) and 7A (other wages and salaries) from the schedule of functional expenses for organizations filing Form 990 and the compensation line from Form 990-EZ. The RTF file was cleaned by replacing all RTF records with the same record from SOI where available. Wage outliers were identified, individually investigated, and manually corrected by reference to the original Form 990 where available, or by interpolation between other years when not available.

NCCS developed the NTEE classification system, which is used to group organizations according to their primary purpose or mission. The NTEE codes were mapped to the NAICS codes. Before assigning the NAICS code, the NTEE industry classification codes were carefully reviewed. During this process, the authors uncovered a few minor discrepancies that change the estimates from the previous version of the *Almanac.* A small number of large organizations had been misclassified and were reclassified according to their correct industries.

While each dataset mentioned sheds some light on nonprofit wages and employment, no single dataset is sufficient to produce estimates of nonprofit wages and employment by industry. The method developed by Kennard T. Wing for *The Nonprofit Almanac 2008* attempts to use the strengths of each while minimizing its weaknesses. The basic approach is to determine the share of nonprofit wages by industry using the Economic Census, CBP, and IRS data and then multiply the tax-exempt share by the value for the whole private industry from QCEW. The authors then attempt to measure total wages, including the imputation for wages not covered by unemployment insurance, by multiplying the nonprofit percentages by wages for each industry.

Calculating Tax-Exempt Share of Wages by Industry

The first step in calculating nonprofit wages by industry is to determine what proportion of total wages is paid by the nonprofit sector for each industry. The authors used the Economic Census, when available, to determine the nonprofit share of wages by industry. When Economic Census data were not available or were questionable, the authors turned to CBP estimates or IRS data.

The Economic Census breaks down wage and employment data for the nonprofit sector for select industries. The industries with a nonprofit breakout in the Economic Census are NAICS 54, 61, 62, 71, and 81. The first step for these industries was to calculate the tax-exempt share of wages from the Economic Census at the six-digit NAICS level.

The Economic Census is conducted every five years, so percentages from the 2002 Census were used for 2002, and percentages for 2007 were used for 2007. Percentages from the 2012 Census were used for 2012 and forward. Percentages for 2000 and 2001 were calculated using linear interpolation between the 1997 and 2002 Census percentages. Likewise, percentages for 2003 through 2006 were interpolated using the 2002 and 2007 Census, and percentages for 2008 through 2011 were interpolated using the 2007 and 2012 Census.

For general medical and surgical hospitals (NAICS 6221), psychiatric and substance abuse hospitals (NAICS 6222), and specialty (except psychiatric and substance abuse) hospitals (NAICS 6223), government hospitals were backed out of the census totals before calculating the nonprofit percentage where possible. Government hospital data for the 2012 Economic Census were not available by the time of publication, so the 2007 nonprofit percentages were used instead for all years following. However the 2007 Census does not break out government hospital data for NAICS 6223, so they are included in the nonprofit percentages for 2007 forward.

Important parts of the educational services and other services industries are excluded from the census, requiring the authors to identify alternative sources for the tax-exempt share. This includes junior colleges (NAICS 6112); colleges, universities, and professional schools (NAICS 6113); elementary and secondary schools (NAICS 6111); labor unions and similar labor organizations (NAICS 81393); political organizations (NAICS 81394); and religious organizations (NAICS 8131). The tax-exempt share for these industries is based on the County Business Patterns annual payroll for nonprofit organizations.

The remaining industries have no nonprofit breakout in the Economic Census. For these, the authors used the NCCS wage dataset based on IRS SOI and RTF files. Wages were totaled by two-digit NAICS industries by reclassifying the NTEE core codes according to the scheme shown in table 2.19. This resulted in the numbers reported in table 2.6.

Creating Wage Estimates

After the tax-exempt shares of wages by industry were calculated, the authors applied these percentages to the QCEW private wages. The authors obtained QCEW private wages at the six-digit NAICS level. Calculations were carried out at the six-digit NAICS level and then aggregated. Also, calculations using IRS Form 990 data were performed at the two-digit NAICS level. Estimated wages covered by unemployment insurance at the six-digit NAICS levels are shown in tables 2.12–2.14.

In 2013, the QCEW reviewed the classification for a number of programs that provide funding for non-medical, home-based services for the elderly and persons with disabilities. In 2012 and previous years, these organizations, which provided over half a million jobs and over $6 billion in wages, had been classified as belonging in the Private Households NAICS category (NAICS 814). Beginning in 2013 and for all following years, these organizations were classified as services for the elderly and persons with disabilities (NAICS 624120). This reclassification resulted in a large increase in wages and employment between the 2012 and 2013 QCEW data sets for the NAICS 624120 category. For more information on this change, see Petty and Hu 2014. After reviewing this discontinuity, the authors of the *Almanac* used QCEW data from 2013 through 2015 to estimate data for 2012 for NAICS 624120. Then the authors used the proportional rates of growth in employment and wages noted in the QCEW for all years prior to 2012 to estimate data for those years.

For most industries in tables 2.12–2.14, the wages covered by unemployment insurance represent the total reported wages for the industry. In a few industries, however, a significant number of nonprofit employees are not covered by unemployment insurance. For these, the authors estimated total reported wages by replacing the QCEW private wages by wage estimates from County Business Patterns. The six main industries in which replacement occurred were elementary and secondary schools; junior colleges; colleges, universities, and professional schools; political organizations; labor unions and similar labor organizations; and religious organizations. These results are shown in table 2.7.

Finally, the authors attempted to measure total wages, including BEA's imputation for unreported wages, by multiplying the nonprofit share of wages by BEA wages by industry. These calculations were carried out at the two-digit NAICS level. These are the wage estimates reported in table 2.1.

Employment Estimates

Employment estimates were developed similarly to wage estimates, with two differences. First, for industries available from the Economic Census, the nonprofit share of employment was used instead of the share of wages, and the share was multiplied by private employment in the industry, rather than wages. Second, because BEA does not provide an estimate of NPISH employment, only two employment estimates were calculated: nonprofit employment covered by unemployment insurance, and total reported nonprofit employment.

For the remaining industries, the authors multiplied the nonprofit share of wages by QCEW private employment. This method is limited because it assumes that wage levels in the nonprofit and for-profit portions within a given industry are similar. If nonprofit wage levels are significantly lower, for example, nonprofit employment will be underestimated.

Comparisons of the wages and employment reported on the same Forms 990 suggested that employment was being underreported to the IRS. Employment numbers reported to the IRS also resulted in lower estimated employment than the estimates from the wage-share method, so this method offered no correction for the suspected underestimation problem. Recognizing its limitations, the authors chose the wage-share approach as the best available at this time. Nonprofit employment data remain the largest missing piece in nonprofit data.

Limitations to the Estimates

There are also some limitations with the wage-share method for estimating nonprofit wages and employment:

- Nonprofit wages may be much lower in some industries than for-profit wages, resulting in significant underestimates.

- IRS data are based on legal entities, whereas QCEW data are based on establishments. A single entity may have multiple establishments, and a single establishment may have multiple legal entities. Where there are multiple establishments or entities, they may be classified into different industry categories. As a result, the IRS and QCEW could be classifying the same organization in different industries.
- IRS data are coded according to the NTEE classification system. QCEW data are coded according to NAICS. The authors' conversion from NTEE to NAICS maps one NTEE code into one NAICS code. This may have reduced the size of some NAICS industries and inflated others.

Alternative Wages and Employment Estimates

The BLS recently released a series of research data on employment, wages, and establishment figures for nonprofit institutions. Like the information presented in this chapter, the new BLS data series relies on QCEW and IRS Forms 990 and 990-EZ data, but the BLS methodology leads to different conclusions than those presented in this chapter. For 2012 (the latest year available for this new dataset), the BLS dataset reports an estimated 11.4 million employees and $532.1 billion in annual wages for organizations exempt under 501(c)(3) of the Internal Revenue Code; both numbers are less than the totals reported in this chapter for 2012 for the nonprofit sector as a whole (14.2 million and $617.3 billion for employees and annual wages, respectively). Among the reasons for the differences in estimates:

- The BLS dataset uses as its base a match of Employer Identification Number between the QCEW and IRS Form 990 at the organizational level.
- The BLS dataset relies on IRS Exempt Organization Business Master File (EOBMF), rather than the SOI or RTF files used in this chapter.
- 501(c)(3) organizations are a subset of the total number of nonprofits in the sector, albeit the largest portion. The employment and wage estimates presented in this chapter encompass the entire nonprofit sector.
- Religious organizations and religiously affiliated organizations (mostly schools) are not required to participate in unemployment insurance, so many are missing from the QCEW data. When creating estimates of nonprofit employment, the authors incorporate data from the QCEW, BEA, Economic Census, and IRS Form 990s to ensure that all industries are included. The BEA's wage and employment estimates are larger than QCEW figures because BEA includes wages for workers not covered by unemployment insurance; BEA also estimates wages earned but not reported to the government.

Additionally, as of publication, this BLS dataset only covers years 2007 to 2012. Furthermore, the information presented by the BLS is not available at the six-digit NAICS level. Due to these limitations and the differences in methodology presented above, the BLS dataset does not facilitate incorporation into the methodology used for the estimates presented in this chapter. For these reasons, the authors opted to continue to use the methodology presented in previous editions of *The Nonprofit Almanac.*

Sources

Boris, Elizabeth T., Erwin de Leon, Katie L. Roeger, and Milena Nikolova. 2010. "Human Service Nonprofits and Government Collaboration: Findings from the 2010 National Survey of Nonprofit Government Contracting and Grants." Washington, DC: The Urban Institute.

Petty, Wade and Patrick Hu. 2014. "CES—National Benchmark Article: BLS Establishment Survey National Estimates Revised to Incorporate March 2013 Benchmarks." U.S. Department of Labor, Bureau of Labor Statistics. http://www.bls.gov/ces/cesbmart13.pdf.

The Urban Institute, National Center for Charitable Statistics. 1998–2013. Core Files.

The Urban Institute, National Center for Charitable Statistics. 1998–2012. Internal Revenue Service Statistics of Income Files.

The Urban Institute, National Center for Charitable Statistics. 2015. NCCS NTEE/NAICS Crosswalk.

U.S. Census Bureau. 1991–2013. County Business Patterns.

U.S. Census Bureau. 1997. Economic Census.

———. 2002. Economic Census.

———. 2007. Economic Census.

———. 2012. Economic Census.

U.S. Department of Commerce, Bureau of Economic Analysis. 2009. "Updated Summary of NIPA Methodologies." http://www.bea.gov/scb/pdf/2009/11%20November/1109_nipa_method.pdf.

———. 2015. National Income and Product Accounts.

U.S. Department of Labor, Bureau of Labor Statistics. 2000–2015. Quarterly Census of Employment and Wages.

———. 2014. "Employment and Wages Online Annual Averages, 2013." http://www.bls.gov/cew/cewbultn13.htm.

Table 2.6. Nonprofit Wages Covered by Unemployment Insurance, for Industries with Tax Status Identified in the Economic Census, 2000–13 (current $ millions)

	NAICS Code and Industry Description					
	54	61	62	71	81	
Year	Professional, scientific, and technical services	Educational services	Health care and social assistance	Arts, entertainment, and recreation	Other services, except public administration	Total
1990	7,455	22,798	98,023	5,705	16,874	150,855
1991	7,814	24,473	107,387	5,779	17,574	163,026
1992	8,050	26,059	117,807	5,658	18,707	176,282
1993	8,319	27,550	123,853	5,686	19,455	184,863
1994	8,610	29,085	130,227	5,926	20,615	194,464
1995	9,103	30,811	137,191	6,202	21,717	205,024
1996	9,284	32,690	144,005	6,657	22,904	215,541
1997	10,097	35,074	152,037	6,928	24,476	228,613
1998	9,796	38,171	161,690	7,585	25,395	242,637
1999	9,435	40,418	168,933	8,143	27,102	254,030
2000	9,438	43,344	178,379	8,898	29,390	269,448
2001	8,345	46,943	192,849	9,481	31,769	289,387
2002	7,037	50,423	207,772	9,780	33,668	308,680
2003	8,370	54,390	221,999	10,318	34,880	329,958
2004	9,884	57,801	235,251	10,829	36,424	350,189
2005	11,803	61,270	246,785	11,269	37,782	368,910
2006	13,761	65,483	262,428	12,051	39,928	393,652
2007	15,804	70,639	278,515	12,800	42,627	420,385
2008	16,323	75,485	297,715	13,574	45,498	448,595
2009	15,769	79,254	311,165	13,112	45,564	464,864
2010	16,017	80,659	319,389	13,224	46,326	475,615
2011	16,459	85,650	329,761	13,777	47,264	492,911
2012	17,099	90,015	341,012	14,427	49,188	511,741
2013	17,544	92,442	351,053	15,113	50,666	526,818

Sources: Authors' estimates based on private wages from U.S. Department of Labor, Bureau of Labor Statistics, Quarterly Census of Employment and Wages (1990–2013). The tax-exempt share of wages is from U.S. Census Bureau, Economic Census (1997, 2002, 2007, and 2012).
Note: Industries are listed as classified by the North American Industry Classification System (NAICS).

Table 2.7. Nonprofit Wages Reported to the U.S. Census Bureau Compared with Covered Wages by Unemployment Insurance, in Select Industries where Many Employees Exempt from Unemployment Insurance, 2000–13 (current $ millions)

	NAICS Code and Industry Description													
	611110		611210		611310		611210+611310		813110		813930		813940	
	Elementary and secondary schools		Junior colleges		Colleges, universities, and professional schools		Junior colleges, colleges, universities, and professional schools		Religious organizations		Labor unions and similar labor organizations		Political organizations	
Year	Reported	Covered	Reported	Covered	Reported	Covered	Reported	Covered	Reported	Covered	Reported	Covered	Reported	Covered
1990	5,817.2	4,847.6	—	182.1	—	16,775.5	18,177.0	16,957.6	10,006.8	1,288.6	2,671.1	2,319.8	143.9	125.3
1991	6,347.2	5,333.3	—	230.5	—	17,871.9	19,673.9	18,102.4	10,923.6	1,307.8	2,791.9	2,438.3	102.7	87.8
1992	7,375.1	5,573.7	—	242.4	—	19,144.6	21,351.1	19,387.0	11,863.9	1,400.7	2,926.2	2,518.5	186.3	142.3
1993	7,661.7	5,962.6	—	249.8	—	20,192.7	23,195.3	20,442.5	12,716.7	1,476.3	2,990.6	2,551.4	145.3	105.1
1994	8,283.7	6,383.0	—	257.9	—	21,244.2	24,330.9	21,502.1	13,540.6	1,565.6	2,961.0	2,603.8	222.8	168.9
1995	9,053.4	6,933.0	—	267.5	—	22,330.0	25,504.5	22,597.5	15,233.9	1,681.5	3,087.3	2,678.2	[illegible]	121.9
1996	9,808.4	7,507.0	—	287.1	—	23,431.2	26,587.2	23,718.3	16,152.5	1,826.9	3,237.4	2,794.1	256.8	189.3
1997	10,606.9	8,240.3	—	303.8	—	24,898.6	28,174.3	25,202.5	17,406.8	2,265.9	3,347.6	2,928.0	178.7	125.1
1998	11,478.6	8,847.2	583.8	317.7	29,043.8	27,215.0	29,627.6	27,532.8	18,721.4	2,245.4	3,487.0	3,036.7	259.1	184.5

1999	12,633.5	9,687.4	599.3	320.7	30,888.5	28,267.8	31,487.8	28,588.5	20,247.7	2,489.2	3,654.1	3,159.9	217.2	154.6
2000	13,676.8	10,614.4	627.8	340.2	32,713.7	30,014.0	33,341.5	30,354.2	21,934.6	2,773.7	3,842.9	3,329.4	29[illegible].2	225.8
2001	14,998.3	11,654.2	645.6	347.2	34,823.8	32,215.8	35,469.4	32,563.0	23,131.4	3,027.0	3,966.5	3,500.1	25[illegible].4	176.2
2002	16,714.9	12,719.5	682.9	341.9	37,188.0	34,350.0	37,870.9	34,691.9	24,669.6	3,287.9	4,274.9	3,646.6	350.4	275.6
2003	17,482.8	13,681.3	778.0	382.7	38,799.7	37,130.8	39,577.7	37,513.5	25,575.5	3,529.2	4,391.7	3,777.1	340.8	203.2
2004	18,219.1	14,612.4	818.5	392.4	41,090.9	39,389.2	41,909.4	39,781.6	26,195.8	3,713.5	4,543.8	3,854.4	50[illegible].7	329.1
2005	18,327.4	15,532.9	856.5	591.3	43,007.1	41,441.4	43,863.6	42,032.7	27,039.8	3,889.8	4,657.4	3,892.8	35[illegible].5	222.2
2006	19,669.0	16,706.4	934.4	638.7	45,461.2	44,070.7	46,395.6	44,709.4	28,109.0	4,140.1	4,790.9	4,033.8	516.2	360.7
2007	21,157.1	18,104.1	984.1	635.0	48,866.7	47,445.0	49,850.7	48,080.0	30,253.2	4,487.1	4,867.2	4,164.6	37[illegible].5	310.1
2008	22,535.1	19,569.7	1,033.6	639.8	52,803.7	50,418.7	53,837.2	51,058.5	31,428.5	4,773.1	5,119.2	4,384.3	50[illegible].2	434.6
2009	23,356.6	20,509.3	1,088.7	681.1	55,179.5	53,083.9	56,268.2	53,765.1	31,663.6	4,630.8	5,147.3	4,390.7	35[illegible].1	278.2
2010	23,794.0	20,655.1	1,039.6	712.1	56,963.3	54,006.8	58,002.9	54,718.9	31,472.9	4,806.1	5,100.8	4,342.1	45[illegible].0	394.2
2011	24,761.7	22,051.0	1,115.4	726.4	59,161.2	57,324.0	60,276.6	58,050.4	31,762.4	4,450.9	5,107.8	4,350.1	30[illegible].7	275.1
2012	26,132.6	23,303.7	1,002.6	675.8	62,064.1	60,169.6	63,066.7	60,845.4	32,631.3	4,558.9	5,120.5	4,391.9	48[illegible].5	449.8
2013	28,110.3	24,151.3	1,007.5	678.2	64,028.5	61,566.7	65,036.0	62,244.9	33,136.2	4,698.8	5,237.6	4,422.0	32[illegible].8	296.0

Sources: Reported wages are authors' estimates based on multiplying tax-exempt shares by national total private wages from U.S. Census Bureau, County Business Patterns (1991–2013). Covered wages are authors' estimates based on multiplying tax-exempt shares by private wages from U.S. Department of Labor, Bureau of Labor Statistics, Quarterly Census of Employment and Wages (1991–2013).

Note: The NAICS 611210+611310 column is the sum of the two columns to its left, except for 1990–97 reported wages, when the more detailed breakout was not available.

— = not available

Table 2.8. Wages Reported to the Internal Revenue Service for Two-Digit Industries Whose Tax Status Is Not Identified in the Economic Census, 2000–13 (current $ millions)

NAICS code	Industry	2000	2001	2002	2003	2004	2005	2006	2007	2008	2009	2010	2011	2012	2013
11	Agriculture, forestry, fishing, and hunting	221.2	264.6	275.8	291.8	284.2	290.4	297.3	313.5	296.4	288.4	301.8	323.9	331.7	362.8
22	Utilities	993.4	1,109.7	1,176.7	1,258.4	1,373.3	1,431.1	1,541.8	1,668.9	2,200.2	2,368.0	2,455.9	2,615.8	2,724.6	2,820.9
48–49	Transportation and warehousing	50.4	34.1	43.8	63.5	63.1	65.6	70.5	78.3	82.0	78.7	68.1	75.1	74.2	75.3
51	Information	1,788.8	2,063.7	2,246.6	2,353.9	2,384.7	2,534.6	2,624.3	2,817.0	2,941.9	2,955.1	2,742.5	2,812.5	2,809.7	2,965.3
52	Finance and insurance	3,227.9	3,859.4	4,124.1	5,304.0	5,656.7	6,044.5	6,750.3	7,470.9	7,331.5	7,100.7	6,968.1	6,752.9	7,109.8	7,120.9
53	Real estate and rental and leasing	111.2	88.1	103.1	131.2	110.0	111.4	122.4	142.6	144.7	132.4	143.4	135.9	136.4	130.7
54	Professional, scientific, and technical services	7,156.4	8,317.2	9,134.1	9,375.4	9,892.1	11,335.0	11,989.5	12,892.1	13,734.0	14,454.2	13,682.7	16,476.4	16,638.0	16,911.5
56	Administrative and waste management services	667.5	714.8	748.5	773.7	767.6	757.2	784.0	860.7	902.0	911.5	1,074.3	1,088.5	1,006.6	1,007.1
72	Accommodation and food services	183.5	205.7	222.2	234.4	246.3	255.8	269.8	285.7	285.9	281.6	303.5	329.6	348.8	362.5

Source: Urban Institute, National Center for Charitable Statistics, Core Files (Public Charities and Others, 2000–13), with error corrections and missing-data interpolations performed by the authors.
Note: Industries are listed as classified by the North American Industry Classification System (NAICS).

Table 2.9. Nonprofit Employees Covered by Unemployment Insurance, for Industries with Tax Status Identified in the Economic Census, 2000–13

	NAICS Code and Industry Description					
	54	61	62	71	81	
Year	Professional, scientific, and technical services	Educational services	Health care and social assistance	Arts, entertainment, and recreation	Other services, except public administration	Total
1990	220,605	1,056,900	4,834,911	467,990	1,039,327	7,619,733
1991	216,694	1,063,276	5,011,825	447,666	1,017,467	7,756,929
1992	214,203	1,071,175	5,203,602	398,349	1,035,742	7,923,071
1993	216,394	1,085,774	5,368,738	377,885	1,050,926	8,099,717
1994	215,214	1,116,078	5,496,232	380,729	1,077,457	8,285,709
1995	213,969	1,141,285	5,630,647	380,543	1,100,687	8,467,131
1996	210,221	1,182,292	5,773,888	382,535	1,121,857	8,670,794
1997	215,527	1,224,878	5,914,178	388,798	1,147,034	8,890,416
1998	203,532	1,278,373	6,073,715	403,242	1,161,731	9,120,593
1999	191,172	1,319,310	6,194,394	415,481	1,194,644	9,315,001
2000	178,657	1,362,885	6,305,850	437,971	1,235,287	9,520,650
2001	162,710	1,414,567	6,504,403	452,120	1,267,662	9,801,462
2002	142,703	1,464,509	6,707,611	460,296	1,292,657	10,067,776
2003	162,496	1,514,588	6,827,773	471,677	1,289,107	10,265,640
2004	183,674	1,555,027	6,893,517	488,167	1,290,923	10,411,307
2005	209,354	1,598,676	6,983,509	498,306	1,291,401	10,581,247
2006	235,341	1,643,801	7,084,871	513,879	1,306,683	10,784,574
2007	256,371	1,700,089	7,215,558	533,318	1,328,047	11,033,382
2008	251,331	1,753,688	7,406,115	545,577	1,358,384	11,315,095
2009	237,421	1,785,514	7,523,140	534,374	1,321,139	11,401,589
2010	230,408	1,784,327	7,610,352	533,742	1,306,131	11,464,961
2011	224,246	1,838,666	7,690,207	543,913	1,309,272	11,606,304
2012	217,403	1,886,618	7,787,704	560,724	1,318,890	11,771,340
2013	216,773	1,904,944	7,902,872	577,786	1,325,118	11,927,494

Sources: Authors' estimates based on private employment from U.S. Department of Labor, Bureau of Labor Statistics, Quarterly Census of Employment and Wages (1990–2014). Tax-exempt share of wages is from U.S. Census Bureau, Economic Census (1997, 2002, 2007, and 2012).
Note: Industries are listed as classified by the North American Industry Classification System (NAICS).

Table 2.10. Nonprofit Employees Reported to the U.S. Census Bureau or Covered by Unemployment Insurance with Many Employees Exempt from Unemployment Insurance, 1990–2013

	NAICS Code and Industry Description							
	611110		611210		611310		611210+611310	
	Elementary and secondary schools		Junior colleges		Colleges, universities, and professional schools		Junior colleges, colleges, universities, and professional schools	
Year	Reported	Covered	Reported	Covered	Reported	Covered	Reported	Covered
1990	397,081	289,560	—	9,484	—	703,830	1,023,410	713,313
1991	413,196	296,460	—	11,295	—	703,183	1,061,539	714,478
1992	461,634	300,477	—	11,229	—	706,590	1,131,568	717,819
1993	474,134	313,702	—	11,293	—	706,009	1,152,942	717,302
1994	495,616	327,596	—	11,365	—	720,293	1,167,809	731,658
1995	517,983	342,472	—	11,138	—	728,292	1,182,774	739,430
1996	535,971	356,674	—	11,270	—	750,446	1,190,759	761,716
1997	562,693	373,665	—	11,666	—	771,413	1,224,713	783,080
1998	580,165	391,305	23,546	11,740	1,215,115	800,408	1,238,661	812,148
1999	611,247	412,408	22,982	11,170	1,242,825	811,627	1,265,808	822,797
2000	637,294	432,679	23,663	11,069	1,259,745	823,716	1,283,408	834,786
2001	657,756	452,064	23,336	11,169	1,270,559	844,685	1,293,894	855,854
2002	698,251	471,661	24,419	10,454	1,300,282	865,305	1,324,701	875,759
2003	707,586	488,708	25,547	11,253	1,331,697	893,355	1,357,244	904,608
2004	711,390	502,340	24,695	11,331	1,390,059	915,875	1,414,754	927,206
2005	687,029	519,167	30,656	16,680	1,401,703	932,373	1,432,359	949,053
2006	706,455	535,151	33,326	17,526	1,427,054	958,080	1,460,380	975,607
2007	727,748	555,785	38,729	20,140	1,463,842	987,480	1,502,571	1,007,620
2008	741,305	576,775	39,821	20,329	1,510,408	1,011,919	1,550,229	1,032,249
2009	751,392	586,046	40,879	21,193	1,547,424	1,032,429	1,588,303	1,053,622
2010	747,963	582,558	36,457	21,375	1,566,631	1,029,819	1,603,088	1,051,194
2011	758,308	608,590	38,556	21,496	1,603,193	1,054,360	1,641,749	1,075,856
2012	783,342	629,009	35,139	19,713	1,639,134	1,078,643	1,674,273	1,098,356
2013	826,081	639,849	33,859	18,504	1,656,197	1,085,119	1,690,056	1,103,624

Sources: Reported employees are authors' estimates based on multiplying tax-exempt shares by national total private employment from U.S. Census Bureau, County Business Patterns (1991–2013). Covered employees are authors' estimates based on multiplying tax-exempt shares by private employment from U.S. Department of Labor, Bureau of Labor Statistics, Quarterly Census of Employment and Wages (1991–2013).

Note: The NAICS 611210+611310 column is the sum of the two columns to its left, except for 1990–97 reported wages, when the more detailed breakout was not available.

— = not available

813110		813930		813940	
Religious organizations		Labor unions and similar labor organizations		Political organizations	
Reported	Covered	Reported	Covered	Reported	Covered
1,089,557	99,521	172,005	134,460	7,027	6,416
1,136,328	98,123	177,053	136,760	5,075	4,069
1,164,829	102,374	180,859	136,428	9,990	6,453
1,236,417	105,226	178,874	136,282	6,393	4,377
1,258,137	108,839	167,882	136,258	9,543	7,412
1,307,797	113,373	163,109	136,587	6,750	4,702
1,372,465	119,034	165,315	138,596	9,000	7,301
1,427,694	129,563	167,487	139,040	6,620	4,538
1,460,331	135,060	163,206	138,195	8,357	6,476
1,508,529	144,456	162,933	138,270	7,100	4,920
1,559,682	150,875	164,152	139,911	9,143	6,878
1,585,180	158,231	159,378	138,819	7,460	4,926
1,628,816	165,757	166,806	137,920	9,723	7,889
1,644,583	171,605	178,522	135,821	8,503	5,203
1,639,328	174,040	174,542	133,242	12,689	9,887
1,621,887	176,201	172,517	129,894	11,446	5,229
1,637,069	178,323	174,971	129,446	13,992	8,853
1,680,761	182,546	168,759	128,243	8,708	6,556
1,688,767	185,231	168,649	130,029	11,695	10,502
1,680,943	183,575	160,872	124,797	8,243	5,598
1,672,520	179,647	157,760	119,302	9,584	8,325
1,648,121	181,061	151,062	116,825	6,561	5,277
1,668,885	180,972	150,916	115,508	9,440	8,891
1,668,685	184,387	147,549	112,001	7,264	5,306

Table 2.11. Estimated Employment for Two-Digit Industries Whose Tax Status Is Not Identified in the Economic Census, 2000–13

NAICS code	Industry	2000	2001	2002	2003	2004
11	Agriculture, forestry, fishing, and hunting	11,386	13,107	13,203	13,659	12,724
22	Utilities	15,748	16,927	17,466	18,331	18,968
48–49	Transportation and warehousing	1,433	942	1,188	1,696	1,625
51	Information	30,534	36,023	40,044	40,584	39,272
52	Finance and insurance	53,670	60,600	65,711	81,656	80,660
53	Real estate and rental and leasing	3,496	2,679	3,039	3,743	2,949
54	Professional, scientific, and technical services	178,657	162,710	142,703	162,496	183,674
56	Administrative and waste management services	28,965	29,241	29,613	29,693	28,190
72	Accommodation and food services	13,716	15,046	15,931	16,475	16,750

Sources: Authors' estimates based on multiplying the tax-exempt wage share by private employment. Tax-exempt wages by industry are from Urban Institute, National Center for Charitable Statistics, Core Files (Public Charities and Others, 2000–13). Private wages and private employment by industry are from U.S. Department of Labor, Bureau of Labor Statistics, Quarterly Census of Employment and Wages (2000–14).
Notes: Industries are listed as classified by the North American Industry Classification System (NAICS). Please see the methodology section of this chapter for a discussion of estimated employment and its limitations.

2005	2006	2007	2008	2009	2010	2011	2012	2013
12,563	12,321	12,447	11,407	11,078	11,331	11,759	11,589	12,320
19,028	19,681	20,285	26,145	27,899	28,297	28,869	29,072	29,645
1,660	1,727	1,837	1,908	1,838	1,541	1,657	1,593	1,587
40,325	39,785	40,743	41,560	41,509	36,864	35,905	34,283	34,168
82,368	85,919	87,942	85,982	88,989	82,445	76,484	77,943	77,517
2,828	2,918	3,281	3,347	3,133	3,274	2,964	2,823	2,652
209,354	235,341	256,371	251,331	237,421	230,408	224,246	217,403	216,773
26,910	26,727	27,858	28,103	27,969	32,284	32,143	28,879	28,796
16,868	17,183	17,463	17,129	16,870	17,669	18,786	19,435	19,947

Table 2.12. Nonprofit Wages Covered by Unemployment Insurance for Six-Digit Industries Whose Tax Status Is Identified in the Economic Census, 1990–97 (current $ millions)

NAICS code	Industry	1990	1991	1992	1993	1994	1995	1996	1997
541110	Offices of lawyers	607.9	621.3	663.9	677.2	694.7	713.1	743.7	791.7
541710	Physical, engineering, and biological research services	5,830.1	6,007.9	6,141.3	6,388.1	6,608.0	7,000.4	7,125.5	7,823.2
541720	Research and development in the social sciences and humanities	1,016.8	1,184.3	1,244.8	1,253.7	1,307.2	1,389.8	1,414.8	1,482.4
611110	Elementary and secondary schools	4,847.6	5,333.3	5,573.7	5,962.6	6,383.0	6,933.0	7,507.0	8,240.3
611210	Junior colleges	182.1	230.5	242.4	249.8	257.9	267.5	287.1	303.8
611310	Colleges, universities, and professional schools	16,775.5	17,871.9	19,144.6	20,192.7	21,244.2	22,330.0	23,431.2	24,898.6
611410	Business and secretarial schools	25.2	21.7	20.2	18.0	17.3	16.9	16.4	16.4
611420	Computer training	2.1	2.3	2.8	3.1	3.8	5.0	6.1	7.6
611430	Professional and management development training	112.5	118.7	137.3	143.3	154.7	168.8	201.5	221.5
611511	Cosmetology and barber schools	6.2	6.3	6.0	5.9	5.5	5.3	5.2	4.8
611512	Flight training	7.4	7.1	6.6	6.1	6.5	6.6	6.6	7.5
611513	Apprenticeship training	174.2	157.4	140.5	127.0	121.8	120.2	125.9	136.6
611519	Other technical and trade schools	118.7	131.8	139.9	148.6	150.6	160.4	180.5	208.3
611610	Fine arts schools	119.3	120.3	127.5	134.2	150.1	162.5	182.0	187.1
611620	Sports and recreation instruction	26.6	27.9	31.2	35.7	39.7	43.4	48.8	49.9
611630	Language schools	19.6	22.2	25.5	27.3	29.6	31.6	36.2	40.1
611691	Exam preparation and tutoring	21.8	22.7	25.1	27.5	29.9	32.8	37.9	43.8
611692	Automobile driving schools	5.6	5.5	5.6	5.8	6.2	6.6	6.9	7.4
611699	All other miscellaneous schools and instruction	86.3	95.0	100.4	114.4	125.0	133.8	152.6	176.0
611710	Educational support services	267.6	298.1	329.5	348.0	359.6	386.4	458.4	524.2

621410	Family planning centers	233.3	264.5	326.4	359.0	384.1	408.2	425.6	449.6
621420	Outpatient mental health and substance abuse centers	1,323.1	1,433.7	1,563.7	1,729.6	1,918.0	2,087.7	2,252.0	2,428.0
621491	HMO medical centers	2,259.0	2,359.2	2,450.9	2,418.4	2,570.1	2,738.2	2,828.8	2,716.7
621492	Kidney dialysis centers	87.6	104.4	124.1	140.6	153.6	172.8	193.3	223.8
621493	Freestanding ambulatory surgical and emergency centers	223.9	305.1	337.6	338.3	359.6	399.5	410.2	413.3
621498	All other outpatient care centers	795.4	759.6	909.3	1,004.3	1,134.4	1,182.4	1,238.6	1,300.3
621610	Home health care services	1,571.1	2,017.0	2,531.0	3,036.5	3,505.5	4,048.8	4,387.2	4,659.6
621910	Ambulance services	133.0	150.6	164.6	177.2	199.2	224.1	260.3	291.0
621991	Blood and organ banks	506.0	561.5	621.1	703.4	777.3	825.7	840.3	892.3
621999	All other miscellaneous ambulatory health care services	25.2	27.7	31.7	34.7	41.7	42.8	52.1	58.9
622110	General medical and surgical hospitals	66,593.5	72,642.9	79,336.9	82,521.6	85,654.6	89,020.9	92,771.0	97,613.1
622210	Psychiatric and substance abuse hospitals	1,092.2	1,168.0	1,199.6	1,153.4	1,139.2	1,133.4	1,089.3	1,094.1
622310	Specialty (except psychiatric and substance abuse) hospitals	1,775.6	1,987.7	2,242.8	2,406.1	2,479.1	2,627.8	2,848.7	3,048.4
623110	Nursing care facilities	4,213.8	4,678.5	5,192.0	5,562.5	6,007.1	6,500.0	6,923.7	7,311.3
623210	Residential mental retardation facilities	1,869.1	2,120.3	2,302.8	2,399.0	2,533.1	2,750.8	2,930.6	3,161.9
623220	Residential mental health and substance abuse facilities	1,003.6	1,113.8	1,173.1	1,255.5	1,332.3	1,464.0	1,558.0	1,692.6
623311	Continuing care retirement communities	1,728.8	1,936.6	2,055.7	2,165.7	2,249.1	2,366.8	2,526.0	2,635.7
623312	Homes for the elderly	554.5	617.8	677.6	722.5	778.0	829.2	978.0	1,034.8
623990	Other residential care facilities	1,221.7	1,344.8	1,511.8	1,636.3	1,751.1	1,960.5	2,129.6	2,324.1
624110	Child and youth services	976.4	1,077.9	1,221.0	1,336.7	1,490.1	1,651.7	1,811.9	2,018.7
624120	Services for the elderly and persons with disabilities	2,701.0	2,940.5	3,308.8	3,513.7	3,766.4	3,922.4	4,094.9	4,316.5
624190	Other individual and family services	1,992.6	2,180.7	2,405.7	2,653.1	2,892.1	3,203.4	3,453.0	3,732.4
624210	Community food services	269.6	346.8	380.4	398.7	424.1	426.4	415.0	391.5

(continued)

Table 2.12. Nonprofit Wages Covered by Unemployment Insurance for Six-Digit Industries Whose Tax Status Is Identified in the Economic Census, 1990–97 (current $ millions) *(continued)*

NAICS code	Industry	1990	1991	1992	1993	1994	1995	1996	1997
624221	Temporary shelters	268.5	318.7	389.5	418.2	474.0	532.6	557.1	608.2
624229	Other community housing services	127.4	152.5	167.1	190.9	229.3	257.0	273.5	304.2
624230	Emergency and other relief services	534.3	491.1	505.5	477.4	476.1	499.0	513.2	522.6
624310	Vocational rehabilitation services	2,405.5	2,548.6	2,731.3	2,935.8	3,109.8	3,290.1	3,428.4	3,704.7
624410	Child day care services	1,537.3	1,736.4	1,945.5	2,163.8	2,398.3	2,624.5	2,814.7	3,088.2
711110	Theater companies and dinner theaters	1,792.9	1,703.2	1,302.6	1,066.0	991.4	907.5	856.5	794.2
711120	Dance companies	132.0	141.0	147.9	157.1	160.7	181.2	183.3	182.7
711130	Musical groups and artists	415.4	430.1	465.1	495.1	494.2	528.5	555.6	602.3
711190	Other performing arts companies	3.4	3.7	3.6	4.2	5.9	6.9	6.5	7.3
711310	Promoters of performing arts, sports, and similar events with facilities	275.3	256.5	224.2	249.3	277.3	321.2	350.2	346.5
711320	Promoters of performing arts, sports, and similar events without facilities	44.4	38.4	43.0	44.4	48.8	56.6	60.4	62.4
712110	Museums	717.9	745.7	799.4	847.4	900.2	946.4	1,143.1	1,121.4
712120	Historical sites	127.3	132.3	133.9	135.0	168.2	169.9	192.4	199.6
712130	Zoos and botanical gardens	220.9	228.4	271.5	294.2	304.1	328.2	351.5	382.3
712190	Nature parks and other similar institutions	28.4	28.7	29.2	33.7	38.1	44.1	45.6	49.5

713910	Golf courses and country clubs	999.6	1,096.3	1,191.9	1,261.7	1,368.9	1,471.1	1,573.5	1,718.0
713940	Fitness and recreational sports centers	817.6	836.2	893.5	930.2	979.9	1,042.0	1,123.5	1,229.8
713990	All other amusement and recreation industries	129.8	139.0	152.5	167.5	188.0	198.6	215.1	232.5
813110	Religious organizations	1,288.6	1,307.8	1,400.7	1,476.3	1,565.6	1,681.5	1,826.9	2,265.9
813211	Grantmaking foundations	594.6	640.3	702.9	781.1	824.9	905.5	991.2	1,077.9
813212	Voluntary health organizations	579.7	552.8	588.2	621.8	773.1	833.4	884.3	912.4
813219	Other grantmaking and giving services	737.0	761.1	836.3	857.6	896.2	944.4	1,001.4	1,096.3
813311	Human rights organizations	523.5	556.5	601.8	628.3	662.3	699.6	746.2	782.6
813312	Environment, conservation, and wildlife organizations	388.7	353.5	366.5	371.0	390.7	423.9	446.7	486.1
813319	Other social advocacy organizations	872.4	883.7	963.6	1,037.9	1,129.3	1,230.9	1,295.1	1,400.7
813410	Civic and social organizations	3,630.6	3,823.6	4,034.7	4,206.4	4,490.5	4,719.2	4,831.2	5,047.5
813910	Business associations	3,004.9	3,174.8	3,374.5	3,526.6	3,686.4	3,900.3	4,096.2	4,307.3
813920	Professional organizations	1,596.8	1,694.1	1,808.3	1,918.2	2,030.6	2,149.9	2,309.6	2,475.2
813930	Labor unions and similar labor organizations	2,319.8	2,438.3	2,518.5	2,551.4	2,603.8	2,678.2	2,794.1	2,928.0
813940	Political organizations	125.3	87.8	142.3	105.1	168.9	121.9	189.3	125.1
813990	Other similar organizations (except business, professional, labor, and political organizations)	1,212.2	1,299.4	1,368.9	1,373.6	1,393.1	1,428.4	1,492.1	1,571.6

Sources: Authors' estimates based on private wages from U.S. Department of Labor, Bureau of Labor Statistics, Quarterly Census of Employment and Wages (1990–2013). Tax-exempt share of wages is from U.S. Census Bureau, Economic Census (1997, 2002, 2007, and 2012).
Note: Industries are listed as classified by the North American Industry Classification System (NAICS).

Table 2.13. Nonprofit Wages Covered by Unemployment Insurance for Six-Digit Industries Whose Tax Status Is Identified in the Economic Census, 1998–2005 (current $ millions)

NAICS code	Industry	1998	1999	2000	2001	2002	2003	2004	2005
541110	Offices of lawyers	848.7	892.6	968.0	1,029.6	1,056.5	1,528.7	2,052.5	2,602.7
541710	Physical, engineering, and biological research services	7,658.8	7,381.4	7,392.1	6,371.9	5,264.7	5,847.0	6,558.6	7,640.2
541720	Research and development in the social sciences and humanities	1,288.8	1,160.8	1,077.7	943.3	715.9	994.7	1,273.2	1,560.4
611110	Elementary and secondary schools	8,847.2	9,687.4	10,614.4	11,654.2	12,719.5	13,681.3	14,612.4	15,532.9
611210	Junior colleges	317.7	320.7	340.2	347.2	341.9	382.7	392.4	591.3
611310	Colleges, universities, and professional schools	27,215.0	28,267.8	30,014.0	32,215.8	34,350.0	37,130.8	39,389.2	41,441.4
611410	Business and secretarial schools	20.0	24.6	30.3	36.4	43.3	43.7	48.3	49.0
611420	Computer training	13.4	20.8	30.2	34.0	32.4	28.5	28.7	30.2
611430	Professional and management development training	265.3	293.0	346.8	366.0	371.3	401.6	417.9	456.8
611511	Cosmetology and barber schools	5.9	7.1	8.7	10.9	13.8	12.5	11.8	10.2
611512	Flight training	8.9	9.9	11.0	11.2	9.9	12.3	15.2	19.6
611513	Apprenticeship training	149.9	174.6	200.1	228.3	269.1	286.5	313.2	333.3
611519	Other technical and trade schools	238.7	256.5	273.6	308.9	336.4	356.8	347.5	358.5
611610	Fine arts schools	202.6	230.3	256.9	291.0	323.7	319.4	312.9	317.9
611620	Sports and recreation instruction	58.1	67.9	82.3	99.5	121.0	129.7	144.7	155.6
611630	Language schools	46.9	52.7	59.2	66.3	65.2	71.5	77.3	75.7
611691	Exam preparation and tutoring	64.3	87.3	123.2	153.6	175.5	197.1	223.1	260.3
611692	Automobile driving schools	9.5	11.4	14.8	18.5	21.8	19.6	18.3	17.5
611699	All other miscellaneous schools and instruction	199.6	247.6	299.1	366.4	413.4	413.8	391.3	420.7
611710	Educational support services	507.7	658.8	639.2	734.4	814.3	902.5	1,056.1	1,199.3

621410	Family planning centers	457.6	459.6	472.4	494.6	523.0	494.8	475.9	440.0
621420	Outpatient mental health and substance abuse centers	2,627.7	2,706.6	2,882.9	3,104.7	3,338.4	3,529.7	3,736.2	3,985.7
621491	HMO medical centers	2,581.5	2,394.9	2,280.9	2,304.0	2,340.5	2,638.5	2,929.3	3,238.5
621492	Kidney dialysis centers	243.2	245.7	263.6	292.2	308.4	322.2	346.4	367.1
621493	Freestanding ambulatory surgical and emergency centers	398.8	376.5	402.0	420.3	444.7	494.6	553.8	614.4
621498	All other outpatient care centers	1,425.0	1,472.0	1,565.5	1,711.2	1,752.9	1,996.3	2,224.2	2,699.5
621610	Home health care services	4,445.1	4,078.2	4,246.3	4,520.9	5,060.2	5,406.9	5,853.0	6,241.7
621910	Ambulance services	342.9	388.8	454.0	528.3	615.6	674.6	727.9	794.6
621991	Blood and organ banks	996.3	1,049.6	1,163.1	1,324.8	1,486.0	1,632.6	1,690.2	1,774.8
621999	All other miscellaneous ambulatory health care services	70.2	73.5	86.3	96.5	109.5	119.4	132.2	151.0
622110	General medical and surgical hospitals	103,905.7	108,306.1	113,633.2	122,564.8	132,416.4	142,529.4	151,939.6	159,630.8
622210	Psychiatric and substance abuse hospitals	1,161.1	1,218.4	1,238.8	1,367.4	1,492.1	1,585.3	1,6[illegible]0.6	1,756.4
622310	Specialty (except psychiatric and substance abuse) hospitals	3,180.3	3,147.4	3,155.9	3,356.1	3,558.4	4,053.0	4,3[illegible]5.9	4,717.5
623110	Nursing care facilities	7,835.5	8,154.4	8,692.6	9,402.5	10,064.8	10,233.3	10,5[illegible]5.1	10,627.0
623210	Residential mental retardation facilities	3,427.2	3,753.1	4,114.9	4,506.9	4,797.6	4,950.8	5,1[illegible]2.2	5,286.6
623220	Residential mental health and substance abuse facilities	1,886.3	2,049.7	2,235.6	2,459.9	2,625.5	2,770.8	2,8[illegible]4.9	2,999.0
623311	Continuing care retirement communities	2,734.7	2,770.8	2,971.7	3,173.0	3,484.1	3,904.1	4,189.1	4,405.0
623312	Homes for the elderly	1,084.6	1,133.7	1,202.2	1,218.0	1,205.3	1,244.8	1,286.7	1,348.5
623990	Other residential care facilities	2,533.9	2,786.5	3,030.4	3,273.3	3,411.6	3,485.0	3,592.6	3,618.1
624110	Child and youth services	2,182.1	2,412.0	2,679.4	3,001.2	3,169.9	3,367.2	3,453.8	3,541.4
624120	Services for the elderly and persons with disabilities	4,593.0	5,076.4	5,201.9	5,599.8	6,117.3	6,548.8	6,870.8	7,202.0
624190	Other individual and family services	4,112.3	4,545.4	5,102.1	5,760.3	6,270.7	6,511.7	6,773.9	7,122.1

(continued)

Table 2.13. Nonprofit Wages Covered by Unemployment Insurance for Six-Digit Industries Whose Tax Status Is Identified in the Economic Census, 1998–2005 (current $ millions) *(continued)*

NAICS code	Industry	1998	1999	2000	2001	2002	2003	2004	2005
624210	Community food services	431.1	460.9	513.7	565.6	546.3	556.3	560.2	562.4
624221	Temporary shelters	696.8	776.1	853.5	959.9	1,064.5	1,125.4	1,185.2	1,240.8
624229	Other community housing services	343.8	387.2	431.4	456.0	529.3	576.6	602.2	641.2
624230	Emergency and other relief services	571.4	631.3	696.2	770.7	851.0	830.2	900.9	898.3
624310	Vocational rehabilitation services	3,996.2	4,305.9	4,636.8	5,009.1	5,255.2	5,380.6	5,569.3	5,609.6
624410	Child day care services	3,425.9	3,771.8	4,171.4	4,606.9	4,933.2	5,036.6	5,129.3	5,271.3
711110	Theater companies and dinner theaters	808.2	795.5	874.8	926.3	954.4	938.5	952.9	916.6
711120	Dance companies	195.1	184.3	199.7	211.7	216.2	230.0	245.2	251.1
711130	Musical groups and artists	646.4	729.7	839.4	881.0	866.7	1,014.3	954.7	960.1
711190	Other performing arts companies	8.4	8.6	11.1	11.1	10.4	11.5	12.1	11.9
711310	Promoters of performing arts, sports, and similar events with facilities	407.8	496.4	471.5	494.1	501.5	529.7	570.4	591.0
711320	Promoters of performing arts, sports, and similar events without facilities	78.0	100.8	144.1	176.5	207.5	176.2	165.1	173.9
712110	Museums	1,243.2	1,350.5	1,483.8	1,619.4	1,677.4	1,728.2	1,789.2	1,880.4
712120	Historical sites	205.5	234.6	268.8	285.6	273.0	279.6	299.9	303.0
712130	Zoos and botanical gardens	418.9	475.8	508.0	546.9	561.1	595.4	638.2	668.6
712190	Nature parks and other similar institutions	55.3	61.4	70.1	80.3	86.3	94.1	92.9	95.7

713910	Golf courses and country clubs	1,864.8	1,995.4	2,176.9	2,278.2	2,399.2	2,567.0	[illegible]	2,936.9
713940	Fitness and recreational sports centers	1,384.4	1,425.6	1,540.7	1,643.5	1,684.7	1,772.8	1,885.7	2,008.6
713990	All other amusement and recreation industries	268.8	284.0	308.8	326.7	341.9	380.7	427.6	471.0
813110	Religious organizations	2,245.4	2,489.2	2,773.7	3,027.0	3,287.9	3,529.2	[illegible]	3,889.8
813211	Grantmaking foundations	1,198.6	1,330.7	1,476.0	1,664.9	1,852.2	1,870.8	1,905.5	2,037.7
813212	Voluntary health organizations	969.4	995.2	1,101.5	1,254.4	1,318.2	1,395.3	[illegible]	1,491.1
813219	Other grantmaking and giving services	1,053.3	1,140.4	1,264.0	1,389.0	1,432.4	1,455.8	[illegible]	1,471.8
813311	Human rights organizations	872.5	948.9	1,018.6	1,113.0	1,185.3	1,240.1	1,303.7	1,333.0
813312	Environment, conservation, and wildlife organizations	528.3	587.8	658.4	732.0	821.8	952.9	[illegible]	1,179.2
813319	Other social advocacy organizations	1,513.6	1,675.4	1,891.2	2,127.5	2,340.1	2,405.5	[illegible]	2,672.2
813410	Civic and social organizations	4,781.5	5,050.9	5,452.9	5,846.9	6,060.0	6,103.3	[illegible]	6,301.3
813910	Business associations	4,612.4	4,890.2	5,148.7	5,468.3	5,632.0	5,840.2	[illegible]	6,458.4
813920	Professional organizations	2,710.1	2,906.4	3,163.9	3,482.7	3,697.6	3,841.0	4,083.2	4,156.0
813930	Labor unions and similar labor organizations	3,036.7	3,159.9	3,329.4	3,500.1	3,646.6	3,777.1	3,854.4	3,892.8
813940	Political organizations	184.5	154.6	225.8	176.2	275.6	203.2	329.1	222.2
813990	Other similar organizations (except business, professional, labor, and political organizations)	1,688.8	1,772.1	1,885.6	1,986.9	2,118.0	2,265.3	[illegible]	2,676.4

Sources: Authors' estimates based on private wages from U.S. Department of Labor, Bureau of Labor Statistics, Quarterly Census of Employment and Wages (1990–2013) Tax-exempt share of wages is from U.S. Census Bureau, Economic Census (1997, 2002, 2007, and 2012).
Note: Industries are listed as classified by the North American Industry Classification System (NAICS).

Table 2.14. Nonprofit Wages Covered by Unemployment Insurance for Six-Digit Industries Whose Tax Status Is Identified in the Economic Census, 2006–13 (current $ millions)

NAICS code	Industry	2006	2007	2008	2009	2010	2011	2012	2013
541110	Offices of lawyers	3,226.1	3,943.1	3,568.4	2,946.5	2,432.8	1,962.6	1,474.6	1,486.3
541710	Physical, engineering, and biological research services	8,623.7	9,415.1	10,290.4	10,475.3	11,189.8	12,122.3	13,063.3	13,509.7
541720	Research and development in the social sciences and humanities	1,911.5	2,445.6	2,464.2	2,347.3	2,394.6	2,374.6	2,560.8	2,548.5
611110	Elementary and secondary schools	16,706.4	18,104.1	19,569.7	20,509.3	20,655.1	22,051.0	23,303.7	24,151.3
611210	Junior colleges	638.7	635.0	639.8	681.1	712.1	726.4	675.8	678.2
611310	Colleges, universities, and professional schools	44,070.7	47,445.0	50,418.7	53,083.9	54,006.8	57,324.0	60,169.6	61,566.7
611410	Business and secretarial schools	46.7	47.4	50.2	58.8	61.4	60.0	48.8	42.8
611420	Computer training	30.1	31.5	34.5	35.0	37.2	42.7	46.0	48.3
611430	Professional and management development training	506.7	550.9	596.7	586.3	626.1	588.9	627.9	641.9
611511	Cosmetology and barber schools	8.6	6.5	6.8	7.1	8.0	8.1	8.1	8.2
611512	Flight training	24.2	30.2	28.7	22.2	16.9	12.5	7.8	8.2
611513	Apprenticeship training	357.3	403.5	443.5	437.0	443.8	437.6	458.2	450.6
611519	Other technical and trade schools	371.5	396.9	392.1	390.4	394.5	354.4	305.0	291.6
611610	Fine arts schools	327.8	334.8	368.8	382.7	411.6	456.7	498.5	529.1
611620	Sports and recreation instruction	169.1	181.1	188.2	185.1	188.0	199.2	215.7	241.8
611630	Language schools	82.7	97.8	108.2	108.8	112.1	117.5	96.3	97.0
611691	Exam preparation and tutoring	293.0	331.4	367.9	378.5	408.8	437.3	456.3	465.4
611692	Automobile driving schools	17.2	16.4	16.0	15.1	14.7	14.7	14.7	14.9
611699	All other miscellaneous schools and instruction	451.1	465.0	475.0	473.4	486.0	533.9	561.5	586.2
611710	Educational support services	1,381.4	1,561.8	1,780.2	1,899.6	2,075.6	2,285.1	2,519.7	2,619.5

621410	Family planning centers	545.4	550.2	585.0	595.6	584.6	580.9	60[illegible].4	628.7
621420	Outpatient mental health and substance abuse centers	4,149.2	4,396.4	4,624.9	4,707.7	4,848.1	5,071.3	5,31[illegible].5	5,607.5
621491	HMO medical centers	3,645.2	3,872.1	3,984.4	4,203.8	7,514.8	8,057.7	8,73[illegible].5	8,966.6
621492	Kidney dialysis centers	412.8	415.1	451.5	461.7	468.4	468.6	49[illegible].8	518.0
621493	Freestanding ambulatory surgical and emergency centers	720.8	789.5	846.4	902.5	930.2	971.0	1,03[illegible].5	1,098.2
621498	All other outpatient care centers	2,938.4	3,133.7	3,428.5	3,678.4	3,961.4	4,247.4	4,55[illegible].5	5,035.6
621610	Home health care services	6,728.9	7,172.9	7,548.1	8,042.5	8,294.5	8,455.6	8,52[illegible].2	8,936.6
621910	Ambulance services	852.7	925.2	995.8	1,052.9	1,086.9	1,126.7	1,16[illegible].2	1,205.5
621991	Blood and organ banks	1,919.3	2,097.1	2,338.2	2,506.0	2,431.8	2,477.7	2,58[illegible].9	2,599.0
621999	All other miscellaneous ambulatory health care services	177.3	200.8	204.2	199.1	214.4	227.4	243.7	286.7
622110	General medical and surgical hospitals	169,815.9	180,124.1	193,118.2	202,458.4	204,576.7	211,229.3	218,70[illegible].5	224,759.2
622210	Psychiatric and substance abuse hospitals	1,876.8	1,986.0	2,127.1	2,200.6	2,238.2	2,342.4	2,38[illegible].3	2,429.4
622310	Specialty (except psychiatric and substance abuse) hospitals	5,210.6	5,818.4	6,683.9	7,188.5	7,653.9	8,186.8	8,78[illegible].8	8,090.4
623110	Nursing care facilities	11,021.9	11,440.9	11,764.0	11,883.2	11,865.8	11,922.1	11,725.5	11,834.0
623210	Residential mental retardation facilities	5,590.4	5,967.4	6,294.5	6,460.3	6,507.2	6,544.4	6,563.0	6,808.4
623220	Residential mental health and substance abuse facilities	3,200.0	3,436.8	3,651.8	3,707.9	3,725.5	3,819.5	3,965.5	4,135.7
623311	Continuing care retirement communities	4,644.5	4,841.8	5,401.0	6,049.3	6,496.8	7,029.8	7,533.9	7,893.2
623312	Homes for the elderly	1,417.4	1,524.1	1,519.6	1,469.3	1,418.6	1,384.7	1,345.3	1,419.9
623990	Other residential care facilities	3,723.6	3,864.8	4,016.4	3,946.0	3,803.5	3,802.4	3,811.2	3,864.1
624110	Child and youth services	3,793.6	4,092.5	4,329.6	4,379.5	4,466.1	4,583.0	4,751.1	4,877.9
624120	Services for the elderly and persons with disabilities	7,652.5	7,976.4	8,690.6	9,224.0	9,603.9	10,024.0	10,4[illegible]6.8	11,583.5
624190	Other individual and family services	7,568.1	8,378.0	8,788.9	9,203.7	9,612.0	9,778.5	10,111.5	10,509.5
624210	Community food services	574.6	622.5	678.8	708.7	764.7	811.1	822.3	862.9
624221	Temporary shelters	1,302.8	1,360.5	1,433.8	1,463.2	1,520.6	1,604.5	1,6[illegible]2.9	1,685.9

(continued)

Table 2.14. Nonprofit Wages Covered by Unemployment Insurance for Six-Digit Industries Whose Tax Status Is Identified in the Economic Census, 2006–13 (current $ millions) *(continued)*

NAICS code	Industry	2006	2007	2008	2009	2010	2011	2012	2013
624229	Other community housing services	698.4	749.3	823.8	891.4	996.6	1,039.9	1,102.8	1,160.5
624230	Emergency and other relief services	939.4	976.3	1,051.3	1,042.4	1,088.1	1,103.1	1,116.2	1,170.2
624310	Vocational rehabilitation services	5,829.2	6,103.1	6,340.5	6,460.3	6,529.3	6,578.3	6,526.9	6,594.0
624410	Child day care services	5,478.7	5,698.8	5,994.3	6,077.8	6,186.2	6,292.6	6,380.1	6,492.0
711110	Theater companies and dinner theaters	945.1	903.2	995.3	972.0	998.8	1,052.8	1,105.8	1,128.3
711120	Dance companies	269.4	293.0	315.9	312.5	314.9	325.8	337.0	350.5
711130	Musical groups and artists	1,094.0	1,148.0	1,260.3	1,074.9	1,084.0	1,129.7	1,199.9	1,291.1
711190	Other performing arts companies	12.7	14.6	17.4	17.9	20.6	24.8	26.0	26.2
711310	Promoters of performing arts, sports, and similar events with facilities	652.5	684.1	771.0	817.1	847.1	965.9	999.9	1,086.0
711320	Promoters of performing arts, sports, and similar events without facilities	166.0	167.3	172.6	159.1	161.8	169.1	197.4	228.4
712110	Museums	1,989.1	2,135.8	2,317.1	2,248.4	2,206.6	2,323.5	2,454.0	2,575.3
712120	Historical sites	317.4	340.7	357.8	353.7	375.2	373.2	377.2	395.9
712130	Zoos and botanical gardens	719.5	778.6	826.1	822.7	844.7	872.1	915.5	962.8
712190	Nature parks and other similar institutions	97.6	117.7	132.2	142.5	153.6	167.2	185.9	187.0

713910	Golf courses and country clubs	3,093.3	3,300.4	3,440.5	3,331.3	3,331.4	3,404.8	3,516.0	3,646.0
713940	Fitness and recreational sports centers	2,155.3	2,316.1	2,347.9	2,247.9	2,240.1	2,290.0	2,372.3	2,455.9
713990	All other amusement and recreation industries	539.3	600.9	620.1	611.7	644.9	678.6	740.5	779.1
813110	Religious organizations	4,140.1	4,487.1	4,773.1	4,630.8	4,806.1	4,450.9	4,558.9	4,698.8
813211	Grantmaking foundations	2,214.3	2,500.4	2,795.9	2,930.4	3,091.3	3,282.1	3,532.0	3,799.2
813212	Voluntary health organizations	1,589.5	1,785.7	1,908.8	1,941.1	1,923.0	1,984.0	2,02[illegible].9	2,104.0
813219	Other grantmaking and giving services	1,499.9	1,554.4	1,621.4	1,600.9	1,564.8	1,592.7	1,635.7	1,691.7
813311	Human rights organizations	1,404.7	1,522.8	1,660.9	1,726.6	1,772.3	1,810.3	1,859.8	1,907.2
813312	Environment, conservation, and wildlife organizations	1,266.6	1,512.4	1,697.6	1,807.5	1,871.7	1,997.3	2,144.2	2,283.4
813319	Other social advocacy organizations	2,806.4	3,033.8	3,343.0	3,471.8	3,668.8	3,791.7	3,982.1	4,220.7
813410	Civic and social organizations	6,526.5	6,770.1	6,969.0	6,754.5	6,679.1	6,807.6	6,964.8	7,004.5
813910	Business associations	6,855.5	7,214.8	7,570.9	7,541.4	7,515.0	7,701.9	8,019.6	8,229.0
813920	Professional organizations	4,361.1	4,678.4	4,997.2	5,135.2	5,261.4	5,581.7	5,92[illegible].0	6,166.8
813930	Labor unions and similar labor organizations	4,033.8	4,164.6	4,384.3	4,390.7	4,342.1	4,350.1	4,39[illegible].9	4,422.0
813940	Political organizations	360.7	310.1	434.6	278.2	394.2	275.1	443.8	296.0
813990	Other similar organizations (except business, professional, labor, and political organizations)	2,869.2	3,092.1	3,341.2	3,355.2	3,436.0	3,638.3	3,705.8	3,842.9

Sources: Authors' estimates based on private wages from U.S. Department of Labor, Bureau of Labor Statistics, Quarterly Census of Employment and Wages (1990–2013). Tax-exempt share of wages is from U.S. Census Bureau, Economic Census (1997, 2002, 2007, and 2012).
Note: Industries are listed as classified by the North American Industry Classification System (NAICS).

Table 2.15. Nonprofit Employment Covered by Unemployment Insurance for Six-Digit Industries with Tax Status Identified in the Economic Census, 1990–97

NAICS code	Industry	1990	1991	1992	1993	1994	1995	1996	1997
541110	Offices of lawyers	21,966	21,648	21,771	21,962	22,038	21,946	22,0[illegible]0	22,482
541710	Physical, engineering, and biological research services	165,555	161,766	156,805	159,184	157,669	156,506	153,4[illegible]1	157,801
541720	Research and development in the social sciences and humanities	33,084	33,281	35,628	35,248	35,507	35,518	34,7[illegible]0	35,244
611110	Elementary and secondary schools	289,560	296,460	300,477	313,702	327,596	342,472	356,6[illegible]4	373,665
611210	Junior colleges	9,484	11,295	11,229	11,293	11,365	11,138	11,2[illegible]0	11,666
611310	Colleges, universities, and professional schools	703,830	703,183	706,590	706,009	720,293	728,292	750,4[illegible]6	771,413
611410	Business and secretarial schools	1,424	1,163	1,031	902	856	803	7[illegible]6	738
611420	Computer training	129	126	140	157	183	226	2[illegible]0	307
611430	Professional and management development training	5,429	5,301	5,664	6,007	6,098	6,417	6,8[illegible]7	7,302
611511	Cosmetology and barber schools	691	653	578	530	500	460	4[illegible]1	401
611512	Flight training	441	411	375	347	351	352	3[illegible]6	354
611513	Apprenticeship training	9,924	8,019	6,952	6,365	5,807	5,550	5,5[illegible]5	5,903
611519	Other technical and trade schools	5,923	5,839	5,840	6,038	6,142	6,365	6,8[illegible]3	7,255
611610	Fine arts schools	8,514	8,504	8,846	9,236	9,931	10,395	10,94[illegible]	11,407
611620	Sports and recreation instruction	2,791	2,823	3,050	3,446	3,886	4,128	4,35[illegible]	4,512
611630	Language schools	1,964	2,212	2,444	2,606	2,761	2,869	3,13[illegible]	3,395
611691	Exam preparation and tutoring	1,700	1,686	1,859	2,109	2,299	2,528	2,83[illegible]	3,232
611692	Automobile driving schools	287	295	309	326	341	360	37[illegible]	394
611699	All other miscellaneous schools and instruction	5,216	5,550	5,677	6,115	6,556	6,897	7,56[illegible]	8,195
611710	Educational support services	9,595	9,756	10,114	10,589	11,113	12,031	13,64[illegible]	14,739

621410	Family planning centers	12,426	14,170	15,925	16,636	17,208	17,839	18,1[illegible]3	18,647
621420	Outpatient mental health and substance abuse centers	67,942	70,394	73,697	79,869	86,216	91,778	95,6[illegible]9	99,845
621491	HMO medical centers	64,728	64,325	63,579	61,342	62,993	64,050	65,0[illegible]4	62,768
621492	Kidney dialysis centers	3,905	4,348	4,716	5,153	5,588	6,067	6,6[illegible]6	7,478
621493	Freestanding ambulatory surgical and emergency centers	6,064	7,914	8,536	8,549	9,135	9,889	10,1[illegible]3	10,026
621498	All other outpatient care centers	33,145	29,918	33,376	35,409	37,580	38,298	39,1[illegible]6	39,993
621610	Home health care services	97,775	115,149	132,902	151,272	171,012	189,312	201,1[illegible]4	209,433
621910	Ambulance services	10,452	11,236	11,707	12,375	13,420	14,490	16,2[illegible]5	17,570
621991	Blood and organ banks	24,607	24,587	25,891	28,543	30,258	31,268	30,9[illegible]0	31,341
621999	All other miscellaneous ambulatory health care services	1,087	1,123	1,168	1,257	1,405	1,476	1,[illegible]5	1,819
622110	General medical and surgical hospitals	2,773,154	2,848,696	2,924,663	2,972,007	2,977,071	2,991,660	3,049,[illegible]8	3,103,347
622210	Psychiatric and substance abuse hospitals	45,923	46,656	45,277	43,059	41,857	39,652	37,[illegible]1	36,060
622310	Specialty (except psychiatric and substance abuse) hospitals	64,735	68,780	73,905	76,683	77,751	79,929	84,[illegible]15	89,041
623110	Nursing care facilities	309,098	320,558	335,935	347,769	360,773	370,478	380,[illegible]73	384,409
623210	Residential mental retardation facilities	134,389	145,844	152,179	155,688	162,972	172,990	178,[illegible]82	185,242
623220	Residential mental health and substance abuse facilities	65,079	68,688	68,441	71,624	73,681	78,304	80,[illegible]51	84,517
623311	Continuing care retirement communities	130,789	138,843	138,398	141,377	141,793	144,261	147,[illegible]85	147,151
623312	Homes for the elderly	39,615	42,657	45,222	47,705	50,193	52,181	56,[illegible]37	60,633
623990	Other residential care facilities	77,107	80,297	87,582	92,840	97,765	106,393	111,[illegible]35	117,640
624110	Child and youth services	66,429	70,448	76,815	83,340	90,699	96,548	100,[illegible]64	104,380
624120	Services for the elderly and persons with disabilities	245,955	261,428	279,956	296,185	309,390	320,342	331,[illegible]36	344,512
624190	Other individual and family services	133,295	136,903	144,449	156,107	167,573	180,086	188,[illegible]13	196,671
624210	Community food services	21,714	25,692	26,923	27,969	28,939	28,205	27,[illegible]01	25,799
624221	Temporary shelters	19,603	22,262	26,180	27,615	30,183	32,855	33,[illegible]45	35,166

(continued)

Table 2.15. Nonprofit Employment Covered by Unemployment Insurance for Six-Digit Industries with Tax Status Identified in the Economic Census, 1990–97 *(continued)*

NAICS code	Industry	1990	1991	1992	1993	1994	1995	1996	1997
624229	Other community housing services	8,565	9,789	10,270	11,360	12,955	14,014	14,437	15,521
624230	Emergency and other relief services	30,906	27,212	26,690	24,760	22,770	23,181	23,120	22,904
624310	Vocational rehabilitation services	197,099	195,323	200,145	209,162	219,109	228,526	228,719	238,753
624410	Child care services	149,323	158,585	169,072	183,081	195,941	206,577	213,679	223,511
711110	Theater companies and dinner theaters	200,771	180,382	124,457	92,607	81,483	67,841	57,630	48,386
711120	Dance companies	4,836	5,113	5,025	5,193	5,132	5,409	5,386	5,794
711130	Musical groups and artists	27,906	25,846	24,990	26,236	27,108	27,435	27,164	27,374
711190	Other performing arts companies	238	285	285	285	329	316	370	406
711310	Promoters of performing arts, sports, and similar events with facilities	13,503	12,538	11,267	11,269	12,143	13,188	14,012	14,216
711320	Promoters of performing arts, sports, and similar events without facilities	3,101	2,378	2,323	2,347	2,565	2,713	2,811	2,950
712110	Museums	42,981	42,400	44,292	46,007	47,820	49,190	51,443	54,370
712120	Historical sites	8,025	8,635	8,525	8,796	9,221	9,334	9,446	9,947
712130	Zoos and botanical gardens	13,512	13,489	15,024	15,817	16,087	16,922	17,810	19,000
712190	Nature parks and other similar institutions	2,431	2,350	2,258	2,552	2,867	3,244	3,294	3,454
713910	Golf course and country clubs	70,534	73,994	77,309	80,575	85,249	90,074	94,238	99,710

713940	Fitness and recreational sports centers	68,100	67,752	69,280	71,935	74,967	78,176	81,503	85,242
713990	All other amusement and recreation industries	12,053	12,503	13,311	14,265	15,758	16,701	17,423	17,950
813110	Religious organizations	99,521	98,123	102,374	105,226	108,839	113,373	119,084	129,563
813211	Grantmaking foundations	26,972	26,395	27,238	28,221	28,828	30,216	32,893	33,614
813212	Voluntary health organizations	28,476	26,542	26,961	28,236	32,783	33,791	33,950	33,467
813219	Other grantmaking and giving services	38,508	36,088	37,425	37,157	37,502	38,450	38,929	40,695
813311	Human rights organizations	30,853	31,085	32,111	32,467	33,644	34,308	35,149	35,615
813312	Environment, conservation, and wildlife organizations	23,531	21,203	20,605	20,241	20,655	21,285	21,792	22,876
813319	Other social advocacy organizations	59,269	55,940	57,075	59,307	61,738	64,231	64,786	66,441
813410	Civic and social organizations	348,733	336,883	342,977	353,242	361,468	371,331	374,021	382,585
813910	Business associations	108,835	108,530	110,222	110,278	111,864	113,867	115,012	115,265
813920	Professional organizations	51,804	52,802	53,048	54,421	55,634	57,410	58,530	60,395
813930	Labor unions and similar labor organizations	134,460	136,760	136,428	136,282	136,258	136,587	138,596	139,040
813940	Political organizations	6,416	4,069	6,453	4,377	7,412	4,702	7,301	4,538
813990	Other similar organizations (except business, professional, labor, and political organizations)	81,949	83,048	82,825	81,471	80,832	81,136	81,854	82,941

Sources: Authors' estimates based on private employment from U.S. Department of Labor, Bureau of Labor Statistics, Quarterly Census of Employment and Wages (1990–2013); and the tax-exempt share of employment from U.S. Census Bureau, Economic Census (1997,2002,2007, and 2012).
Note: Industries are listed as classified by the North American Industry Classification System (NAICS).

Table 2.16. Nonprofit Employment Covered by Unemployment Insurance for Six-Digit Industries with Tax Status Identified in the Economic Census, 1998–2005

NAICS code	Industry	1998	1999	2000	2001	2002	2003	2004	2005
541110	Offices of lawyers	23,195	23,690	24,106	24,669	25,156	37,265	49,[illegible]8	61,430
541710	Physical, engineering, and biological research services	148,927	139,246	128,688	114,806	97,501	102,059	108,2[illegible]8	118,526
541720	Research and development in the social sciences and humanities	31,411	28,236	25,863	23,235	20,045	23,172	26,[illegible]9	29,398
611110	Elementary and secondary schools	391,305	412,408	432,679	452,064	471,661	488,708	502,3[illegible]0	519,167
611210	Junior colleges	11,740	11,170	11,069	11,169	10,454	11,253	11,3[illegible]1	16,680
611310	Colleges, universities, and professional schools	800,408	811,627	823,716	844,685	865,305	893,355	915,8[illegible]5	932,373
611410	Business and secretarial schools	866	999	1,131	1,322	1,490	1,432	1,4[illegible]4	1,419
611420	Computer training	482	705	918	980	964	904	9[illegible]7	958
611430	Professional and management development training	8,076	8,822	10,071	10,372	10,614	10,515	10,0[illegible]8	10,252
611511	Cosmetology and barber schools	437	476	535	629	718	620	5[illegible]6	438
611512	Flight training	391	441	489	493	455	530	6[illegible]9	759
611513	Apprenticeship training	6,182	6,797	7,494	7,972	8,955	9,404	9,7[illegible]	9,803
611519	Other technical and trade schools	7,922	8,503	9,330	10,105	10,746	10,769	10,7[illegible]	10,852
611610	Fine arts schools	12,312	13,449	14,632	15,914	17,174	17,370	17,2[illegible]	17,205
611620	Sports and recreation instruction	5,098	5,827	6,729	7,947	9,410	9,808	10,3[illegible]	10,597
611630	Language schools	3,856	4,321	4,680	5,193	5,139	5,415	5,4[illegible]	5,297
611691	Exam preparation and tutoring	4,387	5,642	7,097	8,363	9,682	10,326	11,3[illegible]	12,587
611692	Automobile driving schools	556	725	925	1,141	1,357	1,189	1,06[illegible]	919
611699	All other miscellaneous schools and instruction	9,023	10,445	12,377	14,579	16,611	16,163	15,68[illegible]	16,192
611710	Educational support services	15,334	16,952	19,012	21,639	23,775	26,827	30,32[illegible]	33,178

621410	Family planning centers	18,573	18,435	18,371	18,386	18,475	16,958	16,[illegible]65	14,963
621420	Outpatient mental health and substance abuse centers	102,474	106,203	109,127	112,214	115,740	119,214	121,242	125,961
621491	HMO medical centers	60,457	55,581	52,409	53,055	53,268	54,620	55,890	57,424
621492	Kidney dialysis centers	7,660	7,671	8,115	8,512	8,640	8,798	8,884	8,937
621493	Freestanding ambulatory surgical and emergency centers	9,989	9,282	9,350	9,313	9,626	10,141	10,923	11,690
621498	All other outpatient care centers	42,079	42,626	44,131	45,545	46,738	50,524	53,[illegible]44	60,534
621610	Home health care services	197,168	181,675	180,117	182,336	194,771	200,033	203,[illegible]30	206,998
621910	Ambulance services	19,894	21,809	24,089	26,761	29,625	30,881	31,[illegible]72	32,301
621991	Blood and organ banks	33,475	34,283	36,489	40,195	43,217	44,657	43,[illegible]77	44,409
621999	All other miscellaneous ambulatory health care services	2,071	2,200	2,522	2,795	3,139	3,307	3,[illegible]58	3,746
622110	General medical and surgical hospitals	3,191,034	3,254,892	3,283,586	3,364,327	3,451,722	3,519,188	3,549,[illegible]04	3,585,376
622210	Psychiatric and substance abuse hospitals	38,814	40,555	40,492	42,843	46,345	47,092	47,[illegible]17	48,143
622310	Specialty (except psychiatric and substance abuse) hospitals	89,559	84,467	81,525	83,229	83,408	89,915	92,[illegible]55	96,736
623110	Nursing care facilities	390,224	388,366	391,024	401,026	410,649	405,663	402,[illegible]11	397,252
623210	Residential mental retardation facilities	189,557	199,429	206,112	216,175	225,300	229,930	233,375	235,896
623220	Residential mental health and substance abuse facilities	89,942	94,816	98,683	103,834	108,064	110,530	111,[illegible]70	112,531
623311	Continuing care retirement communities	145,063	143,281	146,217	149,331	156,890	170,516	177,[illegible]92	184,603
623312	Homes for the elderly	62,153	63,152	64,224	63,302	62,016	62,506	62,[illegible]72	63,642
623990	Other residential care facilities	121,905	128,973	134,302	139,843	141,715	140,378	140,025	139,586
624110	Child and youth services	109,579	116,836	124,075	133,087	133,226	136,737	136,342	137,053
624120	Services for the elderly and persons with disabilities	353,290	358,784	369,202	381,055	407,921	417,768	430,[illegible]33	448,783
624190	Other individual and family services	204,871	216,521	229,538	246,400	260,113	266,157	270,550	276,670
624210	Community food services	27,121	28,324	29,511	30,753	27,940	27,269	26,305	25,956

(continued)

Table 2.16. Nonprofit Employment Covered by Unemployment Insurance for Six-Digit Industries with Tax Status Identified in the Economic Census, 1998–2005 *(continued)*

NAICS code	Industry	1998	1999	2000	2001	2002	2003	2004	2005
624221	Temporary shelters	38,345	40,672	42,656	45,480	48,666	50,085	[illegible]	52,688
624229	Other community housing services	16,530	17,685	18,663	19,002	20,925	21,316	[illegible]	21,455
624230	Emergency and other relief services	23,664	24,905	25,959	27,116	27,933	26,647	[illegible]	25,960
624310	Vocational rehabilitation services	247,782	257,504	264,297	271,434	273,857	274,404	[illegible]	275,667
624410	Child care services	240,445	255,470	271,062	287,053	297,679	292,538	[illegible]	288,549
711110	Theater companies and dinner theaters	44,044	38,278	39,837	40,461	38,762	37,580	[illegible]	33,717
711120	Dance companies	5,835	6,065	6,437	6,748	6,640	6,974	[illegible]	7,339
711130	Musical groups and artists	28,707	29,147	30,229	29,167	28,241	27,291	[illegible]	26,832
711190	Other performing arts companies	398	395	355	325	319	412	[illegible]	441
711310	Promoters of performing arts, sports, and similar events with facilities	13,775	13,719	14,076	14,099	14,289	15,442	[illegible]	17,587
711320	Promoters of performing arts, sports, and similar events without facilities	3,590	4,535	5,914	7,284	8,770	7,559	[illegible]	6,370
712110	Museums	56,872	60,041	62,820	65,620	65,806	65,585	[illegible]	66,515
712120	Historical sites	10,374	10,802	11,466	11,658	11,628	11,859	[illegible]	12,192
712130	Zoos and botanical gardens	20,084	21,794	22,619	22,888	22,679	22,804	[illegible]	24,535
712190	Nature parks and other similar institutions	3,419	3,539	3,917	4,140	4,336	4,477	[illegible]	4,335

713910	Golf course and country clubs	104,501	107,468	112,362	114,112	116,614	120,427	125,358	127,629
713940	Fitness and recreational sports centers	92,136	99,469	106,758	113,596	118,901	126,149	135,006	142,171
713990	All other amusement and recreation industries	19,506	20,228	21,183	22,022	23,313	25,118	27,109	28,642
813110	Religious organizations	135,060	144,456	150,875	158,231	165,757	171,605	174,040	176,201
813211	Grantmaking foundations	35,399	37,747	39,540	42,080	44,396	41,453	40,329	41,819
813212	Voluntary health organizations	33,207	33,734	35,061	37,795	37,295	37,833	36,516	36,831
813219	Other grantmaking and giving services	38,526	40,060	41,903	43,687	43,508	42,527	40,741	39,899
813311	Human rights organizations	37,811	40,621	40,486	41,956	43,282	43,600	43,991	42,842
813312	Environment, conservation, and wildlife organizations	23,856	25,393	26,727	27,991	30,235	33,123	35,585	37,361
813319	Other social advocacy organizations	69,103	73,210	78,308	83,914	85,063	83,602	84,219	85,099
813410	Civic and social organizations	379,212	387,132	401,243	411,679	419,690	416,569	412,083	414,119
813910	Business associations	117,490	119,619	121,378	121,232	119,146	118,583	117,688	118,594
813920	Professional organizations	63,178	65,881	68,051	69,707	72,333	71,708	71,723	70,565
813930	Labor unions and similar labor organizations	138,195	138,270	139,911	138,819	137,920	135,821	133,242	129,894
813940	Political organizations	6,476	4,920	6,878	4,926	7,889	5,203	9,887	5,229
813990	Other similar organizations (except business, professional, labor, and political organizations)	84,218	83,601	84,926	85,646	86,143	87,481	91,479	92,948

Sources: Authors' estimates based on private employment from U.S. Department of Labor, Bureau of Labor Statistics, Quarterly Census of Employment and Wages (1990–2013); and the tax-exempt share of employment from U.S. Census Bureau, Economic Census (1997, 2002, 2007, and 2012).
Note: Industries are listed as classified by the North American Industry Classification System (NAICS).

Table 2.17. Nonprofit Employment Covered by Unemployment Insurance for Six-Digit Industries with Tax Status Identified in the Economic Census, 2006–13

NAICS code	Industry	2006	2007	2008	2009	2010	2011	2012	2013
541110	Offices of lawyers	73,395	85,775	74,044	60,455	48,379	36,947	25,6[illegible]7	25,749
541710	Physical, engineering, and biological research services	128,765	132,028	140,807	142,894	148,581	154,341	158,1[illegible]2	157,738
541720	Research and development in the social sciences and humanities	33,181	38,568	36,480	34,072	33,448	32,958	33,5[illegible]3	33,286
611110	Elementary and secondary schools	535,151	555,785	576,775	586,046	582,558	608,590	629,0[illegible]9	639,849
611210	Junior colleges	17,526	20,140	20,329	21,193	21,375	21,496	19,7[illegible]3	18,504
611310	Colleges, universities, and professional schools	958,080	987,480	1,011,919	1,032,429	1,029,819	1,054,360	1,078,6[illegible]3	1,085,119
611410	Business and secretarial schools	1,287	1,171	1,251	1,446	1,577	1,605	1,3[illegible]2	1,244
611420	Computer training	937	958	988	976	1,008	1,072	1,0[illegible]7	1,063
611430	Professional and management development training	10,474	10,861	11,452	11,303	11,527	10,773	10,5[illegible]3	10,607
611511	Cosmetology and barber schools	336	229	229	232	242	247	2[illegible]6	246
611512	Flight training	861	1,031	896	660	485	328	1[illegible]3	178
611513	Apprenticeship training	9,820	10,774	11,467	11,033	10,850	10,642	11,0[illegible]1	10,774
611519	Other technical and trade schools	10,538	10,584	10,262	9,868	9,790	8,761	7,5[illegible]3	7,293
611610	Fine arts schools	17,067	16,978	17,762	17,901	18,350	19,195	20,14[illegible]	21,159
611620	Sports and recreation instruction	10,761	10,886	11,156	10,971	11,132	11,644	12,5[illegible]	13,819
611630	Language schools	5,530	5,924	6,606	6,370	6,517	6,915	6,64[illegible]	6,814
611691	Exam preparation and tutoring	13,637	15,220	16,338	16,239	16,942	17,507	17,40[illegible]	16,582
611692	Automobile driving schools	808	684	675	663	657	658	67[illegible]	669
611699	All other miscellaneous schools and instruction	16,234	16,151	16,246	16,051	16,313	16,809	17,69[illegible]	18,678
611710	Educational support services	34,752	35,233	39,336	42,134	45,184	48,063	52,05[illegible]	52,347

621410	Family planning centers	15,626	15,252	15,578	15,511	15,443	14,990	15,341	15,804
621420	Outpatient mental health and substance abuse centers	127,122	129,498	133,082	132,856	134,792	139,637	143,853	148,846
621491	HMO medical centers	60,052	59,459	58,821	59,390	87,658	91,436	95,202	96,986
621492	Kidney dialysis centers	9,108	9,252	9,595	9,355	9,281	9,015	8,881	9,281
621493	Freestanding ambulatory surgical and emergency centers	12,848	13,554	14,084	14,528	14,869	15,467	15,993	17,083
621498	All other outpatient care centers	63,367	66,160	68,969	71,500	76,121	79,179	82,[illegible]28	88,819
621610	Home health care services	208,995	209,660	211,973	219,336	222,608	225,520	225,362	232,442
621910	Ambulance services	32,946	33,899	35,233	36,832	38,139	39,333	40,362	41,333
621991	Blood and organ banks	45,641	48,508	52,244	55,162	52,415	52,433	52,848	53,088
621999	All other miscellaneous ambulatory health care services	4,143	4,545	4,569	4,404	4,640	4,917	5,[illegible]40	5,820
622110	General medical and surgical hospitals	3,632,350	3,696,050	3,783,251	3,823,044	3,819,415	3,844,279	3,884,[illegible]91	3,909,227
622210	Psychiatric and substance abuse hospitals	49,585	49,976	51,514	52,235	52,623	53,546	53,728	54,487
622310	Specialty (except psychiatric and substance abuse) hospitals	102,231	110,318	118,504	123,203	129,995	135,414	141,[illegible]82	132,235
623110	Nursing care facilities	393,736	393,934	392,463	391,716	388,045	384,170	375,306	373,546
623210	Residential mental retardation facilities	241,480	248,822	255,615	261,557	263,670	263,430	262,725	269,365
623220	Residential mental health and substance abuse facilities	115,996	121,443	124,518	124,832	124,489	125,614	128,[illegible]78	131,850
623311	Continuing care retirement communities	189,488	191,056	206,616	228,558	245,402	261,746	277,[illegible]62	285,699
623312	Homes for the elderly	64,526	66,439	64,745	62,583	59,970	57,913	55,309	57,838
623990	Other residential care facilities	138,345	138,957	140,524	136,712	132,150	129,763	128,[illegible]45	128,549
624110	Child and youth services	140,738	148,378	151,298	150,875	152,432	153,130	156,[illegible]43	158,325
624120	Services for the elderly and persons with disabilities	458,265	461,060	492,187	518,466	540,976	560,547	589,068	634,802
624190	Other individual and family services	283,416	299,224	307,718	316,119	323,709	322,161	325,248	331,611
624210	Community food services	25,034	25,924	26,634	26,573	27,871	28,471	29,000	29,239
624221	Temporary shelters	53,481	53,630	54,872	55,011	56,624	58,571	58,364	59,451

(continued)

Table 2.17. Nonprofit Employment Covered by Unemployment Insurance for Six-Digit Industries with Tax Status Identified in the Economic Census, 2006–13 *(continued)*

NAICS code	Industry	2006	2007	2008	2009	2010	2011	2012	2013
624229	Other community housing services	22,430	23,069	24,283	25,839	27,897	28,686	29,637	30,764
624230	Emergency and other relief services	25,763	25,442	25,823	25,425	26,106	25,587	24,628	24,445
624310	Vocational rehabilitation services	277,612	280,014	283,953	289,279	292,060	293,138	289,979	290,385
624410	Child care services	290,549	292,036	297,451	292,238	290,950	292,115	291,601	291,551
711110	Theater companies and dinner theaters	33,648	32,876	34,110	32,754	32,807	33,562	34,757	35,137
711120	Dance companies	7,540	7,809	8,368	8,243	8,316	8,448	8,824	9,364
711130	Musical groups and artists	26,620	26,977	26,450	24,436	23,708	23,698	23,076	23,251
711190	Other performing arts companies	502	602	686	715	779	883	914	868
711310	Promoters of performing arts, sports, and similar events with facilities	18,959	20,467	21,216	21,837	21,963	22,651	22,687	25,204
711320	Promoters of performing arts, sports, and similar events without facilities	5,580	5,004	5,090	5,204	5,592	6,087	6,920	7,238
712110	Museums	67,870	70,253	72,764	70,111	69,254	72,070	75,021	77,837
712120	Historical sites	12,231	12,743	12,706	11,880	12,548	12,345	12,452	12,783
712130	Zoos and botanical gardens	25,609	26,963	27,801	27,193	27,963	28,510	29,461	30,808
712190	Nature parks and other similar institutions	4,187	4,711	5,090	5,216	5,408	5,619	6,013	6,099

713910	Golf course and country clubs	129,305	132,390	135,599	131,229	129,756	130,185	132,304	133,961
713940	Fitness and recreational sports centers	150,962	159,467	161,785	161,633	160,025	163,287	168,798	174,592
713990	All other amusement and recreation industries	30,867	33,054	33,911	33,924	35,623	36,568	39,442	40,644
813110	Religious organizations	178,323	182,546	185,231	183,575	179,647	181,061	180,972	184,387
813211	Grantmaking foundations	42,791	45,477	48,537	49,625	51,212	53,561	56,232	58,418
813212	Voluntary health organizations	37,111	39,126	39,776	39,358	37,912	37,935	37,637	37,403
813219	Other grantmaking and giving services	39,404	38,667	38,638	37,362	35,543	35,142	34,647	35,186
813311	Human rights organizations	44,805	45,900	48,226	49,049	48,496	48,971	48,202	47,039
813312	Environment, conservation, and wildlife organizations	39,051	44,064	48,307	49,024	50,302	52,161	54,[illegible]47	56,680
813319	Other social advocacy organizations	84,269	85,755	89,969	90,294	92,772	92,374	93,[illegible]87	94,956
813410	Civic and social organizations	415,395	417,069	418,135	395,833	391,003	392,171	392,[illegible]49	394,895
813910	Business associations	120,451	122,141	123,324	119,320	115,423	114,557	115,[illegible]73	116,189
813920	Professional organizations	71,239	73,364	75,269	75,092	74,244	75,794	78,499	79,699
813930	Labor unions and similar labor organizations	129,446	128,243	130,029	124,797	119,302	116,825	115,508	112,001
813940	Political organizations	8,853	6,556	10,502	5,598	8,325	5,277	8,391	5,306
813990	Other similar organizations (except business, professional, labor, and political organizations)	95,545	99,138	102,441	102,212	101,951	103,443	102,146	102,960

Sources: Authors' estimates based on private employment from U.S. Department of Labor, Bureau of Labor Statistics, Quarterly Census of Employment and Wages (1990–2013); and the tax-exempt share of employment from U.S. Census Bureau, Economic Census (1997, 2002, 2007, and 2012).
Note: Industries are listed as classified by the North American Industry Classification System (NAICS).

Table 2.18. Estimated Wages for Nonprofits Serving Business, 1990–2013 (current $ billions)

	Nonprofit physical, engineering, and biological research services[a]	Nonprofit physical, engineering, and biological research services × 10%[b]	Business associations[c]	Nonprofits serving business[b]	NPISH[d]	Total estimated NPISH
1990	5.8	0.6	3.0	3.6	193.8	197.4
1991	3.0	0.3	3.2	3.5	209.4	212.9
1992	6.1	0.6	3.4	4.0	224.8	228.8
1993	6.4	0.6	3.5	4.2	239.7	243.9
1994	6.6	0.7	3.7	4.3	253.4	257.7
1995	7.0	0.7	3.9	4.6	266.8	271.4
1996	7.1	0.7	4.1	4.8	280.6	285.4
1997	7.8	0.8	4.3	5.1	296.9	302.0
1998	7.7	0.8	4.6	5.4	316.3	321.7
1999	7.4	0.7	4.9	5.6	334.8	340.4
2000	7.4	0.7	5.1	5.9	358.0	363.9
2001	6.4	0.6	5.5	6.1	374.0	380.1
2002	5.3	0.5	5.6	6.2	399.6	405.8
2003	5.8	0.6	5.8	6.4	418.6	425.0
2004	6.6	0.7	6.1	6.8	437.4	444.2
2005	7.6	0.8	6.5	7.2	451.2	458.4
2006	8.6	0.9	6.9	7.7	474.8	482.5
2007	9.4	0.9	7.2	8.2	498.3	506.5
2008	10.3	1.0	7.6	8.6	531.3	539.9
2009	10.5	1.0	7.5	8.6	549.4	558.0
2010	11.2	1.1	7.5	8.6	562.6	571.2
2011	12.1	1.2	7.7	8.9	581.2	590.1
2012	13.1	1.3	8.0	9.3	608.0	617.3
2013	13.5	1.4	8.2	9.6	624.4	634.0

Sources:
a. Authors' estimates based on private wages from U.S. Department of Labor, Bureau of Labor Statistics, Quarterly Census of Employment and Wages (1990–2014), and U.S. Census Bureau, Economic Census (1997, 2002, 2007, and 2012).
b. Authors' estimates. Total estimated NPISH is the sum of data in the nonprofits serving business and NPISH columns.
c. Authors' estimates based on private wages from U.S. Department of Labor, Bureau of Labor Statistics, Quarterly Census of Employment and Wages (1990–2014).
d. U.S. Department of Commerce, Bureau of Economic Analysis, National Income and Product Accounts, table 1.13 (2015).
NPISH = nonprofit institutions serving households

Table 2.19. National Taxonomy of Exempt Entities Core Codes Comprising NAICS Industries Whose Reported Wages Were Aggregated from Internal Revenue Service Data

NAICS 11: Agriculture, forestry, fishing, and hunting
- K20. Agricultural programs
- K25. Farmland preservation
- K26. Animal husbandry
- K99. Food, agriculture, and nutrition n.e.c.

NAICS 22: Utilities
- W80. Public utilities

NAICS 48, 49: Transportation and warehousing
- W40. Public transportation systems

NAICS 51: Information
- A27. Community celebrations
- A30. Media and communications
- A31. Film and video
- A32. Television
- A33. Printing and publishing
- A34. Radio
- B70. Libraries
- W50. Telecommunications
- X80. Religious media and communications
- X81. Religious film and video
- X82. Religious television
- X83. Religious printing and publishing
- X84. Religious radio

NAICS 52: Finance and insurance
- E80. Health (general and financing)
- W60. Financial institutions
- W61. Credit unions
- Y20. Insurance providers
- Y22. Local benevolent life insurance associations, mutual irrigation and telephone companies, and like organizations
- Y23. Mutual insurance companies and associations
- Y30. Pension and retirement funds
- Y33. Teachers' retirement fund associations
- Y34. Employee-funded pension trusts
- Y35. Multiemployer pension plans

NAICS 53: Real estate and rental and leasing
- S47. Real estate associations

NAICS 54: Professional, scientific, and technical services
- I20. Crime prevention
- I21. Youth violence prevention
- I30. Correctional facilities

(continued)

Table 2.19. National Taxonomy of Exempt Entities Core Codes Comprising NAICS Industries Whose Reported Wages Were Aggregated from Internal Revenue Service Data *(continued)*

I40. Rehabilitation services for offenders
I43. Inmate support
I44. Prison alternatives
I50. Administration of justice
I60. Law enforcement
I80. Legal services
I83. Public interest law
I99. Crime and legal related n.e.c.
A02. Management and technical assistance
B02. Management and technical assistance
C02. Management and technical assistance
D02. Management and technical assistance
E02. Management and technical assistance
F02. Management and technical assistance
G02. Management and technical assistance
H02. Management and technical assistance
I02. Management and technical assistance
K02. Management and technical assistance
L02. Management and technical assistance
M02. Management and technical assistance
N02. Management and technical assistance
O02. Management and technical assistance
P02. Management and technical assistance
Q02. Management and technical assistance
R02. Management and technical assistance
S02. Management and technical assistance
T02. Management and technical assistance
U02. Management and technical assistance
V02. Management and technical assistance
W02. Management and technical assistance
X02. Management and technical assistance
Y02. Management and technical assistance
S43. Small business development
S50. Nonprofit management
H20. Birth defects and genetic diseases research
H25. Down syndrome research
H30. Cancer research
H32. Breast cancer research
H40. Diseases of specific organs research
H41. Eye diseases, blindness, and vision impairments research
H42. Ear and throat diseases research
H43. Heart and circulatory system diseases and disorders research
H44. Kidney diseases research
H45. Lung diseases research

(continued)

Table 2.19. National Taxonomy of Exempt Entities Core Codes Comprising NAICS Industries Whose Reported Wages Were Aggregated from Internal Revenue Service Data *(continued)*

H48. Brain disorders research
H50. Nerve, muscle, and bone diseases research
H51. Arthritis research
H54. Epilepsy research
H60. Allergy-related diseases research
H61. Asthma research
H70. Digestive diseases and disorders research
H80. Specifically named diseases research
H81. AIDS research
H83. Alzheimer's disease research
H84. Autism research
H90. Medical disciplines research
H92. Biomedicine and bioengineering research
H94. Geriatrics research
H96. Neurology and neuroscience research
H98. Pediatrics research
H99. Medical research n.e.c.
H9b. Surgical specialties research
U20. General science
U21. Marine science and oceanography
U30. Physical and earth sciences
U31. Astronomy
U33. Chemistry and chemical engineering
U34. Mathematics
U36. Geology
U40. Engineering and technology
U41. Computer science
U42. Engineering
U50. Biological and life sciences
U99. Science and technology n.e.c.
A05. Research institutes and public policy analysis
B05. Research institutes and public policy analysis
C05. Research institutes and public policy analysis
D05. Research institutes and public policy analysis
E05. Research institutes and public policy analysis
F05. Research institutes and public policy analysis
G05. Research institutes and public policy analysis
H05. Research institutes and public policy analysis
I05. Research institutes and public policy analysis
J05. Research institutes and public policy analysis
K05. Research institutes and public policy analysis
L05. Research institutes and public policy analysis
M05. Research institutes and public policy analysis
N05. Research institutes and public policy analysis

(continued)

Table 2.19. National Taxonomy of Exempt Entities Core Codes Comprising NAICS Industries Whose Reported Wages Were Aggregated from Internal Revenue Service Data *(continued)*

O05. Research institutes and public policy analysis
P05. Research institutes and public policy analysis
Q05. Research institutes and public policy analysis
R05. Research institutes and public policy analysis
S05. Research institutes and public policy analysis
T05. Research institutes and public policy analysis
U05. Research institutes and public policy analysis
V05. Research institutes and public policy analysis
W05. Research institutes and public policy analysis
X05. Research institutes and public policy analysis
Y05. Research institutes and public policy analysis
A24. Folk arts
Q35. International democracy and civil society development
Q50. International affairs, foreign policy, and globalization
Q51. International economic and trade policy
V20. Social science
V21. Anthropology and sociology
V22. Economics
V23. Behavioral science
V24. Political science
V25. Population studies
V26. Law and jurisprudence
V30. Interdisciplinary research
V31. Black studies
V32. Women's studies
V33. Ethnic studies
V34. Urban studies
V35. International studies
V36. Gerontology
V37. Labor studies
V99. Social science n.e.c.
D40. Veterinary services
A40. Visual arts

NAICS 56: Administrative and support and waste management and remediation services

C20. Pollution abatement & control
J20. Employment preparation and procurement
J99. Employment n.e.c.

NAICS 72: Accommodation and food services

L40. Temporary housing
N20. Camps

Source: Urban Institute, National Center for Charitable Statistics, NCCS NTEE/NAICS/SIC Crosswalk (2015).
NAICS = North American Industry Classification System
n.e.c. = not elsewhere classified

3

Trends in Private Giving and Volunteering

The nonprofit sector is distinguished from the business and government sectors by the substantial role that donations of time and money play in its financing. Without such donations many nonprofits would cease to exist. This chapter paints a portrait of giving and volunteering in the United States. It provides statistics from various sources on giving from individuals, foundations, and corporations. It also examines who is volunteering at nonprofits, where they are volunteering, and the economic value of volunteer time.

Summary

- Private giving reached an estimated $358.38 billion in 2014. This figure is up from 2013, and has surpassed the pre-recession high of $311.06 billion in 2007.
- Living individuals or households accounted for 72.1 percent of private giving in 2014, donating an estimated $258.51 billion. Individual giving dropped during the recession—by 11.7 percent in 2008 and 5.7 percent in 2009 (in constant dollars)—and has risen in recent years, though not to pre-recession levels.
- In 2013, people who itemized contributions on their income tax forms accounted for 80 percent of total individual or household contributions. Over the past 10 years, itemizers have accounted for approximately 82 percent of individual or household contributions.
- In constant dollars, charitable deductions dropped 14 percent from 2007 to 2008, another 8 percent from 2008 to 2009, and 4 percent between 2012 and 2013, after an increase of 12 percent between 2011 and 2012.
- Grants from foundations account for the second-largest proportion of private giving, contributing $55.3 billion to charities in 2014.
- Foundation assets plummeted 17 percent in 2008 compared to 2007, but reached $46.8 billion in 2008, fueled by increased giving from the Bill and Melinda Gates

Foundation. Since 2008, foundation assets have increased steadily, and foundation assets reached an all-time high of $798.2 billion in 2013.

- While corporate giving dropped around 16 percent from 2007 to 2008, it has risen steadily beginning in 2008. Despite an 11 percent decrease between 2012 and 2013, corporate giving has now surpassed pre-recession (2007) levels.
- Volunteers spent 8.7 billion hours volunteering in 2014, the equivalent of 5.1 million full-time employees. Assuming that these employees would have earned the average private nonfarm hourly wage, volunteers' time contributed $179.2 billion to the nonprofit sector in 2014.

Private Giving

According to *Giving USA*, private giving (comprising giving by living individuals and households, personal bequests, gifts from foundations, and gifts from corporations) reached an estimated $358.4 billion in 2014. This figure is up from 2013, and higher than the pre-recession high of $311.1 billion in 2007. While in constant dollars, private giving declined by 12 percent from 2007 through 2010, it increased 15 percent between 2010 and 2014.

Figure 3.1 displays private giving as a percentage of national income. While this percentage declined since 2005 when it reached a high of 2.60 percent, 2011 marked the low-

Figure 3.1. Private Giving Compared with National Income, 1970–2014 (percent)

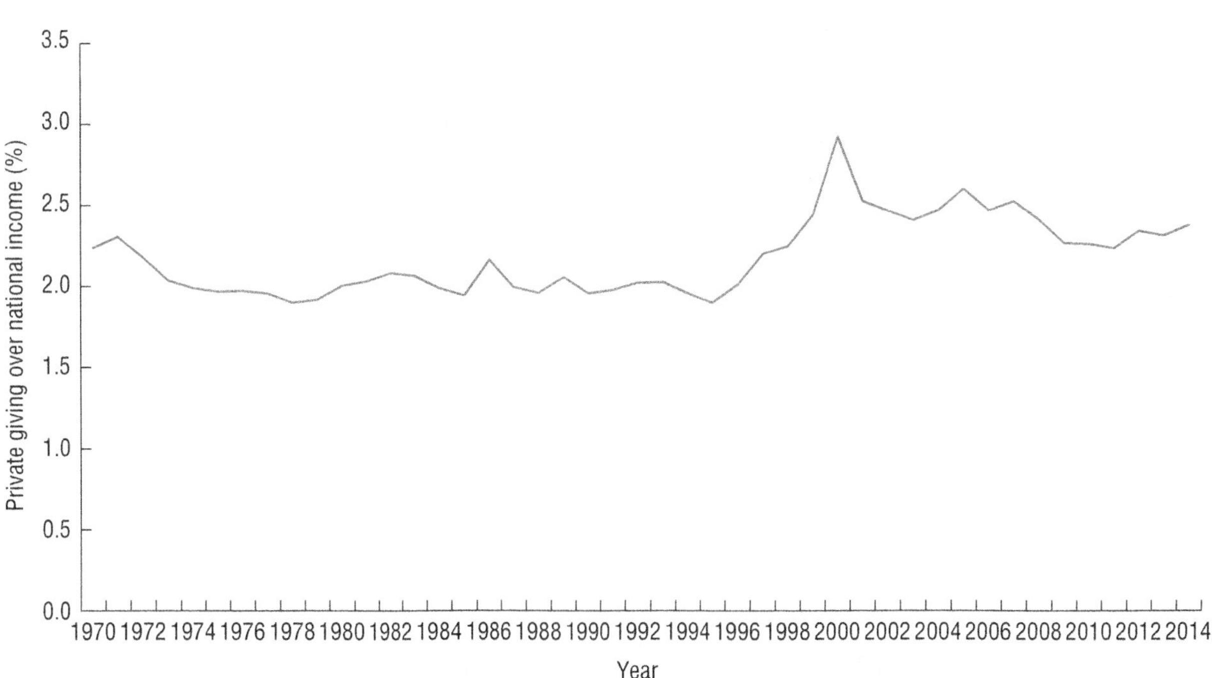

Sources: Authors' calculations based on private giving from Giving USA Foundation, *Giving USA* (2015), and national income from U.S. Department of Commerce, Bureau of Economic Analysis, National Income and Product Accounts, table 1.13 (2015).

est percentage of giving as a share of national income in the past 10 years—2.24 percent. However, in 2012 the percentage of giving increased to 2.34 percent. Although the percentage is still below the pre-recession amount, the data show the percentage of private giving continued to rise, as it was up in 2014 at 2.38 percent.

Private contributions as a percentage of nonprofit expenditures or outlays[1] (consumption expenditures, transfer payments, and savings) have also been on a downward trend after peaking in 2000 at 38.7 percent. While the numbers did trend upward from 2003 to 2005, 2009 marked the lowest percentage seen in over 10 years at 23.5 percent (table 3.1). Since 2009, the numbers have steadily increased, reaching a high of 25.7 percent in 2014. This figure, however, overestimates private philanthropy to the nonprofit sector because the BEA definition of nonprofits excludes organizations that serve business, which generally receive fewer donations from individuals. When calculated using IRS data from Form 990, private contributions account for 14.2 percent of total expenses in 2013 (see chapter 5 for more details). Figure 3.2 shows private contributions in constant 2014 dollars as a percentage of nonprofit outlays, or expenditures, for the last 22 years.

Figure 3.3 shows the distribution of private contributions by recipient type. Once again, religious organizations received the greatest proportion of private giving—32.1 percent in 2014. While religious organizations continue to receive the lion's share of private giving, the percentage going to these organizations began to decline after its peak of 53.3 percent in 1985. Educational organizations received the second-largest percentage of private giving with 15.2 percent of all private contributions, followed by human services organizations (11.7 percent) and gifts to foundations (11.6 percent). The proportion of gifts going to foundations show the largest increase over time from 7.8 percent in 2004 to 11.6 percent in 2014 (table 3.2).

Up to this point, this chapter has discussed private contributions overall. The next four sections look at each component of private giving: by living individuals, personal bequests, foundations, and corporations.

Giving by Living Individuals

Individuals gave an estimated $258.5 billion to charities in 2014, up 24.3 percent since 2010 (14.5 percent in constant dollars). Not surprisingly, individual giving dropped in both 2008 and 2009—down 11.7 percent from 2007 to 2008 and down 5.7 percent from 2008 to 2009 (in constant dollars). While still not up to pre-recession levels, individual giving did increase 20.9 percent from 2011 to 2014 (14.9 percent in constant dollars; figure 3.4, table 3.3).

Giving by living individuals accounted for 72.1 percent of all private giving in 2014. The proportion of giving from individuals began trending downward after 1979,

---

1. The Bureau of Economic Analysis (BEA), which produces the National Income and Product Accounts (NIPA), uses the term *outlays* to discuss expenditures. Outlays include the sum of personal consumption expenditures (expenses to obtain goods and services), personal interest payments (interest payments required to obtain goods and services), and personal current transfer payments (donations, fines, and fees paid to federal, state, and local governments as well as payments to the rest of the world). Outlays reported by the BEA differ from the expenses nonprofit organizations report on their Forms 990. Therefore, expenses discussed in chapter 1 are not comparable to outlays discussed in this chapter. Additional information on BEA data can be found at http://www.bea.gov.

Table 3.1. Private Contributions to Nonprofit Organizations by National Income and Nonprofit Outlays, 1970–2014

	$ Billions (current)			Private Giving as a Percentage of	
Year	Private giving	National income	Nonprofit outlays	National income	Nonprofit outlays
1970	21.0	940	—	2.24	—
1971	23.4	1,017	—	2.30	—
1972	24.4	1,123	—	2.18	—
1973	25.6	1,257	—	2.04	—
1974	26.9	1,351	—	1.99	—
1975	28.6	1,451	—	1.97	—
1976	31.9	1,615	—	1.97	—
1977	35.2	1,799	—	1.96	—
1978	38.6	2,030	—	1.90	—
1979	43.1	2,248	—	1.92	—
1980	48.6	2,427	—	2.00	—
1981	55.3	2,722	—	2.03	—
1982	59.1	2,840	—	2.08	—
1983	63.2	3,061	—	2.07	—
1984	68.6	3,444	—	1.99	—
1985	71.7	3,684	—	1.95	—
1986	83.3	3,848	—	2.16	—
1987	82.2	4,119	—	2.00	—
1988	88.0	4,493	—	1.96	—
1989	98.3	4,782	—	2.06	—
1990	98.5	5,036	—	1.96	—
1991	102.6	5,186	—	1.98	—
1992	111.3	5,500	419.6	2.02	26.52
1993	116.6	5,755	444.9	2.03	26.20
1994	120.1	6,140	468.7	1.96	25.61
1995	123.1	6,480	487.2	1.90	25.27
1996	138.9	6,899	516.6	2.01	26.89
1997	162.5	7,380	539.3	2.20	30.12
1998	176.6	7,857	586.2	2.25	30.12

(continued)

Table 3.1. Private Contributions to Nonprofit Organizations by National Income and Nonprofit Outlays, 1970–2014 *(continued)*

	$ Billions (current)			Private Giving as a Percentage of	
Year	Private giving	National income	Nonprofit outlays	National income	Nonprofit outlays
1999	203.2	8,324	625.1	2.44	32.51
2000	260.3	8,907	673.3	2.92	38.65
2001	232.1	9,185	735.1	2.53	31.57
2002	232.7	9,437	799.0	2.47	29.13
2003	237.5	9,864	840.2	2.41	28.26
2004	260.3	10,541	888.8	2.47	29.28
2005	292.4	11,240	945.8	2.60	30.92
2006	296.1	12,005	1,012.8	2.47	29.23
2007	311.1	12,321	1,070.9	2.52	29.05
2008	299.6	12,428	1,137.8	2.41	26.33
2009	274.8	12,126	1,170.7	2.27	23.47
2010	288.2	12,740	1,208.4	2.26	23.85
2011	298.5	13,352	1,247.4	2.24	23.93
2012	329.3	14,062	1,305.9	2.34	25.22
2013	334.5	14,458	1345.6	2.31	24.86
2014	358.4	15,077	1,394.5	2.38	25.70

Sources: Private giving from Giving USA Foundation, *Giving USA* (2015); national income from U.S. Department of Commerce, Bureau of Economic Analysis, National Income and Product Accounts, table 1.13 (2015); nonprofit outlays from U.S. Department of Commerce, Bureau of Economic Analysis, National Income and Product Accounts, table 2.9 (2015).
— = no data available

when gifts from individuals accounted for about 84.9 percent of total giving. During recessionary times, the proportion of giving from individuals has dropped; during economic expansions, the proportion of gifts from individuals has risen. In 2008, the proportion of private giving (which includes giving by individuals, foundations, and corporations) attributed to individuals declined to 71.3 percent of total giving, the lowest proportion since 2000, the lowest proportion on record.

Per capita contributions also fell during the recession. As displayed in figure 3.5, the per capita contribution (inflation adjusted) increased 11 percent from 2010 to 2014. Giving as a percentage of personal income increased from 1.7 percent to 1.8 percent over this same period (see table 3.4).

In general, contributions per capita increased each year between 1970 and 2010. After adjusting for inflation, contributions per capita increased 65 percent over the period.

Figure 3.2. Private Contributions in Constant 2014 Dollars and as a Percentage of Nonprofit Outlays, 1992–2014

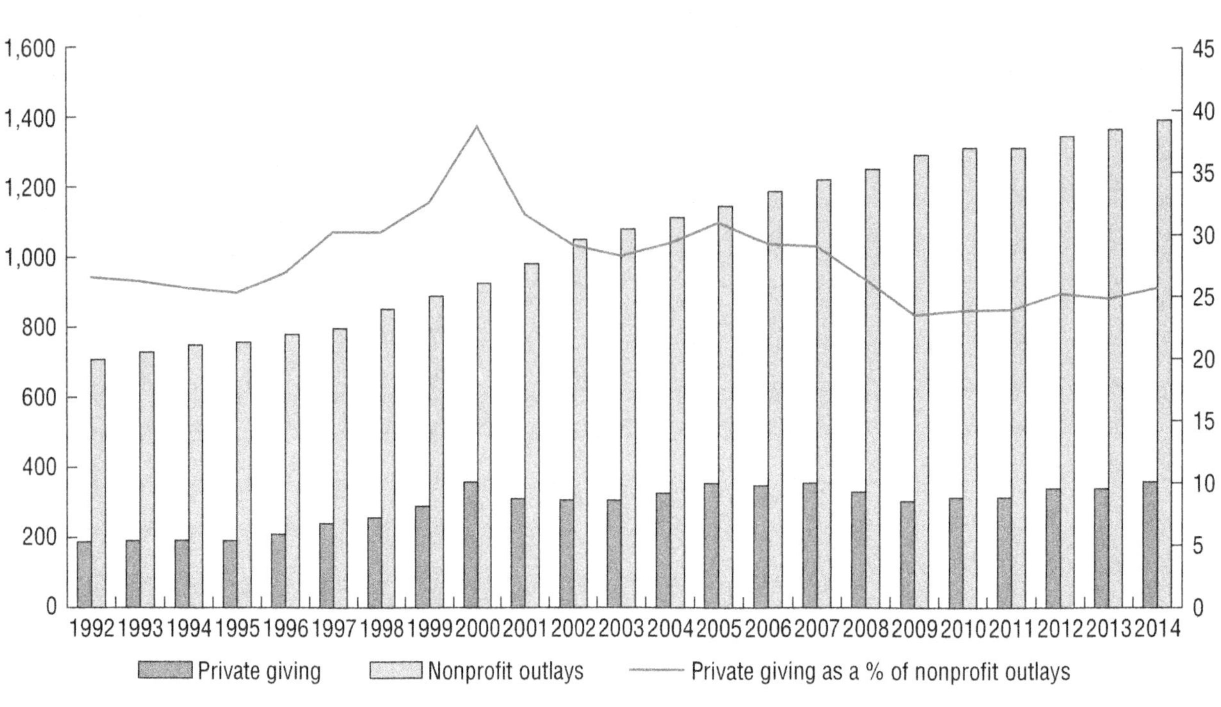

Sources: Authors' calculations based on private giving from Giving USA Foundation, *Giving USA* (2015), and nonprofit outlays from U.S. Department of Commerce, Bureau of Economic Analysis, National Income and Product Accounts, table 2.9 (2015).

Figure 3.3. Distribution of Private Contributions by Recipient Area, 2014

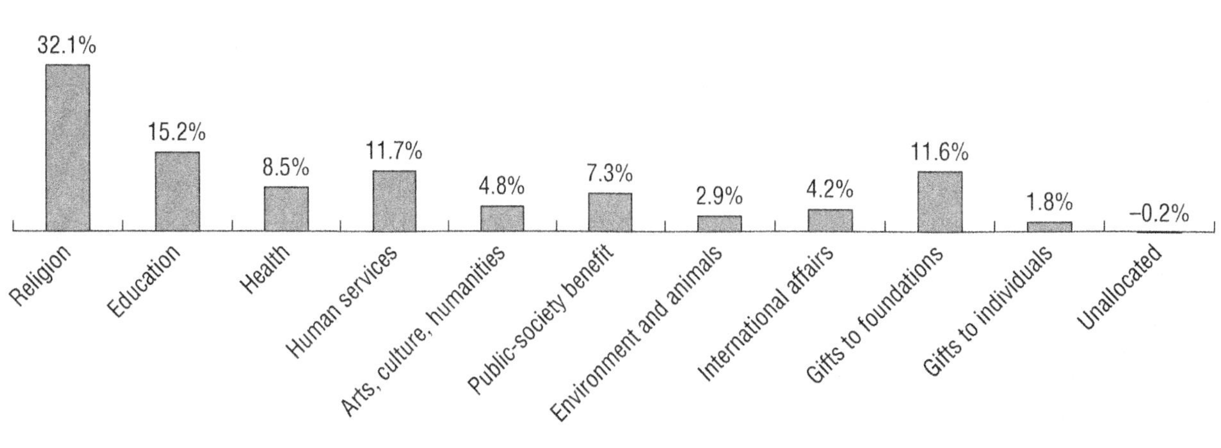

Source: Giving USA Foundation, *Giving USA* (2015).

Table 3.2. Distribution of Private Contributions by Type of Nonprofit, 1970–2014

Year	Total contributions ($ billions)	Percent										
		Religion	Education	Health	Human services	Arts, culture, humanities	Public-society benefit	Environment and animals	International affairs	Gifts to foundations	Gifts to individuals	Unallocated
1970	21.04	44.4	12.4	17.2	14.0	3.1	2.2	—	—	—	—	6.8
1971	23.44	43.0	11.7	16.7	12.9	4.3	2.9	—	—	—	—	8.5
1972	24.44	41.3	12.2	16.7	14.6	4.5	3.4	—	—	—	—	7.3
1973	25.59	41.1	13.0	17.7	15.1	4.9	2.4	—	—	—	—	5.7
1974	26.88	44.05	12.57	13.13	14.51	5.43	3.31	—	—	—	—	6.99
1975	28.56	44.85	11.17	12.82	13.73	5.22	4.27	—	—	—	—	7.95
1976	31.85	44.52	11.27	11.74	12.65	4.84	4.65	—	—	—	—	10.33
1977	35.21	48.22	11.05	11.16	11.64	5.23	3.66	—	—	—	—	9.03
1978	38.57	47.58	11.20	10.63	10.94	4.85	3.89	—	—	4.17	—	6.74
1979	43.11	46.79	10.90	9.93	10.00	4.59	4.22	—	—	5.13	—	8.44
1980	48.63	45.71	10.43	9.21	9.15	4.36	4.69	—	—	4.07	—	12.38
1981	55.28	45.31	10.73	8.38	8.30	4.12	3.85	—	—	4.32	—	14.98
1982	59.11	47.47	8.36	5.18	4.87	1.64	5.43	—	—	6.77	—	20.28
1983	63.21	50.37	8.43	5.47	4.81	2.23	5.96	—	—	4.29	—	18.43
1984	68.58	51.84	9.29	5.64	4.87	2.46	6.82	—	—	4.90	—	14.17
1985	71.69	53.30	9.42	6.40	5.13	2.64	5.71	—	—	6.60	—	10.81
1986	83.25	50.07	10.16	5.25	4.53	3.00	9.20	—	—	5.96	—	11.83
1987	82.20	52.93	9.83	5.73	4.85	3.16	5.91	1.02	1.76	6.28	—	8.52
1988	88.04	51.28	9.98	6.35	5.05	3.42	5.91	1.07	1.66	4.46	—	10.81

(continued)

Table 3.2. Distribution of Private Contributions by Type of Nonprofit, 1970–2014 *(continued)*

		Percent										
Year	Total contributions ($ billions)	Religion	Education	Health	Human services	Arts, culture, humanities	Public-society benefit	Environment and animals	International affairs	Gifts to foundations	Gifts to individuals	Unallocated
1989	98.30	48.60	11.51	6.53	6.63	3.48	6.12	1.10	1.67	4.49	—	9.88
1990	98.48	50.56	12.01	7.87	6.79	3.75	6.66	1.31	2.09	3.89	—	5.07
1991	102.58	48.74	11.80	7.44	7.31	3.72	6.56	1.45	1.58	4.35	—	7.05
1992	111.29	45.78	11.87	7.66	8.21	3.74	6.42	1.43	1.90	4.50	—	8.48
1993	116.58	45.37	12.32	7.54	8.29	3.65	7.09	1.54	1.66	5.37	—	7.16
1994	120.05	47.01	11.74	7.48	8.05	3.83	6.76	1.66	2.06	5.27	—	6.15
1995	123.10	47.17	13.38	14.56	8.67	4.30	7.12	1.81	2.14	6.87	—	–6.01
1996	138.89	44.57	12.92	13.21	8.62	4.31	6.77	1.87	2.15	9.09	—	–3.51
1997	162.46	39.82	13.54	8.38	8.83	4.42	6.91	1.79	1.93	8.59	—	5.77
1998	176.56	38.66	13.58	7.23	9.24	4.59	7.09	2.15	2.33	11.28	—	3.86
1999	203.19	35.07	13.11	6.68	8.64	4.33	6.68	2.22	2.64	14.15	—	6.47

2000	260.26	29.57	11.07	5.88	7.99	4.06	5.76	1.87	2.41	9.49	—	10.14
2001	232.09	34.41	12.09	7.07	10.46	4.19	7.14	2.28	2.88	11.06	—	8.41
2002	232.72	35.66	11.71	6.75	9.76	4.27	6.11	2.00	3.42	8.23	—	12.09
2003	237.45	35.43	12.46	7.49	9.89	4.68	6.72	2.10	3.98	9.11	—	8.15
2004	260.26	33.62	12.16	7.32	10.03	4.31	6.79	2.22	4.43	7.81	0.67	10.64
2005	292.43	31.07	11.97	6.95	10.38	4.25	7.10	2.21	4.35	8.36	1.06	12.30
2006	296.09	31.96	13.53	8.18	10.38	4.70	7.82	2.50	4.56	9.15	1.29	5.92
2007	311.06	31.44	13.72	8.13	10.11	4.80	6.43	2.59	5.07	12.11	1.08	4.52
2008	299.61	32.78	11.98	8.06	11.83	4.10	5.99	2.57	6.87	10.06	1.20	4.56
2009	274.78	36.23	12.72	9.49	13.08	4.58	6.30	2.66	5.96	11.79	1.53	–4.36
2010	288.16	33.85	14.65	9.61	12.76	4.64	6.67	2.75	4.82	9.12	1.62	–0.49
2011	298.45	34.10	14.80	8.72	12.74	4.55	7.45	2.87	5.15	10.17	1.99	–2.55
2012	329.32	32.12	14.65	8.25	12.19	4.63	7.13	2.84	5.11	12.09	1.87	–0.88
2013	334.50	33.51	15.57	8.61	12.15	4.72	7.48	2.93	4.61	12.23	2.14	–3.95
2014	358.38	32.06	15.24	8.47	11.75	4.81	7.34	2.93	4.21	11.61	1.79	–0.21

Source: Giving USA Foundation, *Giving USA* (2015).
— = no data available

Figure 3.4. Private Giving by Living Individuals, 1970–2014 (constant 2014 $)

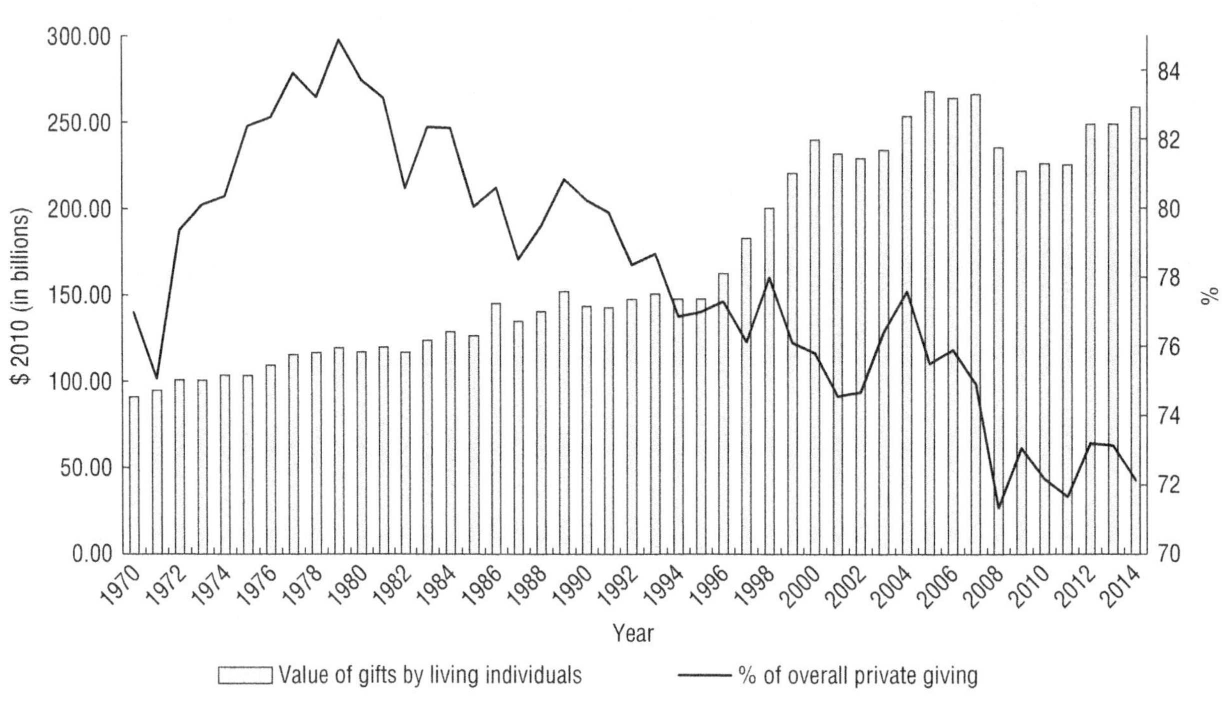

Source: Giving USA Foundation, *Giving USA* (2015).

During the late 1990s, per capita contributions grew steadily, increasing 54 percent between 1995 and 2000 alone. While gifts per capita have increased in dollars, giving as a percentage of income has remained steady at about 1.8 percent over the past 44 years.

Figure 3.6 displays individual giving by recipient organization for 2007, the latest year of data available from the panel study conducted by the Center on Philanthropy at Indiana University. According to this study, religious organizations continue to be the major recipients of donated dollars. Forty-three percent of households report giving to religious organizations, followed by 30.9 percent giving to charities to help the needy.

In addition to the giving estimates based on survey data reported above, the IRS Statistics of Income Division (SOI) provides data on individual giving from individuals who itemized their annual 1040 tax return. This section uses SOI data on deductions taken by personal income tax filers who itemize deductions to get a better picture of individual giving. In addition to the total contributions and average contributions of itemizers, this section presents data on high-income earners and cash versus noncash donations by itemizers.

Table 3.5 displays individual giving broken out by whether the givers itemized deductions on their personal income tax returns. Nonitemizers' contributions are estimated by subtracting itemizers' contributions from the total individual giving found in table 3.3. (Contributions by those who do not file tax returns are not included in the estimates presented in table 3.5.)

Table 3.3. Total Private Contributions by Source, 1970–2014

	Total Private Giving ($ billions)			Gifts by Living Individuals ($ billions)			Personal Bequests ($ billions)			Gifts by Foundations ($ billions)			Gifts by Corporations ($ billions)		
	$	$ 2014	%	$	$ 2014	%	$	$ 2014	%	$	$ 2014	%	$	$ 2014	%
1970	21.04	118.21	100.0	16.20	90.96	77.0	2.10	11.97	10.0	1.90	10.67	9.0	0.80	4.61	3.8
1971	23.44	126.02	100.0	17.60	94.84	75.1	3.00	16.13	12.8	2.00	10.48	8.5	0.90	4.57	3.8
1972	24.44	127.30	100.0	19.40	100.89	79.4	2.10	10.94	8.6	2.00	10.42	8.2	1.00	5.05	4.1
1973	25.59	125.44	100.0	20.50	100.64	80.1	2.00	9.80	7.8	2.00	9.80	7.8	1.10	5.20	4.3
1974	26.88	129.05	100.0	21.60	103.70	80.4	2.07	9.94	7.7	2.11	10.13	7.8	1.10	5.28	4.1
1975	28.56	125.65	100.0	23.53	103.52	82.4	2.23	9.81	7.8	1.65	7.26	5.8	1.15	5.06	4.0
1976	31.85	132.48	100.0	26.32	109.48	82.6	2.30	9.57	7.2	1.90	7.90	6.0	1.33	5.53	4.2
1977	35.21	137.54	100.0	29.55	115.43	83.9	2.12	8.28	6.0	2.00	7.81	5.7	1.54	6.02	4.4
1978	38.57	139.94	100.0	32.10	116.47	83.2	2.60	9.43	6.7	2.17	7.87	5.6	1.70	6.17	4.4
1979	43.11	140.61	100.0	36.59	119.34	84.9	2.23	7.27	5.2	2.24	7.31	5.2	2.05	6.69	4.8
1980	48.63	139.70	100.0	40.71	116.95	83.7	2.86	8.22	5.9	2.81	8.07	5.8	2.25	6.46	4.6
1981	55.28	143.91	100.0	45.99	119.73	83.2	3.58	9.32	6.5	3.07	7.99	5.6	2.64	6.8[illegible]	4.8
1982	59.11	145.01	100.0	47.63	116.85	80.6	5.21	12.78	8.8	3.16	7.75	5.3	3.11	7.63	5.3
1983	63.21	150.25	100.0	52.06	123.75	82.4	3.88	9.22	6.1	3.60	8.56	5.7	3.67	8.7[illegible]	5.8
1984	68.58	156.29	100.0	56.46	128.67	82.3	4.04	9.21	5.9	3.95	9.00	5.8	4.13	9.4[illegible]	6.0
1985	71.69	157.77	100.0	57.39	126.30	80.1	4.77	10.50	6.7	4.90	10.78	6.8	4.63	10.1[illegible]	6.5
1986	83.25	179.80	100.0	67.09	144.90	80.6	5.70	12.31	6.8	5.43	11.73	6.5	5.03	10.8[illegible]	6.0
1987	82.20	171.25	100.0	64.53	134.44	78.5	6.58	13.71	8.0	5.88	12.25	7.2	5.21	10.83	6.3
1988	88.04	176.25	100.0	69.98	140.10	79.5	6.57	13.15	7.5	6.15	12.31	7.0	5.34	10.63	6.1
1989	98.30	187.71	100.0	79.45	151.71	80.8	6.84	13.06	7.0	6.55	12.51	6.7	5.46	10.43	5.6

(continued)

Table 3.3. Total Private Contributions by Source, 1970–2014 *(continued)*

	Total Private Giving ($ billions)			Gifts by Living Individuals ($ billions)			Personal Bequests ($ billions)			Gifts by Foundations ($ billions)			Gifts by Corporations ($ billions)		
	$	$ 2014	%	$	$ 2014	%	$	$ 2014	%	$	$ 2014	%	$	$ 2014	%
1990	98.48	178.43	100.0	79.00	143.14	80.2	6.79	12.30	6.9	7.23	13.10	7.3	5.46	9.89	5.5
1991	102.58	178.31	100.0	81.93	142.41	79.9	7.68	13.35	7.5	7.72	13.42	7.5	5.25	9.13	5.1
1992	111.29	187.77	100.0	87.20	147.12	78.4	9.54	16.10	8.6	8.64	14.58	7.8	5.91	9.97	5.3
1993	116.58	191.05	100.0	91.72	150.31	78.7	8.86	14.52	7.6	9.53	15.62	8.2	6.47	10.60	5.5
1994	120.05	191.75	100.0	92.28	147.39	76.9	11.13	17.78	9.3	9.66	15.43	8.0	6.98	11.15	5.8
1995	123.10	191.24	100.0	94.78	147.24	77.0	10.41	16.17	8.5	10.56	16.41	8.6	7.35	11.42	6.0
1996	138.89	209.61	100.0	107.35	162.01	77.3	12.03	18.16	8.7	12.00	18.11	8.6	7.51	11.33	5.4
1997	162.46	239.61	100.0	123.67	182.40	76.1	16.25	23.97	10.0	13.92	20.53	8.6	8.62	12.71	5.3
1998	176.56	256.40	100.0	137.68	199.94	78.0	13.41	19.47	7.6	17.01	24.70	9.6	8.46	12.29	4.8
1999	203.19	288.79	100.0	154.63	219.77	76.1	17.82	25.33	8.8	20.51	29.15	10.1	10.23	14.54	5.0
2000	229.66	315.72	100.0	174.09	239.33	75.8	20.25	27.84	8.8	24.58	33.79	10.7	10.74	14.76	4.7

2001	232.09	310.28	100.0	173.06	231.36	74.6	20.15	26.94	8.7	27.22	36.39	3.0	11.66	15.59	5.0
2002	232.72	306.29	100.0	173.79	228.73	74.7	21.16	27.85	9.1	26.98	35.51	11.6	10.79	14.29	4.6
2003	237.45	305.56	100.0	181.47	233.52	76.4	18.08	23.27	7.6	26.84	34.54	11.3	11.06	14.23	4.7
2004	260.26	326.18	100.0	201.96	253.11	77.6	18.53	23.22	7.1	28.41	35.61	10.9	11.36	14.24	4.4
2005	292.43	354.50	100.0	220.82	267.69	75.5	24.00	29.09	8.2	32.41	39.29	11.1	15.20	18.43	5.2
2006	296.09	347.73	100.0	224.76	263.96	75.9	21.90	25.72	7.4	34.91	41.00	11.8	14.52	17.05	4.9
2007	311.06	355.17	100.0	233.05	266.10	74.9	23.79	27.16	7.6	40.00	45.67	12.9	14.22	16.24	4.6
2008	299.61	329.42	100.0	213.76	235.03	71.3	31.24	34.35	10.4	42.21	46.41	14.1	12.40	13.63	4.1
2009	274.78	303.22	100.0	200.78	221.56	73.1	19.12	21.10	7.0	41.09	45.34	15.0	13.79	15.22	5.0
2010	288.16	312.85	100.0	207.99	225.81	72.2	23.40	25.40	8.1	40.95	44.46	14.2	15.82	17.13	5.5
2011	298.45	314.10	100.0	213.86	225.07	71.7	25.18	26.50	8.4	43.83	46.13	14.7	15.58	16.40	5.2
2012	329.32	339.58	100.0	241.05	248.56	73.2	24.68	25.45	7.5	46.37	47.81	14.1	17.22	17.75	5.2
2013	334.50	339.94	100.0	244.63	248.61	73.1	24.36	24.76	7.3	49.88	50.69	14.9	15.63	15.83	4.7
2014	358.38	358.38	100.0	258.51	258.51	72.1	28.13	28.13	7.8	53.97	53.97	15.1	17.77	17.77	5.0

Source: Giving USA Foundation, *Giving USA* (2015).

Figure 3.5. Per Capita Individual Charitable Contributions, 1970–2014

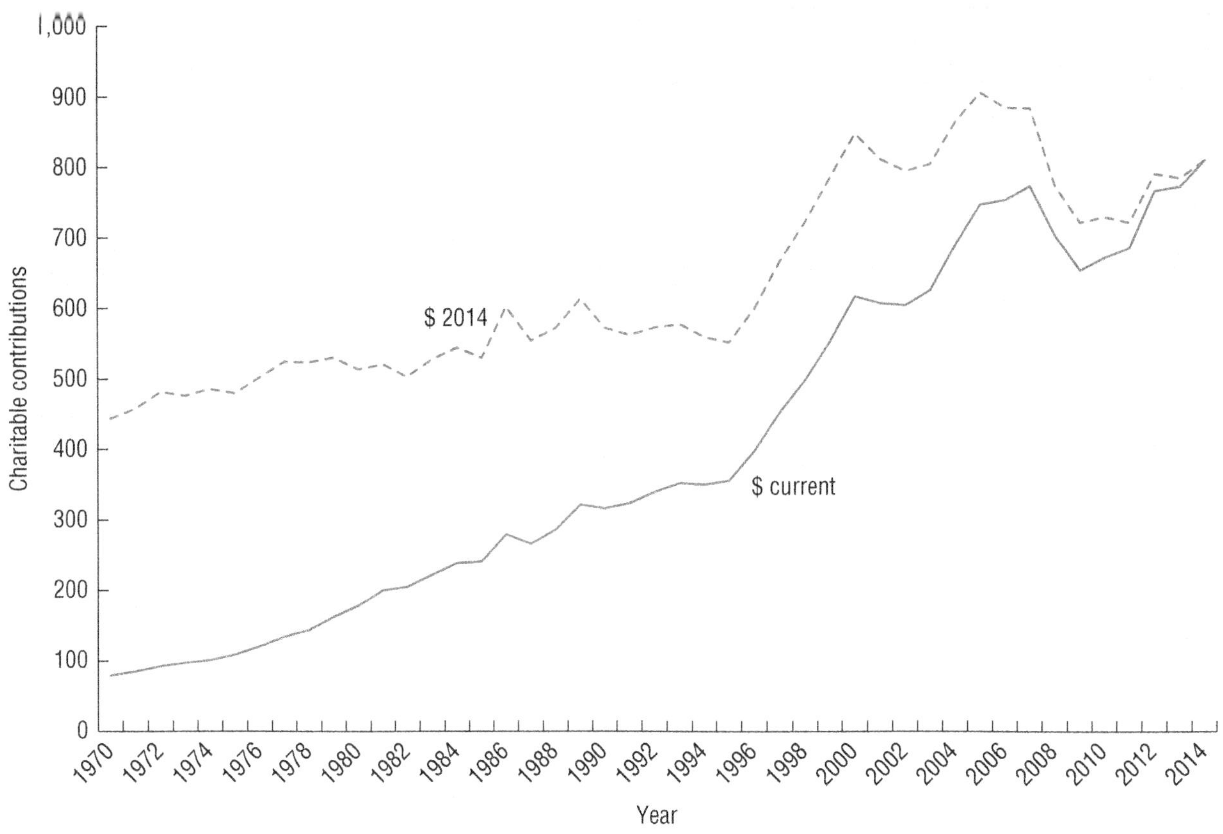

$ 2014

$ current

Charitable contributions

Year

Sources: Private and individual giving from Giving USA Foundation, *Giving USA* (2015); population from Chairman of the Council of Economic Advisors, *Economic Report of the President,* table B-34 (2013); and personal income from U.S. Department of Commerce, Bureau of Economic Analysis, National Income and Product Accounts, table 2.1 (2015).

In 2013, itemizers accounted for 80 percent of total individual contributions. Over the past 10 years, itemizer contributions have accounted for approximately 82 percent of individual contributions. The itemizers' average charitable contributions per return, was about nine times larger than nonitemizers' contributions in 2013. Itemizers typically give twice the percentage of income of nonitemizers.

From 2007 to 2013, the number of itemizers claiming charitable deductions dropped slightly. Approximately 91 percent of itemizers claimed a charitable deduction in 1993 compared with 82 percent in 2013. From 2005 to 2011, the general trend in total charitable contributions on itemized tax returns, measured in constant dollars, was downward. In constant dollars, charitable deductions dropped 14 percent from 2007 to 2008; another 8 percent from 2008 to 2009; and 4 percent between 2012 and 2013, which followed a 12 percent increase between 2011 and 2012. While the average charitable deduction taken by itemizers increased from $4,782 in 2011 to an all-time high of $5,411 in 2012, it declined slightly to $5,343 in 2013 (table 3.6).

Table 3.4. Total Per Capita Contributions and Individual Contributions as a Percentage of National Income, 1970–2014

Year	Private Giving		Population (midyear, millions)	Per Capita Individual Giving		Total personal income ($ billions)	Individual giving as a percentage of income
	Total	By individuals		$	2014		
1970	21.0	16.2	205.1	79.0	443.7	864.6	1.9
1971	23.4	17.6	207.7	84.9	457.4	932.1	1.9
1972	24.4	19.4	209.9	92.3	481.4	1,023.6	1.9
1973	25.6	20.5	211.9	96.9	475.8	1,138.5	1.8
1974	26.9	21.6	213.9	101.0	485.0	1,249.3	1.7
1975	28.6	23.5	216.0	108.9	479.4	1,366.9	1.7
1976	31.9	26.3	218.0	120.7	502.2	1,498.5	1.8
1977	35.2	29.6	220.2	134.2	524.1	1,654.6	1.8
1978	38.6	32.1	222.6	144.2	523.6	1,859.7	1.7
1979	43.1	36.6	225.1	162.6	530.2	2,078.2	1.8
1980	48.6	40.7	227.7	178.8	513.6	2,317.5	1.8
1981	55.3	46.0	230.0	200.0	520.8	2,596.5	1.8
1982	59.1	47.6	232.2	205.1	503.2	2,779.5	1.7
1983	63.2	52.1	234.3	222.2	528.1	2,970.3	1.8
1984	68.6	56.5	236.3	238.9	544.3	3,281.8	1.7
1985	71.7	57.4	238.5	240.7	529.5	3,516.3	1.6
1986	83.3	67.1	240.7	278.8	602.2	3,725.7	1.8
1987	82.2	64.5	242.8	265.8	553.8	3,955.9	1.6
1988	88.0	70.0	245.0	285.6	571.5	4,276.3	1.6
1989	98.3	79.5	247.3	321.2	613.3	4,619.9	1.7
1990	98.5	79.0	250.1	315.8	572.1	4,906.4	1.6
1991	102.6	81.9	253.5	323.2	561.8	5,073.4	1.6
1992	111.3	87.2	256.9	339.4	572.8	5,413.0	1.6
1993	116.6	91.7	260.3	352.4	577.4	5,649.0	1.6
1994	120.1	92.3	263.4	350.3	559.6	5,937.3	1.6
1995	123.1	94.8	266.6	355.6	552.3	6,281.0	1.5
1996	138.9	107.4	269.7	398.1	600.6	6,667.0	1.6
1997	162.5	123.7	272.9	453.1	668.4	7,080.7	1.7
1998	176.6	137.7	276.1	498.6	724.2	7,593.7	1.8
1999	203.2	154.6	279.3	553.6	786.7	7,988.4	1.9
2000	260.3	174.1	282.2	617.0	848.2	8,637.1	2.0
2001	232.1	173.1	285.0	607.3	811.8	8,991.6	1.9

(continued)

Table 3.4. Total Per Capita Contributions and Individual Contributions as a Percentage of National Income, 1970–2014 *(continued)*

Year	Private Giving		Population (midyear, millions)	Per Capita Individual Giving		Total personal income ($ billions)	Individual giving as a percentage of income
	Total	By individuals		$	2014		
2002	232.7	173.8	287.6	604.2	795.1	9,153.9	1.9
2003	237.5	181.5	290.1	625.5	804.8	9,491.1	1.9
2004	260.3	202.0	292.8	689.7	864.4	10,052.9	2.0
2005	292.4	220.8	295.5	747.2	905.8	10,614.0	2.1
2006	296.1	224.8	298.4	753.3	884.6	11,393.9	2.0
2007	311.1	233.1	301.2	773.7	883.3	12,000.2	1.9
2008	299.6	213.8	304.1	702.9	772.9	12,502.2	1.7
2009	274.8	200.8	306.8	654.5	722.2	12,094.8	1.7
2010	288.2	208.0	309.3	672.4	729.9	12,477.1	1.7
2011	298.5	213.9	311.7	686.1	722.0	13,254.5	1.6
2012	329.3	241.1	314.1	767.4	791.3	13,915.1	1.7
2013	334.5	244.6	316.5	772.9	785.5	14,068.4	1.7
2014	358.4	258.5	318.9	810.7	810.7	14,694.2	1.8

Sources: Private and individual giving from Giving USA Foundation, *Giving USA* (2015); population from Chairman of the Council of Economic Advisors, *Economic Report of the President*, table B-34 (2013) for years 1970–2009, years 2010–2014 from U.S. Census Bureau Monthly Population Estimates for the United States: April 1, 2010, to December 1, 2015; personal income from U.S. Department of Commerce, Bureau of Economic Analysis, National Income and Product Accounts, table 2.1 (2015).

Figure 3.6. Household Charitable Giving by Recipient Organization, 2007 (percent)

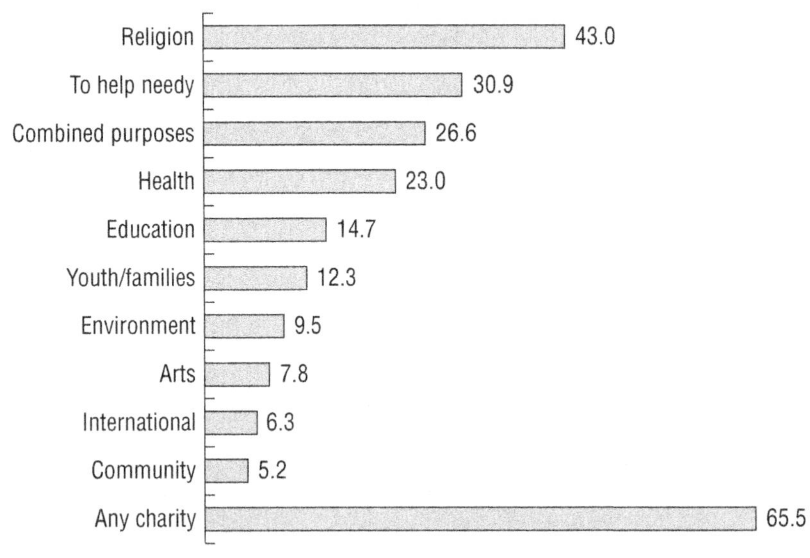

Source: Center on Philanthropy, Center on Philanthropy Panel Study (2007).

Table 3.5. Estimates of Individual Charitable Contributions by Tax-Itemization Status, 1985–2013 (current $)

	Returns	Adjusted gross income ($ millions)	Adjusted gross income per return	Charitable contributions ($ millions)	Charitable contributions per return	As a percentage of adjusted gross income
1985						
All	**101,660,287**	**2,305,952**	**22,683**	**57,390**	**565**	**2.49**
Itemizer	39,848,184	1,582,587	39,715	47,963	1,204	3.03
Nonitemizer	61,812,103	723,365	11,703	9,427	153	1.30
1986						
All	**103,045,170**	**2,481,681**	**24,083**	**67,090**	**651**	**2.70**
Itemizer	40,667,008	1,725,714	42,435	53,816	1,323	3.12
Nonitemizer	62,378,162	755,967	12,119	13,274	213	1.76
1987						
All	**106,996,270**	**2,772,824**	**25,915**	**64,530**	**603**	**2.33**
Itemizer	35,627,790	1,799,048	50,496	49,624	1,393	2.76
Nonitemizer	71,368,480	973,776	13,644	14,906	209	1.53
1988						
All	**109,708,280**	**3,083,020**	**28,102**	**69,980**	**638**	**2.27**
Itemizer	31,902,985	1,887,494	59,164	50,949	1,597	2.70
Nonitemizer	77,805,295	1,195,526	15,366	19,031	245	1.59
1989						
All	**112,135,673**	**3,256,359**	**29,039**	**79,450**	**709**	**2.44**
Itemizer	31,972,317	1,971,222	61,654	55,459	1,735	2.81
Nonitemizer	80,163,356	1,285,137	16,031	23,991	299	1.87
1990						
All	**113,717,136**	**3,405,428**	**29,946**	**79,000**	**695**	**2.32**
Itemizer	32,174,938	2,046,651	63,610	57,243	1,779	2.80
Nonitemizer	81,542,198	1,358,777	16,663	21,757	267	1.60
1991						
All	**114,730,124**	**3,464,524**	**30,197**	**81,930**	**714**	**2.36**
Itemizer	32,489,919	2,056,805	63,306	60,574	1,864	2.95
Nonitemizer	82,240,205	1,407,719	17,117	21,356	260	1.52
1992						
All	**113,604,503**	**3,629,129**	**31,945**	**87,200**	**768**	**2.40**
Itemizer	32,540,614	2,183,969	67,115	63,843	1,962	2.92
Nonitemizer	81,063,889	1,445,160	17,827	23,357	288	1.62

(continued)

Table 3.5. Estimates of Individual Charitable Contributions by Tax-Itemization Status, 1985–2013 (current $) *(continued)*

	Returns	Adjusted gross income ($ millions)	Adjusted gross income per return	Charitable contributions ($ millions)	Charitable contributions per return	As a percentage of adjusted gross income
1993						
All	**114,601,819**	**3,723,340**	**32,489**	**91,720**	**800**	**2.46**
Itemizer	32,821,464	2,241,087	68,281	68,354	2,083	3.05
Nonitemizer	81,780,355	1,482,253	18,125	23,366	286	1.58
1994						
All	**115,943,131**	**3,907,518**	**33,702**	**92,280**	**796**	**2.36**
Itemizer	33,017,754	2,342,834	70,957	70,545	2,137	3.01
Nonitemizer	82,925,377	1,564,684	18,869	21,735	262	1.39
1995						
All	**118,218,327**	**4,189,354**	**35,437**	**94,780**	**802**	**2.26**
Itemizer	34,007,717	2,542,781	74,771	74,992	2,205	2.95
Nonitemizer	84,210,610	1,646,573	19,553	19,788	235	1.20
1996						
All	**120,351,208**	**4,535,974**	**37,689**	**107,350**	**892**	**2.37**
Itemizer	35,414,589	2,812,927	79,428	86,159	2,433	3.06
Nonitemizer	84,936,619	1,723,047	20,286	21,191	249	1.23
1997						
All	**122,421,991**	**4,969,950**	**40,597**	**123,670**	**1,010**	**2.49**
Itemizer	36,624,595	3,130,184	85,467	99,192	2,708	3.17
Nonitemizer	85,797,396	1,839,766	21,443	24,478	285	1.33
1998						
All	**124,770,662**	**5,415,973**	**43,407**	**137,680**	**1,103**	**2.54**
Itemizer	38,186,186	3,466,035	90,767	109,240	2,861	3.15
Nonitemizer	86,584,476	1,949,938	22,521	28,440	328	1.46
1999						
All	**127,075,145**	**5,855,468**	**46,079**	**154,630**	**1,217**	**2.64**
Itemizer	40,244,305	3,853,151	95,744	125,799	3,126	3.26
Nonitemizer	86,830,840	2,002,317	23,060	28,831	332	1.44

(continued)

Table 3.5. Estimates of Individual Charitable Contributions by Tax-Itemization Status, 1985–2013 (current $) *(continued)*

	Returns	Adjusted gross income ($ millions)	Adjusted gross income per return	Charitable contributions ($ millions)	Charitable contributions per return	As a percentage of adjusted gross income
2000						
All	**129,373,500**	**6,365,377**	**49,202**	**174,090**	**1,346**	**2.73**
Itemizer	42,534,320	4,294,262	100,960	140,682	3,307	3.28
Nonitemizer	86,839,180	2,071,115	23,850	33,408	385	1.61
2001						
All	**130,255,237**	**6,170,604**	**47,373**	**173,060**	**1,329**	**2.80**
Itemizer	44,562,308	4,164,470	93,453	139,241	3,125	3.34
Nonitemizer	85,692,929	2,006,134	23,411	33,819	395	1.69
2002						
All	**130,076,443**	**6,033,586**	**46,385**	**173,790**	**1,336**	**2.88**
Itemizer	45,647,551	4,080,678	89,395	140,571	3,079	3.44
Nonitemizer	84,428,892	1,952,908	23,131	33,219	393	1.70
2003						
All	**130,423,626**	**6,207,109**	**47,592**	**181,470**	**1,391**	**2.92**
Itemizer	43,949,591	4,103,653	93,372	145,702	3,315	3.55
Nonitemizer	86,474,035	2,103,456	24,325	35,768	414	1.70
2004						
All	**132,226,042**	**6,788,805**	**51,342**	**201,960**	**1,527**	**2.97**
Itemizer	46,335,237	4,643,404	100,213	165,564	3,573	3.57
Nonitemizer	85,890,805	2,145,401	24,978	36,396	424	1.70
2005						
All	**134,372,678**	**7,422,496**	**55,238**	**220,820**	**1,643**	**2.98**
Itemizer	47,755,427	5,185,666	108,588	183,391	3,840	3.54
Nonitemizer	86,617,251	2,236,830	25,824	37,429	432	1.67
2006						
All	**138,394,754**	**8,030,843**	**58,029**	**224,760**	**1,624**	**2.80**
Itemizer	49,123,555	5,703,411	116,103	186,647	3,800	3.27
Nonitemizer	89,271,199	2,327,432	26,071	38,113	427	1.64

(continued)

Table 3.5. Estimates of Individual Charitable Contributions by Tax-Itemization Status, 1985–2013 (current $) *(continued)*

	Returns	Adjusted gross income ($ millions)	Adjusted gross income per return	Charitable contributions ($ millions)	Charitable contributions per return	As a percentage of adjusted gross income
2007						
All	**142,978,806**	**8,687,719**	**60,762**	**233,050**	**1,630**	**2.68**
Itemizer	50,544,470	6,187,836	122,424	193,604	3,830	3.13
Nonitemizer	92,434,336	2,499,883	27,045	39,446	427	1.58
2008						
All	**142,450,569**	**8,262,860**	**58,005**	**213,760**	**1,501**	**2.59**
Itemizer	48,167,223	5,731,767	118,997	172,936	3,590	3.02
Nonitemizer	94,283,346	2,531,093	26,846	40,824	433	1.61
2009						
All	**140,494,127**	**7,626,431**	**54,283**	**200,780**	**1,429**	**2.63**
Itemizer	45,695,736	5,098,314	111,571	158,017	3,458	3.10
Nonitemizer	94,798,391	2,528,116	26,668	42,763	451	1.69
2010						
All	**142,892,051**	**8,089,142**	**56,610**	**207,990**	**1,456**	**2.57**
Itemizer	46,644,509	5,498,594	117,883	170,236	3,650	3.10
Nonitemizer	96,247,542	2,590,548	26,915	37,754	392	1.46
2011						
All	**145,370,240**	**8,374,143**	**57,606**	**213,860**	**1,471**	**2.55**
Itemizer	46,293,834	5,664,555	122,361	174,474	3,769	3.08
Nonitemizer	99,076,406	2,709,588	27,348	39,386	398	1.45
2012						
All	**144,928,472**	**9,100,131**	**62,791**	**241,050**	**1,663**	**2.65**
Itemizer	45,581,697	6,225,505	136,579	199,270	4,372	3.20
Nonitemizer	99,346,775	2,874,627	28,935	41,780	421	1.45
2013						
All	**147,351,299**	**9,093,629**	**61,714**	**244,630**	**1,660**	**2.69**
Itemizer	44,330,496	5,930,724	133,784	194,664	4,391	3.28
Nonitemizer	103,020,803	3,162,905	30,702	49,966	485	1.58

Sources: U.S. Department of the Treasury, Internal Revenue Service, Statistics of Income, table 1.2 (1985–2013) and table 2.1 (1985–2013); Giving USA Foundation, *Giving USA* (2015).
Note: Nonitemizer giving is the difference between individual giving from table 3.3 and itemizer giving.

Table 3.6. Average Charitable Deduction of All Itemizers and Itemizers with Charitable Deductions, 1985–2013

	Returns		Total Charitable Deductions		Average Charitable Contribution			
					All Returns		With Charitable Deductions	
Year	All	With charitable contributions	Current $, millions	Constant 2013 $, millions	Current dollars	Constant 2013 dollars	Current dollars	Constant 2013 dollars
1985	39,848,184	36,228,636	47,963	103,841	1,204	2,606	1,324	2,866
1986	40,667,008	36,857,590	53,816	114,387	1,323	2,813	1,460	3,103
1987	35,627,790	32,229,545	49,624	101,763	1,393	2,856	1,540	3,157
1988	31,902,985	29,110,570	50,949	100,330	1,597	3,145	1,750	3,447
1989	31,972,317	29,132,485	55,459	104,190	1,735	3,259	1,904	3,576
1990	32,174,938	29,230,264	57,243	102,028	1,779	3,171	1,958	3,491
1991	32,489,919	29,551,348	60,574	103,605	1,864	3,189	2,050	3,506
1992	32,540,614	29,603,407	63,843	106,007	1,962	3,258	2,157	3,581
1993	32,821,464	29,799,001	68,354	110,198	2,083	3,357	2,294	3,698
1994	33,017,754	29,848,727	70,545	110,890	2,137	3,358	2,363	3,715
1995	34,007,717	30,540,637	74,992	114,631	2,205	3,371	2,455	3,753
1996	35,414,589	31,591,983	86,159	127,925	2,433	3,612	2,727	4,049
1997	36,624,595	32,612,634	99,192	143,972	2,708	3,931	3,042	4,415
1998	38,186,186	33,835,992	109,240	156,124	2,861	4,088	3,229	4,614
1999	40,244,305	35,523,471	125,799	175,904	3,126	4,371	3,541	4,952
2000	42,534,320	37,524,825	140,682	190,318	3,307	4,474	3,749	5,072
2001	44,562,308	39,386,782	139,241	183,158	3,125	4,110	3,535	4,650
2002	45,647,551	40,399,695	140,571	182,029	3,079	3,988	3,480	4,506
2003	43,949,591	38,626,902	145,702	184,469	3,315	4,197	3,772	4,776
2004	46,335,237	40,623,426	165,564	204,179	3,573	4,407	4,076	5,026
2005	47,755,427	41,381,465	183,391	218,751	3,840	4,581	4,432	5,286
2006	49,123,555	41,437,749	186,647	215,678	3,800	4,391	4,504	5,205
2007	50,544,470	41,119,033	193,604	217,522	3,830	4,304	4,708	5,290
2008	48,167,223	39,250,369	172,936	187,116	3,590	3,885	4,406	4,767
2009	45,695,736	37,243,302	158,017	171,584	3,458	3,755	4,243	4,607
2010	46,644,509	38,143,170	170,236	181,869	3,650	3,899	4,463	4,768
2011	46,293,834	37,789,956	174,474	180,693	3,769	3,903	4,617	4,782
2012	45,581,697	37,367,247	199,270	202,189	4,372	4,436	5,333	5,411
2013	44,330,496	36,430,878	194,664	194,664	4,391	4,391	5,343	5,343

Source: U.S. Department of the Treasury, Internal Revenue Service, Statistics of Income, Individual Complete Report (Publication 1304), table 2.1 (1985–2013).

Table 3.7 displays charitable contributions for itemizers with adjusted gross incomes of $1 million or more. Itemizers at this income level in 2013 who claimed charitable deductions accounted for less than 1 percent of all itemized returns with charitable deductions and 26 percent of total charitable contributions reported. In 2013, these high-income earners reported total contributions of nearly $50.5 billion. This accounts for about 5 percent of the total adjusted gross income of high-income item-

Table 3.7. Charitable Contributions of Itemizers with Adjusted Gross Income of $1 Million or More, 1993–2013

Year	Returns filed	Returns with charitable deductions	Percentage of returns with contribution deductions	Percentage of all returns filed with contribution deductions	$ Thousands (current)	
					Adjusted gross income	Total contributions
1993	62,392	60,904	97.6	0.20	163,049,402	7,050,906
1994	64,814	63,323	97.7	0.21	172,014,314	7,872,412
1995	80,362	78,447	97.6	0.26	214,365,387	8,845,408
1996	102,129	99,728	97.6	0.32	296,349,836	13,648,238
1997	132,072	128,684	97.4	0.39	397,475,502	18,618,418
1998	155,879	151,683	97.3	0.45	496,505,525	21,141,556
1999	186,729	181,701	97.3	0.51	610,730,186	27,245,122
2000	218,949	212,157	96.9	0.57	770,956,226	32,633,045
2001	178,520	173,957	97.4	0.44	547,369,318	24,932,570
2002	155,055	151,300	97.6	0.37	447,482,537	20,811,652
2003	165,399	161,136	97.4	0.42	503,009,522	24,196,568
2004	219,411	214,027	97.5	0.53	718,083,999	34,123,211
2005	278,701	271,010	97.2	0.65	970,597,258	45,412,078
2006	338,761	326,164	96.3	0.79	1,177,100,230	48,977,919
2007	375,567	361,317	96.2	0.88	1,363,116,669	55,491,266
2008	310,829	298,432	96.0	0.76	1,051,670,613	39,133,378
2009	230,323	220,455	95.7	0.59	711,598,278	29,181,815
2010	274,826	261,081	95.0	0.68	911,289,193	36,569,958
2011	294,685	282,120	95.7	0.75	933,278,553	37,913,968
2012	383,511	367,587	95.8	0.98	1,357,109,036	59,416,092
2013	317,637	305,984	96.3	0.84	1,029,533,256	50,495,671

Source: U.S. Department of the Treasury, Internal Revenue Service, Statistics of Income, Individual Complete Report (Publication 1304), table 2.1 (1985–2013).
Note: The sum of cash and noncash contributions may not sum to total contributions because the values are derived from Form 8283, which is filed by itemizers that report more than $500 of non-cash contributions.
AGI = adjusted gross income

izers. Between 2007 and 2008, adjusted gross income declined roughly 23 percent and the amount of contributions dropped a little more than $16.3 billion, a 29 percent decline in itemized donations. Subsequently, adjusted gross income increased 28 percent between 2009 and 2010 and 45 percent between 2011 and 2012. By the next year it declined 24 percent between 2012 and 2013, and the amount of contributions dropped nearly $9 billion, a 15 percent decline in itemized donations. The average charitable

Average Contributions		Contributions as a percentage of AGI	Cash Contributions		Noncash Contributions	
Current $	Constant 2013 $		$ thousands	%	$ thousands	%
113,010	182,190	4.3	3,907,828	54.5	3,265,085	45.5
121,462	190,927	4.6	3,882,070	48.7	4,092,446	51.3
110,070	168,252	4.1	4,667,770	59.6	3,168,163	40.4
133,637	198,417	4.6	5,808,136	43.7	7,479,736	56.3
140,972	204,613	4.7	7,365,764	38.8	11,641,343	61.2
135,628	193,837	4.3	9,299,041	45.3	11,238,947	54.7
145,907	204,022	4.5	10,208,251	38.9	16,021,218	61.1
149,044	201,631	4.2	12,384,192	32.9	25,304,866	67.1
139,663	183,712	4.6	11,772,323	43.0	15,576,513	57.0
134,221	173,806	4.7	11,159,827	53.1	9,843,792	46.9
146,292	185,216	4.8	12,169,102	49.8	12,255,944	50.2
155,522	191,794	4.8	17,231,783	50.4	16,958,795	49.6
162,942	194,360	4.5	25,960,921	54.6	21,547,363	45.4
144,580	167,068	4.2	27,269,896	49.8	27,451,809	50.2
147,753	166,007	4.1	30,864,409	51.1	29,552,084	48.9
125,900	136,223	3.7	28,273,674	63.8	16,013,777	36.2
126,700	137,578	4.1	21,610,432	66.9	10,677,556	33.1
133,066	142,159	4.0	23,862,533	58.1	17,190,780	41.9
128,659	133,245	4.1	26,194,425	59.5	17,808,428	40.5
154,927	157,196	4.4	36,365,534	62.3	22,030,483	37.7
158,973	158,973	4.9	30,043,569	56.3	23,336,104	43.7

contribution, in constant dollars, for these donors peaked in 1997 at $204,613. Since then, however, tax data show a generally downward trend. Since 2000, the average charitable contribution declined by 21 percent from $201,631 in 2000 to $158,973 in 2013 (in constant dollars).

Gifts to charities can be either cash contributions or noncash contributions such as vehicles or investments. While cash contributions have always accounted for most itemizer deductions, the proportion of cash contributions had been trending generally downward since peaking in 1987 at 88 percent. However, cash contributions temporarily rose during the recession period: by 2009, 82 percent of itemizer contributions were in cash. This is the highest proportion of cash contributions in the past 10 years (figure 3.7, table 3.8). Since 2009, the percentage of itemizer contributions in cash has slightly declined, dropping to 76 percent in 2013. For itemizers with $1 million or more in adjusted gross income, cash contributions accounted for 67 percent of reported donations in 2009, the highest value on record. By 2013, cash contributions had dropped to 56 percent for itemizers with $1 million or more in adjusted gross income. This rate is slightly higher than the pre-recession level: in 2007, 51 percent of contributions were cash gifts (table 3.7).

The shift from noncash to cash contributions may result partly from the recession. Investments account for a large proportion of noncash donations, and include stocks, mutual funds, real estate, and other investments. The market value of these types of

Figure 3.7. Cash Versus Noncash Charitable Contributions, 1985–2013

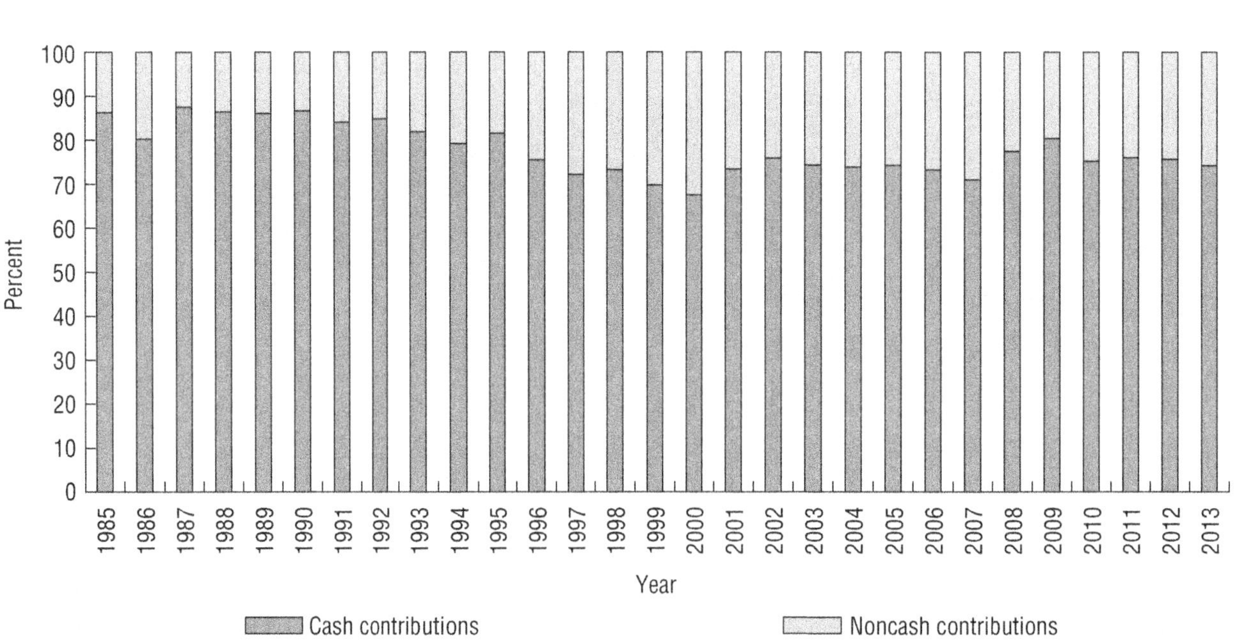

Source: U.S. Department of the Treasury, Internal Revenue Service, Statistics of Income, Individual Complete Report (Publication 1304), table 2.1 (1985–2014).

Table 3.8. Distribution of Itemizers' Cash and Noncash Charitable Contributions, 1985–2013 (current $)

	Total Charitable Contributions		Cash Contributions		Noncash Contributions	
Year	$ thousands	%	$ thousands	%	$ thousands	%
1985	47,962,848	100.0	41,371,619	86.3	6,591,229	13.7
1986	53,815,978	100.0	43,168,816	80.2	10,647,169	19.8
1987	49,623,906	100.0	43,448,099	87.6	6,175,807	12.4
1988	50,949,273	100.0	42,834,342	84.1	6,711,616	13.2
1989	55,459,205	100.0	46,553,194	83.9	7,550,914	13.6
1990	57,242,767	100.0	48,485,664	84.7	7,494,016	13.1
1991	60,573,565	100.0	51,277,927	84.7	9,681,786	16.0
1992	63,843,281	100.0	53,647,612	84.0	9,632,779	15.1
1993	68,354,293	100.0	55,784,521	81.6	12,278,893	18.0
1994	70,544,542	100.0	56,229,759	79.7	14,739,299	20.9
1995	74,991,519	100.0	59,589,837	79.5	13,521,937	18.0
1996	86,159,305	100.0	65,658,168	76.2	21,298,819	24.7
1997	99,191,962	100.0	72,425,402	73.0	27,961,174	28.2
1998	109,240,078	100.0	80,114,372	73.3	29,255,985	26.8
1999	125,798,548	100.0	88,276,422	70.2	38,286,580	30.4
2000	140,681,631	100.0	98,247,539	69.8	47,256,104	33.6
2001	139,241,476	100.0	104,747,173	75.2	37,997,546	27.3
2002	140,571,365	100.0	108,130,267	76.9	34,293,125	24.4
2003	145,702,137	100.0	110,336,696	75.7	38,041,067	26.1
2004	165,564,388	100.0	122,874,926	74.2	43,373,209	26.2
2005	183,390,686	100.0	139,054,112	75.8	48,056,520	26.2
2006	186,646,644	100.0	144,223,015	77.3	52,631,443	28.2
2007	193,603,968	100.0	143,826,766	74.3	58,747,438	30.3
2008	172,936,002	100.0	139,159,654	80.5	40,421,411	23.4
2009	158,016,526	100.0	129,946,302	82.2	31,816,050	20.1
2010	170,235,681	100.0	134,800,994	79.2	44,321,908	26.0
2011	174,474,029	100.0	138,608,769	79.4	43,639,867	25.0
2012	199,270,460	100.0	152,157,640	76.4	49,047,100	24.6
2013	194,664,317	100.0	148,440,964	76.3	51,591,496	26.5

Source: U.S. Department of the Treasury, Internal Revenue Service, Statistics of Income, Individual Complete Report (Publication 1304), table 2.1 (1985–2013).
Note: Due to treatment of tax-year carryovers by the IRS, the sum of cash and noncash contributions may not equal total contributions.

gifts likely declined during the recession, so some donors were more reluctant to use these assets for charitable donations or simply had fewer assets to donate.

The American Jobs Creation Act of 2004, which changed how deductions in donations of vehicle, boats, and planes were valued, may also have contributed to the decline of noncash contributions. Under the new rules, if the charity sold the motor vehicle, the taxpayer could claim only the gross proceeds from the sale. Previously, the taxpayer could claim the fair-market value of the car, boat, or plane. The amount of vehicle donations reported dropped 76 percent from 2003 to 2008.

Internal Revenue Service (IRS) Form 8283 details the types, amounts, and recipients of noncash contributions from itemizers who donated more than $500 in noncash property. Donated property includes clothing, motor vehicles, real estate, and corporate stock, mutual funds, and other investments. Table 3.9 shows the composition of noncash gifts. In 2012, $42.9 billion in noncash contributions was reported on Form 8283. Investments such as corporate stocks, mutual funds, and other investments account for the largest proportion of noncash contributions, about 51 percent. Clothing donations account for the second-largest type of noncash gift at 22 percent. Earners with adjusted gross income of $1 million or more contributed about 44 percent of all noncash donations in 2012 (table 3.7).

Table 3.9. Individual Noncash Charitable Contributions, All Itemized Returns with Donations Reported on Form 8283, by Donation Type, 2003–12

		Percent						
Year	Total noncash donations	Corporate stock, mutual funds, and other investments	Real estate and easements	Food	Clothing	Household items	Other	Cars and other vehicles
2003	36,902,794	41.7	20.0	0.2	15.8	8.7	7.1	6.4
2004	37,189,160	44.5	12.3	0.3	17.0	9.3	9.5	7.1
2005	41,070,632	45.2	15.2	0.3	17.2	9.4	11.2	1.5
2006	46,841,245	55.7	11.4	0.2	13.4	8.2	9.9	1.2
2007	52,827,286	51.3	15.4	0.2	14.6	7.4	9.8	1.3
2008	34,597,290	43.0	10.3	0.3	22.9	9.1	12.7	1.7
2009	27,986,691	39.7	9.3	0.3	27.2	11.5	10.7	1.4
2010	34,898,507	48.6	6.0	0.3	23.9	9.3	10.8	1.1
2011	38,698,506	47.6	6.9	0.3	23.4	9.3	11.2	1.3
2012	42,913,291	51.4	6.4	0.3	21.9	8.7	10.2	1.1

Source: U.S. Department of Treasury, Internal Revenue Service, Statistics of Income Division, SOI Bulletin, Publication 1136 (2006–15).
Note: All figures reported are the amount carried to Schedule A from Form 8283.

Giving by Bequests

Many individuals leave stocks, bonds, or other property such as land or artwork to charitable organizations in their wills or trusts. This form of donation is known as a bequest. The proportion of private giving accounted for by personal bequests spiked in 2008 at 10.4 percent, up almost 3 percentage points from 2007 (see table 3.3). After 2008, personal bequests as a percentage of private giving returned to pre-recession levels of between 7.0 and 8.4 percent.

The number of estate returns filed decreased 81 percent in the past 10 years—a drastic decline. Given this, it is of no surprise that the number of bequests recorded by the IRS has also declined—from 18,652 in 2001 to 2,743 in 2014 (see table 3.10). The sharp decline in estate returns is primarily due to changes with the estate tax. The Economic Growth and Tax Relief Reconciliation Act of 2001 set forth incremental increases in the estate tax exemption levels while simultaneously decreasing the highest marginal tax rates for estates. In 2008, bequest giving was at its highest since 1987, at $28 billion (figure 3.8, table 3.10). Bequests accounted for an estimated $7.2 billion

Table 3.10. Estate Tax Returns and Charitable Bequests, Selected Years, 1987–2014

		Gross Estate				Value of Bequests		
Year	Number of returns	$ billions	$ billions (2014)	Number of bequests	Percentage of total returns	$ billions	$ billions (2014)	Percentage of gross estate
1987	45,113	66.6	138.8	8,967	19.9	4.0	8.3	6.0
1990	50,367	87.1	157.8	9,709	19.3	5.5	10.0	6.3
1992	59,176	98.9	166.9	11,053	18.7	6.8	11.5	6.9
1993	60,211	103.7	169.9	11,119	18.5	7.3	12.0	7.0
1994	68,595	117.0	186.9	11,869	17.3	9.3	14.9	7.9
1995	69,755	117.7	182.8	13,039	18.7	8.7	13.5	7.4
1996	79,321	137.4	207.3	14,233	17.9	10.2	15.4	7.4
1997	90,006	162.3	239.4	15,575	17.3	14.3	21.1	8.8
1998	97,856	173.8	252.4	16,982	17.4	10.9	15.8	6.2
1999	103,979	196.4	279.1	17,554	16.9	14.6	20.7	7.4
2000	108,322	217.4	298.9	18,011	16.6	16.1	22.1	7.4
2001	106,885	214.8	287.1	18,652	17.5	16.1	21.5	7.5
2002	98,356	211.2	277.9	16,104	16.4	17.8	23.4	8.4
2003	66,042	194.5	250.2	12,492	18.9	14.6	18.8	7.5
2004	62,718	192.6	241.4	11,599	18.5	15.0	18.8	7.8
2005	45,070	184.7	223.9	8,785	19.5	19.8	24.0	10.7

(continued)

Table 3.10. Estate Tax Returns and Charitable Bequests, Selected Years, 1987–2014 *(continued)*

Year	Number of returns	Gross Estate $ billions	Gross Estate $ billions (2014)	Number of bequests	Percentage of total returns	Value of Bequests $ billions	Value of Bequests $ billions (2014)	Percentage of gross estate
2006	49,050	211.5	248.3	9,522	19.4	17.6	20.7	8.3
2007	38,000	203.0	231.8	7,666	20.2	19.7	22.5	9.7
2008	38,354	228.3	251.0	7,199	18.8	28.1	30.9	12.3
2009	33,515	194.6	214.7	6,242	18.6	16.0	17.7	8.2
2010	15,191	130.2	141.3	3,061	20.2	11.5	12.5	8.8
2011	4,588	48.0	50.5	1,039	22.6	7.2	7.6	15.1
2012	9,412	124.3	128.2	2,399	25.5	14.1	14.6	11.4
2013	10,568	138.7	141.0	2,528	23.9	13.6	13.8	9.8
2014	11,931	169.5	169.5	2,743	23.0	18.4	18.4	10.9

Source: U.S. Department of the Treasury, Internal Revenue Service, Statistics of Income, Estate Tax Returns (1987, 1990, 1992–2014).

Figure 3.8. Number and Amount of Charitable Bequests by Year Filed, 1987–2014

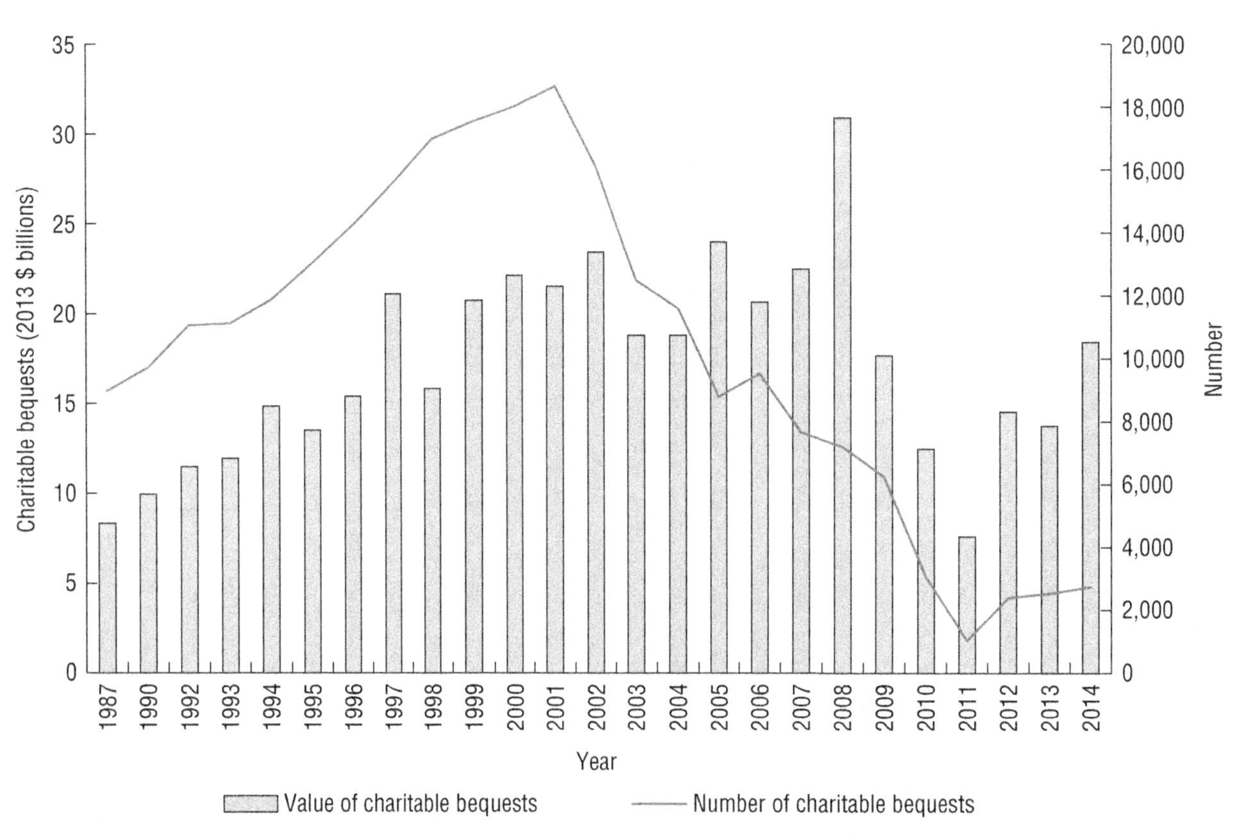

Source: U.S. Department of the Treasury, Internal Revenue Service, Statistics of Income, Individual Complete Report (Publication 1304), table 2.1 (1987, 1990, 1992–2014).

of private giving in 2011. In constant dollars, this amount is the lowest since 1987. However, between 2011 and 2012 bequest giving almost doubled—in 2012 it was $14 billion—and continued to increase, to $18 billion in 2014. In 2014, five estates listed in the Chronicle of Philanthropy's Philanthropy 50 list bequeathed $1.6 billion, led by the estate of Ralph C. Wilson, Jr., which donated $1 billion to the Ralph C. Wilson, Jr. Foundation in Detroit.

Given the nature of charitable bequests, which are most likely to be from the wealthiest people, their number and dollar value vary each year. There is no way to predict the number of bequests that will occur each year because it depends on the number of donor deaths. Changes in the economy and changes in estate tax law are factors in the dollar value of bequests.

Giving by Foundations

Giving by foundations accounts for the second-largest proportion of private giving, contributing $55.3 billion to charities in 2014. Table 3.11 displays the overall picture

Table 3.11. Foundation Giving: Grants Made, Gifts Received, and Assets, 1975–2013

Year	Number of grantmaking foundations	Grants Made		Gifts Received		Assets	
		$ billions	1975[a]	$ billions	1978[b]	$ billions	1975[a]
1975	21,877	1.9	100.0	—	—	30.1	100.0
1976	21,447	2.2	114.9	—	—	34.8	115.4
1977	22,152	2.4	121.1	—	—	35.4	117.4
1978	22,484	2.6	131.4	1.6	100.0	37.3	123.7
1979	22,535	2.9	146.9	2.2	137.3	41.6	138.0
1980	22,088	3.4	176.8	2.0	123.0	48.2	159.9
1981	21,967	3.8	195.4	2.4	148.4	47.6	157.9
1982	23,770	4.5	231.4	4.0	248.4	58.7	194.7
1983	24,261	4.5	230.9	2.7	168.3	67.9	225.3
1984	24,859	5.0	259.8	3.4	208.7	74.1	245.8
1985	25,639	6.0	310.8	5.2	321.7	102.1	338.7
1986	—	—	—	—	—	—	—
1987	27,661	6.7	343.3	5.0	308.1	115.4	383.1
1988	30,338	7.4	382.5	5.2	320.5	122.1	405.2
1989	31,990	7.9	407.7	5.5	342.9	137.5	456.5

(continued)

Table 3.11. Foundation Giving: Grants Made, Gifts Received, and Assets, 1975–2013 *(continued)*

Year	Number of grantmaking foundations	Grants Made		Gifts Received		Assets	
		$ billions	1975[a]	$ billions	1978[b]	$ billions	1975[a]
1990	32,401	8.7	447.4	5.0	308.7	142.5	472.9
1991	33,356	9.2	474.7	5.5	339.8	162.9	540.7
1992	35,765	10.2	526.3	6.2	383.9	176.8	586.9
1993	37,571	11.1	572.7	7.8	482.0	189.2	628.0
1994	38,807	11.3	582.0	8.1	501.9	195.8	649.8
1995	40,140	12.3	632.0	10.3	637.3	226.7	752.5
1996	41,588	13.8	713.4	16.0	995.0	267.6	888.1
1997	44,146	16.0	824.2	15.8	983.2	329.9	1,095.0
1998	46,832	19.5	1,003.1	22.6	1,401.9	385.1	1,278.0
1999	50,201	23.3	1,202.1	32.1	1,992.5	448.6	1,488.9
2000	56,582	27.6	1,420.6	27.6	1,714.9	486.1	1,613.3
2001	61,810	30.5	1,572.2	28.7	1,783.2	467.3	1,551.1
2002	64,843	30.4	1,568.6	22.2	1,376.4	435.2	1,444.4
2003	66,398	30.3	1,562.4	24.9	1,544.1	476.7	1,582.2
2004	67,736	31.8	1,641.2	24.0	1,490.1	510.5	1,694.3
2005	71,095	36.4	1,876.3	31.5	1,954.7	550.6	1,827.2
2006	72,477	39.0	2,010.3	36.6	2,271.4	614.7	2,040.0
2007	75,187	44.4	2,288.1	46.8	2,909.3	682.2	2,264.3
2008	75,595	46.8	2,411.3	39.6	2,456.5	565.0	1,875.0
2009	76,545	45.8	2,359.8	40.9	2,537.9	590.2	1,958.8
2010	76,610	45.9	2,366.0	38.0	2,360.2	644.0	2,137.4
2011	81,777	49.0	2,525.8	42.2	2,621.1	662.3	2,198.1
2012	86,192	51.8	2,670.1	52.1	3,236.0	715.5	2,374.7
2013	87,142	55.3	2,850.5	56.2	3,490.7	798.2	2,649.2

Source: Foundation Center, "Research Studies: National Trends" and "Foundation Stats" (2015).
Notes: Grants made include grants, scholarships, employee-matching gifts, and other amounts separated as "grants and contributions paid during the year" on Form 990-PF. Asset figures represent the market value of assets.
a. Figures from the first column, rebased to 1978 = 100.
b. Figures from the first column, rebased to 1978 = 100.
— = data not available

of foundations in the United States since 1975. The data reported on foundations in this section are drawn from the Foundation Center and are based on a sample of all U.S. independent, corporate, community, and grantmaking operating foundations. One caveat when comparing the Foundation Center data to *Giving USA* is that *Giving USA* classifies gifts from corporate foundations under giving by corporations while the Foundation Center reports these as gifts from foundations.

According to the Foundation Center, there were 87,142 U.S. grantmaking foundations in 2013—a 31 percent increase over the past 10 years. Foundation assets have steadily increased since 2008, reaching an all-time high at $798.2 billion in 2013. Foundation giving accounted for a greater proportion of private giving during both 2013 and 2014 than it had in previous years. From 2008 to 2013, foundation giving hovered around 14 percent of private giving—up just over 1 percent from 2007. Foundation giving has increased by 52 percent (after inflation adjustments) from 2004 to 2014. Foundation assets plummeted 17 percent in 2008 compared to 2007. In 2008, however, foundation giving reached $46.8 billion, fueled by increased giving from the Bill and Melinda Gates Foundation. Since 2008, foundation assets have increased steadily, and foundation giving also reached an all-time high of $55.3 billion in 2013 (figure 3.9).

Foundations continue to receive contributions and bequests from donors and estates. In 2013, these gifts to foundations totaled $56.2 billion. Gifts received by foundations more than doubled between 2003 and 2013, increasing by 126 percent.

Figure 3.9. Foundation Assets and Amount of Grants Made by Year, 2003–13

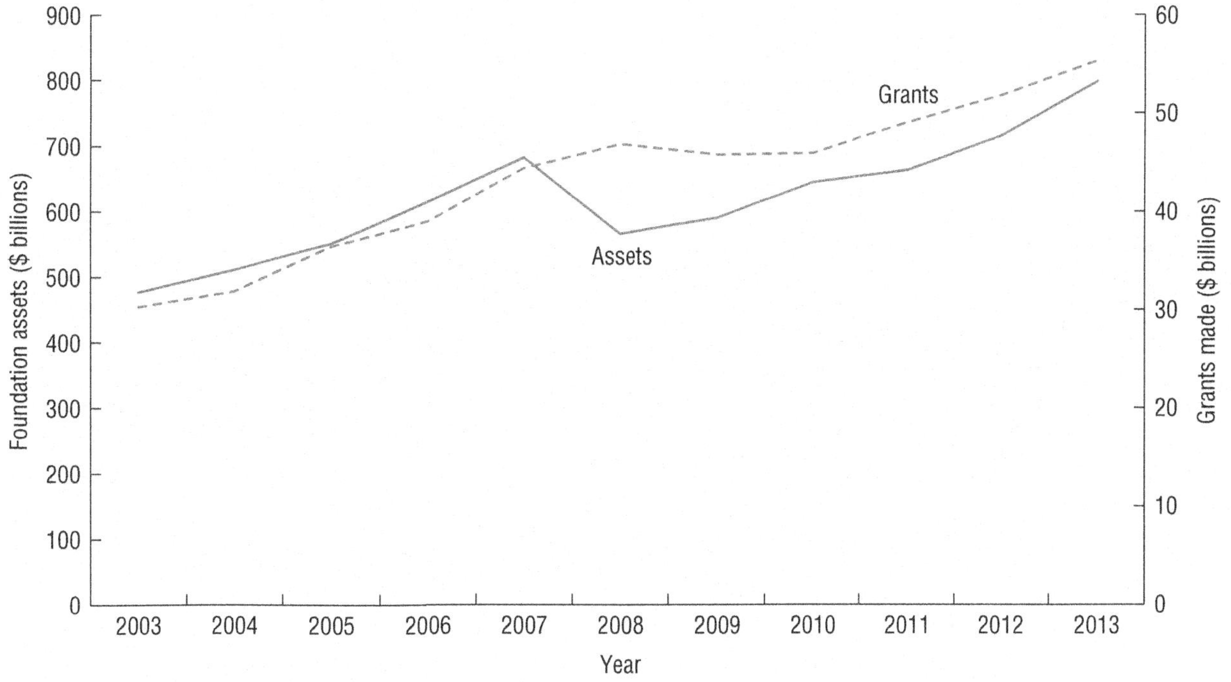

Source: Foundation Center, "Foundation Stats" (2015).

One important trend in foundation grantmaking is the increase in the number, assets, and grantmaking by family foundations. The Foundation Center reported that 63 percent of dollars given by independent foundations came from so-called family foundations, and that one-third of family foundations have been established since 2000. The Foundation Center defines family foundations as those grantmaking independent foundations with measurable donor or donor-family involvement. These include foundations with "family" or "families" in their name, a living donor whose surname matches the foundation name, or at least two trustee surnames that match a living or deceased donor's name, along with any independent foundations that self-identify as family foundations on annual Foundation Center surveys.

In 2013, independent foundations accounted for about 91.4 percent of all foundations, followed by operating foundations (4.8 percent), corporate foundations (3 percent), and community foundations (0.9 percent). Independent foundations also hold the majority of foundation assets (82 percent) and give the greatest proportion of grants (67.2 percent). Community foundations, while representing just under 1 percent of foundations, gave over 9 percent of foundation grant dollars, practically the same as corporate foundations (figure 3.10, table 3.12).

Figure 3.11 displays the proportion of both the number of grants and value of grants by type of recipient organization. Human service organizations received over a quarter of all grants in terms of numbers in 2013. However, these organizations received only 16 percent of the amount of grants given by foundations. Health and education organizations combined received about 45 percent of the total grant dollars given (table 3.13).

Figure 3.10. Distribution of Foundations by Number, Assets, and Grants, 2013 (percent)

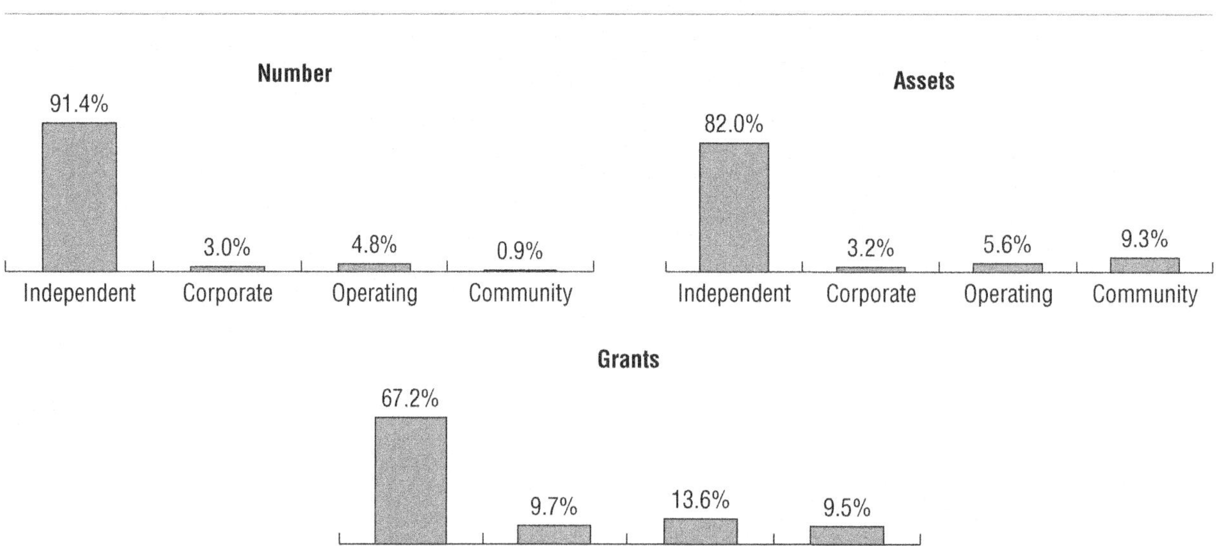

Source: Foundation Center, "Foundation Stats" (2015).

Table 3.12. Foundation Giving: Number, Assets, Gifts Received, and Grants Made by Type of Foundation, 2001–13

	Foundations		Grants Made		Gifts Received		Assets	
	Number	%	$ millions	%	$ millions	%	$ millions	%
2001								
Independent	55,125	89.2	23,710	77.7	20,545	71.5	403,541	84.6
Corporate	2,170	3.5	3,284	10.8	3,040	10.6	15,578	3.3
Operating	3,918	6.3	1,110	3.6	1,950	6.8	27,384	5.7
Community	604	1.0	2,404	7.9	3,186	11.1	30,318	6.4
Total	**61,817**	**100.0**	**30,508**	**100.0**	**28,720**	**100.0**	**476,820**	**100.0**
2002								
Independent	57,840	89.2	23,020	76.3	13,957	63.0	360,404	83.5
Corporate	2,357	3.6	3,433	11.4	3,002	13.5	14,428	3.3
Operating	3,987	6.1	1,195	4.0	2,037	9.2	27,214	6.3
Community	661	1.0	2,526	8.4	3,175	14.3	29,772	6.9
Total	**64,845**	**100.0**	**30,174**	**100.0**	**22,170**	**100.0**	**431,818**	**100.0**
2003								
Independent	58,993	88.8	22,568	74.4	15,846	63.7	399,140	83.7
Corporate	2,549	3.8	3,466	11.4	3,234	13.0	15,447	3.2
Operating	4,159	6.3	1,744	5.8	2,302	9.3	27,975	5.9
Community	700	1.1	2,545	8.4	3,481	14.0	34,302	7.2
Total	**66,401**	**100.0**	**30,322**	**100.0**	**24,863**	**100.0**	**476,864**	**100.0**
2004								
Independent	60,031	88.6	23,334	73.3	13,655	56.9	425,103	83.3
Corporate	2,596	3.8	3,430	10.8	3,667	15.3	16,645	3.3
Operating	4,409	6.5	2,164	6.8	2,808	11.7	29,951	5.9
Community	700	1.0	2,916	9.2	3,859	16.1	38,782	7.6
Total	**67,736**	**100.0**	**31,844**	**100.0**	**23,989**	**100.0**	**510,481**	**100.0**
2005								
Independent	63,060	88.7	25,199	69.2	17,366	55.2	455,570	82.7
Corporate	2,607	3.7	3,996	11.0	4,008	12.7	17,795	3.2
Operating	4,722	6.6	3,990	11.0	4,505	14.3	32,603	5.9
Community	708	1.0	3,217	8.8	5,587	17.8	44,585	8.1
Total	**71,097**	**100.0**	**36,402**	**100.0**	**31,465**	**100.0**	**550,553**	**100.0**

(continued)

Table 3.12. Foundation Giving: Number, Assets, Gifts Received, and Grants Made by Type of Foundation, 2001–13 *(continued)*

	Foundations		Grants Made		Gifts Received		Assets	
	Number	%	$ millions	%	$ millions	%	$ millions	%
2006								
Independent	64,405	88.9	27,457	70.4	21,591	59.0	509,077	82.8
Corporate	2,548	3.5	4,098	10.5	4,374	12.0	19,730	3.2
Operating	4,807	6.6	3,853	9.9	4,571	12.5	35,906	5.8
Community	717	1.0	3,596	9.2	6,033	16.5	49,942	8.1
Total	**72,477**	**100.0**	**39,004**	**100.0**	**36,569**	**100.0**	**614,656**	**100.0**
2007								
Independent	67,034	89.2	32,220	72.6	31,279	66.8	564,216	82.7
Corporate	2,498	3.3	4,397	9.9	4,418	9.4	21,924	3.2
Operating	4,938	6.6	3,429	7.7	4,915	10.5	39,403	5.8
Community	717	1.0	4,348	9.8	6,232	13.3	56,680	8.3
Total	**75,187**	**100.0**	**44,394**	**100.0**	**46,844**	**100.0**	**682,222**	**100.0**
2008								
Independent	67,379	89.1	33,819	72.3	24,068	60.9	456,025	80.7
Corporate	2,742	3.6	4,559	9.7	4,610	11.7	20,335	3.6
Operating	4,762	6.3	3,900	8.3	5,250	13.3	38,968	6.9
Community	709	0.9	4,492	9.6	5,620	14.2	49,623	8.8
Total	**75,592**	**100.0**	**46,770**	**100.0**	**39,549**	**100.0**	**564,951**	**100.0**
2009								
Independent	68,508	89.5	32,753	71.5	27,054	66.2	482,954	81.8
Corporate	2,733	3.6	4,691	10.2	3,966	9.7	19,299	3.3
Operating	4,567	6.0	4,161	9.1	5,027	12.3	38,444	6.5
Community	737	1.0	4,174	9.1	4,814	11.8	49,491	8.4
Total	**76,545**	**100.0**	**45,778**	**100.0**	**40,862**	**100.0**	**590,188**	**100.0**
2010								
Independent	68,211	89.0	32,475	70.8	21,350	56.2	527,164	81.9
Corporate	2,718	3.5	4,908	10.7	5,410	14.3	21,917	3.4

(continued)

Table 3.12. Foundation Giving: Number, Assets, Gifts Received, and Grants Made by Type of Foundation, 2001–13 *(continued)*

	Foundations		Grants Made		Gifts Received		Assets	
	Number	%	$ millions	%	$ millions	%	$ millions	%
Operating	4,947	6.5	4,261	9.3	6,449	17.0	39,337	6.1
Community	734	1.0	4,213	9.2	4,752	12.5	55,556	8.6
Total	**76,610**	**100.0**	**45,858**	**100.0**	**37,961**	**100.0**	**643,974**	**100.0**
2011								
Independent	73,764	90.2	33,910	69.2	25,697	61.0	540,154	81.6
Corporate	2,689	3.3	5,168	10.5	4,362	10.3	22,195	3.4
Operating	4,574	5.6	5,610	11.4	6,665	15.8	42,049	6.3
Community	750	0.9	4,311	8.8	5,434	12.9	57,938	8.7
Total	**81,777**	**100.0**	**48,999**	**100.0**	**42,159**	**100.0**	**662,336**	**100.0**
2012								
Independent	78,582	91.2	35,403	68.3	32,224	61.9	584,007	81.6
Corporate	2,629	3.1	5,458	10.5	4,617	8.9	23,161	3.2
Operating	4,218	4.9	6,025	11.6	7,763	14.9	43,347	6.1
Community	763	0.9	4,938	9.5	7,492	14.4	64,940	9.1
Total	**86,192**	**100.0**	**51,824**	**100.0**	**52,096**	**100.0**	**715,456**	**100.0**
2013								
Independent	79,616	91.4	37,118	67.2	33,277	59.2	654,309	82.0
Corporate	2,577	3.0	5,384	9.7	6,193	11.0	25,512	3.2
Operating	4,169	4.8	7,499	13.6	8,420	15.0	44,505	5.6
Community	780	0.9	5,262	9.5	8,350	14.8	73,849	9.3
Total	**87,142**	**100.0**	**55,263**	**100.0**	**56,241**	**100.0**	**798,176**	**100.0**

Source: Foundation Center, "Research Studies: National Trends" and "Foundation Stats" (2015).
Notes: Grants made include grants, scholarships, and employee-matching gifts. They do not include program-related investments (such as loans, loan guarantees, equity investments, and other investments made by foundations to organizations to forward their charitable purposes), set-asides, or program expenses. Asset figures represent the market value of assets.

Figure 3.11. Distribution of the Number and Value of Grants Given by Type of Organization, 2013 (percent)

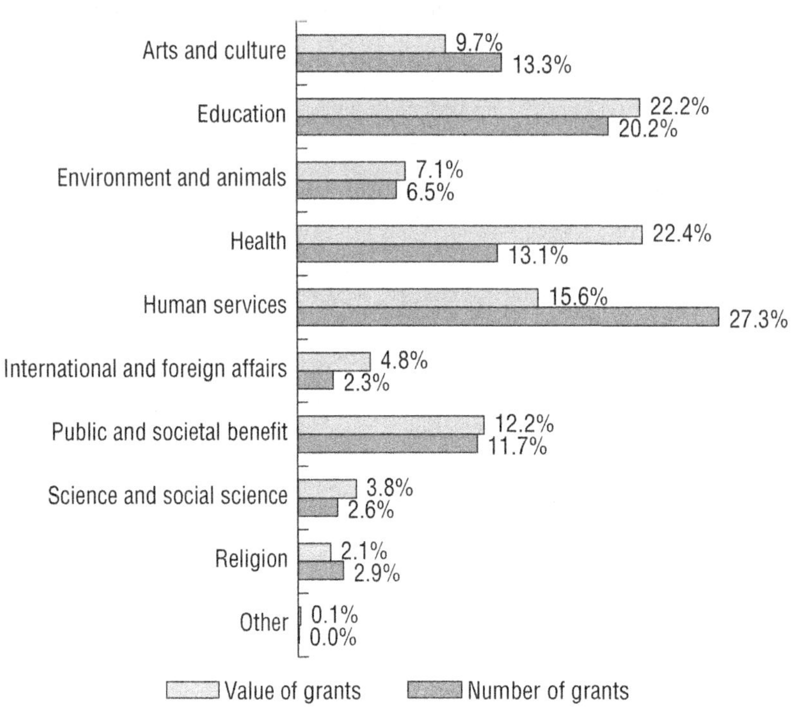

Source: Foundation Center, "Foundation Stats" (2015).
Notes: The data are based on all grants of $10,000 or more awarded by a sample of 1,000 larger foundations. These grants totaled $22.35 billion and represented more than a third of total grant dollars awarded by all U.S. independent, corporate, community, and grantmaking operating foundations. Subtotals may not add to total because of rounding. The other categories include civil rights and social action, community improvement and development, philanthropy and voluntarism, and public affairs.

Giving by Corporations

Giving by corporations is the final component of private giving. Corporate contributions can be made directly by the corporation or through a corporate foundation. According to *Giving USA*, corporate giving reached an estimated $17.8 billion in 2014. This represents 5 percent of private giving. While corporate giving dropped around 16 percent from 2007 to 2008, despite an 11 percent decrease between 2012 and 2013, it has overall been rising since 2008 and has now surpassed 2007's pre-recession levels (figure 3.12).

Volunteering

Volunteering is just as important as gifts of cash or goods for many nonprofit organizations. Many charities rely on volunteers to help further their mission. Whether volunteers are stuffing envelopes, serving food, serving on the governing boards of a charity, or organizing a public relations campaign, they are a vital component of the nonprofit sector.

Table 3.13. Foundation Giving: Number and Value of Grants by Type of Organization, 2002–12

	Number of Grants		$ Value of Grants		Average value of grants ($)
	Number	%	$ thousands	%	
2002					
Arts and culture	17,945	14.9	1,898,091	9.6	105,773
Education	24,904	20.7	4,064,268	20.5	163,197
Environment and animals	7,173	6.0	931,963	4.7	129,927
Health	14,471	12.0	2,910,720	14.7	201,142
Human services	30,932	25.7	2,298,812	11.6	74,318
International and foreign affairs	2,667	2.2	348,110	1.8	130,525
Public and societal benefit	14,836	12.3	1,731,138	8.7	116,685
Science and social science	3,734	3.1	849,066	4.3	227,388
Religion	3,508	2.9	403,061	2.0	114,898
Other	91	0.1	16,042	0.1	176,291
Total	**120,261**	**100.0**	**15,451,271**	**100.0**	**128,481**
2003					
Arts and culture	16,815	14.8	1,928,043	13.7	114,662
Education	23,664	20.8	3,537,206	25.1	149,476
Environment and animals	6,663	5.9	847,753	6.0	127,233
Health	13,997	12.3	2,703,250	19.2	193,131
Human services	28,906	25.4	1,958,091	13.9	67,740
International and foreign affairs	2,551	2.2	399,409	2.8	156,569
Public and societal benefit	14,300	12.6	1,802,794	12.8	126,070
Science and social science	3,240	2.9	559,710	4.0	172,750
Religion	3,445	3.0	330,624	2.3	95,972
Other	77	0.1	8,467	0.1	109,967
Total	**113,658**	**100.0**	**14,075,347**	**100.0**	**123,839**
2004					
Arts and culture	14,267	14.8	1,406,264	11.4	98,568
Education	19,704	20.5	2,877,621	23.4	146,042
Environment and animals	5,449	5.7	702,378	5.7	128,900
Health	12,388	12.9	2,903,047	23.6	234,344

(continued)

Table 3.13. Foundation Giving: Number and Value of Grants by Type of Organization, 2002–12 *(continued)*

	Number of Grants		$ Value of Grants		Average value of grants ($)
	Number	%	$ thousands	%	
Human services	24,293	25.2	1,525,608	12.4	62,800
International and foreign affairs	2,147	2.2	327,963	2.7	152,754
Public and societal benefit	12,104	12.6	1,583,501	12.9	130,825
Science and social science	2,825	2.9	636,499	5.2	225,310
Religion	3,031	3.1	310,067	2.5	102,298
Other	58	0.1	8,843	0.1	152,469
Total	**96,266**	**100.0**	**12,281,792**	**100.0**	**127,582**
2005					
Arts and culture	16,856	14.0	2,069,551	13.1	122,778
Education	23,898	19.8	3,765,016	23.9	157,545
Environment and animals	7,398	6.1	990,741	6.3	133,920
Health	16,676	13.8	3,338,063	21.2	200,172
Human services	31,208	25.9	2,348,348	14.9	75,248
International and foreign affairs	3,222	2.7	570,770	3.6	177,148
Public and societal benefit	14,557	12.1	1,633,522	10.4	112,216
Science and social science	3,165	2.6	661,427	4.2	208,982
Religion	3,574	3.0	384,852	2.4	107,681
Other	89	0.1	12,185	0.1	136,907
Total	**120,643**	**100.0**	**15,774,475**	**100.0**	**130,753**
2006					
Arts and culture	18,368	14.1	2,169,548	11.7	118,116
Education	25,979	20.0	4,234,357	22.8	162,992
Environment and animals	7,917	6.1	1,121,647	6.0	141,676
Health	17,385	13.4	4,432,770	23.9	254,977
Human services	33,903	26.1	2,387,184	12.9	70,412
International and foreign affairs	3,141	2.4	907,166	4.9	288,814
Public and societal benefit	15,243	11.7	2,040,501	11.0	133,865
Science and social science	3,808	2.9	836,867	4.5	219,765

(continued)

Table 3.13. Foundation Giving: Number and Value of Grants by Type of Organization, 2002–12 *(continued)*

	Number of Grants		$ Value of Grants		Average value of grants ($)
	Number	%	$ thousands	%	
Religion	4,198	3.2	425,732	2.3	101,413
Other	94	0.1	20,474	0.1	217,810
Total	**130,036**	**100.0**	**18,576,245**	**100.0**	**142,855**
2007					
Arts and culture	19,550	14.3	2,767,434	12.5	141,557
Education	27,097	19.9	4,925,633	22.2	181,778
Environment and animals	8,742	6.4	1,471,693	6.6	168,347
Health	18,263	13.4	5,148,021	23.2	281,883
Human services	35,114	25.7	2,926,887	13.2	83,354
International and foreign affairs	3,276	2.4	1,086,254	4.9	331,579
Public and societal benefit	15,578	11.4	2,306,974	10.4	148,092
Science and social science	3,803	2.8	905,636	4.1	238,137
Religion	4,975	3.6	545,603	2.5	109,669
Other	93	0.1	68,410	0.3	735,592
Total	**136,491**	**100.0**	**22,152,545**	**100.0**	**162,300**
2008					
Arts and culture	19,204	13.7	2,352,774	10.5	122,515
Education	27,076	19.3	4,794,402	21.4	177,072
Environment and animals	9,325	6.6	2,004,334	9.0	214,942
Health	18,416	13.1	5,274,276	23.6	286,396
Human services	37,786	26.9	2,842,066	12.7	75,215
International and foreign affairs	3,790	2.7	1,352,186	6.0	356,777
Public and societal benefit	16,427	11.7	2,357,530	10.5	143,516
Science and social science	3,726	2.7	894,944	4.0	240,189
Religion	4,620	3.3	487,621	2.2	105,546
Other	94	0.1	8,471	0.0	90,119
Total	**140,464**	**100.0**	**22,368,605**	**100.0**	**159,248**

(continued)

Table 3.13. Foundation Giving: Number and Value of Grants by Type of Organization, 2002–12 *(continued)*

	Number of Grants		$ Value of Grants		Average value of grants ($)
	Number	%	$ thousands	%	
2009					
Arts and culture	16,851	13.0	2,046,689	10.3	121,458
Education	25,553	19.7	4,636,987	23.4	181,465
Environment and animals	8,321	6.4	1,332,799	6.7	160,173
Health	17,140	13.2	4,662,899	23.5	272,048
Human services	35,873	27.7	2,576,433	13.0	71,821
International and foreign affairs	3,556	2.7	965,077	4.9	271,394
Public and societal benefit	15,269	11.8	2,385,874	12.0	156,256
Science and social science	2,983	2.3	811,105	4.1	271,909
Religion	4,126	3.2	397,303	2.0	96,293
Other	60	0.0	12,923	0.1	215,376
Total	**129,732**	**100.0**	**19,828,087**	**100.0**	**152,839**
2010					
Arts and culture	17,790	13.4	3,307,595	16.5	185,924
Education	25,396	19.2	4,520,763	22.6	178,011
Environment and animals	8,818	6.7	1,271,999	6.4	144,250
Health	16,789	12.7	4,124,639	20.6	245,675
Human services	36,890	27.8	2,859,382	14.3	77,511
International and foreign affairs	3,531	2.7	670,810	3.4	189,977
Public and societal benefit	15,913	12.0	2,124,109	10.6	133,483
Science and social science	3,145	2.4	660,503	3.3	210,017
Religion	4,211	3.2	441,446	2.2	104,832
Other	63	0.0	6,653	0.0	105,611
Total	**132,546**	**100.0**	**19,987,900**	**100.0**	**150,800**
2011					
Arts and culture	18,572	13.4	2,074,488	9.2	111,700
Education	27,375	19.7	4,869,225	21.5	177,871

(continued)

Table 3.13. Foundation Giving: Number and Value of Grants by Type of Organization, 2002–12 *(continued)*

	Number of Grants		$ Value of Grants		Average value of grants ($)
	Number	%	$ thousands	%	
Environment and animals	9,103	6.6	1,333,154	5.9	146,452
Health	18,264	13.1	6,424,001	28.4	351,730
Human services	38,382	27.6	3,404,340	15.1	88,696
International and foreign affairs	3,182	2.3	932,740	4.1	293,130
Public and societal benefit	16,148	11.6	2,393,985	10.6	148,253
Science and social science	3,455	2.5	726,750	3.2	210,347
Religion	4,412	3.2	430,464	1.9	97,567
Other	51	0.0	8,212	0.0	161,029
Total	**138,944**	**100.0**	**22,597,360**	**100.0**	**162,636**
2012					
Arts and culture	20,518	13.3	2,166,039	9.7	105,568
Education	31,050	20.2	4,969,634	22.2	160,053
Environment and animals	10,007	6.5	1,585,794	7.1	158,468
Health	20,102	13.1	5,001,049	22.4	248,784
Human services	42,023	27.3	3,497,761	15.6	83,234
International and foreign affairs	3,554	2.3	1,064,885	4.8	299,630
Public and societal benefit	18,004	11.7	2,715,989	12.2	150,855
Science and social science	3,973	2.6	848,815	3.8	213,646
Religion	4,527	2.9	468,398	2.1	103,468
Other	63	0.0	31,649	0.1	502,370
Total	**153,821**	**100.0**	**22,350,013**	**100.0**	**145,299**

Source: Foundation Center, "Aggregate Fiscal Data of Grants from FC 1000 Foundations" (2002–12).
Notes: Major categories are defined by the National Taxonomy of Exempt Entities. The data are based on all grants of $10,000 or more awarded by 1,000 of the largest U.S. foundations by giving. Subtotals may not add to total because of rounding. "Other" includes civil rights and social action, community improvement and development, philanthropy and voluntarism, and public affairs.

Using data collected from the Current Population Survey (CPS) and the American Time Use Survey (ATUS), this section estimates the number of people volunteering, who is volunteering, where they are volunteering, how volunteers spend their time, the amount of hours volunteered, and the economic value of volunteers to the sector.

Table 3.14 provides key indicators from the two major government surveys that collect data on volunteering, the CPS and the ATUS. These data can be used to calculate

Figure 3.12. Corporate Giving, 2004–14

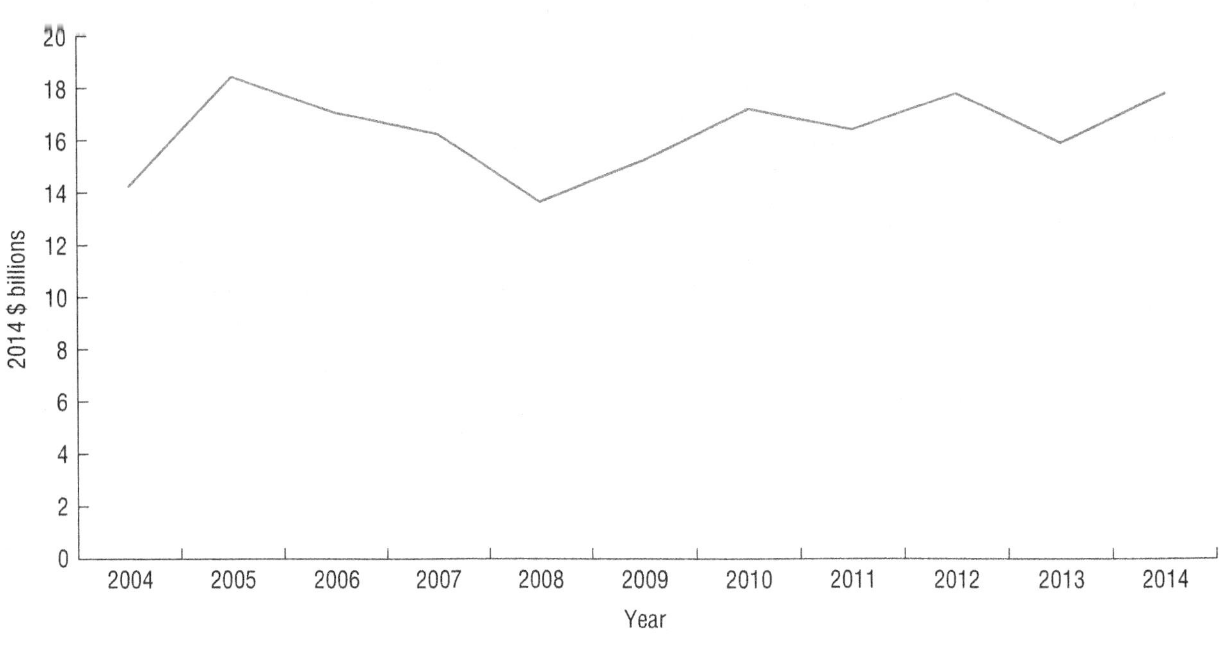

Source: Giving USA Foundation, *Giving USA* (2015).

the economic value of volunteering. While the CPS asks questions on volunteering throughout the year, the ATUS asks in greater detail how people spent the past 24 hours. Therefore, the survey shows volunteer activity on an average day.

According to the CPS, 25.3 percent of the civilian population age 16 and older volunteered in 2014. This translates to 62.8 million volunteers. When asked how many hours they volunteered in that year, volunteers' median response was 50 hours. The rate and amount of time volunteered in 2014 are similar to the numbers reported from 2008 onward.

According to the ATUS, 6.4 percent of the adult population volunteered on an average day in 2014. This translates into 16 million volunteers a day. These people spent 2.4 hours, on average, volunteering a day.

Data from the CPS also show that volunteers spent an estimated 8.7 billion hours volunteering in 2014. Assuming that a full-time employee works 1,700 hours a year, those volunteer hours were the equivalent of 5.1 million full-time employees. Further assuming that those employees would have earned the average private nonfarm hourly wage, volunteers' time contributed $179.2 billion in 2014.

The CPS asks various demographic questions that allow researchers to see who is volunteering. The 2014 data show no major changes in the demographics of volunteers. In general, women are more likely to volunteer than men. The peak ages for volunteering are between 35 and 54 years old. Whites volunteer at higher rates than other racial/ethnic groups. College graduates volunteer at higher rates that those with less schooling. Part-time employees continue to be more likely to volunteer than those with

Table 3.14. Volunteers: Number, Hours, and Dollar Value, 2008–14

	2008	2009	2010	2011	2012	2013	2014
Per year							
Percent of population volunteering	26.4	26.8	26.3	26.8	26.5	25.4	25.3
Number of volunteers	61.8 million	63.4 million	62.8 million	64.3 million	64.5 million	62.6 million	62.8 million
Hours volunteered	8.0 billion	8.1 billion	8.1 billion	8.5 billion	8.5 billion	8.3 billion	8.7 billion
Average hours per volunteer	129	127	128	132	132	133	139
Median hours per volunteer	52	52	52	51	50	50	50
Per average day							
Percent of population volunteering	68%	71%	68%	60%	58%	61%	64%
Number of volunteers	16.2 million	17.1 million	16.6 million	14.6 million	14.3 million	15.1 million	16.0 million
Hours per day per volunteer	2.43	2.39	2.46	2.84	2.48	2.57	2.41
Value of volunteers							
Population age 16 and over	234.4 million	236.3 million	238.3 million	240.0 million	243.8 million	246.2 million	243.4 million
Full-time-equivalent employees	4.7 million	4.8 million	4.8 million	5.0 million	5.0 million	4.9 million	5.1 million
Assigned hourly wages for volunteers	$18.08	$18.63	$19.07	$19.47	$19.75	$20.16	$20.59
Assigned value of volunteer time	$144.7 billion	$150.7 billion	$154.1 billion	$164.8 billion	$168.3 billion	$167.2 billion	$179.2 billion

Sources: Authors' calculations based on data from U.S. Department of Labor, Bureau of Labor Statistics, Current Population Survey, Volunteer Supplement (2008–14); U.S. Department of Labor, Bureau of Labor Statistics, American Time Use Survey (2008–14); and U.S. Department of Labor, Bureau of Labor Statistics, Current Employment Statistics (2014).

any other employment status. Married people are more likely to volunteer than single people or people with another marital status (table 3.15).

While the CPS and the ATUS both ask about the types of activities volunteers are performing, the ATUS asks how much time they are spending on various volunteer activities. Because the CPS asks questions about time spent volunteering throughout the year, the survey asks people to choose the organizations where they spent the most hours volunteering. As displayed in figure 3.13, 33.3 percent of volunteers volunteered at a religious organization in 2014. Another 25.1 percent report volunteering at an educational or youth service organization, followed by 14.4 percent of volunteers spending time at a social or community service organization (table 3.16).

Whereas the CPS asks where volunteers are spending their time, the ATUS asks about the types of activities volunteers are performing. Measured as the average amount of time across all volunteers, the single largest use of volunteers in 2014 was for social service and care. Social service and care includes preparing food and cleaning up, collecting and delivering clothing or other goods, providing direct care or services, teaching, leading, counseling, and mentoring. Administration and support is the second-largest

Table 3.15. Percent Volunteering by Demographic Group, 2005–14

	2005	2006	2007	2008	2009	2010	2011	2012	2013	2014
Total	28.8	26.7	26.2	26.4	26.8	26.3	26.8	26.5	25.4	25.3
Gender										
Male	25.0	23.0	22.9	23.2	23.3	23.2	23.5	23.2	22.2	22.0
Female	32.4	30.1	29.3	29.4	30.1	29.3	29.9	29.5	28.4	28.3
Race/Ethnicity										
White	30.4	28.3	27.9	27.9	28.3	27.8	28.2	27.8	27.1	26.7
Black or African American	22.1	19.2	18.2	19.1	20.2	19.4	20.3	21.1	18.5	19.7
Asian	20.7	18.5	17.7	18.7	19.0	19.6	20.0	19.6	19.0	18.2
Hispanic or Latino	15.4	13.9	13.5	14.4	14.0	14.7	14.9	15.2	15.5	15.5
Age										
16 and older	28.8	26.7	26.2	26.4	26.8	26.3	26.8	26.5	25.4	25.3
16–24	24.4	21.7	20.8	21.9	22.0	21.9	22.5	22.6	21.8	21.9
25–34	25.3	23.1	22.6	22.8	23.5	22.3	23.3	23.2	21.9	22.0
35–44	34.5	31.2	30.5	31.3	31.5	32.2	31.8	31.6	30.6	29.8
45–54	32.7	31.2	30.1	29.9	30.8	30.3	30.6	29.3	28.2	28.5
55–64	30.2	27.9	28.4	28.1	28.3	27.2	28.1	27.6	26.0	25.9
65 and older	24.8	23.8	23.8	23.5	23.9	23.6	24.0	24.4	24.1	23.6

(continued)

Table 3.15. Percent Volunteering by Demographic Group, 2005–14 *(continued)*

	2005	2006	2007	2008	2009	2010	2011	2012	2013	2014
Education										
Less than high school diploma	10.0	9.3	9.0	9.4	8.6	8.8	9.8	8.8	9.0	8.8
High school graduate, no college	21.2	19.2	18.6	18.1	18.8	17.9	18.2	17.3	16.7	16.4
Less than a bachelor's degree	33.7	30.9	30.7	30.0	30.5	29.2	29.5	28.7	27.7	27.3
College graduate	45.8	43.3	41.8	42.2	42.8	42.3	42.4	42.2	39.8	39.4
Employment										
Civilian labor force	31.1	28.5	28.1	28.5	29.0	28.7	29.1	28.7	27.5	27.3
Employed	31.3	28.7	28.3	28.9	29.7	29.2	29.6	29.1	27.7	27.5
Full time	29.8	27.3	26.9	27.8	28.7	28.2	28.7	28.1	26.8	26.5
Part time	38.2	35.5	35.4	34.2	33.7	33.2	33.3	33.4	31.7	31.7
Unemployed	26.4	23.8	23.2	22.3	22.9	23.8	23.8	23.8	24.1	24.0
Not in the labor force	24.4	23.1	22.3	22.2	22.6	22.0	22.5	22.4	21.9	21.8
Marital status										
Single, never married	23.0	20.3	19.2	20.4	20.6	20.3	20.9	20.7	20.0	20.2
Married, spouse present	34.1	32.2	31.9	31.6	32.3	32.0	32.3	31.9	30.7	30.0
Other marital status	23.1	21.3	20.9	20.9	21.5	20.9	21.5	21.3	20.5	21.1

Source: U.S. Department of Labor, Bureau of Labor Statistics, Current Population Survey, Volunteer Supplement (2005–14).

Figure 3.13. Volunteers by Their Main Organization, 2014 (percent)

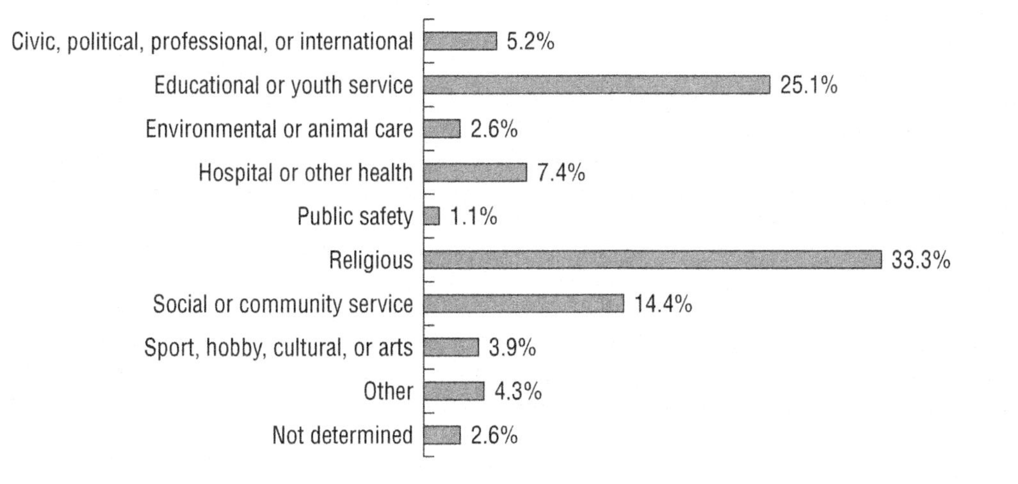

Source: U.S. Department of Labor, Bureau of Labor Statistics, Current Population Survey, Volunteer Supplement (2014).

Table 3.16. Volunteers by Main Type of Organization, 2005–14 (percent)

Main type of organization	2005	2006	2007	2008	2009	2010	2011	2012	2013	2014
All	28.8	26.7	26.2	26.4	26.8	26.3	26.8	26.5	25.4	25.3
Civic, political, professional, or international	6.4	6.1	5.1	5.5	5.5	5.3	5.4	5.5	5.1	5.2
Educational or youth service	26.2	26.4	26.2	26.0	26.1	26.5	25.7	25.5	25.6	25.1
Environmental or animal care	1.8	1.6	1.9	2.0	2.2	2.4	2.3	2.6	2.7	2.6
Hospital or other health	7.7	8.1	7.8	8.2	8.5	7.9	7.7	7.8	7.3	7.4
Public safety	1.3	1.3	1.3	1.3	1.2	1.3	1.3	1.2	1.1	1.1
Religious	34.8	35.0	35.6	35.1	34.0	33.8	33.2	33.1	33.0	33.3
Social or community service	13.4	12.7	13.1	13.5	13.9	13.6	14.3	14.2	14.7	14.4
Sport, hobby, cultural, or arts	3.3	3.7	3.5	3.3	3.4	3.3	3.8	3.8	4.0	3.9
Other	3.5	3.4	3.7	3.3	3.4	3.7	3.9	4.0	3.9	4.3
Not determined	1.7	1.5	1.7	1.9	1.9	2.2	2.4	2.3	2.5	2.6

Source: U.S. Department of Labor, Bureau of Labor Statistics, Current Population Survey, Volunteer Supplement (2005–14).

activity reported among volunteers and includes fundraising, office work, computer use, making phone calls, writing, editing, and reading (figure 3.14, table 3.17).

When the percentage of volunteers who performed each activity is considered instead of the average time, travel emerges as the most common activity. While the majority of individuals who volunteered spent some time traveling, time spent traveling is less than time spent in many other categories (figure 3.15, table 3.18).

Figure 3.14. Distribution of Average Volunteer Time by Activity, 2014

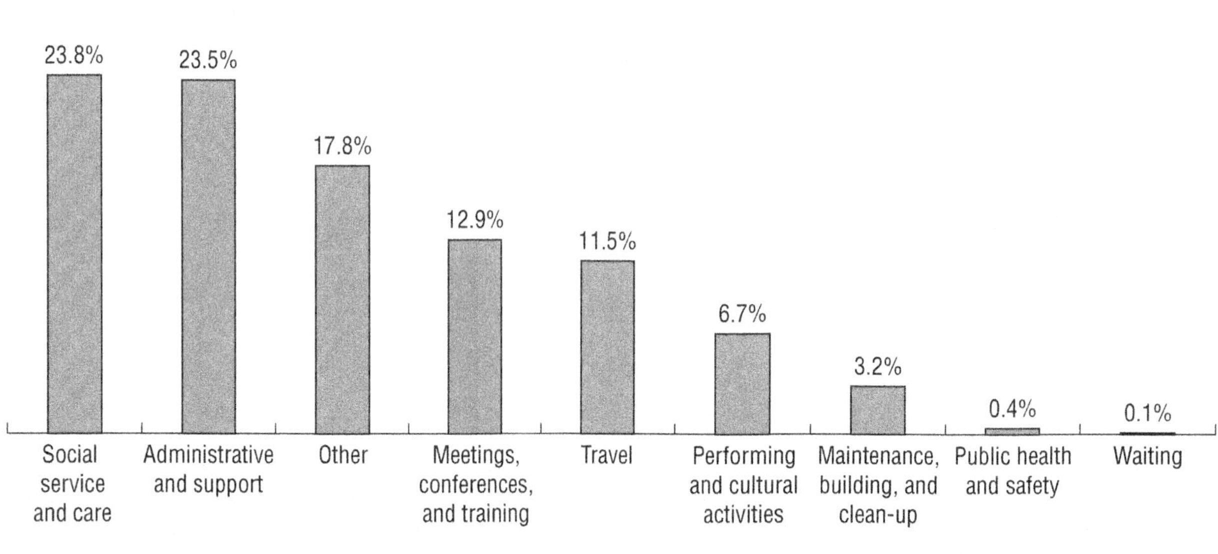

Source: Authors' calculations based on U.S. Department of Labor, Bureau of Labor Statistics, American Time Use Survey (2014).

Table 3.17. Distribution of Average Annual Volunteer Time by Activity, 2003–14

%	2003	2004	2005	2006	2007	2008	2009	2010	2011	2012	2013	2014
Administrative and support	28.0	24.8	24.4	20.6	16.8	22.4	26.3	21.7	23.6	26.1	22.0	23.5
Social service and care	21.1	22.7	20.2	17.8	22.3	21.8	21.8	24.3	20.0	20.6	27.5	23.8
Maintenance, building, and clean-up	6.1	6.0	3.7	5.7	5.1	7.2	4.3	6.6	5.6	4.4	3.4	3.2
Performing and cultural activities	5.9	4.3	9.1	6.9	5.9	5.7	4.8	5.4	6.6	7.6	8.7	6.7
Meetings, conferences, and training	11.2	11.1	11.1	10.6	11.7	8.5	11.1	10.6	9.3	12.5	10.3	12.9
Public health and safety	1.3	2.4	1.1	0.9	0.4	2.0	0.7	0.4	1.4	1.2	0.8	0.4
Waiting	—	0.0	0.1	0.3	0.1	0.1	0.2	0.5	0.2	0.1	0.1	0.1
Security	—	—	—	—	0.0	0.0	0.0	0.1	0.1	—	—	—
Other	15.3	17.0	17.9	22.9	25.0	21.4	19.1	19.7	19.9	15.9	16.5	17.8
Travel	11.1	11.6	12.3	14.2	12.8	10.8	11.7	10.8	13.5	11.7	10.8	11.5
Total	**100.0**	**100.0**	**100.0**	**100.0**	**100.0**	**100.0**	**100.0**	**100.0**	**100.0**	**100.0**	**100.0**	**100.0**

Source: Authors' calculations based on U.S. Department of Labor, Bureau of Labor Statistics, American Time Use Survey (2003–14).
Notes: Waiting was not a separate category in 2003, so wait time was distributed across the other categories. Security was not a separate category until 2007, so time spent on security procedures related to the volunteer activity was distributed across the other categories.
— = no data available

Figure 3.15. Percentage of Volunteers Who Performed Each Activity, 2014 (percent)

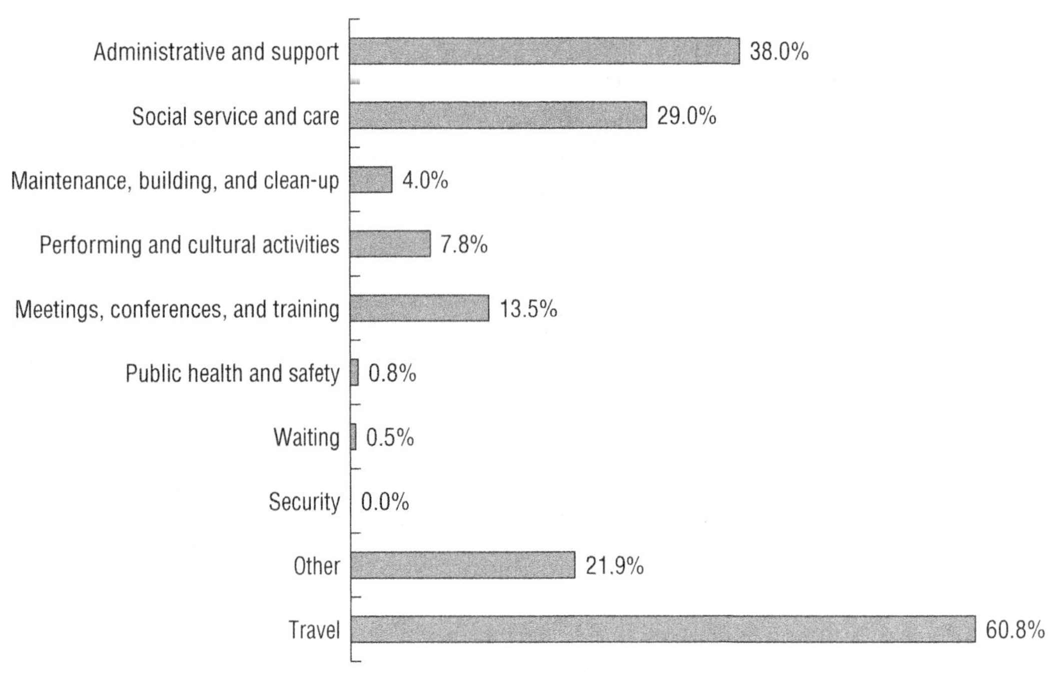

Source: Authors' calculations based on U.S. Department of Labor, Bureau of Labor Statistics, American Time Use Survey (2014).

Table 3.18. Percentage of Volunteers Who Performed Each Activity, 2003–14

%	2003	2004	2005	2006	2007	2008	2009	2010	2011	2012	2013	2014
Administrative and support	43.6	44.1	40.4	37.3	34.2	37.3	41.4	35.4	36.6	39.7	42.7	38.0
Social service and care	25.6	28.1	27.5	23.8	25.7	26.3	28.3	26.0	26.7	27.3	30.3	29.0
Maintenance, building, and clean-up	7.5	8.5	5.5	6.7	8.6	7.7	7.8	9.0	7.4	6.6	5.0	4.0
Performing and cultural activities	7.2	5.5	9.7	8.9	6.5	6.4	6.1	6.4	7.2	7.5	9.4	7.8
Meetings, conferences, and training	13.2	12.5	11.9	13.1	14.5	11.6	13.6	14.2	12.5	15.8	14.1	13.5
Public health and safety	1.8	2.3	1.6	1.3	0.9	2.5	1.4	0.7	2.6	1.0	0.8	0.8
Waiting	—	0.3	0.5	2.0	0.3	0.6	1.1	1.8	0.3	0.8	0.8	0.5
Security	—	—	—	—	0.2	0.3	0.3	0.1	0.6	0.0	0.8	0.0
Other	21.3	20.2	20.7	25.3	30.1	25.6	21.6	25.3	27.0	19.9	19.5	21.9
Travel	63.6	65.0	60.9	65.7	67.2	63.1	62.4	63.4	69.1	59.8	62.0	60.8

Source: Authors' calculations based on U.S. Department of Labor, Bureau of Labor Statistics, American Time Use Survey (2003–14).
Notes: Multiple responses were allowed. Waiting was not a separate category in 2003, so wait time was distributed across the other categories. Security was not a separate category until 2007, so time spent on security procedures related to the volunteer activity was distributed across the other categories.
— = no data available

Sources

The Bill and Melinda Gates Foundation. 2007. "Annual Report." http://www.gatesfoundation.org/Who-We-Are/Resources-and-Media/Annual-Reports (accessed August 19, 2016).

Center on Philanthropy at Indiana University. 2007. "Center on Philanthropy Panel Study." https://scholarworks.iupui.edu/handle/1805/6310 (accessed August 19, 2016).

Centre for Time Use Research. 2006. "American Heritage Time Use Study (AHTUS)." https://www.ahtusdata.org/ahtus/ (accessed August 19, 2016).

Chairman of the Council of Economic Advisers. 2011. *Economic Report of the President.* Washington, DC: U.S. Government Printing Office. https://www.whitehouse.gov/administration/eop/cea/economic-report-of-the-President/2011 (accessed August 19, 2016).

Foundation Center. 2011. "Research Studies: National Trends." http://foundationcenter.org/gainknowledge/research/nationaltrends.html (accessed May 16, 2012).

Giving USA Foundation. 2015. *Giving USA 2015: The Annual Report on Philanthropy for the Year 2014.* http://www.givinginstitute.org/?page=GUSA2015Release (accessed August 22, 2016).

U.S. Department of Commerce, Bureau of Economic Analysis. 2011. "National Income and Product Accounts Tables." http://www.bea.gov/iTable/iTable.cfm?ReqID=9&step=1 (accessed May 17, 2012).

U.S. Department of Labor, Bureau of Labor Statistics. 2005–2010. "American Time Use Survey." http://www.bls.gov/tus/home.htm (accessed May 17, 2012).

———. 2005–2010. "Current Population Survey." http://www.bls.gov/cps/home.htm (accessed May 17, 2012).

———. 2011. "Employment, Hours, and Earnings from the Current Employment Statistics Survey (National)." http://www.bls.gov/ces/home.htm (13 1301 May 17, 2012).

———. 2012. "Consumer Price Indexes." http://www.bls.gov/cpi/home.htm (accessed May 17, 2012).

U.S. Department of the Treasury, Internal Revenue Service. 1985–2013. "SOI Tax Stats—Individual Income Tax Returns Publication 1304 (Complete Report)." https://www.irs.gov/uac/soi-tax-stats-individual-income-tax-returns-publication-1304-complete-report (accessed August 22, 2016).

———. 1987, 1990, 1992–2014. "SOI Tax Stats—Estate Tax Statistics Filing Year Table 3." https://www.irs.gov/uac/soi-tax-stats-estate-tax-statistics-filing-year-table-3 (accessed August 19, 2016).

———. 2007–2013. "Individual Noncash Contributions." https://www.irs.gov/uac/soi-tax-stats-special-studies-on-individual-tax-return-data#noncash (accessed August 19, 2016).

Technical Notes

The following explains the methodology for calculating volunteer values in tables 3.14, 3.17, and 3.18.

Per day values in table 3.14 are based on author calculations and do not match published numbers from the American Time Use Survey because ATUS includes travel time only in major categories and not in subcategories, thus excluding travel time associated with volunteering. Table 3.14 includes all time in the 2010 ATUS activity codes 15xxxx (volunteering) and 1815xx (travel associated with volunteering) and the analogous codes for 2005–2010. Participation rates are calculated by summing the weights (*TUFINLWGT*) for all respondents with any time in the above categories and dividing by the sum of the weights of all respondents. The number of volunteers is calculated by summing the weights for all respondents with volunteer time and dividing by 365. Hours per day per volunteer result from a two-step process: Average minutes across the whole population are calculated by multiplying each respondent's minutes in the above categories by that respondent's weight, summing those products, and dividing by the sum of the weights of all respondents. This is converted to hours per day by dividing by 60, and to hours per day per volunteer by dividing by the volunteer participation rate calculated above. These are standard calculations, documented in ATUS codebooks.

The per year calculations at the bottom of table 3.14 are also author calculations. Population is calculated by dividing the sum of *TUFINLWGT* by 365. Total annual volunteer hours is calculated by multiplying population times the percent of population volunteering on an average day times 365, times the average hours volunteered per day per volunteer. Full-time-equivalent employment is calculated by dividing total annual volunteer hours per year by 1,700 working hours per full-time employee per year. Total assigned value of volunteer time is total annual volunteer hours times the average private nonfarm hourly wage.

Tables 3.17 and 3.18 are also based on author calculations using the ATUS. The categories shown in table 3.17 correspond to the activity codes given above—15xxxx and

1815xx—summed to the four-digit level. For each category shown, each respondent's time was multiplied by that respondent's weight (*TUFINLWGT*) and the results summed. The sum was divided by the sum of weights of all volunteers, even those who did not perform that particular activity on the diary day. The result is the average minutes per day per volunteer for each activity. Converted to hours, these totals would sum to the average hours volunteered per volunteer per day in table 3.14.

In table 3.18, which also uses data from the ATUS, participation rates for each activity are calculated by summing *TUFINLWGT* of respondents who reported any time in that activity and dividing by the sum of the weights of all volunteers.

4
Financial Trends

In this chapter, we seek to understand the nonprofit sector's revenue and expenses by examining revenue sources and types of expenditures, and how these have changed over time. We pay special attention to pre- and post-recession figures to assess any lingering effects of the recession. As in chapter 1, the primary source of data is the Bureau of Economic Analysis's (BEA) National Income and Product Accounts. The analysis, therefore, is limited to Nonprofit Institutions Serving Households (NPISH). Because this chapter focuses on trends, all figures have been adjusted for inflation and are shown in 2014 dollars.

Summary

- NPISH revenue was $1.32 trillion in 2014, a 19 percent growth since 2004, when adjusting for inflation.
- NPISH revenue growth has not yet fully recovered from the recession. The average annual revenue growth rate pre-recession (2004 to 2007) was 3.1 percent compared to 2.1 percent post-recession (2009 to 2014).
- In 2014, sales receipts or fee-for-service revenue accounted for 72 percent of nonprofit revenues; transfer receipts[1] accounted for 24 percent; and asset income, such as interest, dividends, or rental income, accounted for another 4 percent.
- Asset income still remains below pre-recession levels. In 2008, asset income declined 28 percent after adjustments for inflation and has declined in 4 of the 7 years since 2008. In 2014, asset income was at $56.6 billion, 21 percent lower than the $71.7 billion reported in 2007 after adjustments for inflation.

1. The BEA defines transfer receipts as funds that NPISHs receive from private and public sources, such as donations and grants. The author uses the BEA's terminology in this chapter.

- NPISHs had $1.41 trillion in outlays or expenditures in 2014. Ninety-two percent of nonprofit funds were spent directly,[2] and the remaining 8 percent were given away.[3] NPISH does include grantmaking foundations in these figures.
- In 2014, NPISHs outlays exceeded revenues by $69.9 billion. In fact, total NPISH expenditures have exceeded revenues resulting in a deficit each year since 2008.
- More than half of NPISH consumption expenditures were in the health care field in 2014. Another 14 percent were in education, and 9 percent were in social services.
- In 2014, more than three-quarters of nonprofit transfer payments (79 percent) went to households in the United States. Twenty-one percent of these payments went to help people internationally, and 0.4 percent went to pay excise taxes.
- International transfer payments as a proportion of transfer payments increased from 11.2 percent in 2004 to 20.9 percent in 2014.

Nonprofit Institutions Serving Households

The BEA's National Income and Product Accounts provide data on nonprofit institutions serving households. What is included in the BEA's definition of NPISH? Nonprofit organizations serving households, such as social service organizations or museums, would fall under the criteria. For a nonprofit to be included in the NPISH definition, it needs to provide services in one of the following five categories (Mead et al. 2003):

1. religious and welfare, which includes human services, grantmaking foundations, libraries, and some fraternal organizations;
2. recreation, such as athletic organizations or cultural activities;
3. education and research;
4. medical care; and
5. personal business, which includes labor unions, legal aid, and professional associations.

Nonprofit organizations that serve business, such as chambers of commerce, trade associations, and homeowners associations, are excluded from the NPISH figures; they are included in the business sector. In addition, nonprofits that sell goods and services in the same way as for-profit organizations are excluded. These include tax-exempt cooperatives, credit unions, mutual financial institutions, and tax-exempt manufac-

2. The BEA describes funds spent directly by NPISHs to obtain goods and provide services as consumption expenditures. The authors use the BEA's terminology in this chapter.
3. The BEA describes funds transferred from NPISHs to households as transfer payments. The authors use the BEA's terminology in this chapter.

turers like university presses. NPISH figures, therefore, do not encompass the entire nonprofit sector.

Trends in Revenues

In 2014, NPISH revenue was $1.32 trillion, an inflation-adjusted increase of 2.3 percent from 2013 (figure 4.1). From 2004 to 2014, revenue grew 19 percent after adjusting for inflation. Not surprisingly, NPISH revenues declined in 2008 during the recession, dropping by 3.5 percent. Revenues remained below 2007 levels until 2010, when revenues exceeded $1.2 trillion. Although revenue figures may be back up to pre-recession levels, post-recession average annual growth is still recovering. The average annual growth rate in NPISH revenue from 2009 to 2014 was 2.1 percent compared to 3.1 percent from 2004 to 2007.

Figure 4.2 displays the sources of revenue for NPISHs in 2014. Revenues are generated from three primary sources: sales receipts, asset income, or transfer payments (grants and donations). Sales receipts, or fees for services and goods, which includes hospital payments, tuition payments, and entrance fees, accounted for the lion's share of nonprofit revenue—72 percent. Transfer payments, which consist of contributions from public and private sources, accounted for 24 percent, and asset income accounted for another 4 percent. Nonprofit organizations providing health services, such as hospitals, nursing care facilities, mental health centers, home health care services, and senior care account for the bulk of fee-for-service revenue, 76 percent in 2014 (table 4.1). Education, a distant second, collected $103.8 billion, or 11 percent of total NPISH sales receipts, in tuition and other sales receipts in 2014. (The industries included in each subsector are listed in table 4.5.)

Figure 4.1. Revenue of Nonprofit Institutions Serving Households, 2004–14 (2014 $ billions)

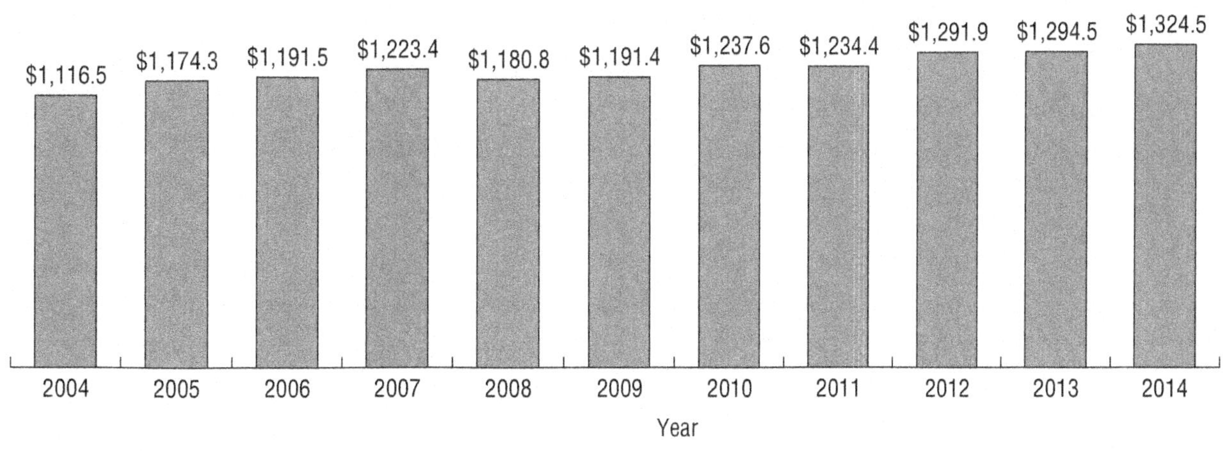

Source: U.S. Department of Commerce, Bureau of Economic Analysis, National Income and Product Accounts, table 2.9 (2015).
Notes: Estimates in this figure exclude nonprofit institutions serving business and government. Values are adjusted for inflation.

Figure 4.2. Sources of Revenue of Nonprofit Institutions Serving Households, 2014 (percent)

Category	Percent
Sales receipts (public and private)	72.2%
Transfer receipts (grants and donations, public and private)	23.6%
Asset income	4.3%

Source: U.S. Department of Commerce, Bureau of Economic Analysis, National Income and Product Accounts, table 2.9 (2015).
Notes: Estimates in this figure exclude nonprofit institutions serving business and government. Values are adjusted for inflation.

Figure 4.3 shows the value of total sales receipts, transfer receipts, and asset income since 2004. Sales receipts had the greatest growth, increasing 25 percent from 2004 to 2014. Asset income grew by 7 percent over the 10-year period, and transfer receipts grew 5 percent. Foundations and grantmaking/giving establishments showed the largest growth in sales receipts since 2004, increasing by 86 percent (table 4.1). These organizations, however, account for less than 1 percent of all sales receipts for the sector. Health care organizations, which account for more than three-quarters of sales receipts for the sector, also saw strong growth, increasing 29 percent since 2004.

Sales receipts, transfer receipts, and asset income each declined during the recession (2008). Sales receipts saw a less than 1 percent decline in 2008 and have been increasing steadily since 2009. Asset income and transfer receipts, on the other hand, were hit much harder by the recession. Asset income declined 28 percent in 2008 and has shown decline in four of the seven years since 2008. In 2014, asset income was at $56.6 billion, 21 percent lower than the $71.7 billion reported in 2007. Transfer receipts also saw decline in four of the last seven years since 2008. However, the $312 billion in transfer receipts in 2014 are within 1 percent of 2007 levels.

As displayed in figure 4.4, the composition of nonprofit revenue has changed only slightly since 2004. Sales receipts, which accounted for 69 percent of revenue in 2004, accounted for 72 percent in 2014. Over the same period, transfer receipts dropped from 26 percent of revenue to 24 percent of revenue, and asset income dropped from 5 percent to 4 percent.

The next few paragraphs focus more specifically on the components of transfer receipts and asset income. While the BEA breaks out transfer receipts into public and private sources, a similar breakout is not provided for sales receipts.

Table 4.1. Revenues of Nonprofit Institutions Serving Households, 2004–14 (2014 $ billions)

	2004	2005	2006	2007	2008	2009	2010	2011	2012	2013	2014
Sales receipts (public and private)[a]	767.7	797.8	813.8	838.5	834.3	878.9	901.6	909.9	928.1	944.4	956.0
Health	565.6	591.1	603.3	623.2	619.6	659.3	678.5	687.7	704.9	718.6	728.4
Education	83.0	85.3	87.6	90.5	92.4	96.4	98.8	100.3	102.0	103.3	103.8
Social services	53.9	54.4	54.0	54.6	54.3	55.8	57.5	56.6	55.1	54.8	54.9
Professional advocacy	29.3	29.5	30.1	30.5	30.2	30.7	30.5	29.9	30.2	30.6	31.0
Recreation	18.3	20.2	21.1	21.4	20.2	19.3	19.0	18.5	19.0	19.3	19.8
Civic and social organizations	7.9	7.4	7.2	7.1	6.7	6.5	6.6	6.4	6.5	6.7	6.7
Religious organizations	6.6	6.5	6.6	6.9	6.6	6.5	6.3	6.0	6.1	6.4	6.4
Social advocacy establishments	2.5	2.5	2.7	3.0	3.0	3.1	3.3	3.3	3.3	3.4	3.6
Foundations and grantmaking/giving establishments	0.8	0.8	1.2	1.5	1.3	1.2	1.2	1.3	1.2	1.3	1.4
Transfer receipts	295.8	315.8	307.5	313.3	295.2	261.4	285.1	272.9	305.5	294.4	312.0
From households[b]	261.0	276.5	272.1	279.0	262.2	225.6	245.3	235.0	265.5	255.0	272.6
From government	21.8	21.2	20.7	20.0	20.7	22.4	22.9	22.5	23.0	22.7	22.3
From business (net)	12.8	18.2	14.8	14.3	12.3	13.5	16.9	15.3	17.0	16.8	17.0
Asset income	53.0	60.7	70.2	71.7	51.3	51.0	50.7	51.6	58.1	55.8	56.6
Interest income	28.1	32.1	37.8	38.0	25.0	23.7	20.1	19.0	20.6	20.3	20.4
Dividend income	18.9	22.7	26.5	27.3	19.6	19.2	21.9	22.8	27.5	25.7	26.1
Rental income	6.0	5.9	5.9	6.4	6.8	8.1	8.7	9.7	9.9	9.8	10.1
Total	**1,116.5**	**1,174.3**	**1,191.5**	**1,223.5**	**1,180.9**	**1,191.3**	**1,237.4**	**1,234.4**	**1,291.7**	**1,294.6**	**1,324.6**

Source: U.S. Department of Commerce, Bureau of Economic Analysis, National Income and Product Accounts, table 2.9 (2015).
Notes: Estimates in this table exclude nonprofit institutions serving business and government. Values are adjusted for inflation.
a. Sales receipts exclude unrelated sales, secondary sales, and sales to business, government, and the rest of the world; includes membership dues and fees.
b. Transfer receipts from households include individual contributions and bequests from households.

Figure 4.3. Revenue of Nonprofit Institutions Serving Households by Source, 2004–14 (2014 $ billions)

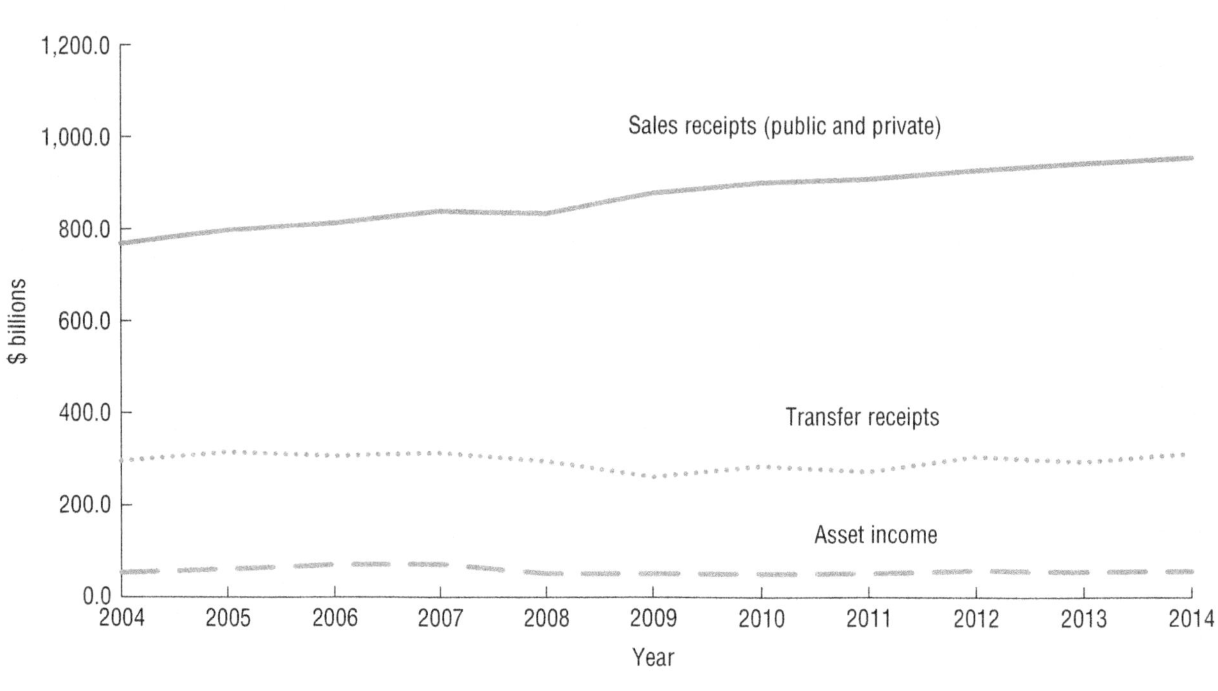

Source: U.S. Department of Commerce, Bureau of Economic Analysis, National Income and Product Accounts, table 2.9 (2015).
Notes: Estimates in this figure exclude nonprofit institutions serving business and government. Values are adjusted for inflation.

Figure 4.4. Types of Revenue for Nonprofit Institutions Serving Households, 2004–14 (percent)

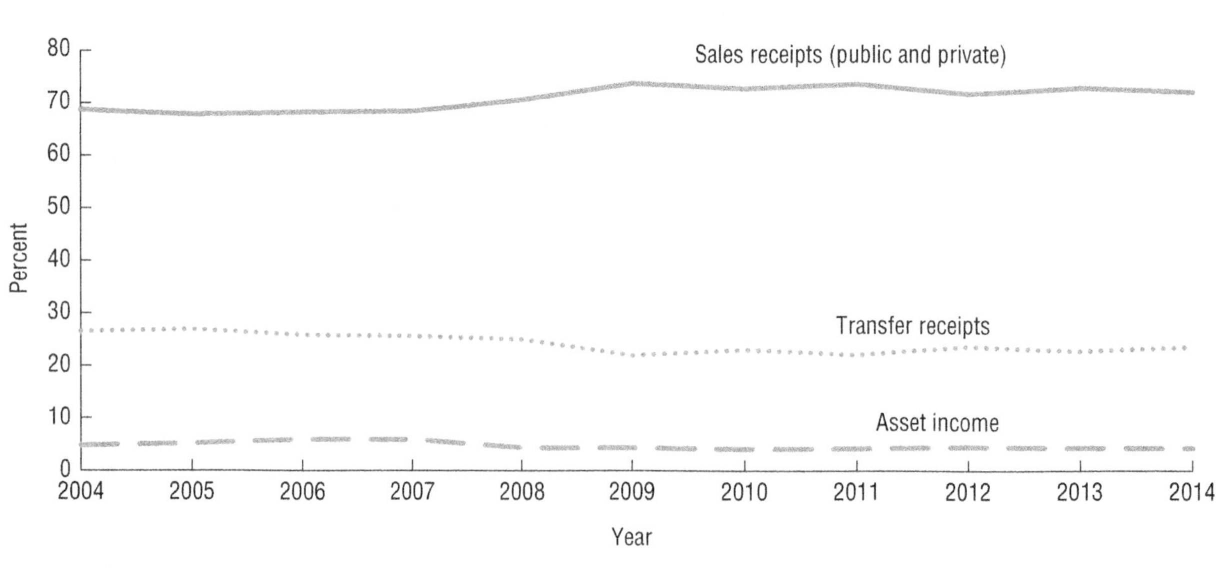

Source: U.S. Department of Commerce, Bureau of Economic Analysis, National Income and Product Accounts, table 2.9 (2015).
Notes: Estimates in this figure exclude nonprofit institutions serving business and government. Values are adjusted for inflation.

In 2014, transfer receipts contributed $312 billion to NPISH revenue. Contributions from households accounted for 87 percent of all transfer receipts, government accounted for 7 percent, and business accounted for 5 percent. Figure 4.5 displays the trend in transfer receipts by funding source. Transfer receipts from business saw the largest growth from 2004 to 2014, increasing by 33 percent, followed by transfer receipts from households (4 percent). Transfer receipts from government increased by 2 percent.

Examining pre- and post-recession transfer receipts by source reveals that transfer receipts from households are still below pre-recession levels. In 2014, transfer receipts from households totaled $272.6 billion—still 2 percent below 2007 levels. Growth in transfer receipts from government and businesses, however, has exceeded pre-recession levels. The average annual growth rate post-recession (2009 to 2014) was –0.1 percent for transfer receipts from government and 4.8 percent for those from businesses compared to average pre-recession (2004 to 2007) growth rates of –2.9 percent and 3.7 percent, respectively.

Figure 4.6 displays the shares of transfer receipts by source from 2004 to 2014. The percentage of transfer receipts from all sources remained remarkably steady over the 10 years, staying within 1 to 2 percentage points.

In 2014, nonprofits reported $56.6 billion in asset income. As displayed in figure 4.7, dividend income accounted for 46 percent of this income, followed by interest income at 36 percent and rental income at 18 percent. Figure 4.8 shows how interest income, dividend income, and rental income have changed since 2004. Not surprisingly, both dividend and interest income declined drastically in 2008. Interest income, which includes interest earned from savings accounts, certificates of deposits, or other temporary cash

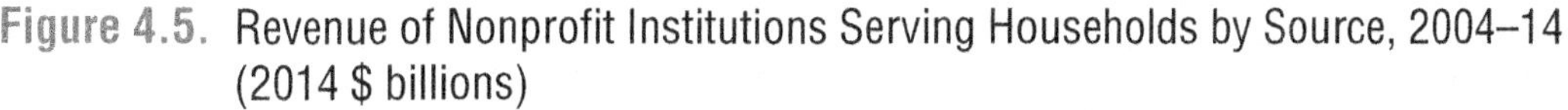

Figure 4.5. Revenue of Nonprofit Institutions Serving Households by Source, 2004–14 (2014 $ billions)

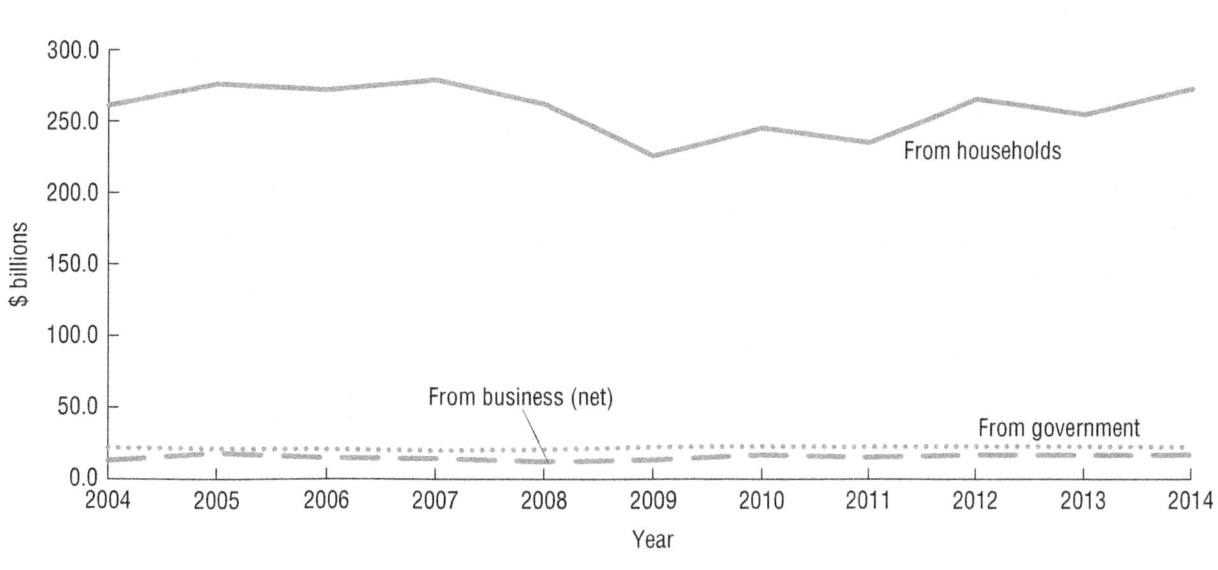

Source: U.S. Department of Commerce, Bureau of Economic Analysis, National Income and Product Accounts, table 2.9 (2015).
Notes: Estimates in this figure exclude nonprofit institutions serving business and government. Values are adjusted for inflation.

Figure 4.6. Transfer Receipts for Nonprofit Organizations Serving Households by Source, 2004–14 (percent)

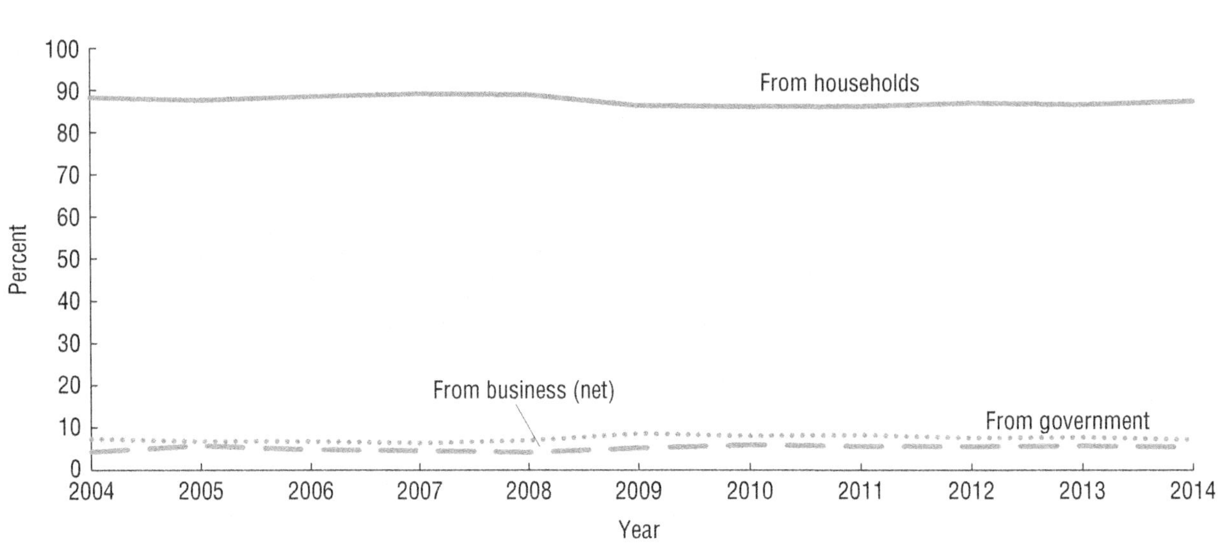

Source: U.S. Department of Commerce, Bureau of Economic Analysis, National Income and Product Accounts, table 2.9 (2015).
Notes: Estimates in this figure exclude nonprofit institutions serving business and government. Values are adjusted for inflation.

Figure 4.7. Asset Income for Nonprofit Institutions Serving Households by Source, 2014 (percent)

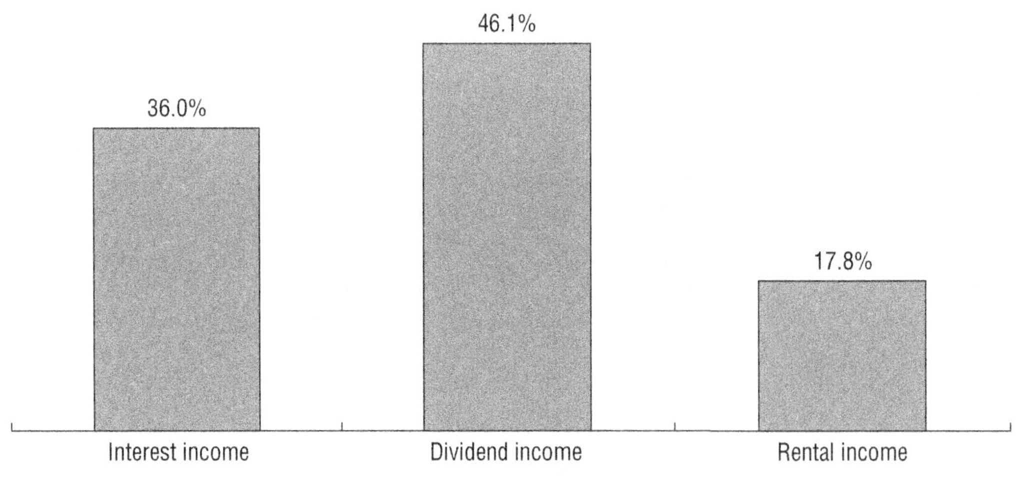

Source: U.S. Department of Commerce, Bureau of Economic Analysis, National Income and Product Accounts, table 2.9 (2015).
Notes: Estimates in this figure exclude nonprofit institutions serving business and government. Values are adjusted for inflation.

Figure 4.8. Asset Income of Nonprofit Institutions Serving Households by Source, 2004–14 (2014 $ billions)

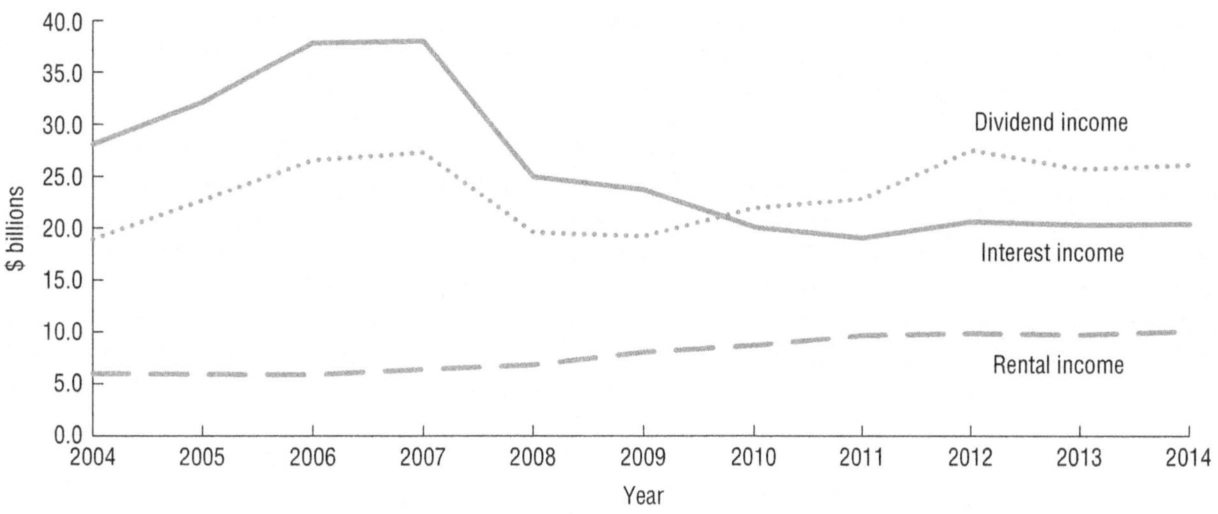

Source: U.S. Department of Commerce, Bureau of Economic Analysis, National Income and Product Accounts, table 2.9 (2015).
Notes: Estimates in this figure exclude nonprofit institutions serving business and government. Values are adjusted for inflation.

investments, plummeted 34 percent from 2007 to 2008 and continued to decline through 2011. Interest income has yet to return to pre-recession levels. In fact, interest income is 46 percent below its 2007 level. Dividend income from stocks, mutual funds, and other investments declined 28 percent between 2007 and 2008 and continued to decline through 2009. Although dividend income is still below 2007 levels, it is within 5 percent of the $27.3 billion reported just before the recession. Rental income, on the other hand, has been steadily increasing since 2004, increasing by 68 percent since 2004. The three components of asset income—dividends, interest, and rental income—are not growing as fast as nonprofit sector income. This suggests that the nonprofit sector may be undercapitalized.

Trends in Outlays

Now that we know where nonprofit funds come from, we turn our attention to how these funds are spent. In 2014, NPISHs had $1.39 trillion in outlays—a 25 percent increase since 2004. Figure 4.9 displays how funds were spent. Ninety-two percent of nonprofit funds were spent directly to obtain goods and provide services (consumption expenditures), and the remaining 8 percent were given to the government, domestic households, or internationally (transfer payments). Comparing total NPISH revenue and outlays, outlays exceeded revenues by $69.9 billion, or 5 percent, in 2014. This indicates that nonprofit organizations either used reserves to fund their activities or were running deficits.

Figure 4.10 and table 4.2 show nonprofit outlays from 2004 to 2014. Consumption expenditures grew 25 percent and transfer payments grew 33 percent since 2004. Unlike

Figure 4.9. Uses of Funds by Nonprofit Institutions Serving Households, 2014 (percent)

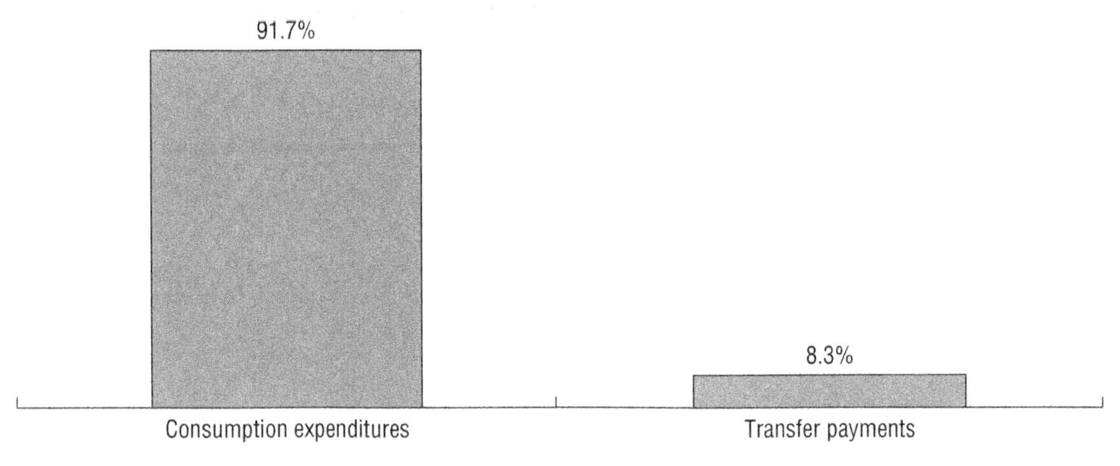

Source: U.S. Department of Commerce, Bureau of Economic Analysis, National Income and Product Accounts, table 2.9 (2015).
Notes: Estimates in this figure exclude nonprofit institutions serving business and government. Values are adjusted for inflation.

Figure 4.10. Outlays from Nonprofit Institutions Serving Households by Use, 2000–14 (2014 $ billions)

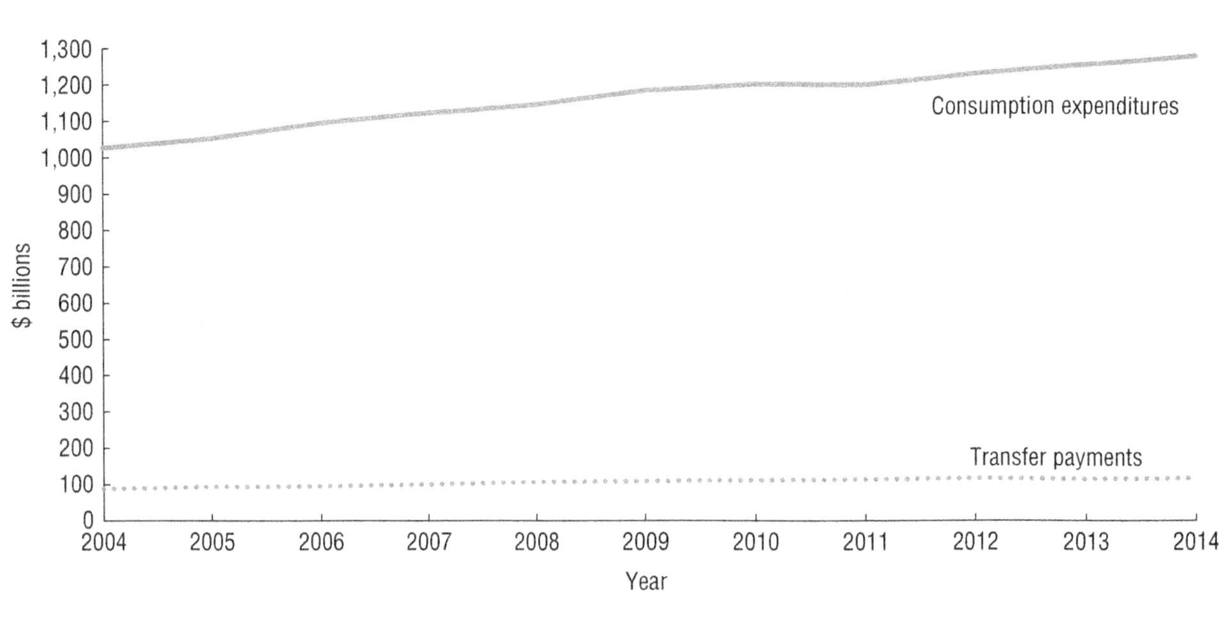

Source: U.S. Department of Commerce, Bureau of Economic Analysis, National Income and Product Accounts, table 2.9 (2015).
Notes: Estimates in this figure exclude nonprofit institutions serving business and government. Values are adjusted for inflation.

Table 4.2. Outlays from Nonprofit Institutions Serving Households, 2004–14 (2014 $ billions)

	2004	2005	2006	2007	2008	2009	2010	2011	2012	2013	2014
Consumption expenditures[a]	1,026.4	1,052.8	1,094.7	1,122.5	1,144.5	1,183.6	1,200.6	1,199.4	1,230.1	1,253.2	1,278.3
Health	571.1	594.4	617.3	630.4	639.7	678.3	690.6	698.7	718.6	740.7	754.1
Education	140.5	142.2	147.6	154.9	157.7	162.7	164.2	166.3	168.0	171.0	174.4
Social services	106.7	109.2	110.9	113.4	115.8	120.2	123.7	121.1	118.8	118.0	117.8
Professional advocacy	38.9	34.5	40.2	36.4	43.4	36.3	40.8	35.7	44.9	36.8	42.3
Recreation	37.8	39.5	41.5	43.2	44.2	43.8	42.1	41.3	42.4	43.2	43.6
Civic and social organizations	12.0	11.2	10.9	10.4	10.4	10.3	10.1	10.0	9.9	10.1	10.2
Religious organizations	83.6	84.4	84.7	88.3	84.1	83.9	80.9	77.0	78.4	81.9	82.6
Social advocacy establishments	12.9	13.7	15.4	17.4	18.7	19.2	19.5	19.8	19.9	20.3	21.1
Foundations and grantmaking/giving establishments	22.8	23.5	26.4	28.3	30.5	29.1	28.7	29.5	29.4	31.2	32.3
Transfer payments	87.5	93.7	94.6	100.2	106.5	108.3	111.3	113.5	116.4	114.2	116.2
To households[b]	77.1	81.1	82.2	84.5	81.5	82.2	85.4	85.2	89.2	89.3	91.4
To the rest of the world (net)	9.8	11.9	11.4	14.8	24.6	25.7	25.4	27.8	26.7	24.4	24.3
To government[c]	0.6	0.7	0.9	1.0	0.3	0.2	0.4	0.4	0.4	0.5	0.5
Total NPISH outlays	**1,113.9**	**1,146.5**	**1,189.3**	**1,222.7**	**1,251.1**	**1,291.8**	**1,311.9**	**1,312.8**	**1,346.5**	**1,367.4**	**1,394.5**

Source: U.S. Department of Commerce, Bureau of Economic Analysis, National Income and Product Accounts, table 2.9 (2015).
NPISH = nonprofit institutions serving households
Notes: Estimates in this table exclude nonprofit institutions serving business and government. Values are adjusted for inflation. Outlays have been revised from the 2008 Almanac.
a. Gross output is net of unrelated sales, secondary sales, and sales to business, government, and the rest of the world; excludes own-account investment (construction and software).
b. Transfer payments to households include benefits paid to members, specific assistance to individuals, and grants and allocations.
c. Transfer payments to government consist of excise taxes paid by nonprofit institutions serving households.
d. Includes grants and allocations made by nonprofit institutions that indirectly support households through the support of other nonprofit institutions, plus their payments to affiliates.

revenue trends, NPISH outlays continued to grow throughout the recession. In fact, both consumption expenditures and transfer payments have only seen one year of negative growth since 2007. Consumption expenditures declined 0.1 percent in 2011 and transfer payments declined by 1.9 percent in 2013. Annual growth in both consumption expenditures and transfer payments, however, is lower post-recession. Between 2004 and 2007 the average annual growth in consumption expenditures and transfer payments was 3 percent and 5 percent, respectively, compared with 2 percent and 1 percent from 2009 to 2014.

Figure 4.11 shows the proportion of each type of outlay from 2004 to 2014. Over the years, consumption expenditures accounted for the largest proportion of outlays, hovering just above 90 percent. The share of transfer payments has remained relatively steady over the 10-year period at 8 percent.

Diving deeper into consumption expenditures and transfer payments, figure 4.12 shows consumption expenditures by type of organization, or subsector, in 2014. Health care organizations accounted for more than half of NPISH expenditures. Another 14 percent were in education, and 9 percent were in social services. As displayed in table 4.3, the proportion of total NPISH expenditures by most subsectors has remained fairly consistent since 2004—usually staying within 1 to 2 percentage points. The proportion of NPISH consumption expenditures accounted for by health organizations has changed slightly more than other subsectors over the 10-year period, increasing by 3 percent.

Table 4.4 displays the amount of money spent by type of organization, or subsector, since 2004. (The industries included in each subsector are listed in table 4.5.) Health care nonprofits reported consumption expenditures of $754.1 billion in 2014, the highest

Figure 4.11. Outlays from Nonprofit Institutions Serving Households by Use, 2004–14 (percent)

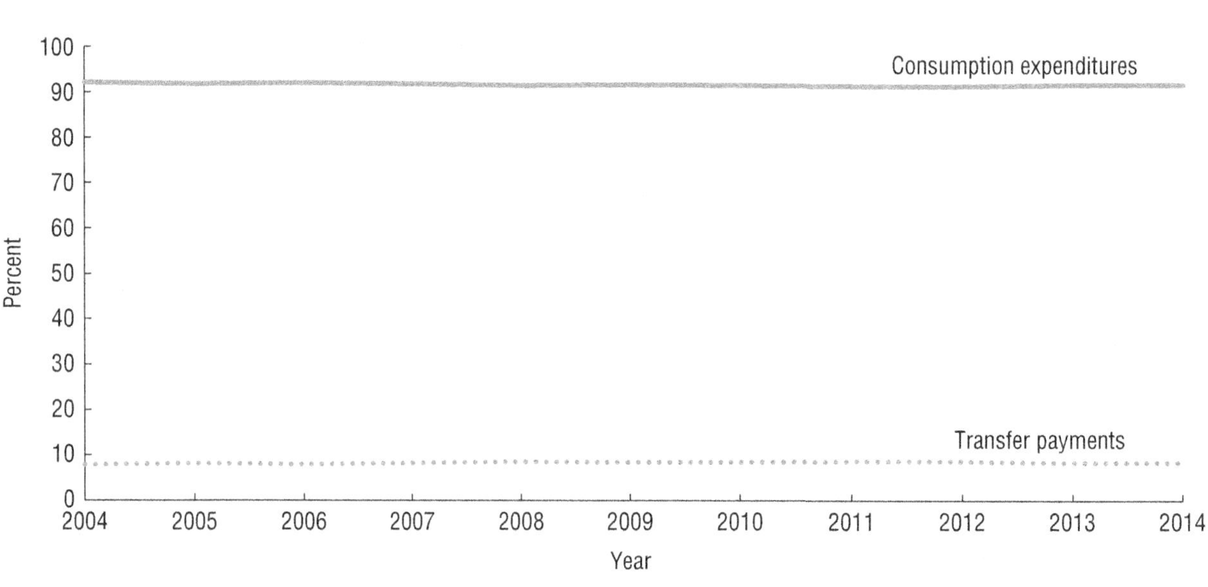

Source: U.S. Department of Commerce, Bureau of Economic Analysis, National Income and Product Accounts, table 2.9 (2015).
Notes: Estimates in this figure exclude nonprofit institutions serving business and government. Values are adjusted for inflation.

Figure 4.12. Consumption Expenditures for Nonprofit Institutions Serving Households by Subsector, 2014 (percent)

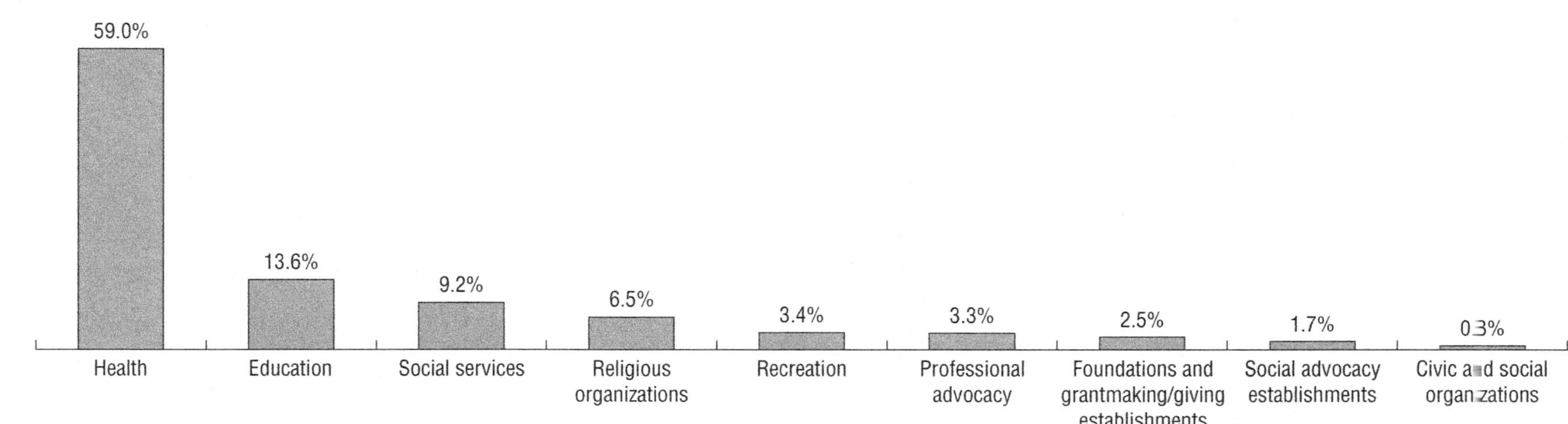

Source: U.S. Department of Commerce, Bureau of Economic Analysis, National Income and Product Accounts, table 2.9 (2015).
Notes: Estimates in this figure exclude nonprofit institutions serving business and government. Values are adjusted for inflation.

Table 4.3. Consumption Expenditures for Nonprofit Institutions Serving Households by Subsector, 2004–14 (percent)

	2004	2005	2006	2007	2008	2009	2010	2011	2012	2013	2014
Health	55.6	56.5	56.4	56.2	55.9	57.3	57.5	58.3	58.4	59.1	59.0
Education	13.7	13.5	13.5	13.8	13.8	13.7	13.7	13.9	13.7	13.6	13.6
Social services	10.4	10.4	10.1	10.1	10.1	10.2	10.3	10.1	9.7	9.4	9.2
Religious organizations	8.1	8.0	7.7	7.9	7.3	7.1	6.7	6.4	6.4	6.5	6.5
Recreation	3.7	3.8	3.8	3.8	3.9	3.7	3.5	3.4	3.4	3.4	3.4
Professional advocacy	3.8	3.3	3.7	3.2	3.8	3.1	3.4	3.0	3.6	2.9	3.3
Foundations and grantmaking/giving establishments	2.2	2.2	2.4	2.5	2.7	2.5	2.4	2.5	2.4	2.5	2.5
Social advocacy establishments	1.3	1.3	1.4	1.5	1.6	1.6	1.6	1.6	1.6	1.6	1.7
Civic and social organizations	1.2	1.1	1.0	0.9	0.9	0.9	0.8	0.8	0.8	0.8	0.8
Total NPISH consumption expenditures	**100.0**	**100.0**	**100.0**	**100.0**	**100.0**	**100.0**	**100.0**	**100.0**	**100.0**	**100.0**	**100.0**

Source: U.S. Department of Commerce, Bureau of Economic Analysis, National Income and Product Accounts, table 2.9 (2015).
Notes: Estimates exclude nonprofit institutions serving business and government. Values are adjusted for inflation.

Table 4.4. Consumption Expenditures for Nonprofit Institutions Serving Households by Subsector, 2004–14 (2014 $ billions)

	2004	2005	2006	2007	2008	2009	2010	2011	2012	2013	2014
Health	571.1	594.4	617.3	630.4	639.7	678.3	690.6	698.7	718.6	740.7	754.1
Education	140.5	142.2	147.6	154.9	157.7	162.7	164.2	166.3	168.0	171.0	174.4
Social services	106.7	109.2	110.9	113.4	115.8	120.2	123.7	121.1	118.8	118.0	117.8
Religious organizations	83.6	84.4	84.7	88.3	84.1	83.9	80.9	77.0	78.4	81.9	82.6
Recreation	37.8	39.5	41.5	43.2	44.2	43.8	42.1	41.3	42.4	43.2	43.6
Professional advocacy	38.9	34.5	40.2	36.4	43.4	36.3	40.8	35.7	44.9	36.8	42.3
Foundations and grantmaking/giving establishments	22.8	23.5	26.4	28.3	30.5	29.1	28.7	29.5	29.4	31.2	32.3
Social advocacy establishments	12.9	13.7	15.4	17.4	18.7	19.2	19.5	19.8	19.9	20.3	21.1
Civic and social organizations	12.0	11.2	10.9	10.4	10.4	10.3	10.1	10.0	9.9	10.1	10.2
Total NPISH consumption expenditures	**1,026.3**	**1,052.6**	**1,094.8**	**1,122.6**	**1,144.5**	**1,183.7**	**1,200.5**	**1,199.4**	**1,230.1**	**1,253.2**	**1,278.4**

Source: U.S. Department of Commerce, Bureau of Economic Analysis, National Income and Product Accounts, table 2.9 (2015).
Notes: Estimates exclude nonprofit institutions serving business and government. Values are adjusted for inflation.

Table 4.5. NAICS Industries Included in Bureau of Economic Analysis Consumption Categories, 2010

Health	
621410	Family planning centers
621420	Outpatient mental health
621491	HMO medical centers
621492	Kidney dialysis centers
621493	Freestanding ambulatory surgical and emergency centers
621498	All other outpatient care centers
621610	Home health care services
621910	Ambulance services
621999	All other miscellaneous ambulatory services
622119	General medical and surgical hospitals
622219	Psychiatric and substance abuse hospitals
622319	Specialty hospitals, excluding psychiatric and substance abuse
623110	Nursing care facilities
623210	Residential mental retardation facilities
623311	Continuing care retirement communities
Education	
541710	Research and development in life sciences, physical sciences, and engineering
541720	Research and development in social sciences and humanities
611110	Elementary and secondary education services
611210	Private higher education services
611310	Colleges, universities, professional schools, and junior colleges
611400	Professional/management, business/secretarial, and computer schools
611500	Apprenticeship, flight, cosmetology, and other training schools
611600	Art/drama/music, language, exam preparation, auto driving, and all other misc. schools, and incidental and support services
611710	Educational support services
624410	Child day care services
Social services	
623220	Residential mental health and substance abuse facilities
623312	Homes for the elderly
623900	Other residential care facilities

(continued)

Table 4.5. NAICS Industries Included in Bureau of Economic Analysis Consumption Categories, 2010 *(continued)*

624110	Child and youth services
624120	Services for the elderly and persons with disabilities
624190	Other individual and family services
624210	Community food services
624221	Temporary shelters
624229	Other community housing services
624230	Emergency and other relief services
624300	Vocational rehabilitation services
624400	Child day care services
Religious organizations	
813110	Religious organizations
Foundations and grantmaking and giving establishments	
813211	Grantmaking foundations
813212	Voluntary health organizations, grantmaking and giving
813219	Other grantmaking and giving services
Social advocacy establishments	
813311	Human rights organizations
813312	Environment, conservation, and wildlife organizations
813319	Social advocacy organizations
Civic and social organizations	
813400	Civic and social organizations
Professional advocacy	
541110	Legal aid societies and similar legal services
813920	Professional associations
813930	Labor organizations
813940	Political organizations
813990	All other similar organizations, excl. condos and homeowners association services to households

Source: Private communication from analysts at the Bureau of Economic Analysis, October 2011.
NAICS = North American Industry Classification System

of any subsector. Education followed with $174.4 billion. Expenditures of civic and social organizations were the smallest, spending $10.2 billion in 2014.

Expenditures of social advocacy establishments grew by 63 percent in the past 10 years, after adjusting for inflation. Over the same period, foundations and grantmaking organizations also saw tremendous growth in expenditures, increasing 42 percent. Civic and social organizations saw a decline of approximately $2 billion dollars since 2004, a 15 percent drop over the 10-year period. Religious organizations also saw a slight decline in expenditures decreasing by 1 percent since 2004.

Transfer payments from nonprofits, which include benefits paid to members, specific assistance to individuals, and grants and allocations, can go to U.S. households, to government, or outside the United States. As displayed in figure 4.13, over three-quarters of transfer payments (79 percent) went to households in the United States in 2014. Twenty-one percent of payments went to help people internationally, such as assistance provided by relief organizations. Finally, the BEA treats the excise taxes paid by grantmaking foundations as transfer payments to government. These taxes accounted for less than 1 percent of total transfer payments.

Figure 4.14 shows the dollar trend of transfer payments by type from 2004 to 2014. International transfer payments saw the greatest growth over the decade, increasing by 149 percent. Transfer payments to households grew 19 percent, and transfer payments to government declined by 20 percent over the 10 years.

Although the dollar amount of transfer payments to households in the United States has been on the rise, the share of transfer payments going to households has declined by nearly 10 percentage points since 2004 (figure 4.15). This reduction likely

Figure 4.13. Transfer Payments from Nonprofit Institutions Serving Households by Recipient, 2014 (percent)

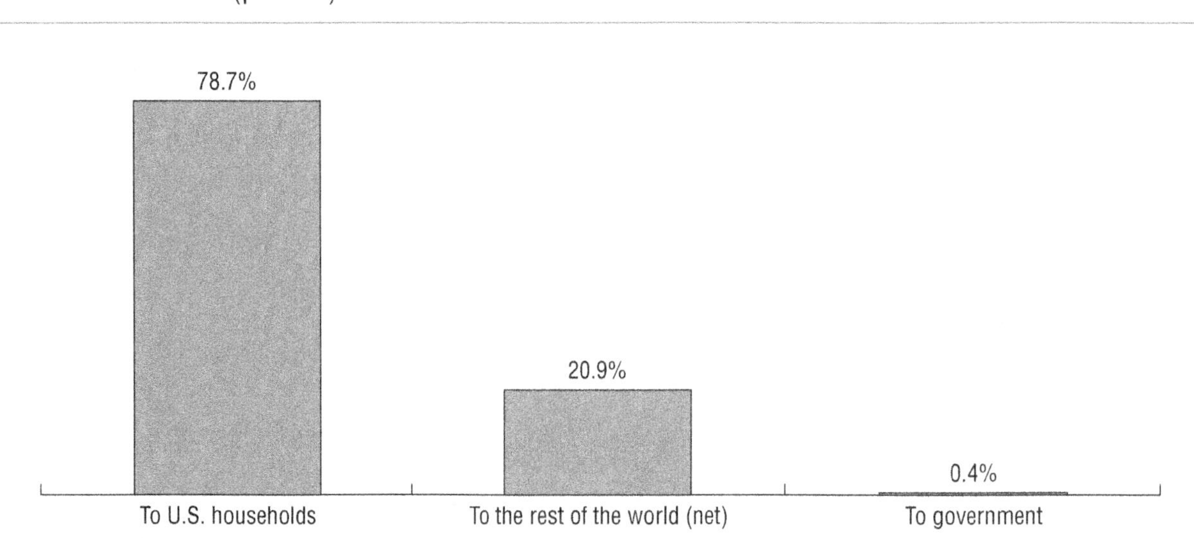

Source: U.S. Department of Commerce, Bureau of Economic Analysis, National Income and Product Accounts, table 2.9 (2015).
Notes: Estimates in this figure exclude nonprofit institutions serving business and government. Values are adjusted for inflation.

Figure 4.14. Transfer Payments from Nonprofit Institutions Serving Households by Recipient, 2004–14 (2014 $ billions)

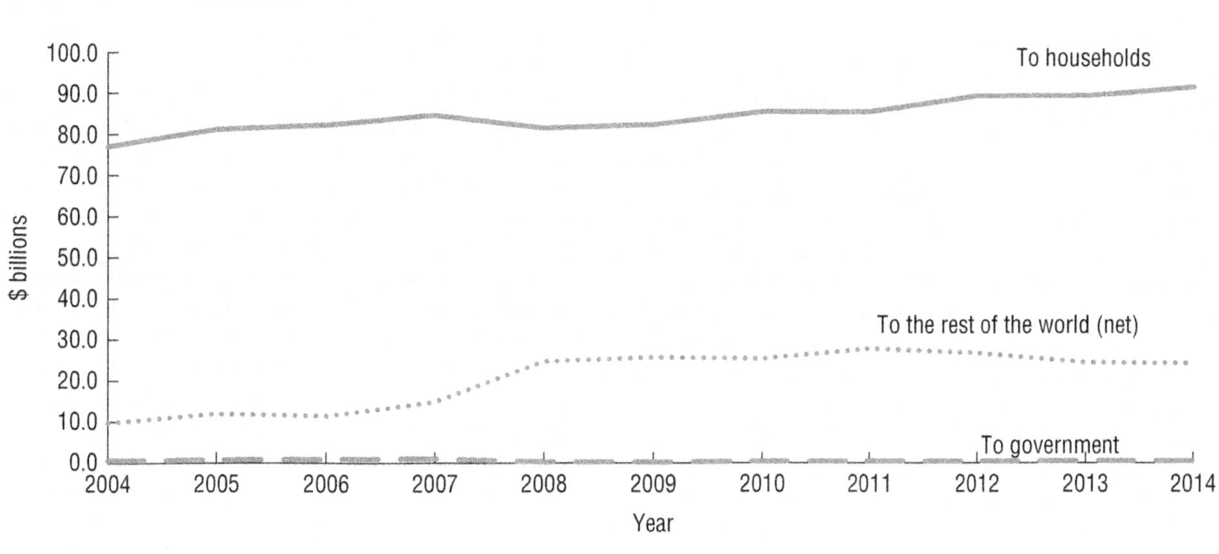

Source: U.S. Department of Commerce, Bureau of Economic Analysis, National Income and Product Accounts, table 2.9 (2015).
Notes: Estimates in this figure exclude nonprofit institutions serving business and government. Values are adjusted for inflation.

Figure 4.15. Transfer Payments from Nonprofit Institutions Serving Households by Recipient, 2004–14 (percent)

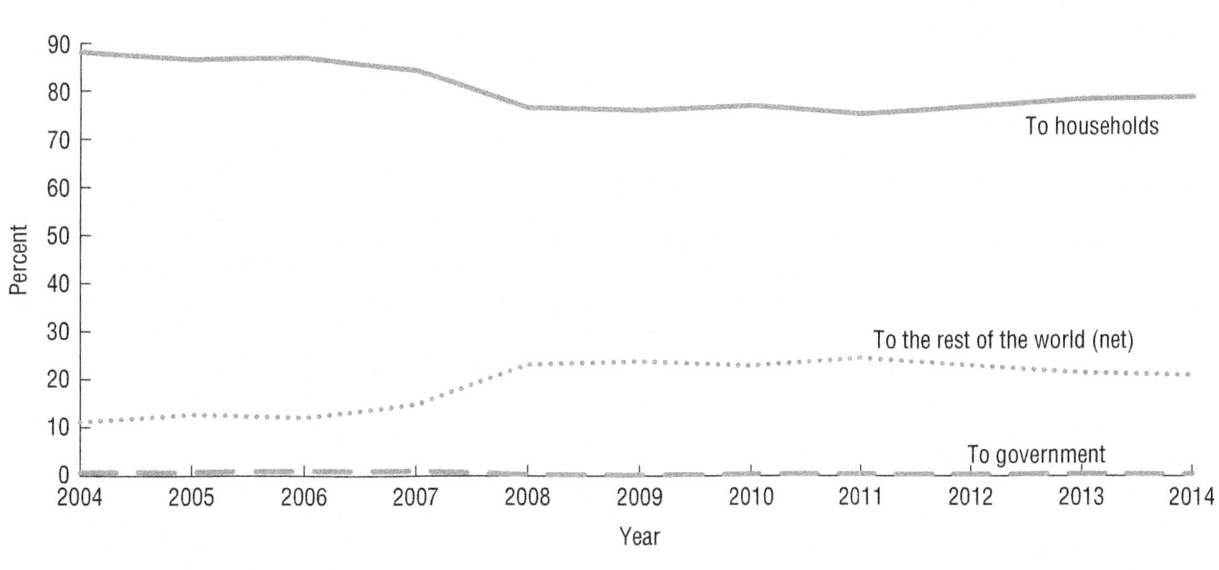

Source: U.S. Department of Commerce, Bureau of Economic Analysis, National Income and Product Accounts, table 2.9 (2015).
Notes: Estimates in this figure exclude nonprofit institutions serving business and government. Values are adjusted for inflation.

Table 4.6. Consumption Expenditures for Nonprofit Institutions Serving Households by Subsector, 2004–14 (2014 $ billions)

	2004	2005	2006	2007	2008	2009	2010	2011	2012	2013	2014
Revenue	1,116.5	1,174.3	1,191.5	1,223.5	1,180.9	1,191.3	1,237.4	1,234.4	1,291.7	1,294.6	1,324.6
Outlays	1,113.9	1,146.5	1,189.3	1,222.7	1,251.1	1,291.8	1,311.9	1,312.8	1,346.5	1,367.4	1,394.5
Savings	2.6	27.9	2.2	0.8	–70.2	–100.5	–74.5	–78.4	–54.9	–72.9	–69.9

Source: U.S. Department of Commerce, Bureau of Economic Analysis, National Income and Product Accounts, table 2.9 (2015).
Notes: Estimates exclude nonprofit institutions serving business and government. Values are adjusted for inflation.

stems from the huge growth in transfer payments going outside the United States. International transfer payments as a proportion of transfer payments increased from 11.2 percent in 2004 to 20.9 percent in 2014. The percentage of transfers going to the government declined slightly, from 0.7 percent in 2004 to 0.4 percent in 2014.

Table 4.6 shows NPISH savings from 2004 to 2014. The BEA defines saving as total revenue minus consumption expenditures and transfer payments. As shown, savings by nonprofits have been declining steadily since 2008. In 2014, NPISHs ran a deficit of $69.9 billion. This indicates that many nonprofit organizations are spending more money than they are able to generate, highlighting a major financial problem for the sector. Those that are able to sustain operations may be drawing down reserves or taking out lines of credit.

Conclusion

Analysis of nonprofit revenue and outlays shows that both have increased from 2004 to 2014. However, a look at average annual growth rates pre-recession and post-recession reveals lingering effects of the recession. A more concerning issue for the sector, though, is a gap between total NPISH revenues and outlays. Since 2008, the sector has been running deficits between 4 to 8 percent of its total revenue each year. Nonprofits may be drawing down savings or taking out lines of credit to sustain their operations.

Sources

Mead, Charles Ian, Clinton P. McCully, and Marshall B. Reindorf. "Income and Outlays of Households and of Nonprofit Institutions Serving Households." April 2003.

U.S. Department of Commerce, Bureau of Economic Analysis. 2011. "National Income and Product Accounts Tables." http://www.bea.gov/iTable/iTable.cfm?ReqID=9&step=1 (accessed May 17, 2016).

———. 2011. Private communication from analysts at the Bureau of Economic Analysis, October 2011.

5

The Size, Scope, and Finances of Public Charities

This chapter examines the size, scope, and financial conditions of public charities, those organizations exempt from taxation under section 501(c)(3) of the Internal Revenue Code. We begin with an overview of the general characteristics of public charities and position them within the broader nonprofit sector. Then we discuss the characteristics of public charities in detail, including a look at these organizations by subsector, state, and metropolitan area.

Summary

- More than 1.4 million nonprofits were registered with the Internal Revenue Service (IRS) in 2013; about 1 million of these were registered as 501(c)(3) public charities.
- The 293,102 reporting public charities took in $1.73 trillion in revenue, spent $1.62 trillion in expenses, and had $3.22 trillion in assets in 2013.
- Public charities with $10 million or more in expenses accounted for 87 percent of total public charity expenses, despite only representing 5 percent of total public charities by number. Conversely, while over 77 percent of all public charities reported less than $500,000 in expenses, these organizations accounted for only 3 percent of total public charity expenses.
- Sixty-four percent of public charities have been founded since 1990.
- The largest subsector of public charities is the human services subsector; this subsector, which accounts for more than one-third of public charities, includes organizations that provide job training, legal aid, housing and disaster assistance, youth development, and food distribution programs, among others. Education, with a little less than one-fifth of organizations, is the second largest subsector.

- Fees for services and goods from private sources and government account for 72 percent of public charity revenues. If hospitals and higher education institutions are excluded, the proportion of revenue from fees for services and goods drops from 72 percent to 54 percent.
- The number of reporting public charities grew from 237,524 in 2003 to 293,102 in 2013, an increase of 23 percent.
- Over this same 10-year period, revenues of reporting public charities grew by 79 percent (an inflation-adjusted 42 percent), public support grew by 71 percent (an inflation-adjusted 35 percent), expenses grew by 73 percent (an inflation-adjusted 37 percent), and assets grew by 85 percent (an inflation-adjusted 46 percent).
- The number of reporting public charities per state ranged from 866 in Wyoming to 34,068 in California. Highly populated states like California, New York, and Texas have the most charities, while less populated states like Wyoming and North Dakota have fewer.
- Less populated states have more reporting public charities on a per capita basis than the more populated states. Vermont, Montana, Alaska, Maine, and Wyoming are the top five states in terms of nonprofit density per person.

Overview of the Nonprofit Sector

Approximately 1.4 million nonprofit organizations were registered with the IRS in 2013. This figure includes a wide variety of organizations, ranging from hospitals and educational institutions to social service organizations and performing arts groups. It excludes organizations that are not required to register with the Internal Revenue Service, such as nonprofits with less than $5,000 in annual revenue or religious congregations (although many congregations choose to register), and organizations whose tax-exempt status was revoked for failing to file a financial return for three consecutive years. See the section on Reporting Public Charities and tables 5.2 and 5.3 for more information on changes to filing requirements for nonprofit organizations.

The Internal Revenue Code defines more than 30 different categories of tax-exempt organizations. The largest group—501(c)(3) public charities—accounts for 67 percent of all nonprofit organizations and holds most of the sector's revenues and assets, over three-quarters and three-fifths, respectively. Other categories of nonprofit organizations include social welfare organizations (501(c)(4)), labor and agricultural associations (501(c)(5)), business leagues (501(c)(6)), and fraternal beneficiary societies (501(c)(8)), among others; see table 1.1 for a complete listing.

Approximately 35 percent of nonprofit organizations registered with the IRS were required to file a Form 990 (Form 990, Form 990-EZ, or Form 990-PF) in 2013. Private foundations, regardless of size, were required to file, as were other organizations that collected more than $50,000 in gross receipts. We refer to these 500,395 entities as reporting nonprofits. Reporting nonprofits accounted for approximately $2.26 trillion in revenue, $2.10 trillion in expenses, and $5.17 trillion in assets.

As displayed in table 5.1, while the overall number of nonprofits registered with the IRS grew by only 3 percent from 2003 to 2013, the number of reporting nonprofits grew by 14 percent.[1] Most growth in the sector occurred between 2003 and 2008. When only 501(c)(3) public charities registered with the IRS are considered, we see a 20 percent increase—about 17 percentage points greater than the growth rate for all registered nonprofits over the decade. Public charities increased from about 58 percent of all nonprofits in 2003 to about 67 percent of nonprofits by 2013.

Despite covering a period of economic recession, revenues and assets for reporting nonprofits grew at respectable rates over the last 10 years—31 percent and 33 percent, respectively—after adjusting for inflation. This compares to a 14 percent inflation-adjusted growth rate of the U.S. gross domestic product over the same time period.

Reporting Public Charities

The remainder of this chapter focuses on reporting public charities. These are 501(c)(3) organizations that have charitable purposes (i.e., assisting the poor and underprivileged; advancing religion, education, health, science, art, or culture; protecting the environment; or other purposes beneficial to the community), rely primarily on support from the general public or government, and are required to file Form 990 or Form 990-EZ with the IRS. Table 5.2 outlines the registration and filing requirements for all 501(c)(3) nonprofits.

Congregations, most religious primary and secondary schools, and other religious organizations are not required to apply for tax-exempt status with the IRS, so most do not register. Financial figures in this chapter include religious organizations that nonetheless filed Forms 990 or Forms 990-EZ.

The Pension Protection Act of 2006 mandated that nonprofits with less than $25,000 in annual gross receipts file a Form 990-N, also known as the e-Postcard.[2] The act also called for automatic revocation of tax-exempt status for nonprofits that failed to file a return for three consecutive years. These smaller organizations previously had no reporting responsibilities to the IRS, but they are now required to file annually. As an alternative to Form 990-N, these smaller organizations can opt to complete Form 990 or Form 990-EZ to satisfy their filing requirement.

In addition, the IRS redesigned Form 990 for organizations starting with tax year 2008. Given the extent of the changes on the form, the IRS adjusted the filing thresholds to allow organizations additional time to collect the information needed to complete the redesigned Form 990. Table 5.3 lists the filing thresholds for tax years 2007 through 2013.

Before tax year 2010, nonprofits with gross receipts of $25,000 or more (excluding religious congregations) were required to file a Form 990 or Form 990-EZ. Beginning

1. See the next section, "Reporting Public Charities," for details regarding the definition of reporting public charities used in this chapter.
2. The threshold for filing increased to $50,000 starting in tax year 2010.

Table 5.1. Size and Financial Scope of the Nonprofit Sector, 2003–13

	2003	2008	Percentage change, 2003–08	Percentage change, 2003–08 (inflation adjusted)	2013	Percentage change, 2003–13	Percentage change, 2003–13 (inflation adjusted)
All registered nonprofits	**1.38 million**	**1.54 million**	**11.7**	—	**1.41 million**	**2.8**	—
Reporting nonprofits	437,364	510,089	16.6	—	500,395	14.4	—
Revenues ($)	1.36 trillion	1.93 trillion	42.2	21.5	2.26 trillion	66.3	31.4
Expenses ($)	1.30 trillion	1.82 trillion	40.0	19.6	2.10 trillion	61.5	27.6
Assets ($)	3.06 trillion	4.33 trillion	41.5	20.9	5.17 trillion	68.8	33.3
Public charities, 501(c)(3)	**798,987**	**975,770**	**22.1**	—	**954,476**	**19.5**	—
Reporting public charities	237,524	286,500	20.6	—	293,102	23.4	—
Revenues ($)	968 billion	1.44 trillion	48.7	27.1	1.73 trillion	79.2	41.5
Expenses ($)	938 billion	1.34 trillion	42.9	22.1	1.62 trillion	73.1	36.7
Assets ($)	1.74 trillion	2.59 trillion	48.6	27.0	3.22 trillion	85.0	46.[illegible]

Sources: Urban Institute, National Center for Charitable Statistics, Core Files (Public Charities, 2003, 2008, and 2013); Internal Revenue Service Business Master Files, Exempt Organizations (2003–13).

Notes: Reporting public charities include only organizations that both reported (filed IRS Forms 990) and were required to do so (had $25,000 or more in gross receipts). Organizations that had their tax-exempt status revoked for failing to file a financial return for three consecutive years have been removed from the 2009 nonprofit total. The following were also excluded: foreign organizations, government-associated organizations, and organizations without state identifiers. All amounts are in current dollars and are not adjusted for inflation.

— = not applicable

Table 5.2. Registration and Filing Requirements for 501(c)(3) Organizations, 2013

	One-time registration for tax exemption	Annual reporting to IRS
Nonreligious public charities		
Less than $5,000 in annual gross receipts	Optional	Required
$5,000 to $24,999 in annual gross receipts	Required	Required
$25,000 or more in annual gross receipts	Required	Required
Religious public charities		
Congregations, religious primary and secondary schools, denominations and integrated auxiliaries	Optional	Optional
Religiously affiliated hospitals, universities, human service organizations, and others	Required to follow nonreligious public charity regulations	Required to follow nonreligious public charity regulations
Private foundations	Required regardless of size	Required regardless of size

Source: Internal Revenue Service (www.irs.gov).

Table 5.3. IRS Filing Requirements for Tax-Exempt Organizations, Tax Years 2007–Present

	Form to file
2007 tax year (filed in 2008 or 2009)	
Gross receipts normally less than or equal to $25,000	990-N or 990-EZ or 990
Gross receipts less than $100,000, and Total assets less than $250,000	990-EZ or 990
Gross receipts greater than or equal to $100,000, or Total assets greater than or equal to $250,000	990
Private foundation	990-PF
2008 tax year (filed in 2009 or 2010)	
Gross receipts normally less than or equal to $25,000	990-N or 990-EZ or 990
Gross receipts less than $1 million, and Total assets less than $2.5 million	990-EZ or 990
Gross receipts greater than or equal to $1 million, or Total assets greater than or equal to $2.5 million	990
Private foundation	990-PF
2009 tax year (filed in 2010 or 2011)	
Gross receipts normally less than or equal to $25,000	990-N or 990-EZ or 990
Gross receipts less than $500,000, and Total assets less than $1.25 million	990-EZ or 990

(continued)

Table 5.3. IRS Filing Requirements for Tax-Exempt Organizations, Tax Years 2007–Present *(continued)*

	Form to file
Gross receipts greater than or equal to $500,000, or Total assets greater than or equal to $1.25 million	990
Private foundation	990-PF
2010 and later tax years (filed in 2011 and later)	
Gross receipts normally less than or equal to $50,000	990-N or 990-EZ or 990
Gross receipts less than $200,000, and Total assets less than $500,000	990-EZ or 990
Gross receipts greater than or equal to $200,000, or Total assets greater than or equal to $500,000	990
Private foundation	990-PF

Source: Internal Revenue Service (www.irs.gov).

in 2010, only organizations with $50,000 or more in gross receipts (excluding religious congregations) were required to file a Form 990 or Form 990-EZ. This change could have led some readers to draw inaccurate conclusions regarding the change in the number and finances of reporting public charities when comparing figures from years prior to 2010 with those in 2010 and later years, since these changes would have also reflected the raising of the minimum threshold. To facilitate accurate comparison between years, the authors elected to include only organizations reporting $50,000 or more in gross receipts in the analysis presented in this chapter, regardless of the filing requirements of that year. Consequently, readers should be aware that the definition of "reporting public charities" used in this chapter does exclude some organizations that were required to file with the IRS, namely those that filed with gross receipts between $25,000 and $50,000 in years prior to 2010.

Reporting Public Charities by Size and Age

In 2013, public charities reported $1.73 trillion in revenue, $1.62 trillion in expenses, and $3.22 trillion in total assets. The largest organizations, primarily hospitals and higher education organizations, dominate these figures. About two-thirds of public charities reported less than $500,000 in total expenses (figure 5.1). In 2013, 30 percent of organizations reported less than $100,000 in expenses and another 37 percent reported between $100,000 and $500,000 in expenses. Twenty-three percent of public charities reported expenses greater than $1 million. These larger organizations, however, account for the vast majority of total expenditures. Organizations with $10 million or more in expenses account for just 5 percent of all nonprofits but more than 86 percent of total

Figure 5.1. Number and Expenses of Reporting Public Charities, 2013

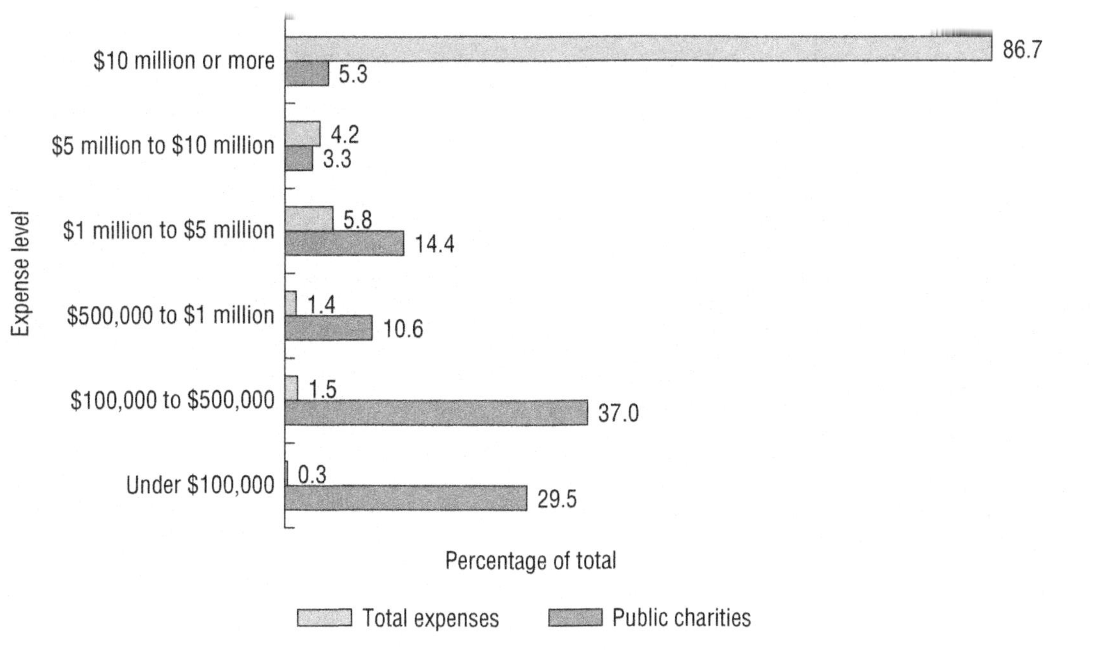

Source: National Center for Charitable Statistics, Core Files (2013).

expenses. Conversely, organizations reporting under $500,000 in total expenses account for approximately 66 percent of all charities but less than 2 percent of total expenditures.

Not surprisingly, the larger organizations tend to be older. Fifty-three percent of organizations with $10 million or more in total expenses report a founding date prior to 1980. Over two-thirds of organizations with less than $500,000 in total expenses report a founding date after 1989 (table 5.4).

Reporting Public Charities by Subsector

Over one-third of all public charities are human service providers, which includes organizations that provide job training, legal aid, housing, youth development services, disaster assistance, food distribution, and other similar programs (table 5.5). Education organizations account for the second largest group at 17 percent. This category includes higher education as well as preschools, parent-teacher organizations, and alumni associations. Health organizations such as hospitals, blood banks, medical research, and mental health centers account for the third-highest percentage at 13 percent.

Table 5.5 also distinguishes operating public charities from supporting public charities. Supporting public charities primarily distribute funds to operating public charities. Such charities can support a particular operating public charity or a group of public charities. In 2013, supporting organizations accounted for 19 percent of all public charities. The education subsector reported the largest number of supporting

Table 5.4. Reporting Public Charities by Founding Date, 2013 (percent)

Total expenses	Before 1950	1950–59	1960–69	1970–79	1980–89	1990–99	2000–10	2010–13	Unknown	Total
Under $100,000	1.8	1.5	4.8	6.8	11.7	20.5	33.3	19.3	0.2	100.0
$100,000 to $499,999	1.7	1.7	4.0	8.1	14.4	24.2	32.7	13.1	0.2	100.0
$500,000 to $999,999	2.9	2.5	5.1	11.9	18.7	25.4	25.6	7.9	0.1	100.0
$1 million to $4.99 million	5.0	3.5	7.1	15.1	19.4	22.9	20.7	6.2	0.2	100.0
$5 million to $9.99 million	9.0	5.0	11.0	16.7	17.9	18.9	16.6	4.8	0.2	100.0
$10 million or more	19.4	8.1	11.1	14.5	15.8	15.7	11.1	4.1	0.2	100.0
All public charities	**3.5**	**2.5**	**5.4**	**9.7**	**15.0**	**22.4**	**28.7**	**12.6**	**0.2**	**100.0**

Source: Urban Institute, National Center for Charitable Statistics, Core Files (Public Charities, 2013).
Note: The founding date is the year in which the organization officially received tax-exempt status from the IRS and may not be the year in which the organization was founded.

Table 5.5. Reporting Public Charities by Subsector, 2013

Subsector	Operating public charities	%	Supporting public charities	%	Total public charities	%
Arts, culture, and humanities	25,984	10.9	3,153	5.7	29,137	9.9
Education	34,639	14.6	15,623	28.2	50,262	17.1
Environment and animals	10,938	4.6	2,345	4.2	13,283	4.5
Health	28,483	12.0	9,249	16.7	37,732	12.9
Human services	94,440	39.7	9,564	17.2	104,004	35.5
International and foreign affairs	5,538	2.3	767	1.4	6,305	2.2
Other public and societal benefit	21,205	8.9	12,872	23.2	34,077	11.6
Religion-related	16,405	6.9	1,897	3.4	18,302	6.2
Total	**237,632**	**100.0**	**55,470**	**100.0**	**293,102**	**100.0**

Source: Urban Institute, National Center for Charitable Statistics, Core Files (Public Charities, 2013).

organizations. Education support organizations include school booster clubs, college fundraising organizations, and public education funds that raise money to help public school districts. Other supporting organizations include community foundations and federation giving programs such as United Way organizations.

Finances of Reporting Public Charities

In 2013, public charities reported total revenues of $1.73 trillion. The single largest source of funding for the nonprofit sector is fee-for-service revenue from private sources, which includes tuition payments, hospital patient revenues (excluding Medicare and Medicaid), and ticket sales. Fee-for-service revenue from private sources accounted for 48 percent of total nonprofit revenues in 2013. Fees from government sources, such as Medicare and Medicaid payments and government contracts, accounted for another 24 percent of revenue. Private contributions, including individual contributions and grants from foundations and corporations, accounted for 13 percent, and government grants accounted for another 8 percent of total revenue. Funding from government, both fees for services and government grants, accounted for nearly one-third of all nonprofit revenue (32 percent). Other income, which includes dues and assessments, rental income, and income from special events accounted for less than 2 percent of revenue (figure 5.2). Investment income, which has continued to recover from stock market losses caused by the recession, accounted for 5 percent of nonprofit revenue in 2013.

Since hospitals and higher education make up such a large proportion of total public charity revenue, the distribution of sources of revenue changes significantly if they are excluded. Hospitals and higher education rely heavily on revenue from fees

Figure 5.2. Sources of Revenue for Reporting Public Charities, 2013 (percent)

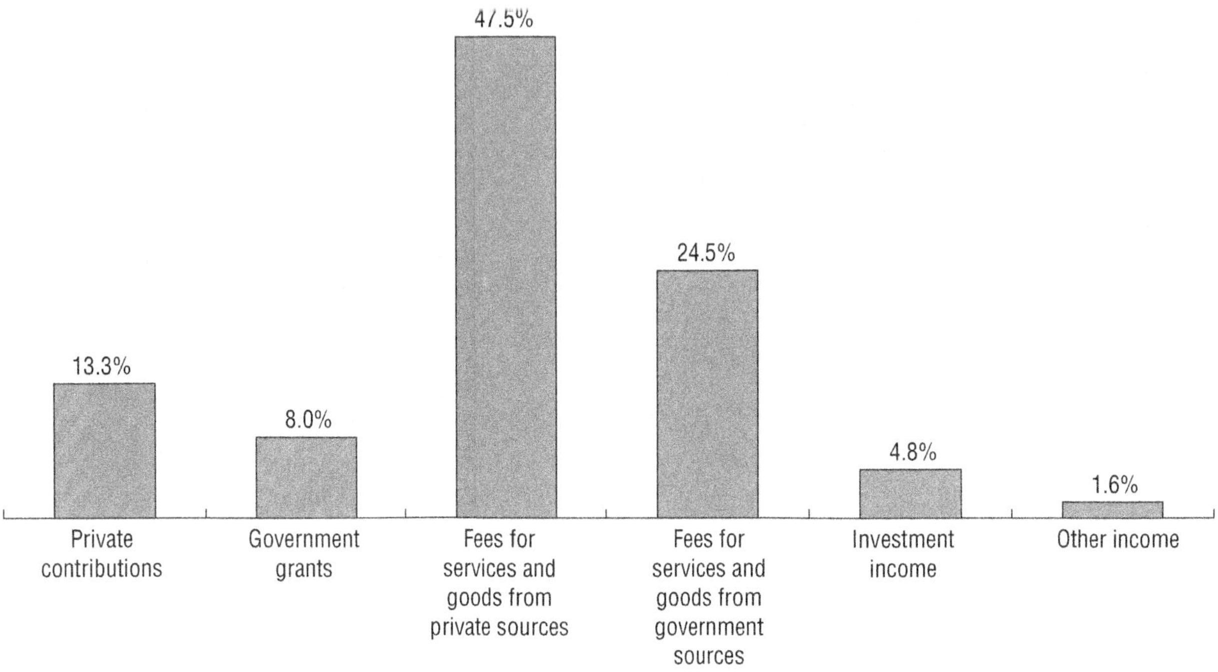

Sources: NCCS calculations of IRS Statistics of Income Division Exempt Organizations Sample (2009, 2011); Urban Institute, National Center for Charitable Statistics, Core Files (Public Charities, 2013); American Hospital Association (AHA) 2012 survey; and National Health Accounts, produced by CMS.

for services and goods from government; when these organizations are excluded from the public charity totals, the proportion of revenue from these sources drops from 72 percent to 54 percent. Hospitals and higher education also derive a lower proportion of their revenue from public support (private contributions and government grants combined) than the rest of the nonprofit sector. Public support accounts for 21 percent of nonprofit revenue when hospitals and higher education are included, compared with 38 percent when they are removed (figure 5.3).

Table 5.6 presents a detailed view of public charities' revenue, expenses, and assets. Revenues generated from contributions, fees for services, investment income, and government grants are included. Expenses are broken down into wages, benefits, fees, interest, and more.

Revenues, expenses, and assets are further separated by supporting public charities and operating public charities, which have distinct differences in their distribution of revenue and expenses. Supporting organizations rely more heavily on private contributions than operating public charities (28 percent versus 11 percent) and less on fees for services (51 percent versus 76 percent).

Ninety percent of the over $1.62 trillion in expenses reported by public charities in 2013 was used for operating expenses such as wages, supplies, and fees. Expenses for paid personnel (which includes salaries, wages, benefits, and payroll tax) accounted

Figure 5.3. Sources of Revenue for Reporting Public Charities, Excluding Hospitals and Higher Education, 2013 (percent)

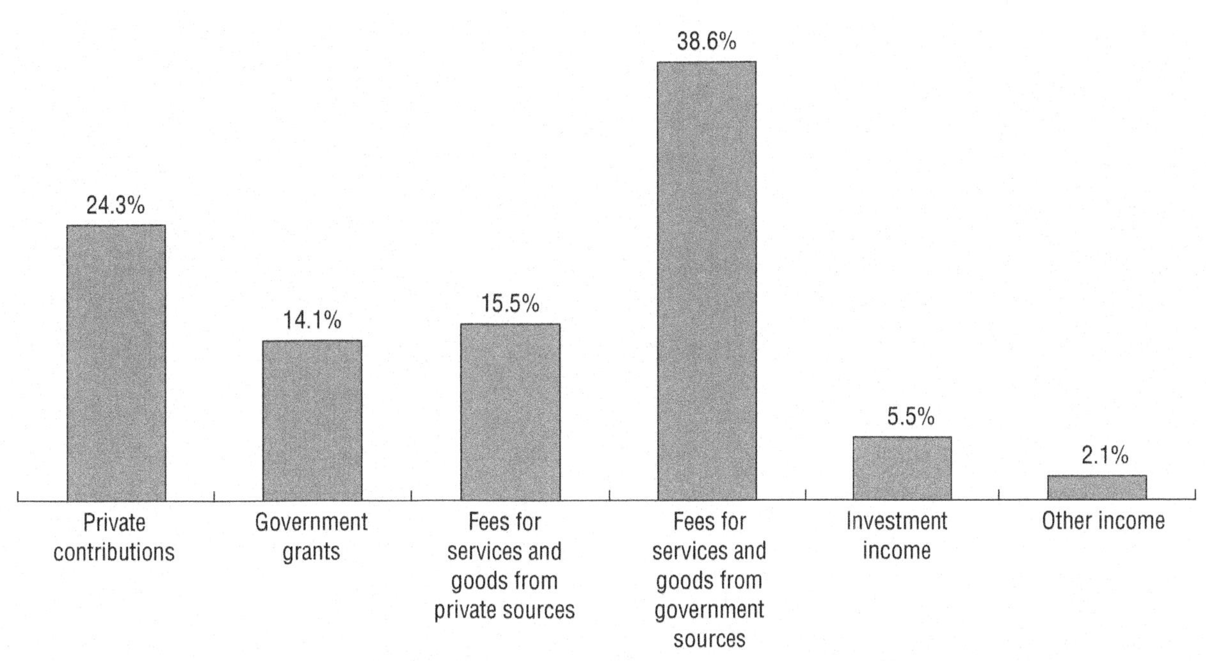

Sources: NCCS calculations of IRS Statistics of Income Division Exempt Organizations Sample (2009, 2011); Urban Institute, National Center for Charitable Statistics, Core Files (Public Charities, 2013); American Hospital Association (AHA) 2012 survey; and National Health Accounts, produced by CMS.

for 46 percent of total expenses. "Other expenses" was the second-largest category at 22 percent. While IRS Form 990 provides more than 25 separate expense breakdowns designed to cover most expenses that nonprofits incur, over two-thirds of organizations reported "other" expenses in 2013. Often the expenses listed in the "other" category can be allocated to an existing line item. Common types of expenses reported as "other" include consulting and insurance.

Operating expenses also vary between operating and supporting organizations. Operating organizations spend more on salaries and benefits than supporting organizations (48 percent versus 37 percent) and less on grants (7 percent versus 23 percent).

Growth in the Number of Reporting Public Charities, 2003–13

The number of reporting public charities grew 23 percent from 2003 to 2013, increasing by 55,578 organizations.[3] Growth among individual subsectors varied greatly over this

3. See section entitled "Reporting Public Charities" at the beginning of this chapter for an important note regarding the definition of reporting public charities used in this analysis.

Table 5.6. Revenues and Expenses for Reporting Public Charities, 2013

	All Organizations		Operating Organizations		Supporting Organizations	
	$ millions	%	$ millions	%	$ millions	%
Public support	368,323.7	21	285,663.0	19	82,660.7	35
Private contributions	230,295.5	13	163,170.7	11	67,124.8	28
Direct contributions	209,050.4	12	147,792.8	10	61,257.6	26
Indirect contributions	21,245.1	1	15,377.9	1	5,867.2	2
Government grants	138,028.5	8	122,492.4	8	15,536.2	7
Fee for service	1,254,990.9	72	1,134,089.6	76	120,901.3	51
Fees from government sources	424,443.7	24	385,639.3	26	38,804.4	16
Fees from private sources	824,335.0	48	742,238.1	50	82,096.9	35
Net income from sale of inventory	6,212.2	0	5,013.5	0	1,198.8	1
Investment income	83,760.0	5	54,113.1	4	29,646.9	12
Dividends, interest, and other similar amounts	30,471.8	2	19,546.3	1	10,925.4	5
Net gain on sale of assets or securities	50,154.1	3	32,139.7	2	18,014.4	8
Other investment income	3,134.2	0	2,427.1	0	707.1	0
Other income	28,456.8	2	23,416.2	2	5,040.6	2
Net income from special events	2,947.4	0	2,398.1	0	549.2	0
Other revenue	25,509.4	1	21,018.0	1	4,491.4	2
Total revenue	**1,734,101.6**	**100**	**1,496,805.7**	**100**	**237,295.9**	**100**
Paid personnel	750,792.2	46	676,251.0	48	74,541.2	37
Wages and salaries	604,339.0	37	542,933.1	38	61,405.9	30
Compensation of officers	73,437.0	5	60,749.0	4	12,688.0	6
Other wages and salaries	530,902.0	33	482,184.1	34	48,717.9	24
Fringe benefits and payroll tax	146,453.2	9	133,317.9	9	13,135.3	6
Pension plan contributions	28,009.2	2	25,315.2	2	2,694.0	1
Other employee benefits	79,449.4	5	72,481.1	5	6,968.3	3
Payroll taxes	38,994.6	2	35,521.6	2	3,473.0	2
Supplies	54,386.9	3	50,026.8	4	4,360.1	2
Communications (printing, phone, etc.)	46,534.8	3	38,645.3	3	7,889.5	4
Professional fees	127,558.5	8	110,525.9	8	17,032.6	8

(continued)

Table 5.6. Revenues and Expenses for Reporting Public Charities, 2013 *(continued)*

	All Organizations		Operating Organizations		Supporting Organizations	
	$ millions	%	$ millions	%	$ millions	%
Occupancy	49,256.5	3	44,339.0	3	4,917.5	2
Interest	22,574.2	1	19,393.8	1	3,180.4	2
Depreciation and depletion	67,376.1	4	60,754.5	4	6,621.6	3
Other	350,001.8	22	313,338.2	22	36,663.5	18
Total current operating expenses	1,468,480.9	90	1,313,274.5	92	155,206.4	77
Grants and benefits	149,835.1	9	103,532.3	7	46,302.8	23
Grants and allocations	88,380.1	5	47,087.8	3	41,292.4	20
Specific assistance to individuals	46,966.4	3	44,367.5	3	2,598.9	1
Benefits paid to members	14,488.5	1	12,077.0	1	2,411.6	1
Payments to affiliates	5,472.2	0	4,407.5	0	1,064.7	1
Total expenses	**1,623,788.2**	**100**	**1,421,214.3**	**100**	**202,573.9**	**100**
Net income (revenue – expenses)	110,313.5		75,591.5		34,722.0	
Total assets	**3,224,987.3**		**2,466,703.0**		**758,284.4**	
Total liabilities	1,245,828.1		1,007,944.5		237,883.6	
Net assets (assets – liabilities)	**1,979,134.0**		**1,458,736.2**		**520,397.8**	

Sources: Urban Institute, National Center for Charitable Statistics, Core Files (Public Charities, 2013), Core Full 990 Files (Public Charities, 2012–13) and Core Supplement Files (2013); and Internal Revenue Service, Statistics of Income Sample Files (Public Charities, 2007–12).

Notes: Authors' calculations are based on U.S. Internal Revenue Service Forms 990 and 990-EZ, classified according to the National Taxonomy of Exempt Entities—Core Codes, and adjusted by the National Center for Charitable Statistics based on available data. See the methodology section at the end of the chapter for more information on how the estimates were created. Reporting public charities include only organizations that both reported (filed IRS Forms 990) and were required to do so. The following were excluded: foreign organizations, government-associated organizations, organizations without state identifiers, and organizations excluded by the authors' discretion. Organizations not required to report include religious congregations and organizations with less than $25,000 in gross receipts. The table includes separate analyses for operating public charities and supporting organizations to clarify the distribution of funds and to avoid double-counting the financial information for supporting organizations (see the methodology section at the end of this chapter for a detailed description of the methodology). The sum of the dollar amounts may not equal due to rounding. Percentages for revenue items and net income are expressed as percentages of total revenue. Program service revenue figures may include sizable income via government contracts, which the data source is unable to differentiate from funds raised via the public (i.e., fees for services). Percentages for current operating expense items are expressed as percentages of total current operating expenses. Percentages for other expense items, assets, and liabilities are expressed as percentages of total expenses.

time period. Health organizations saw the smallest growth at 8 percent, while the number of environmental and animal-related organizations increased 51 percent (table 5.7).

The three smallest subsectors—environment and animal, international, and religion-related—exhibited the greatest growth in number of organizations over the 10 years. Environment and animals increased by 51 percent, for an average annual increase of 4.2 percent; international and foreign affairs grew by 46 percent, for an average annual increase of 3.8 percent; and religion-related organizations grew 43 percent, for an average annual increase of 3.6 percent.

Human services, the largest subsector, grew 24 percent from 2003 to 2013. Within the human services, three subsectors actually experienced small amounts of decline: children and youth services organizations declined by 6 percent, residential and custodial care organizations declined by 3 percent, and employment and job-related organizations declined by less than 1 percent. Growth was greatest among food, agriculture, and nutrition organizations, which increased in number by 58 percent. Public safety and disaster preparedness organizations and recreation and sports organizations (which include amateur sports leagues, Special Olympics, fairs, and playgrounds) also experienced marked growth, increasing by 57 and 55 percent, respectively (table 5.8).

The health subsector showed the least growth in number of public charities from 2003 to 2013: 8 percent. Despite the low growth, only nursing service organizations and hospitals and primary treatment facilities saw outright decline. The former experienced a decline of 12 percent and the latter a decline of less than 1 percent. Disease-specific

Table 5.7. Change in the Number of Reporting Public Charities, by Subsector, 2003, 2008, and 2013

				Total Percentage Change	Average Annual Percentage Change		
Subsector	2003	2008	2013	2003–13	2003–13	2003–08	2008–13
Arts, culture, and humanities	24,013	29,301	29,137	21.3	2.0	4.1	–0.1
Education	40,194	49,422	50,262	25.0	2.3	4.2	0.3
Environment and animal-related	8,821	11,874	13,283	50.6	4.2	6.1	2.3
Health	34,847	38,580	37,732	8.3	0.8	2.1	–0.4
Human services	83,644	99,468	104,004	24.3	2.2	3.5	0.9
International and foreign affairs	4,329	5,553	6,305	45.6	3.8	5.1	2.6
Public and societal benefit	28,838	35,122	34,077	18.2	1.7	4.0	–0.6
Religion-related	12,838	17,180	18,302	42.6	3.6	6.0	1.3
All	**237,524**	**286,500**	**293,102**	**23.4**	**2.1**	**3.8**	**0.5**

Source: Urban Institute, National Center for Charitable Statistics, Core Files (Public Charities, 2003, 2008, and 2013).

Table 5.8. Change in the Number of Reporting Public Charities, by Detailed Subsector, 2003, 2008, and 2013

				Total Percentage Change	Average Annual Percentage Change		
Subsector	2003	2008	2013	2003–13	2003–13	2003–08	2008–13
All public charities	**237,524**	**286,500**	**293,102**	**23.4**	**2.1**	**3.8**	**0.5**
Arts, culture, and humanities	**24,013**	**29,301**	**29,137**	**21.3**	**2.0**	**4.1**	**–0.1**
Performing arts organizations	8,091	10,049	10,226	26.4	2.4	4.4	0.3
Historical societies and related	3,452	4,195	3,907	13.2	1.2	4.0	–1.4
Museums and museum activities	2,703	3,217	3,168	17.2	1.6	3.5	–0.3
Other arts, culture, and humanities	9,767	11,840	11,836	21.2	1.9	3.9	0.0
Education	**40,194**	**49,422**	**50,262**	**25.0**	**2.3**	**4.2**	**0.3**
Higher education institutions	1,782	1,961	2,050	15.0	1.4	1.9	0.9
Student services and organizations	4,319	5,582	5,240	21.3	2.0	5.3	–1.3
Elementary and secondary education	10,065	11,761	12,721	26.4	2.4	3.2	1.6
Other education	24,028	30,118	30,251	25.9	2.3	4.6	0.1
Environment and animal-related	**8,821**	**11,874**	**13,283**	**50.6**	**4.2**	**6.1**	**2.3**
Environment	5,049	6,433	6,460	27.9	2.5	5.0	0.1
Animal-related	3,772	5,441	6,823	80.9	6.1	7.6	4.6

(continued)

Table 5.8. Change in the Number of Reporting Public Charities, by Detailed Subsector, 2003, 2008, and 2013 *(continued)*

				Total Percentage Change	Average Annual Percentage Change		
Subsector	2003	2008	2013	2003–13	2003–13	2003–08	2008–13
Health	**34,847**	**38,580**	**37,732**	**8.3**	**0.8**	**2.1**	**-0.4**
Nursing services	2,709	2,616	2,375	–12.3	–1.3	–0.7	–1.9
Hospitals and primary treatment facilities	3,847	3,933	3,827	–0.5	–0.1	0.4	–0.5
Treatment facilities—outpatient	2,794	3,072	3,158	13.0	1.2	1.9	0.6
Mental health	7,497	8,156	7,720	3.0	0.3	1.7	–1.1
Disease-specific-general	5,308	6,931	7,344	38.4	3.3	5.5	1.2
Medical research	1,713	1,903	1,736	1.3	0.1	2.1	–1.8
Other health	10,979	11,969	11,572	5.4	0.5	1.7	-0.7
Human services	**83,644**	**99,468**	**104,004**	**24.3**	**2.2**	**3.5**	**0.9**
Crime and legal-related	4,387	4,991	5,054	15.2	1.4	2.6	0.3
Employment and job-related	3,739	3,798	3,725	–0.4	0.0	0.3	–0.4
Food, agriculture, and nutrition	2,288	2,905	3,615	58.0	4.7	4.9	4.5
Housing and shelter	13,790	15,621	15,978	15.9	1.5	2.5	0.5

Public safety and disaster preparedness	3,661	5,083	5,744	56.9	4.6	6.8	2.5
Recreation and sports	16,081	22,261	24,950	55.2	4.5	6.7	2.3
Youth development	6,065	7,054	7,061	16.4	1.5	3.1	0.0
Children and youth services	6,537	6,844	6,165	–5.7	–0.6	0.9	–2.1
Family services	3,729	4,209	4,158	11.5	1.1	2.5	–0.2
Residential and custodial care	5,397	5,557	5,219	–3.3	–0.3	0.6	–1.2
Services promoting independence	7,838	8,692	8,717	11.2	1.1	2.1	0.1
Other human services	10,132	12,453	13,618	34.4	3.0	4.2	1.8
International and foreign affairs	**4,329**	**5,553**	**6,305**	**45.6**	**3.8**	**5.1**	**2.6**
Public and societal benefit	**28,838**	**35,122**	**34,077**	**18.2**	**1.7**	**4.0**	**-0.6**
Civil rights and advocacy	1,622	1,922	1,907	17.6	1.6	3.5	–0.2
Community improvement	10,819	13,118	13,124	21.3	2.0	3.9	0.0
Philanthropy and voluntarism	11,392	13,645	12,061	5.9	0.6	3.7	–2.4
Science and technology	1,507	1,787	1,782	18.2	1.7	3.5	–0.1
Social science	595	732	759	27.6	2.5	4.2	0.7
Other public and societal benefit	2,903	3,918	4,444	53.1	4.4	6.2	2.6
Religion-related	**12,838**	**17,180**	**18,302**	**42.6**	**3.6**	**6.0**	**1.3**

Source: Urban Institute, National Center for Charitable Statistics, Core Files (Public Charities, 2003, 2008, and 2013).

organizations contributed to most of the increase in the number of organizations, with a 38 percent increase.

Growth in Revenue of Reporting Public Charities

Total revenue grew from about $968 billion in 2003 to about $1.73 trillion in 2013, an increase of 79 percent, or an average annual growth of roughly 6 percent (table 5.9). This represents a 42 percent inflation-adjusted increase over the last 10 years.

Growth varied widely across the subsectors. Arts, culture, and humanities organizations had the smallest growth in revenue at 52 percent (20 percent after adjusting for inflation). Within this group, museums grew faster than average at approximately 71 percent (about 35 percent after adjusting for inflation), while performing arts organizations grew more slowly than average (only 44 percent, or 13 percent after adjusting for inflation) (table 5.10). Human services organizations experienced the second-slowest revenue growth over the 10 years, with revenue growing by 59 percent (26 percent after adjusting for inflation). Within this subsector, children and youth services and family services had the smallest overall growth, at 27 percent and 33 percent, respectively (the

Table 5.9. Change in Total Revenue for Reporting Public Charities, by Subsector, 2003, 2008, and 2013 ($ millions)

				Total Percentage Change	Average Annual Percentage Change		
Subsector	2003	2008	2013	2003–13	2003–13	2003–08	2008–13
Arts, culture, and humanities	22,046	31,962	33,596	52.4	4.3	7.7	1.0
Education	159,645	266,339	296,282	85.6	6.4	10.8	2.2
Environment and animal-related	9,006	13,716	16,691	85.3	6.4	8.8	4.0
Health	565,964	816,899	1,025,317	81.2	6.1	7.6	4.6
Human services	134,574	180,843	214,195	59.2	4.8	6.1	3.4
International and foreign affairs	17,074	31,812	32,420	89.9	6.6	13.3	0.4
Public and societal benefit	51,798	86,063	100,245	93.5	6.8	10.7	3.1
Religion-related	7,833	12,101	15,355	96.0	7.0	9.1	4.9
All public charities	**967,941**	**1,439,735**	**1,734,102**	**79.2**	**6.0**	**8.3**	**3.8**

Source: Urban Institute, National Center for Charitable Statistics, Core Files (Public Charities, 2003, 2008, and 2013).
Note: Figures are shown in current dollars and are not adjusted for inflation.

Table 5.10. Change in Total Revenue for Reporting Public Charities, by Detailed Subsector, 2003, 2008, and 2013 ($ millions)

Subsector	2003	2008	2013	Total Percentage Change	Average Annual Percentage Change		
				2003–13	2003–13	2003–08	2008–13
All public charities	**967,941**	**1,439,735**	**1,734,102**	**79.2**	**6.0**	**8.3**	**3.8**
Arts, culture, and humanities	**22,046**	**31,962**	**33,596**	**52.4**	**4.3**	**7.7**	**1.0**
Performing arts organizations	7,149	9,704	10,267	43.6	3.7	6.3	1.1
Historical societies and related	1,608	2,445	2,507	55.9	4.5	8.7	0.5
Museums and museum activities	4,838	7,753	8,253	70.6	5.5	9.9	1.3
Other arts, culture, and humanities	8,452	12,060	12,569	48.7	4.0	7.4	0.8
Education	**159,645**	**266,339**	**296,282**	**85.6**	**6.4**	**10.8**	**2.2**
Higher education institutions	104,628	168,414	188,094	79.8	6.0	10.0	2.2
Student services and organizations	3,253	5,088	5,339	64.1	5.1	9.4	1.0
Elementary and secondary education	23,449	37,248	48,958	108.8	7.6	9.7	5.6
Other education	28,316	55,588	53,891	90.3	6.6	14.4	–0.6
Environment and animal-related	**9,006**	**13,716**	**16,691**	**85.3**	**6.4**	**8.8**	**4.0**
Environment	5,126	8,173	9,220	79.9	6.0	9.8	2.4
Animal-related	3,880	5,543	7,471	92.6	6.8	7.4	6.2

(continued)

Table 5.10. Change in Total Revenue for Reporting Public Charities, by Detailed Subsector, 2003, 2008, and 2013 ($ millions) *(continued)*

Subsector	2003	2008	2013	Total Percentage Change	Average Annual Percentage Change		
				2003–13	2003–13	2003–08	2008–13
Health	**565,964**	**816,899**	**1,025,317**	**81.2**	**6.1**	**7.6**	**4.6**
Nursing services	21,319	26,829	29,059	36.3	3.1	4.7	1.6
Hospitals and primary treatment facilities	417,553	589,961	724,027	73.4	5.7	7.2	4.2
Treatment facilities—outpatient	60,338	95,682	138,180	129.0	8.6	9.7	7.6
Mental health	22,092	28,161	30,811	39.5	3.4	5.0	1.8
Disease-specific-general	10,071	15,093	17,581	74.6	5.7	8.4	3.1
Medical research	5,592	11,469	10,517	88.1	6.5	15.4	–1.7
Other health	29,000	49,704	75,142	159.1	10.0	11.4	8.6
Human services	**134,574**	**180,843**	**214,195**	**59.2**	**4.8**	**6.1**	**3.4**
Crime and legal-related	5,177	6,849	7,356	42.1	3.6	5.8	1.4
Employment and job-related	9,998	12,847	16,037	60.4	4.8	5.1	4.5
Food, agriculture, and nutrition	4,769	6,588	11,979	151.2	9.6	6.7	12.7
Housing and shelter	13,551	20,544	24,179	78.4	6.0	8.7	3.3
Public safety and disaster preparedness	1,292	1,926	2,503	93.8	6.8	8.3	5.4

Recreation and sports	7,577	11,528	16,114	112.7	7.8	8.8	6.9
Youth development	5,314	7,082	7,840	47.5	4.0	5.9	2.1
Children and youth services	9,853	12,395	12,510	27.0	2.4	4.7	0.2
Family services	5,247	6,578	6,957	32.6	2.9	4.6	1.1
Residential and custodial care	24,376	32,827	37,380	53.4	4.4	6.1	2.6
Services promoting independence	20,967	28,132	32,933	57.1	4.6	6.1	3.2
Other human services	26,453	33,549	38,406	45.2	3.8	4.9	2.7
International and foreign affairs	**17,074**	**31,812**	**32,420**	**89.9**	**6.6**	**13.3**	**0.4**
Public and societal benefit	**51,798**	**86,063**	**100,245**	**93.5**	**6.8**	**10.7**	**3.1**
Civil rights and advocacy	1,553	2,136	2,553	64.4	5.1	6.6	3.6
Community improvement	11,307	16,583	18,474	63.4	5.0	8.0	2.2
Philanthropy and voluntarism	17,888	33,004	42,221	136.0	9.0	13.0	5.0
Science and technology	11,296	18,277	20,582	82.2	6.2	10.1	2.4
Social science	1,273	2,357	2,866	125.2	8.5	13.1	4.0
Other public and societal benefit	8,482	13,706	13,549	59.7	4.8	10.1	–0.2
Religion-related	**7,833**	**12,101**	**15,355**	**96.0**	**7.0**	**9.1**	**4.9**

Source: Urban Institute, National Center for Charitable Statistics, Core Files (Public Charities, 2003, 2008, and 2013).
Note: Figures are not adjusted for inflation.

growth for children and youth services is just barely positive after adjusting for inflation, while family services grew 5 percent after adjusting for inflation). Religion-related organizations experienced the largest growth in revenues, at 96 percent during the time period (55 percent after adjusting for inflation). Health, which accounts for over half the sector's revenue, experienced what was, for the sector, slightly above average growth in revenue at 81 percent (43 percent after adjusting for inflation).

It is evident in the last two columns of table 5.10 that most of the revenue growth occurred between 2003 and 2008, the years leading up to the recession. The average annual change dropped from 8.3 percent for the years 2003 to 2008 to 3.8 percent for 2008 to 2013. Every subsector witnessed a similar drop in the latter span. International and foreign affairs organizations saw the largest decline in growth when comparing the two periods, dropping from a well above average annual percentage change of 13.3 percent for 2003 to 2008 to a minimal growth of 0.4 percent change for 2008 to 2013. Human services organizations, although experiencing below average growth in both the years leading up to the recession (6.1 percent annual growth) and the years following (3.4 percent annual growth) were the most resilient, as the difference between the two periods is less than 3 percent.

Growth in Public Support for Reporting Public Charities

Table 5.11 displays the growth in public support for reporting public charities from 2003 to 2013. A major component of revenue for many public charities, public support consists of private contributions from individuals, foundations, corporations, and other public charities as well as government grants. It does not include government contracts, Medicare or Medicaid funding, or program service revenue.

Public support grew from $215.9 billion in 2003 to $368.3 billion in 2013. This represents a 71 percent increase (35 percent increase after adjusting for inflation). Arts, culture, and humanities organizations experienced the least growth over the 10 years at 45 percent (14 percent after adjusting for inflation). Public and societal benefit organizations saw the largest increase in public support: 97 percent (56 percent after adjusting for inflation). Religion-related organizations followed with a 92 percent increase (52 percent after adjusting for inflation).

Human services organizations, which receive just under a quarter of all public support in the sector, saw a 63 percent increase in public support—growing from $55.2 billion in 2003 to $90.1 billion in 2013. This is a 29 percent increase after adjusting for inflation. Within the human services subsector, food, agriculture, and nutrition organizations had the largest increase in public support: 163 percent, or 107 percent after adjusting for inflation (table 5.12). Recreation and sports organizations and public safety and disaster preparedness organizations also more than doubled in contributions from 2003 to 2013. Overall, public support grew more robustly from 2003 to 2008 than from 2008 to 2013.

Table 5.11. Change in Public Support for Reporting Public Charities, by Subsector, 2003, 2008, and 2013 ($ millions)

				Total Percentage Change	Average Annual Percentage Change		
Subsector	2003	2008	2013	2003–13	2003–13	2003–08	2008–13
Arts, culture, and humanities	12,583	17,771	18,186	44.5	3.8	7.1	0.5
Education	49,738	82,807	81,406	63.7	5.1	10.7	–0.3
Environment and animal-related	5,637	8,662	10,648	88.9	6.6	9.0	4.2
Health	41,964	59,175	70,107	67.1	5.3	7.1	3.4
Human services	55,213	73,359	90,052	63.1	5.0	5.8	4.2
International and foreign affairs	15,077	28,337	27,738	84.0	6.3	13.5	–0.4
Public and societal benefit	30,801	49,016	60,777	97.3	7.0	9.7	4.4
Religion-related	4,892	7,715	9,409	92.3	6.8	9.5	4.0
All	**215,905**	**326,841**	**368,324**	**70.6**	**5.5**	**8.6**	**2.4**

Source: Urban Institute, National Center for Charitable Statistics, Core Files (Public Charities, 2003, 2008, and 2013).
Note: Figures are not adjusted for inflation.

Growth in Expenses of Reporting Public Charities

Public charity expenses grew from $938 billion in 2003 to $1.62 trillion in 2013 (table 5.13). This is a 73 percent increase, or a 37 percent inflation-adjusted increase. The growth in expenses grew slightly slower than the growth in revenue over the same period: 37 percent compared to 42 percent (inflation adjusted). Expenses grew more slowly between 2008 and 2013 than they did between 2003 and 2008.

The change in total expenses for each subsector is shown in detail in table 5.14. Expenses for environmental and animal organizations and international and foreign affairs organizations saw the most proportional growth of any of the subsectors: 87 percent for environmental and animal organizations (48 percent after adjusting for inflation) followed closely by international and foreign affairs organizations at 86 percent (47 percent after inflation adjustments). Education and health nonprofits experienced slightly above average growth in expenses. The expenses for health organizations, which account for about 60 percent of total public charity expenses, grew from $553.3 billion in 2003 to $975.8 billion in 2013, an increase of 76 percent (39 percent after adjusting

Table 5.12. Change in Public Support for Reporting Public Charities, by Detailed Subsector, 2003, 2008, and 2013 ($ millions)

Subsector	2003	2008	2013	Total Percentage Change 2003–13	Average Annual Percentage Change 2003–13	2003–08	2008–13
All public charities	**215,905**	**326,841**	**368,324**	**70.6**	**5.5**	**8.6**	**2.4**
Arts, culture, and humanities	**12,583**	**17,771**	**18,186**	**44.5**	**3.8**	**7.1**	**0.5**
Performing arts organizations	3,238	4,505	4,598	42.0	3.6	6.8	0.4
Historical societies and related	1,006	1,579	1,406	39.7	3.4	9.4	–2.3
Museums and museum activities	3,206	4,721	5,016	56.5	4.6	8.0	1.2
Other arts, culture, and humanities	5,132	6,966	7,165	39.6	3.4	6.3	0.6
Education	**49,738**	**82,807**	**81,406**	**63.7**	**5.1**	**10.7**	**–0.3**
Higher education institutions	24,860	34,195	34,866	40.2	3.4	6.6	0.4
Student services and organizations	1,460	2,202	2,510	71.9	5.6	8.6	2.7
Elementary and secondary education	6,910	11,936	16,589	140.1	9.2	11.6	6.8
Other education	16,507	34,474	27,441	66.2	5.2	15.9	–4.5
Environment and animal-related	**5,637**	**8,662**	**10,648**	**88.9**	**6.6**	**9.0**	**4.2**
Environment	3,340	5,416	6,131	83.6	6.3	10.2	2.5
Animal-related	2,297	3,246	4,517	96.6	7.0	7.2	6.8
Health	**41,964**	**59,175**	**70,107**	**67.1**	**5.3**	**7.1**	**3.4**
Nursing services	1,180	1,299	1,142	–3.2	–0.3	1.9	–2.5
Hospitals and primary treatment facilities	11,123	15,568	18,713	68.2	5.3	7.0	3.7
Treatment facilities—outpatient	3,670	5,032	7,216	96.6	7.0	6.5	7.5
Mental health	8,331	9,750	9,778	17.4	1.6	3.2	0.1
Disease-specific-general	6,061	8,775	9,084	49.9	4.1	7.7	0.7

Medical research	3,753	6,976	6,609	76.1	5.8	13.2	–1.1
Other health	7,847	11,774	17,565	123.8	8.4	8.5	8.3
Human services	**55,213**	**73,359**	**90,052**	**63.1**	**5.0**	**5.8**	**4.2**
Crime and legal-related	3,469	4,529	5,112	47.4	4.0	5.5	2.4
Employment and job-related	4,149	5,131	6,216	49.8	4.1	4.3	3.9
Food, agriculture, and nutrition	4,072	5,569	10,692	162.6	10.1	6.5	13.9
Housing and shelter	4,275	6,965	8,502	98.9	7.1	10.3	4.1
Public safety and disaster preparedness	683	1,059	1,422	108.3	7.6	9.2	6.1
Recreation and sports	2,132	3,271	4,477	110.0	7.7	8.9	6.5
Youth development	2,964	4,079	4,643	56.7	4.6	6.6	2.6
Children and youth services	4,388	6,062	6,208	41.5	3.5	6.7	0.5
Family services	2,732	3,458	3,737	36.8	3.2	4.8	1.6
Residential and custodial care	3,078	3,783	4,322	40.4	3.5	4.2	2.7
Services promoting independence	9,621	12,070	14,290	48.5	4.0	4.6	3.4
Other human services	13,651	17,383	20,430	49.7	4.1	5.0	3.3
International and foreign affairs	**15,077**	**28,337**	**27,738**	**84.0**	**6.3**	**13.5**	**–0.4**
Public and societal benefit	**30,801**	**49,016**	**60,777**	**97.3**	**7.0**	**9.7**	**4.4**
Civil rights and advocacy	1,260	1,687	2,015	59.9	4.8	6.0	3.6
Community improvement	6,783	9,598	10,031	47.9	4.0	7.2	0.9
Philanthropy and voluntarism	14,655	23,995	31,891	117.6	8.1	10.4	5.9
Science and technology	5,413	9,012	10,569	95.3	6.9	10.7	3.2
Social science	806	1,671	2,017	150.3	9.6	15.7	3.8
Other public and societal benefit	1,883	3,054	4,254	125.9	8.5	10.1	6.9
Religion-related	**4,892**	**7,715**	**9,409**	**92.3**	**6.8**	**9.5**	**4.0**

Source: Urban Institute, National Center for Charitable Statistics, Core Files (Public Charities, 2003, 2008, and 2013).
Note: Figures are not adjusted for inflation.

Table 5.13. Change in Total Expenses for Reporting Public Charities, by Subsector, 2003, 2008, and 2013 ($ millions)

				Total Percentage Change	Average Annual Percentage Change		
Subsector	2003	2008	2013	2003–13	2003–13	2003–08	2008–13
Arts, culture, and humanities	20,615	27,944	30,184	46.4	3.9	6.3	1.6
Education	151,800	221,340	269,150	77.3	5.9	7.8	4.0
Environment and animal-related	7,854	11,805	14,713	87.3	6.5	8.5	4.5
Health	553,366	788,179	975,813	76.3	5.8	7.3	4.4
Human services	132,032	174,887	206,851	56.7	4.6	5.8	3.4
International and foreign affairs	16,596	30,844	30,826	85.7	6.4	13.2	0.0
Public and societal benefit	48,230	73,928	82,762	71.6	5.5	8.9	2.3
Religion-related	7,521	11,328	13,489	79.4	6.0	8.5	3.6
All public charities	**938,014**	**1,340,254**	**1,623,788**	**73.1**	**5.6**	**7.4**	**3.9**

Source: Urban Institute, National Center for Charitable Statistics, Core Files (Public Charities, 2003, 2008, and 2013).
Note: Figures are not adjusted for inflation.

for inflation). Expenses increased the least for arts, culture, and humanities organizations: 46 percent (16 percent after adjusting for inflation).

Growth in Assets of Reporting Public Charities

As displayed in table 5.15, total assets grew from roughly $1.74 trillion in 2003 to $3.22 trillion in 2013, an 85 percent increase (46 percent increase after adjusting for inflation). International and foreign affairs organizations, health organizations, and religion-related organizations all experienced above average growth over the 10 years, doubling (or more than doubling) between 2003 and 2013. International organizations saw an increase of 117 percent (71 percent after adjusting for inflation), and religion-related organizations and health organizations both grew by about 100 percent (58 percent after adjusting for inflation). Arts organizations experienced the lowest increase in assets over the period, growing 64 percent (30 percent after adjusting for inflation). Health organizations account for over 43 percent of the sector's assets.

For all subsectors, assets averaged greater annual growth between 2003 and 2008 than between 2008 and 2013. Table 5.16 shows that growth of assets in health was

Table 5.14. Change in Total Expenses for Reporting Public Charities, by Detailed Subsector, 2003, 2008, and 2013 ($ millions)

				Total Percentage Change	Average Annual Percentage Change		
Subsector	2003	2008	2013	2003–13	2003–13	2003–08	2008–13
All public charities	**938,014**	**1,340,254**	**1,623,788**	**73.1**	**5.6**	**7.4**	**3.9**
Arts, culture, and humanities	**20,615**	**27,944**	**30,184**	**46.4**	**3.9**	**6.3**	**1.6**
Performing arts organizations	6,736	8,919	9,617	42.8	3.6	5.8	1.5
Historical societies and related	1,465	1,877	2,090	42.7	3.6	5.1	2.2
Museums and museum activities	4,488	6,158	6,788	51.3	4.2	6.5	2.0
Other arts, culture, and humanities	7,927	10,990	11,689	47.5	4.0	6.8	1.2
Education	**151,800**	**221,340**	**269,150**	**77.3**	**5.9**	**7.8**	**4.0**
Higher education institutions	101,673	141,325	174,582	71.7	5.6	6.8	4.3
Student services and organizations	2,917	4,658	4,961	70.0	5.5	9.8	1.3
Elementary and secondary education	22,536	33,792	45,449	101.7	7.3	8.4	6.1
Other education	24,674	41,565	44,159	79.0	6.0	11.0	1.2
Environment and animal-related	**7,854**	**11,805**	**14,713**	**87.3**	**6.5**	**8.5**	**4.5**
Environment	4,415	6,762	8,129	84.1	6.3	8.9	3.8
Animal-related	3,439	5,043	6,585	91.5	6.7	8.0	5.5

(continued)

Table 5.14. Change in Total Expenses for Reporting Public Charities, by Detailed Subsector, 2003, 2008, and 2013 ($ millions) *(continued)*

Subsector	2003	2008	2013	Total Percentage Change	Average Annual Percentage Change		
				2003–13	2003–13	2003–08	2008–13
Health	**553,366**	**788,179**	**975,813**	**76.3**	**5.8**	**7.3**	**4.4**
Nursing services	21,468	26,050	28,478	32.7	2.9	3.9	1.8
Hospitals and primary treatment facilities	406,433	569,843	683,282	68.1	5.3	7.0	3.7
Treatment facilities—outpatient	60,259	94,646	138,908	130.5	8.7	9.5	8.0
Mental health	21,630	27,784	30,137	39.3	3.4	5.1	1.6
Disease-specific-general	9,895	14,447	16,747	69.2	5.4	7.9	3.0
Medical research	5,814	9,641	9,857	69.5	5.4	10.6	0.4
Other health	27,867	45,769	68,404	145.5	9.4	10.4	8.4
Human services	**132,032**	**174,887**	**206,851**	**56.7**	**4.6**	**5.8**	**3.4**
Crime and legal-related	5,078	6,566	7,105	39.9	3.4	5.3	1.6
Employment and job-related	9,760	12,379	15,438	58.2	4.7	4.9	4.5
Food, agriculture, and nutrition	4,659	6,222	11,629	149.6	9.6	6.0	13.3
Housing and shelter	12,989	19,364	23,171	78.4	6.0	8.3	3.7
Public safety and disaster preparedness	1,240	1,794	2,272	83.3	6.2	7.7	4.8

Recreation and sports	7,259	10,714	14,970	106.2	7.5	8.1	6.9
Youth development	5,039	6,711	7,311	45.1	3.8	5.9	1.7
Children and youth services	9,702	12,181	12,280	26.6	2.4	4.7	0.2
Family services	5,169	6,351	6,754	30.7	2.7	4.2	1.2
Residential and custodial care	24,311	32,215	36,616	50.6	4.2	5.8	2.6
Services promoting independence	20,573	27,518	32,196	56.5	4.6	6.0	3.2
Other human services	26,255	32,873	37,111	41.3	3.5	4.6	2.5
International and foreign affairs	**16,596**	**30,844**	**30,826**	**85.7**	**6.4**	**13.2**	**0.0**
Public and societal benefit	**48,230**	**73,928**	**82,762**	**71.6**	**5.5**	**8.9**	**2.3**
Civil rights and advocacy	1,499	2,022	2,399	60.0	4.8	6.2	3.5
Community improvement	10,338	14,487	16,944	63.9	5.1	7.0	3.2
Philanthropy and voluntarism	16,436	25,233	29,331	78.5	6.0	9.0	3.1
Science and technology	10,892	17,202	19,458	78.6	6.0	9.6	2.5
Social science	1,257	2,093	2,688	113.8	7.9	10.7	5.1
Other public and societal benefit	7,808	12,890	11,944	53.0	4.3	10.5	–1.5
Religion-related	**7,521**	**11,328**	**13,489**	**79.4**	**6.0**	**8.5**	**3.6**

Source: Urban Institute, National Center for Charitable Statistics, Core Files (Public Charities, 2003, 2008, and 2013).
Note: Figures are not adjusted for inflation.

Table 5.15. Change in Total Assets for Reporting Public Charities, by Subsector, 2003, 2008, and 2013

				Total Percentage Change	Average Annual Percentage Change		
Subsector	2003	2008	2013	2003–13	2003–13	2003–08	2008–13
Arts, culture, and humanities	67,458	97,790	110,689	64.1	5.1	7.7	2.5
Education	538,166	844,354	958,091	78.0	5.9	9.4	2.6
Environment and animals-related	22,132	32,709	41,400	87.1	6.5	8.1	4.8
Health	697,971	1,011,652	1,392,790	99.5	7.2	7.7	6.6
Human services	196,440	273,271	331,481	68.7	5.4	6.8	3.9
International and foreign affairs	18,148	31,336	39,343	116.8	8.0	11.5	4.7
Public and societal benefit	185,214	273,428	315,210	70.2	5.5	8.1	2.9
Religion-related	17,972	26,339	35,984	100.2	7.2	7.9	6.4
All public charities	**1,743,501**	**2,590,879**	**3,224,987**	**85.0**	**6.3**	**8.2**	**4.5**

Source: Urban Institute, National Center for Charitable Statistics, Core Files (Public Charities, 2003, 2008, and 2013).
Note: Figures are not adjusted for inflation.

fueled by hospitals, which more than doubled in assets between 2003 and 2013, growing from $522.43 million in 2003 to $1.05 trillion in 2013 (an increase of 102 percent, or 59 percent after adjusting for inflation).

Tables 5.17 and 5.18 display the growth in net assets, defined as total assets minus liabilities, between 2003 and 2013. Net assets grew from $1.1 trillion in 2003 to about $2.0 trillion in 2013, an increase of 87 percent (48 percent after adjusting for inflation). This is approximately the same as the growth in total assets, indicating that liabilities and assets grew at similar rates over the same period.

International and foreign affairs organizations exhibited the greatest increase in net assets. Net assets for these organizations increased from $14.1 billion in 2003 to $30.3 billion in 2013, an increase of 115 percent (an inflation-adjusted 70 percent). Health organizations also had a large increase in net assets, growing 103 percent (60 percent after adjusting for inflation).

Reporting Public Charities by Major Subsector

We now turn to covering the specific public charity subsectors in more detail. We begin by giving a financial snapshot for 2013 for each subsector. Then, we break the subsector

Table 5.16. Change in Total Assets for Reporting Public Charities, by Detailed Subsector, 2003, 2008, and 2013 ($ millions)

				Total Percentage Change	Average Annual Percentage Change		
Subsector	2003	2008	2013	2003–13	2003–13	2003–08	2008–13
All public charities	**1,743,501**	**2,590,879**	**3,224,987**	**85.0**	**6.3**	**8.2**	**4.5**
Arts, culture, and humanities	**67,458**	**97,790**	**110,689**	**64.1**	**5.1**	**7.7**	**2.5**
Performing arts organizations	14,010	20,774	23,302	66.3	5.2	8.2	2.3
Historical societies and related	6,962	9,470	11,792	69.4	5.4	6.3	4.5
Museums and museum activities	27,088	39,840	45,239	67.0	5.3	8.0	2.6
Other arts, culture, and humanities	19,398	27,706	30,356	56.5	4.6	7.4	1.8
Education	**538,166**	**844,354**	**958,091**	**78.0**	**5.9**	**9.4**	**2.6**
Higher education institutions	377,860	562,441	617,743	63.5	5.0	8.3	1.9
Student services and organizations	12,135	20,975	23,799	96.1	7.0	11.6	2.6
Elementary and secondary education	59,013	89,524	111,427	88.8	6.6	8.7	4.5
Other education	89,158	171,414	205,122	130.1	8.7	14.0	3.7
Environment and animal-related	**22,132**	**32,709**	**41,400**	**87.1**	**6.5**	**8.1**	**4.8**
Environment	13,368	20,440	24,980	86.9	6.5	8.9	4.1
Animal-related	8,764	12,269	16,420	87.4	6.5	7.0	6.0

(continued)

Table 5.16. Change in Total Assets for Reporting Public Charities, by Detailed Subsector, 2003, 2008, and 2013 ($ millions) *(continued)*

Subsector	2003	2008	2013	Total Percentage Change	Average Annual Percentage Change		
				2003–13	2003–13	2003–08	2008–13
Health	**697,971**	**1,011,652**	**1,392,790**	**99.5**	**7.2**	**7.7**	**6.6**
Nursing services	22,707	27,162	31,232	37.5	3.2	3.6	2.8
Hospitals and primary treatment facilities	522,341	754,653	1,053,172	101.6	7.3	7.6	6.9
Treatment facilities—outpatient	28,212	44,769	78,495	178.2	10.8	9.7	11.9
Mental health	16,491	21,591	25,205	52.8	4.3	5.5	3.1
Disease-specific-general	12,480	19,913	23,057	84.8	6.3	9.8	3.0
Medical research	26,647	39,314	39,608	48.6	4.0	8.1	0.1
Other health	69,093	104,250	142,022	105.6	7.5	8.6	6.4
Human services	**196,440**	**273,271**	**331,481**	**68.7**	**5.4**	**6.8**	**3.9**
Crime and legal-related	4,089	6,164	7,387	80.7	6.1	8.6	3.7
Employment and job-related	7,541	10,233	14,326	90.0	6.6	6.3	7.0
Food, agriculture, and nutrition	2,434	3,807	6,097	150.5	9.6	9.4	9.9
Housing and shelter	46,374	67,374	81,469	75.7	5.8	7.8	3.9
Public safety and disaster preparedness	2,863	4,565	6,147	114.7	7.9	9.8	6.1

Recreation and sports	10,449	16,045	21,154	102.4	7.3	9.0	5.7
Youth development	9,485	13,107	15,560	64.0	5.1	6.7	3.5
Children and youth services	6,114	8,336	9,446	54.5	4.4	6.4	2.5
Family services	4,190	5,799	6,871	64.0	5.1	6.7	3.5
Residential and custodial care	52,145	69,652	80,476	54.3	4.4	6.0	2.9
Services promoting independence	15,534	21,470	27,741	78.6	6.0	6.7	5.3
Other human services	35,222	46,719	54,807	55.6	4.5	5.8	3.2
International and foreign affairs	**18,148**	**31,336**	**39,343**	**116.8**	**8.0**	**11.5**	**4.7**
Public and societal benefit	**185,214**	**273,428**	**315,210**	**70.2**	**5.5**	**8.1**	**2.9**
Civil rights and advocacy	1,640	2,496	3,148	91.9	6.7	8.8	4.7
Community improvement	39,656	43,604	45,516	14.8	1.4	1.9	0.9
Philanthropy and voluntarism	78,841	124,474	174,479	121.3	8.3	9.6	7.0
Science and technology	14,077	19,748	23,706	68.4	5.3	7.0	3.7
Social science	2,554	3,949	4,854	90.1	6.6	9.1	4.2
Other public and societal benefit	48,446	79,156	63,508	31.1	2.7	10.3	–4.3
Religion-related	**17,972**	**26,339**	**35,984**	**100.2**	**7.2**	**7.9**	**6.4**

Source: Urban Institute, National Center for Charitable Statistics, Core Files (Public Charities, 2003, 2008 and 2013).
Note: Figures are not adjusted for inflation.

Table 5.17. Change in Net Assets for Reporting Public Charities, by Type of Organization, 2003, 2008, and 2013 ($ millions)

				Total Percentage Change	Average Annual Percentage Change		
Subsector	2003	2008	2013	2003–13	2003–13	2003–08	2008–13
Arts, culture, and humanities	55,570	78,767	90,515	62.9	5.0	7.2	2.8
Education	379,157	626,629	681,983	79.9	6.0	10.6	1.7
Environment and animal-related	18,211	27,082	34,995	92.2	6.7	8.3	5.3
Health	356,396	508,155	723,013	102.9	7.3	7.4	7.3
Human services	95,364	130,607	167,744	75.9	5.8	6.5	5.1
International and foreign affairs	14,132	23,852	30,328	114.6	7.9	11.0	4.9
Public and societal benefit	125,500	171,324	223,776	78.3	6.0	6.4	5.5
Religion-related	13,807	19,483	26,780	94.0	6.8	7.1	6.6
All public charities	**1,058,139**	**1,585,900**	**1,979,134**	**87.0**	**6.5**	**8.4**	**4.5**

Source: Urban Institute, National Center for Charitable Statistics, Core Files (Public Charities, 2003, 2008, and 2013).
Note: Figures are shown in current dollars and are not adjusted for inflation.

into its component parts, or industries, and discuss the proportion of each subsector's resources belonging to each industry.

Arts, Culture and Humanities

In 2013, arts, culture, and humanities organizations accounted for nearly 10 percent of all reporting public charities, but just 2 percent of revenues and expenses. This subsector includes organizations such as museums, performing arts groups, folk life organizations, historical societies, and supporting organizations such as local arts agencies. In 2013, arts, culture, and humanities nonprofits accounted for roughly 3 percent of public charity assets.

Arts, culture, and humanities groups reported $33.6 billion in revenue and $30.2 billion in total expenses in 2013 (table 5.19). Donations are the largest source of revenue for arts, culture, and humanities organizations. Contributions from individuals, foundations, corporations, and government grants accounted for 54 percent of arts, culture, and humanities revenues in 2013 (figure 5.4). This sector is the third-most dependent on private contributions (44 percent) behind international and foreign affairs and

Table 5.18. Change in Net Assets for Reporting Public Charities, by Subsector, 2003, 2008, and 2013 ($ millions)

Subsector	2003	2008	2013	Total Percentage Change	Average Annual Percentage Change		
				2003–13	2003–13	2003–08	2008–13
All public charities	**1,058,139**	**1,585,900**	**1,979,134**	**87.0**	**6.5**	**8.4**	**4.5**
Arts, culture, and humanities	**55,570**	**78,767**	**90,515**	**62.9**	**5.0**	**7.2**	**2.8**
Performing arts organizations	10,712	15,678	17,568	64.0	5.1	7.9	2.3
Historical societies and related	6,137	8,250	10,477	70.7	5.5	6.1	4.9
Museums and museum activities	23,236	33,340	38,462	65.5	5.2	7.5	2.9
Other arts, culture, and humanities	15,485	21,498	24,008	55.0	4.5	6.8	2.2
Education	**379,157**	**626,629**	**681,983**	**79.9**	**6.0**	**10.6**	**1.7**
Higher education institutions	254,757	412,909	430,664	69.0	5.4	10.1	0.8
Student services and organizations	8,743	12,965	14,219	62.6	5.0	8.2	1.9
Elementary and secondary education	43,715	64,503	80,050	83.1	6.2	8.1	4.4
Other education	71,942	136,252	157,050	118.3	8.1	13.6	2.9
Environment and animal-related	**18,211**	**27,082**	**34,995**	**92.2**	**6.7**	**8.3**	**5.3**
Environment	11,107	17,048	21,488	93.5	6.8	8.9	4.7
Animal-related	7,104	10,034	13,508	90.1	6.6	7.2	6.1

(continued)

Table 5.18. Change in Net Assets for Reporting Public Charities, by Subsector, 2003, 2008, and 2013 ($ millions) *(continued)*

Subsector	2003	2008	2013	Total Percentage Change	Average Annual Percentage Change		
				2003–13	2003–13	2003–08	2008–13
Health	**356,396**	**508,155**	**723,013**	**102.9**	**7.3**	**7.4**	**7.3**
Nursing services	8,785	11,118	14,109	60.6	4.9	4.8	4.9
Hospitals and primary treatment facilities	246,491	346,681	511,322	107.4	7.6	7.1	8.1
Treatment facilities—outpatient	10,060	17,227	32,017	218.2	12.3	11.4	13.2
Mental health	9,706	12,643	15,629	61.0	4.9	5.4	4.3
Disease-specific-general	8,305	12,255	14,918	79.6	6.0	8.1	4.0
Medical research	20,632	29,500	31,474	52.6	4.3	7.4	1.3
Other health	52,417	78,731	103,543	97.5	7.0	8.5	5.6
Human services	**95,364**	**130,607**	**167,744**	**75.9**	**5.8**	**6.5**	**5.1**
Crime and legal-related	2,816	4,438	5,387	91.3	6.7	9.5	4.0
Employment and job-related	4,822	6,796	9,942	106.2	7.5	7.1	7.9
Food, agriculture, and nutrition	2,061	3,197	5,164	150.5	9.6	9.2	10.1
Housing and shelter	11,591	17,612	23,260	100.7	7.2	8.7	5.7
Public safety and disaster preparedness	2,235	3,525	4,814	115.4	8.0	9.5	6.4

Recreation and sports	7,895	11,733	15,863	100.9	7.2	8.2	6.2
Youth development	8,264	11,207	12,672	53.3	4.4	6.3	2.5
Children and youth services	4,040	5,566	6,364	57.5	4.6	6.6	2.7
Family services	2,998	4,108	4,984	66.3	5.2	6.5	3.9
Residential and custodial care	15,846	18,859	25,494	60.9	4.9	3.5	6.2
Services promoting independence	9,515	12,761	17,882	87.9	6.5	6.0	7.0
Other human services	23,282	30,807	35,918	54.3	4.4	5.8	3.1
International and foreign affairs	**14,132**	**23,852**	**30,328**	**114.6**	**7.9**	**11.0**	**4.9**
Public and societal benefit	**125,500**	**171,324**	**223,776**	**78.3**	**6.0**	**6.4**	**5.5**
Civil rights and advocacy	1,269	1,962	2,498	96.8	7.0	9.1	4.9
Community improvement	29,949	29,304	26,299	–12.2	–1.3	–0.4	–2.1
Philanthropy and voluntarism	69,589	109,368	155,492	123.4	8.4	9.5	7.3
Science and technology	9,809	13,681	16,193	65.1	5.1	6.9	3.4
Social science	1,753	2,826	3,493	99.2	7.1	10.0	4.3
Other public and societal benefit	13,131	14,184	19,802	50.8	4.2	1.6	6.9
Religion-related	**13,807**	**19,483**	**26,780**	**94.0**	**6.8**	**7.1**	**6.6**

Source: Urban Institute, National Center for Charitable Statistics, Core Files (Public Charities, 2003, 2008, and 2013).
Note: Figures are not adjusted for inflation.

Table 5.19. Revenues and Expenses for Reporting Public Charities in Arts, Culture, and Humanities, 2013

	All Organizations	
	$ millions	%
Public support	18,186	54
Private contributions	14,738	44
Direct contributions	14,157	42
Indirect contributions	581	2
Government grants	3,448	10
Fee for service	11,631	35
Fees from government sources	381	1
Fees from private sources	10,685	32
Net income from sale of inventory	566	2
Investment income	2,972	9
Dividends, interest, and other similar amounts	976	3
Net gain on sale of assets or securities	1,779	5
Other investment income	217	1
Other income	841	3
Net income from special events	239	1
Other revenue	602	2
Total revenue	**33,596**	**100**
Paid personnel	13,110	43
Wages and salaries	11,019	37
Compensation of officers	3,022	10
Other wages and salaries	7,996	26
Fringe benefits and payroll tax	2,091	7
Pension plan contributions	353	1
Other employee benefits	1,001	3
Payroll taxes	738	2
Supplies	853	3
Communications (printing, phone, etc.)	1,680	6
Professional fees	2,270	8
Occupancy	1,486	5

(continued)

Table 5.19. Revenues and Expenses for Reporting Public Charities in Arts, Culture, and Humanities, 2013 *(continued)*

	All Organizations	
	$ millions	%
Interest	351	1
Depreciation and depletion	1,961	6
Other	6,430	21
Total current operating expenses	28,142	93
Grants and benefits	1,982	7
Grants and allocations	1,747	6
Specific assistance to individuals	226	1
Benefits paid to members	9	0
Payments to affiliates	60	0
Total expenses	**30,184**	**100**
Net income (revenue – expenses)	3,412	
Total assets	**110,689**	
Total liabilities	20,162	
Net assets (assets – liabilities)	**90,515**	

Sources: Urban Institute, National Center for Charitable Statistics, Core Files (Public Charities, 2013), Core Full 990 Files (Public Charities, 2012–13) and Core Supplement Files (2013); and Internal Revenue Service, Statistics of Income Sample Files (Public Charities, 2007–12).

Notes: Authors' calculations are based on U.S. Internal Revenue Service Forms 990 and 990-EZ, classified according to the National Taxonomy of Exempt Entities—Core Codes, and adjusted by the National Center for Charitable Statistics based on available data. See the methodology section at the end of the chapter for more information on how the estimates were created. Reporting public charities include only organizations that both reported (filed IRS Forms 990) and were required to do so. The following were excluded: foreign organizations, government-associated organizations, organizations without state identifiers, and organizations excluded by the authors' discretion. Organizations not required to report include religious congregations and organizations with less than $25,000 in gross receipts. The table includes separate analyses for operating public charities and supporting organizations to clarify the distribution of funds and to avoid double-counting the financial information for supporting organizations (see the methodology section at the end of this chapter for a detailed description of the methodology). The sum of the dollar amounts may not equal due to rounding. Percentages for revenue items and net income are expressed as percentages of total revenue. Program service revenue figures may include sizable income via government contracts, which the data source is unable to differentiate from funds raised via the public (i.e., fees for services). Percentages for current operating expense items are expressed as percentages of total current operating expenses. Percentages for other expense items, assets, and liabilities are expressed as percentages of total expenses.

Figure 5.4. Sources of Revenue for Arts, Culture, and Humanities Reporting Public Charities, 2013

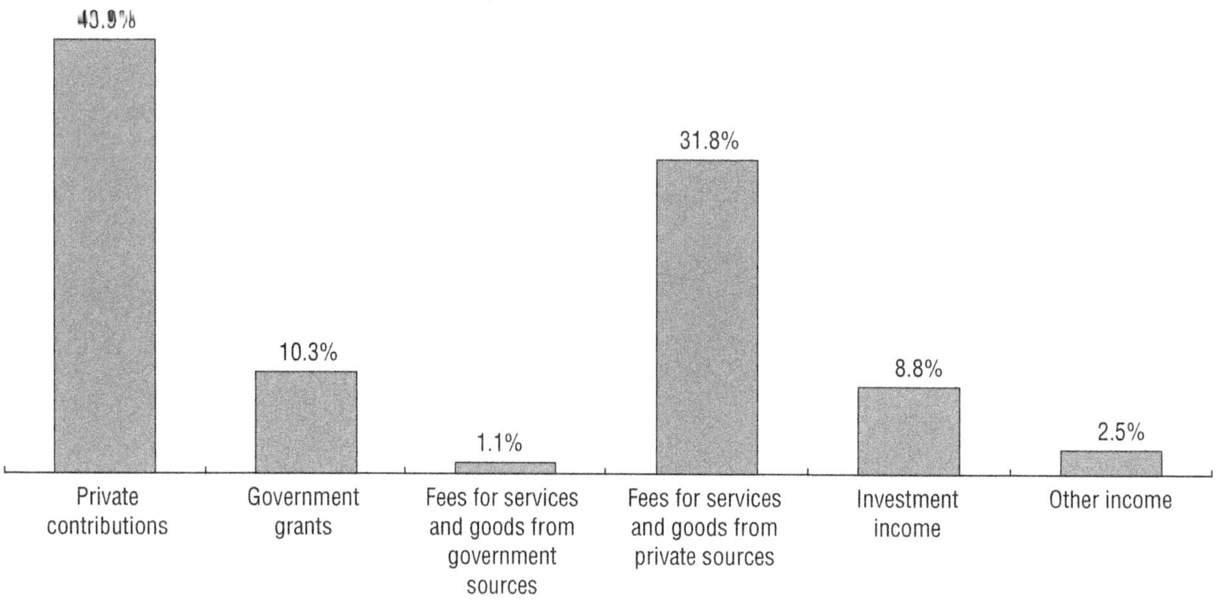

Source	Percent
Private contributions	40.9%
Government grants	10.3%
Fees for services and goods from government sources	1.1%
Fees for services and goods from private sources	31.8%
Investment income	8.8%
Other income	2.5%

Sources: NCCS calculations of IRS Statistics of Income Division Exempt Organizations Sample (2009, 2011); Urban Institute, National Center for Charitable Statistics, Core Files (2013).

environment and animal subsectors. About 43 percent of total operating costs of arts, culture, and humanities organizations were spent on wages, salaries, and other personnel costs.

The arts, culture, and humanities subsector had net income of $3.4 billion. Additionally, it held $110.7 billion in total assets and had net assets (assets minus liabilities) of $90.5 billion.

Figure 5.5 displays the number, assets, revenues, and expenses of major types of organizations within the arts, culture, and humanities subsectors. "Other" organizations, which include arts service organizations, arts education organizations, media and communications organizations, and arts councils and agencies, account for 41 percent of the subsector. These organizations also account for the highest proportion of revenues and expenses within the subsector, at 37 and 39 percent, respectively. Museums, while accounting for only 11 percent of organizations in the subsector, account for 41 percent of total assets, mainly land and buildings.

Education

The education subsector includes higher education institutions, student service organizations, elementary and secondary institutions, libraries, and parent-teacher groups. In 2013, these organizations accounted for 17 percent of public charities, 17 percent of total revenue and expenses, and 30 percent of assets.

Figure 5.5. Assets, Revenue, and Expenses for Arts, Culture, and Humanities Public Charities, 2013

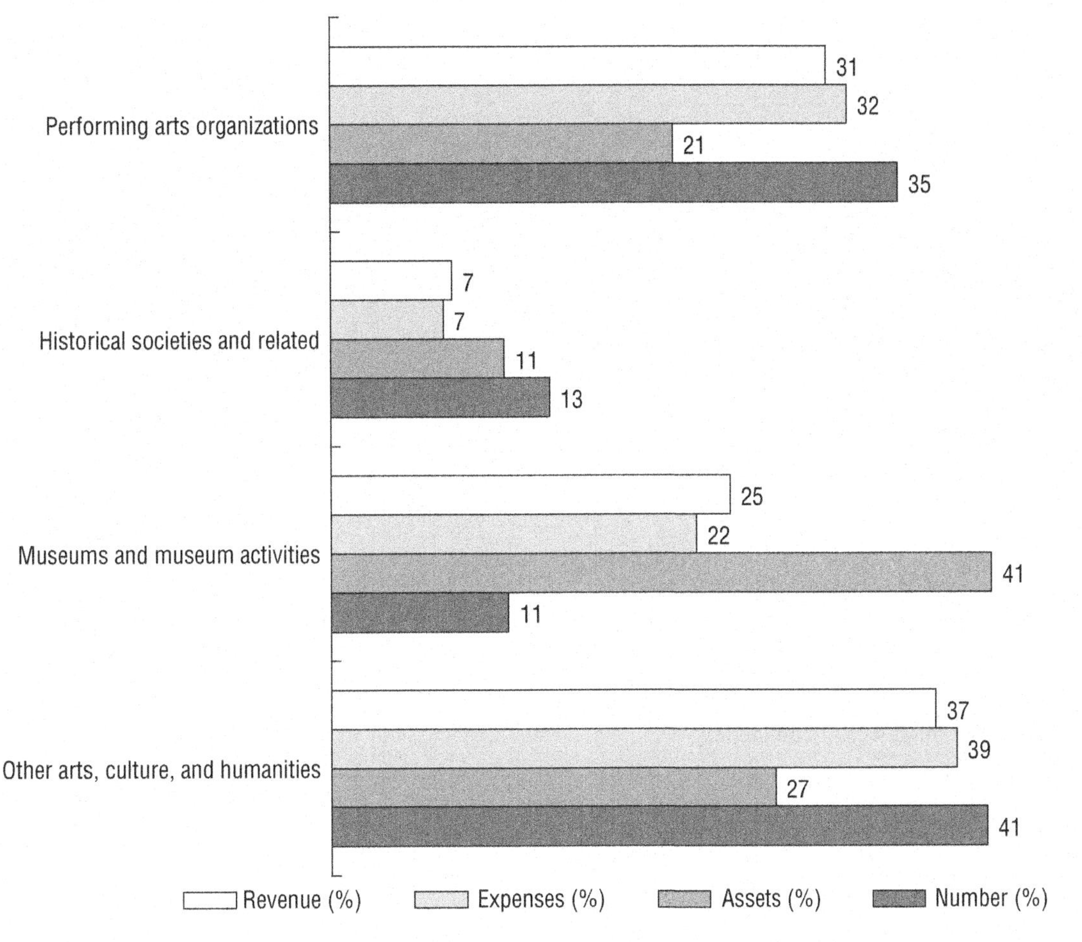

Source: Urban Institute, National Center for Charitable Statistics, Core Files (Public Charities, 2013).

Education public charities reported $296.3 billion in revenue and $269.2 billion in expenses in 2013 (table 5.20). Figure 5.6 shows sources of income for the education subsector. Education organizations count on fees for services (such as tuition) for a high proportion of their total revenue—60 percent, overall. This makes education the second-most-dependent sector on fee revenue, behind the health subsector. Wages, salaries, and other personnel costs account for nearly half of education expenses.

Revenues exceeded expenses in the education subsector by $27.1 billion in 2013. These organizations reported $958.1 billion in total assets and had net assets (assets minus liabilities) of $682.0 billion.

The number, assets, revenues, and expenses of organizations within the education subsector are displayed in figure 5.7. The "other" category accounts for 60 percent of total organizations. This category includes special education programs, libraries, adult continuing education programs, and parent-teacher groups. Elementary and secondary education organizations account for another 25 percent of organizations.

Table 5.20. Revenues and Expenses for Reporting Public Charities in Education, 2013

	All Organizations	
	$ millions	%
Public support	81,406	27
Private contributions	48,023	16
Direct contributions	44,750	15
Indirect contributions	3,272	1
Government grants	33,383	11
Fee for service	179,759	61
Fees from government sources	7,225	2
Fees from private sources	171,777	58
Net income from sale of inventory	757	0
Investment income	31,976	11
Dividends, interest, and other similar amounts	9,023	3
Net gain on sale of assets or securities	22,226	8
Other investment income	727	0
Other income	4,376	1
Net income from special events	717	0
Other revenue	3,659	1
Total revenue	**296,282**	**100**
Paid personnel	132,217	49
Wages and salaries	106,612	40
Compensation of officers	13,831	5
Other wages and salaries	92,781	34
Fringe benefits and payroll tax	25,605	10
Pension plan contributions	5,712	2
Other employee benefits	13,521	5
Payroll taxes	6,371	2
Supplies	8,442	3
Communications (printing, phone, etc.)	9,269	3
Professional fees	14,294	5
Occupancy	10,435	4
Interest	5,602	2
Depreciation and depletion	12,773	5

(continued)

Table 5.20. Revenues and Expenses for Reporting Public Charities in Education, 2013 *(continued)*

	All Organizations	
	$ millions	%
Other	28,768	11
Total current operating expenses	221,800	82
Grants and benefits	46,850	17
Grants and allocations	14,298	5
Specific assistance to individuals	32,493	12
Benefits paid to members	59	0
Payments to affiliates	499	0
Total expenses	**269,150**	**100**
Net income (revenue – expenses)	27,132	
Total assets	**958,091**	
Total liabilities	276,106	
Net assets (assets – liabilities)	**681,983**	

Sources: Urban Institute, National Center for Charitable Statistics, Core Files (Public Charities, 2013), Core Full 990 Files (Public Charities, 2012–13) and Core Supplement Files (2013); and Internal Revenue Service, Statistics of Income Sample Files (Public Charities, 2007–12).
Notes: Authors' calculations are based on U.S. Internal Revenue Service Forms 990 and 990-EZ, classified according to the National Taxonomy of Exempt Entities—Core Codes, and adjusted by the National Center for Charitable Statistics based on available data. See the methodology section at the end of the chapter for more information on how the estimates were created. Reporting public charities include only organizations that both reported (filed IRS Forms 990) and were required to do so. The following were excluded: foreign organizations, government-associated organizations, organizations without state identifiers, and organizations excluded by the authors' discretion. Organizations not required to report include religious congregations and organizations with less than $25,000 in gross receipts. The table includes separate analyses for operating public charities and supporting organizations to clarify the distribution of funds and to avoid double-counting the financial information for supporting organizations (see the methodology section at the end of this chapter for a detailed description of the methodology). The sum of the dollar amounts may not equal due to rounding. Percentages for revenue items and net income are expressed as percentages of total revenue. Program service revenue figures may include sizable income via government contracts, which the data source is unable to differentiate from funds raised via the public (i.e., fees for services). Percentages for current operating expense items are expressed as percentages of total current operating expenses. Percentages for other expense items, assets, and liabilities are expressed as percentages of total expenses.

Higher education organizations, while accounting for only 4 percent of total organizations within the subsector, account for about two-thirds of revenue, assets, and expenses.

Total assets for education organizations were $958.1 billion for 2013. Assets among education organizations ranged from $23.8 billion for student services organizations to $617.7 billion for higher education organizations.

Figure 5.6. Sources of Revenue for Education Reporting Public Charities, 2013

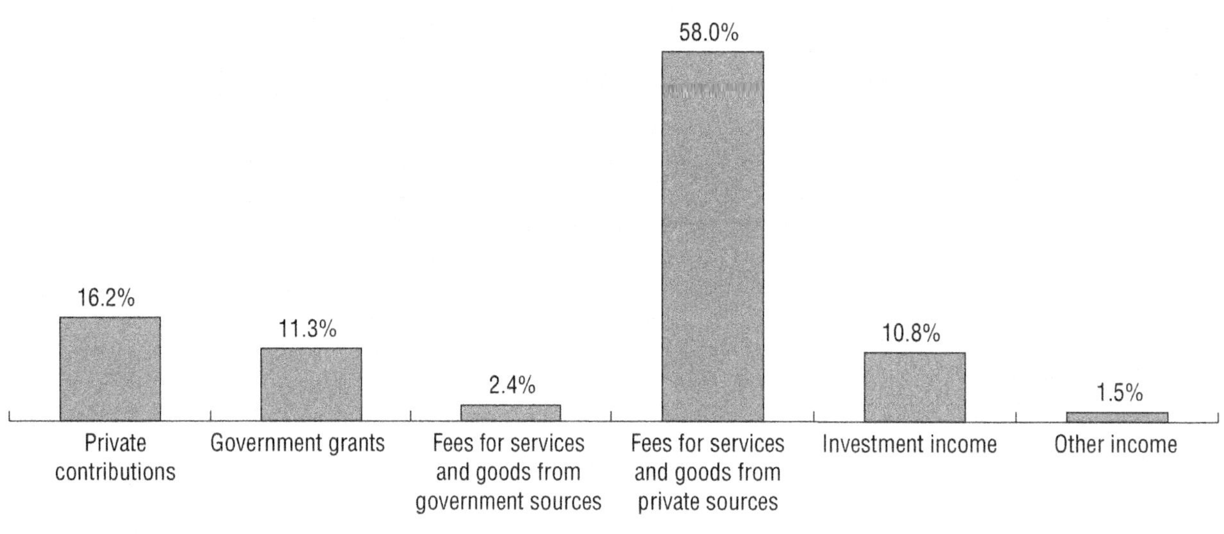

Sources: NCCS calculations of IRS Statistics of Income Division Exempt Organizations Sample (2009, 2011); Urban Institute, National Center for Charitable Statistics, Core Files (2013).

Figure 5.7. Assets, Revenue, and Expenses for Education Public Charities, 2013

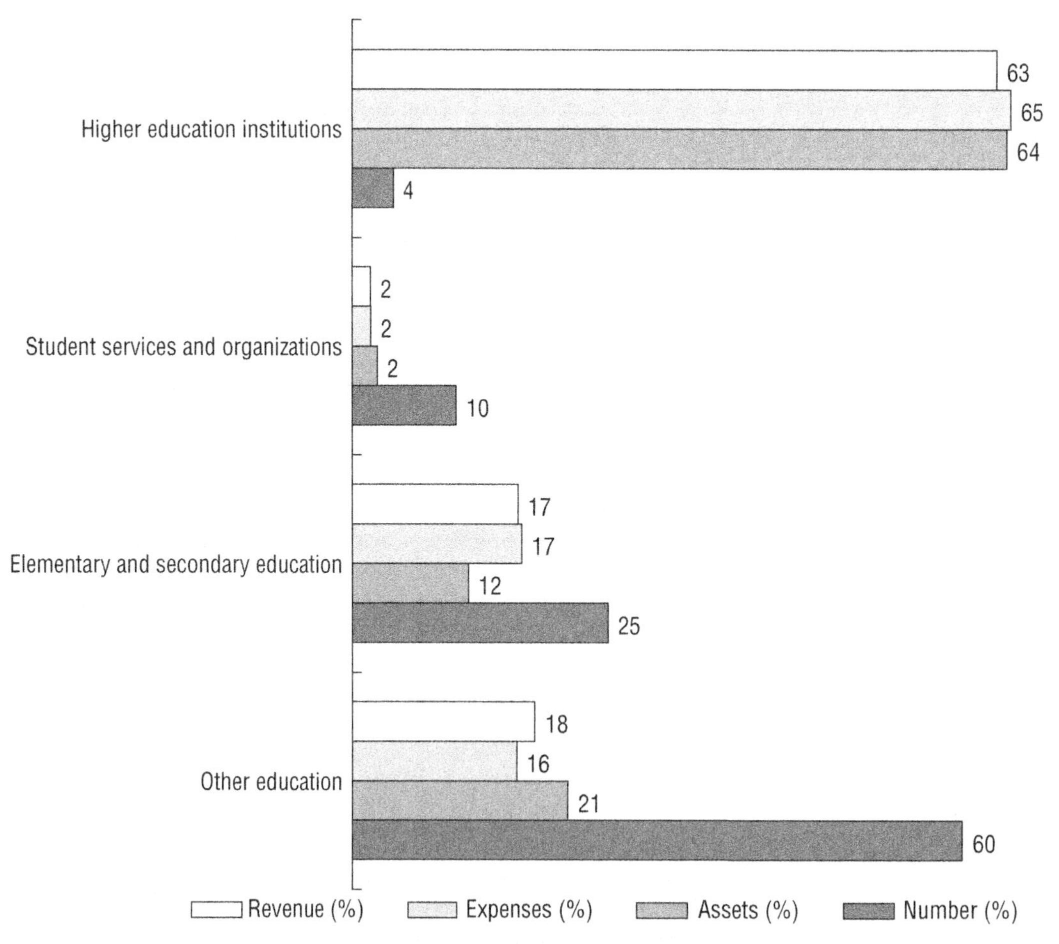

Source: Urban Institute, National Center for Charitable Statistics, Core Files (2013).

Environment and Animals

Organizations focusing on environmental preservation, recycling, pollution abatement, animal protection, and wildlife preservation make up the environment and animal subsector. In 2013, environment and animal organizations accounted for 5 percent of public charities and 1 percent of revenues, expenses, and total assets of all public charities.

Environment and animal-related organizations reported $16.7 billion in revenue and $14.7 billion in expenses. Donations are a major source of revenue. Total contributions from individuals, foundations, corporation, and government grants accounted for 64 percent of environment and animal-related revenue in 2013 (figure 5.8). The environment and animals subsector is the second most dependent on contributions (50 percent) behind international and foreign affairs.

As exhibited in table 5.21, wages, salaries, and other personnel costs accounted for 35 percent of expenses for environment and animal-related revenue in 2013.

The environment and animal subsector reported a surplus of revenue in 2013. This subsector reported net income of $2 billion. Environment and animal organizations held $41.4 billion in assets and had net assets (assets minus liabilities) of $35.0 billion.

Figure 5.8. Sources of Revenue for Environment and Animal-Related Reporting Public Charities, 2013

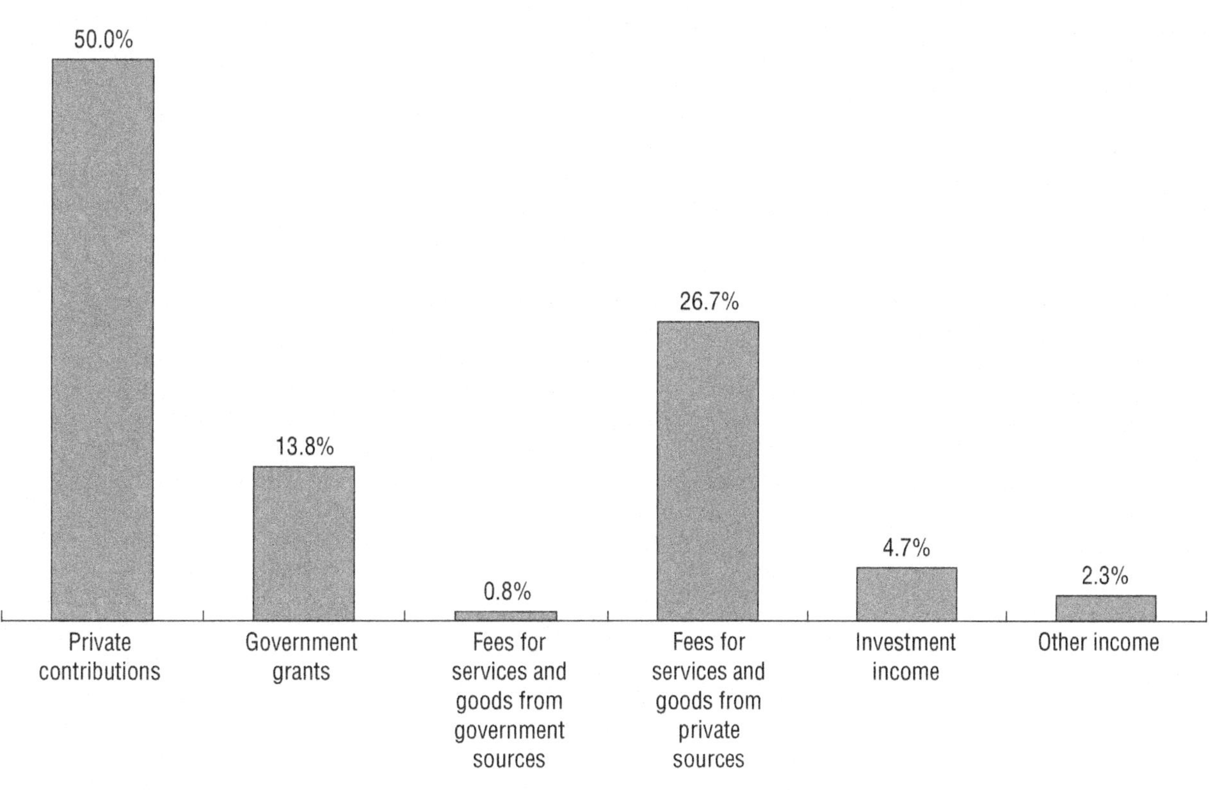

Sources: NCCS calculations of IRS Statistics of Income Division Exempt Organizations Sample (2009, 2011); Urban Institute, National Center for Charitable Statistics, Core Files (2013).

Table 5.21. Revenues and Expenses for Reporting Public Charities in Environment and Animal-Related, 2013

	All Organizations	
	$ millions	%
Public support	10,648	64
Private contributions	8,352	50
Direct contributions	8,115	49
Indirect contributions	237	1
Government grants	2,296	14
Fee for service	4,833	29
Fees from government sources	137	1
Fees from private sources	4,453	27
Net income from sale of inventory	243	1
Investment income	791	5
Dividends, interest, and other similar amounts	312	2
Net gain on sale of assets or securities	423	3
Other investment income	56	0
Other income	376	2
Net income from special events	201	1
Other revenue	175	1
Total revenue	**16,691**	**100**
Paid personnel	6,219	42
Wages and salaries	5,206	35
Compensation of officers	1,381	9
Other wages and salaries	3,825	26
Fringe benefits and payroll tax	1,013	7
Pension plan contributions	157	1
Other employee benefits	502	3
Payroll taxes	354	2
Supplies	434	3
Communications (printing, phone, etc.)	791	5

(continued)

Table 5.21. Revenues and Expenses for Reporting Public Charities in Environment and Animal-Related, 2013 *(continued)*

	All Organizations	
	$ millions	%
Professional fees	1,273	9
Occupancy	468	3
Interest	74	1
Depreciation and depletion	550	4
Other	3,583	24
Total current operating expenses	13,391	91
Grants and benefits	1,301	9
Grants and allocations	1,245	8
Specific assistance to individuals	53	0
Benefits paid to members	3	0
Payments to affiliates	21	0
Total expenses	**14,713**	**100**
Net income (revenue – expenses)	1,978	
Total assets	**41,400**	
Total liabilities	6,405	
Net assets (assets – liabilities)	**34,995**	

Sources: Urban Institute, National Center for Charitable Statistics, Core Files (Public Charities, 2013), Core Full 990 Files (Public Charities, 2012–13) and Core Supplement Files (2013); and Internal Revenue Service, Statistics of Income Sample Files (Public Charities, 2007–12).

Notes: Authors' calculations are based on U.S. Internal Revenue Service Forms 990 and 990-EZ, classified according to the National Taxonomy of Exempt Entities—Core Codes, and adjusted by the National Center for Charitable Statistics based on available data. See the methodology section at the end of the chapter for more information on how the estimates were created. Reporting public charities include only organizations that both reported (filed IRS Forms 990) and were required to do so. The following were excluded: foreign organizations, government-associated organizations, organizations without state identifiers, and organizations excluded by the authors' discretion. Organizations not required to report include religious congregations and organizations with less than $25,000 in gross receipts. The table includes separate analyses for operating public charities and supporting organizations to clarify the distribution of funds and to avoid double-counting the financial information for supporting organizations (see the methodology section at the end of this chapter for a detailed description of the methodology). The sum of the dollar amounts may not equal due to rounding. Percentages for revenue items and net income are expressed as percentages of total revenue. Program service revenue figures may include sizable income via government contracts, which the data source is unable to differentiate from funds raised via the public (i.e., fees for services). Percentages for current operating expense items are expressed as percentages of total current operating expenses. Percentages for other expense items, assets, and liabilities are expressed as percentages of total expenses.

Figure 5.9 displays the number, assets, revenue, and expenses of organizations in the environment and animal subsector. Animal protection and welfare organizations account for over one third of organizations within the subsector, followed by natural resources conservation and protection nonprofits (23 percent). Natural resources conservation and protection nonprofits account for the largest proportion of assets (34 percent), revenue (27 percent), and expenses (27 percent).

Figure 5.9. Number, Assets, Revenue, and Expenses for Environment and Animal-Related Public Charities, 2013

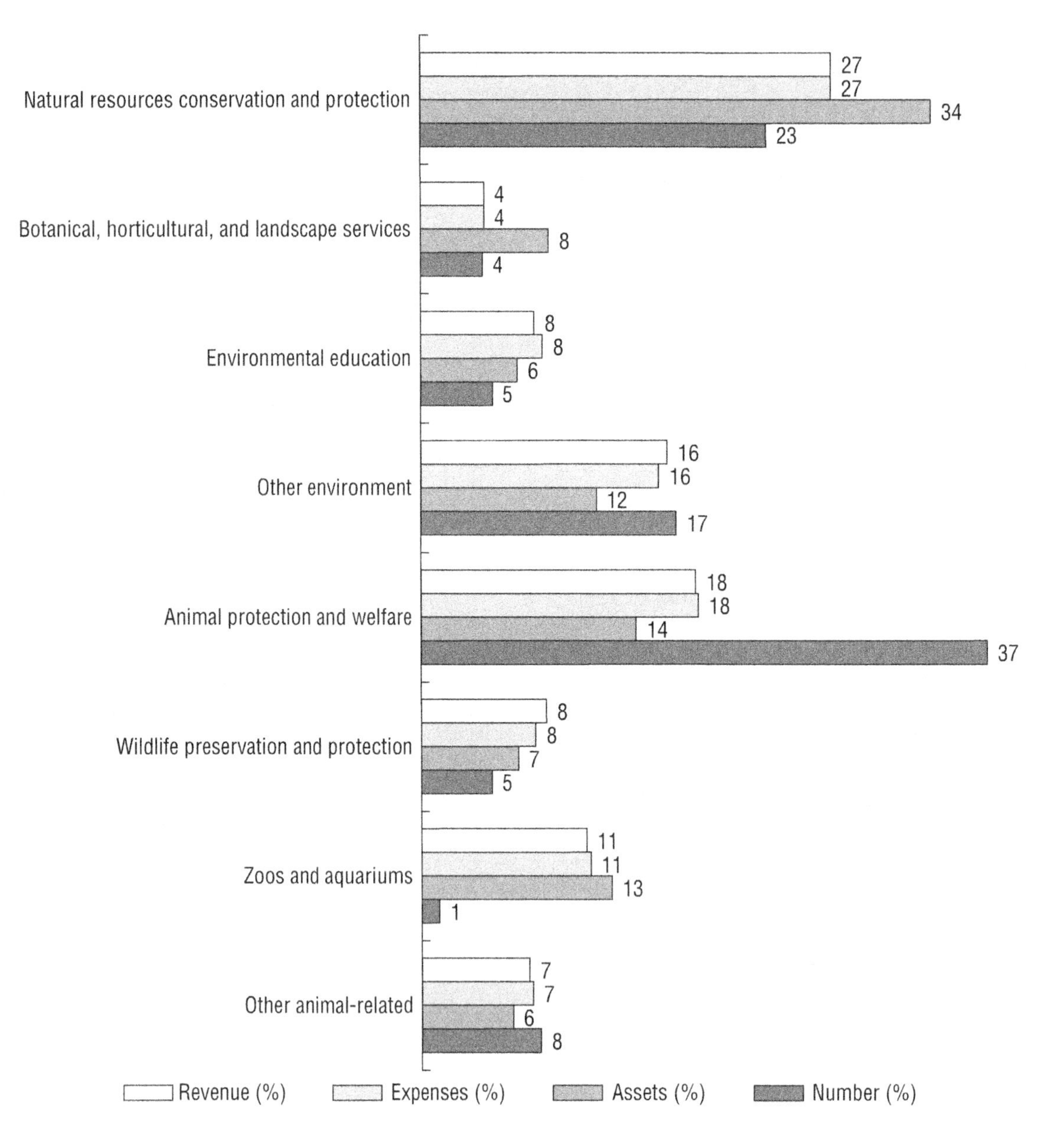

Source: Urban Institute, National Center for Charitable Statistics, Core Files (Public Charities, 2013).

Environmental organizations reported $1.1 billion in net income, and animal-related organizations reported $886.7 million in net income. Environmental organizations held $25 billion in assets, and animal-related organizations held $16.4 billion in assets.

Health

The health subsector, which includes hospitals, nursing facilities, mental health organizations, and medical research organizations, accounts for 13 percent of all public charities, 59 percent of total revenue, 60 percent of total expenses, and 43 percent of total assets.

In 2013, health nonprofits reported $1.0 trillion in total revenues and $975.8 billion in total expenses (table 5.22), higher than all the other subsectors combined. About 88 percent of revenue in the health subsector comes from fees for goods and services such as patient revenue (figure 5.10). The health subsector is the most reliant on fee-for-service revenue, which includes Medicare and Medicaid payments, and is the least reliant of all subsectors on donations (at 7 percent of total revenues). Private contributions accounted for 4 percent of revenue in 2013, and government grants accounted for 3 percent. Wages, salaries, and personnel costs accounted for 47 percent of expenses in the health sector followed by "other" expenses at 26 percent. The health subsector spends less on grants and benefits than any other subsector, just 3 percent in 2013.

The health subsector had net income of $49.5 billion as of 2013. Organizations in this subsector held over $1.4 trillion in total assets.

Figure 5.11 displays the number, assets, revenues, and expenses of public charities within the health subsector. Other health organizations, which include family planning organizations, blood banks, public health organizations, and patient and family support organizations, account for 31 percent of organizations within the health subsector. Mental health organizations account for another 20 percent of health organizations, while disease-specific organizations (which include organizations like the March of Dimes and American Cancer Society) account for approximately 19 percent. Hospitals and primary treatment facilities, while accounting for only 10 percent of organizations, account for approximately three-quarters of assets, and over 70 percent of expenses and revenues.

Outpatient treatment facilities report a negative net income for health organizations at –$728 million. Hospitals and primary treatment facilities have the highest net income by far, $40.7 billion.

Hospitals and primary treatment facilities had $1.1 trillion in assets, well more than the "other" health organizations, which have the next largest amount of assets ($142.0 billion).

Human Services

The human services subsector, which accounts for just over one-third of all reporting public charities, includes a broad array of organizations ranging from soup kitchens

Table 5.22. Revenues and Expenses for Reporting Public Charities in Health, 2013

	All Organizations	
	$ millions	%
Public support	70,107	7
Private contributions	42,684	4
Direct contributions	33,141	3
Indirect contributions	9,543	1
Government grants	27,423	3
Fee for service	907,525	89
Fees from government sources	355,772	35
Fees from private sources	550,438	54
Net income from sale of inventory	1,315	0
Investment income	29,862	3
Dividends, interest, and other similar amounts	13,135	1
Net gain on sale of assets or securities	15,412	2
Other investment income	1,316	0
Other income	17,417	2
Net income from special events	363	0
Other revenue	17,054	2
Total revenue	**1,025,317**	**100**
Paid personnel	462,011	47
Wages and salaries	369,190	38
Compensation of officers	35,381	4
Other wages and salaries	333,808	34
Fringe benefits and payroll tax	92,821	10
Pension plan contributions	18,420	2
Other employee benefits	50,868	5
Payroll taxes	23,533	2
Supplies	38,049	4
Communications (printing, phone, etc.)	23,744	2
Professional fees	88,707	9
Occupancy	23,140	2

(continued)

Table 5.22. Revenues and Expenses for Reporting Public Charities in Health, 2013 *(continued)*

	All Organizations	
	$ millions	%
Interest	11,705	1
Depreciation and depletion	41,086	4
Other	250,074	26
Total current operating expenses	938,516	96
Grants and benefits	33,227	3
Grants and allocations	18,145	2
Specific assistance to individuals	2,768	0
Benefits paid to members	12,314	1
Payments to affiliates	4,071	0
Total expenses	**975,813**	**100**
Net income (revenue – expenses)	49,504	
Total assets	**1,392,790**	
Total liabilities	669,776	
Net assets (assets – liabilities)	**723,013**	

Sources: Urban Institute, National Center for Charitable Statistics, Core Files (Public Charities, 2013), Core Full 990 Files (Public Charities, 2012–13) and Core Supplement Files (2013); and Internal Revenue Service, Statistics of Income Sample Files (Public Charities, 2007–12).

Notes: Authors' calculations are based on U.S. Internal Revenue Service Forms 990 and 990-EZ, classified according to the National Taxonomy of Exempt Entities—Core Codes, and adjusted by the National Center for Charitable Statistics based on available data. See the methodology section at the end of the chapter for more information on how the estimates were created. Reporting public charities include only organizations that both reported (filed IRS Forms 990) and were required to do so. The following were excluded: foreign organizations, government-associated organizations, organizations without state identifiers, and organizations excluded by the authors' discretion. Organizations not required to report include religious congregations and organizations with less than $25,000 in gross receipts. The table includes separate analyses for operating public charities and supporting organizations to clarify the distribution of funds and to avoid double-counting the financial information for supporting organizations (see the methodology section at the end of this chapter for a detailed description of the methodology). The sum of the dollar amounts may not equal due to rounding. Percentages for revenue items and net income are expressed as percentages of total revenue. Program service revenue figures may include sizable income via government contracts, which the data source is unable to differentiate from funds raised via the public (i.e., fees for services). Percentages for current operating expense items are expressed as percentages of total current operating expenses. Percentages for other expense items, assets, and liabilities are expressed as percentages of total expenses.

Figure 5.10. Sources of Revenue for Health Reporting Public Charities, 2013

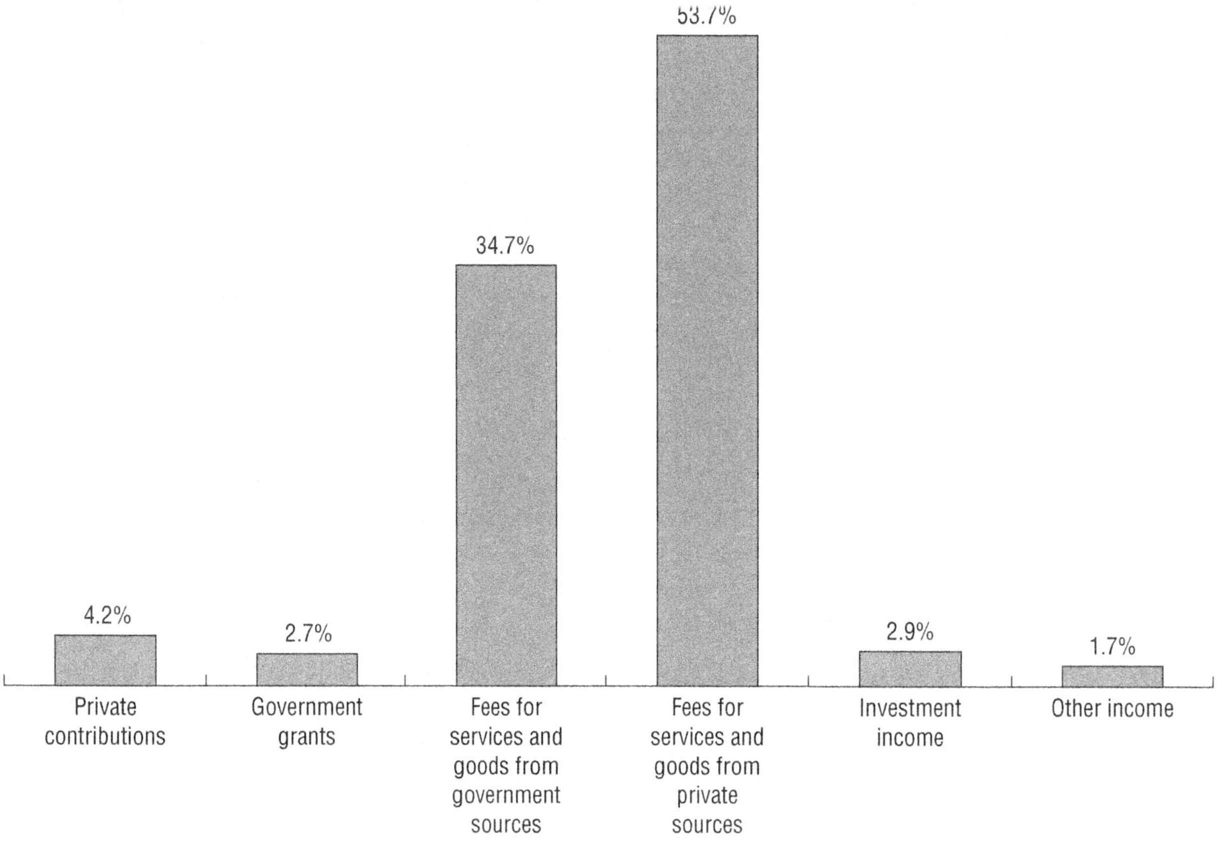

Source	Percent
Private contributions	4.2%
Government grants	2.7%
Fees for services and goods from government sources	34.7%
Fees for services and goods from private sources	53.7%
Investment income	2.9%
Other income	1.7%

Sources: NCCS calculations of IRS Statistics of Income Division Exempt Organizations Sample (2009, 2011); Urban Institute, National Center for Charitable Statistics, Core Files (2013).

and youth development groups to farmland preservation alliances and amateur sporting clubs. In 2013, human service organizations accounted for 12 percent of total revenue, 13 percent of total expenses, and 10 percent of total assets.

The largest subsector by numbers, human services reported $214.2 billion in revenue and $206.9 billion in expenses in 2013 (table 5.23). Figure 5.12 displays the sources of revenue for these organizations. Fees for services and goods account for 53 percent of human services revenue, making the human services sector the third-most-dependent on fees, behind health and education.

The number, assets, revenue, and expenses of reporting public charities in the human services subsector are displayed in figure 5.13. Recreation and sports organizations account for a quarter of human services organizations (the greatest number of reporting public charities in this subsector) but only a modest proportion of resources. Housing and shelter organizations follow with 15 percent of organizations. Youth development (7 percent), children and youth services (6 percent), and family services (4 percent) are smaller subsectors, but they include some of the most

Figure 5.11. Assets, Revenue, and Expenses for Health Public Charities, 2013

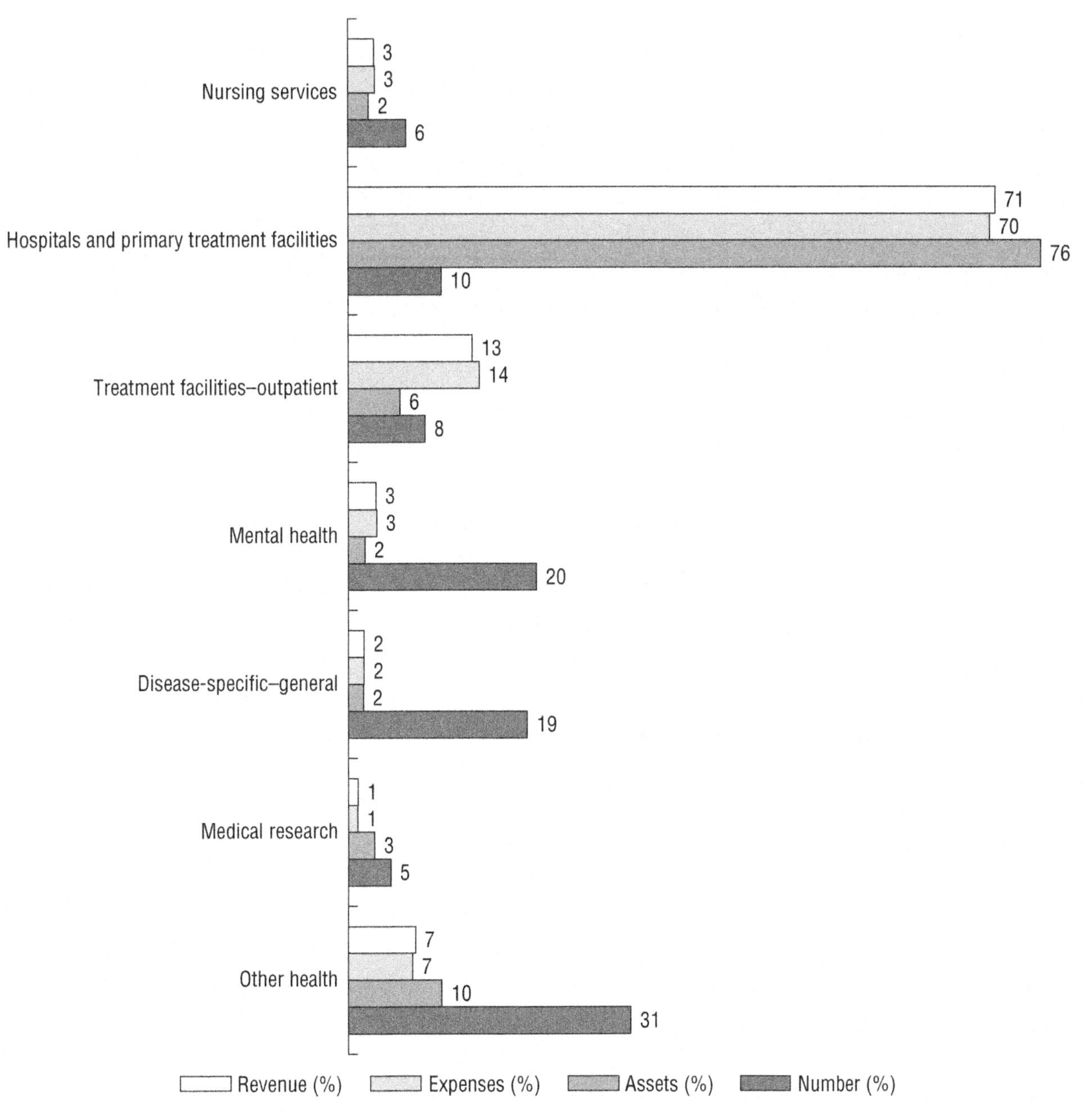

Source: Urban Institute, National Center for Charitable Statistics, Core Files (Public Charities, 2013).

recognized human services organizations, such as Boy Scouts, Girl Scouts, Big Brothers and Big Sisters, Harlem Children's Zone, and Jewish Family and Children's services.

Housing and shelter as well as residential and custodial care organizations account for the highest proportion of assets, about 25 percent each. These groups of organizations are closely followed by "other" human service organizations (including multiservice, financial counseling, and transportation assistance), which account for 17 percent.

Table 5.23. Revenues and Expenses for Reporting Public Charities in Human Services, 2013

	All Organizations	
	$ millions	%
Public support	90,052	42
Private contributions	44,736	21
Direct contributions	41,345	19
Indirect contributions	3,390	2
Government grants	45,317	21
Fee for service	115,298	54
Fees from government sources	55,351	26
Fees from private sources	57,725	27
Net income from sale of inventory	2,223	1
Investment income	5,704	3
Dividends, interest, and other similar amounts	2,229	1
Net gain on sale of assets or securities	2,953	1
Other investment income	521	0
Other income	3,405	2
Net income from special events	1,090	1
Other revenue	2,316	1
Total revenue	**214,195**	**100**
Paid personnel	96,686	47
Wages and salaries	78,901	38
Compensation of officers	10,379	5
Other wages and salaries	68,521	33
Fringe benefits and payroll tax	17,785	9
Pension plan contributions	1,956	1
Other employee benefits	9,733	5
Payroll taxes	6,096	3
Supplies	4,376	2
Communications (printing, phone, etc.)	5,171	3
Professional fees	11,512	6

(continued)

Table 5.23. Revenues and Expenses for Reporting Public Charities in Human Services, 2013 *(continued)*

	All Organizations	
	$ millions	%
Occupancy	10,386	5
Interest	3,493	2
Depreciation and depletion	8,451	4
Other	42,823	21
Total current operating expenses	182,898	88
Grants and benefits	23,568	11
Grants and allocations	13,409	6
Specific assistance to individuals	8,831	4
Benefits paid to members	1,328	1
Payments to affiliates	385	0
Total expenses	**206,851**	**100**
Net income (revenue – expenses)	7,344	
Total assets	**331,481**	
Total liabilities	163,723	
Net assets (assets – liabilities)	**167,744**	

Sources: Urban Institute, National Center for Charitable Statistics, Core Files (Public Charities, 2013), Core Full 990 Files (Public Charities, 2012–13) and Core Supplement Files (2013); and Internal Revenue Service, Statistics of Income Sample Files (Public Charities, 2007–12).

Notes: Authors' calculations are based on U.S. Internal Revenue Service Forms 990 and 990-EZ, classified according to the National Taxonomy of Exempt Entities—Core Codes, and adjusted by the National Center for Charitable Statistics based on available data. See the methodology section at the end of the chapter for more information on how the estimates were created. Reporting public charities include only organizations that both reported (filed IRS Forms 990) and were required to do so. The following were excluded: foreign organizations, government-associated organizations, organizations without state identifiers, and organizations excluded by the authors' discretion. Organizations not required to report include religious congregations and organizations with less than $25,000 in gross receipts. The table includes separate analyses for operating public charities and supporting organizations to clarify the distribution of funds and to avoid double-counting the financial information for supporting organizations (see the methodology section at the end of this chapter for a detailed description of the methodology). The sum of the dollar amounts may not equal due to rounding. Percentages for revenue items and net income are expressed as percentages of total revenue. Program service revenue figures may include sizable income via government contracts, which the data source is unable to differentiate from funds raised via the public (i.e., fees for services). Percentages for current operating expense items are expressed as percentages of total current operating expenses. Percentages for other expense items, assets, and liabilities are expressed as percentages of total expenses.

Figure 5.12. Sources of Revenue for Human Services Reporting Public Charities, 2013

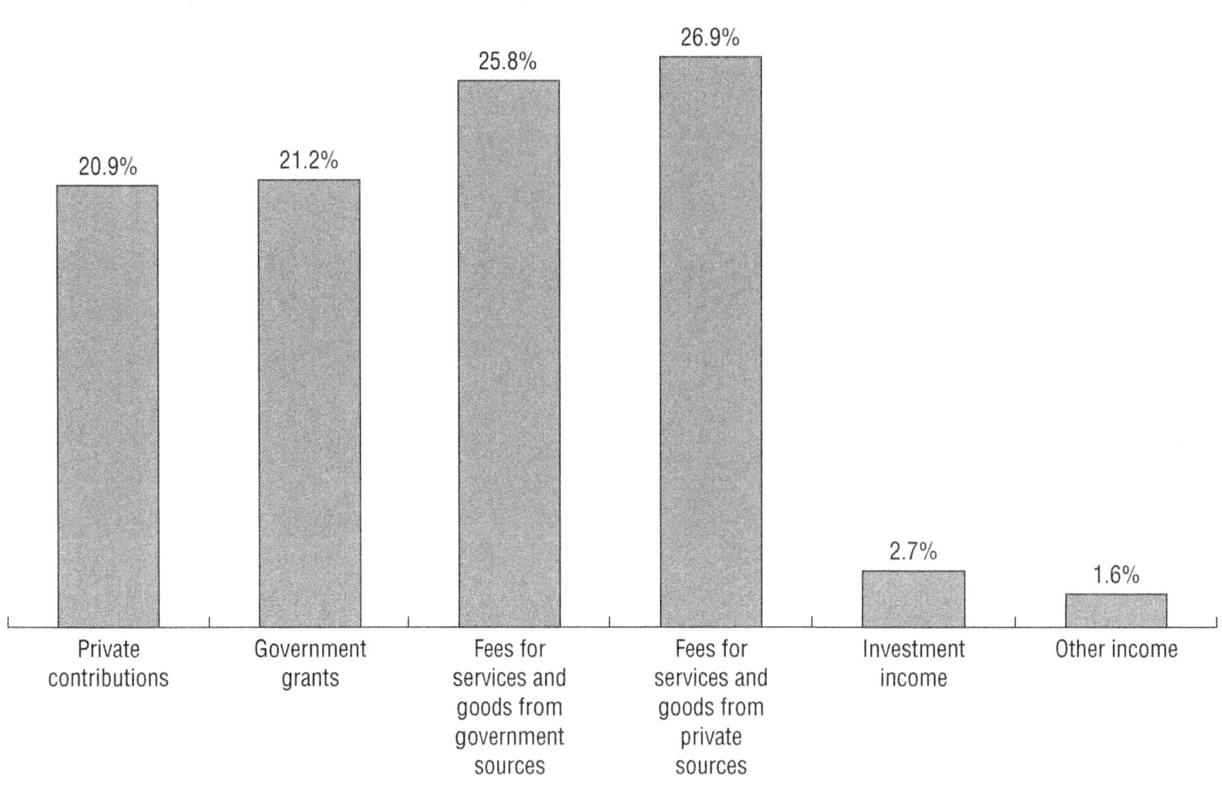

Sources: NCCS calculations of IRS Statistics of Income Division Exempt Organizations Sample (2009, 2011); Urban Institute, National Center for Charitable Statistics, Core Files (2013).

The human services subsector reported net income of $7.3 billion in 2013. These organizations held $331.4 billion in total assets and had net assets (assets minus liabilities) of $167.7 billion. Contributions from individuals, foundations, and corporations accounted for 21 percent of revenue for human services organizations in 2013. Grants from the government account for 21 percent of total revenue, making human services organizations the subsector most reliant on government grants.

"Other" human services organizations reported the highest net income in 2013: $1.3 billion.

International and Foreign Affairs

International and foreign affairs organizations, which include international exchange programs, international development and relief services, international peace and security organization, and international human rights organizations, accounted for 2 percent of reporting public charities. In 2013, these organizations accounted for 2 percent of the nonprofits sector's revenues and expenses and 1 percent of total assets.

Figure 5.13. Number, Assets, Revenue, and Expenses for Human Services Public Charities, 2013

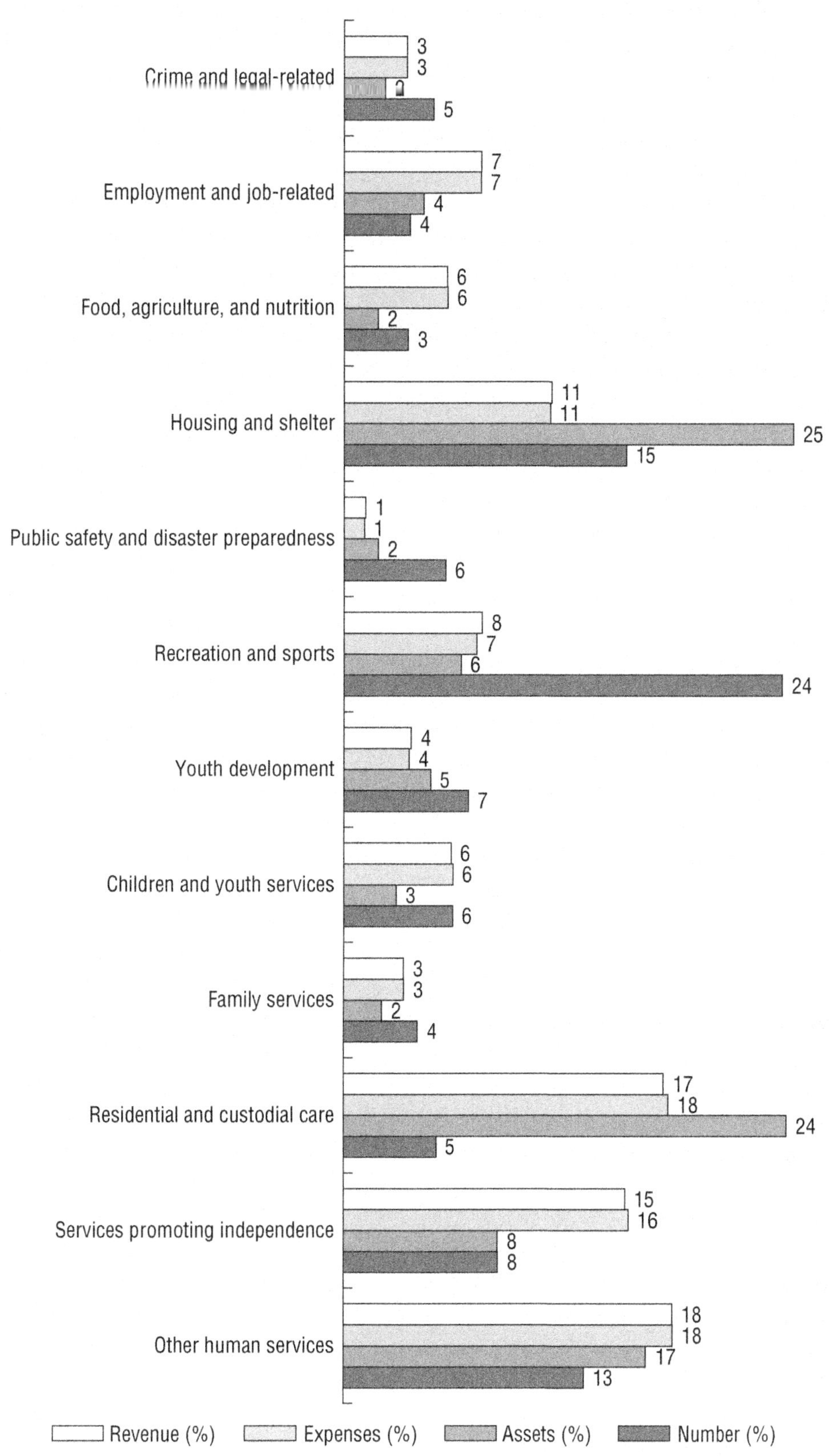

Source: Urban Institute, National Center for Charitable Statistics, Core Files (Public Charities, 2013).

In 2013, international and foreign affairs organizations reported $32.4 billion in total revenue and $30.8 billion in expenses (table 5.24). Contributions from foundations, individuals, and corporations accounted for 65 percent of all revenue for international and foreign affairs organizations, far higher than that of any subsector (figure 5.14). Government grants accounted for about 20 percent. Combined, roughly 86 percent of revenue for international and foreign affairs organizations comes from public support, making this the subsector most dependent on contributions.

Table 5.24. Revenues and Expenses for Reporting Public Charities in International and Foreign Affairs, 2013

	All Organizations	
	$ millions	%
Public support	27,738	86
Private contributions	21,193	65
Direct contributions	19,361	60
Indirect contributions	1,832	6
Government grants	6,545	20
Fee for service	3,618	11
Fees from government sources	534	2
Fees from private sources	3,030	9
Net income from sale of inventory	53	0
Investment income	1,096	3
Dividends, interest, and other similar amounts	299	1
Net gain on sale of assets or securities	770	2
Other investment income	27	0
Other income	187	1
Net income from special events	21	0
Other revenue	166	1
Total revenue	**32,420**	**100**
Paid personnel	7,406	24
Wages and salaries	6,219	20
Compensation of officers	2,213	7
Other wages and salaries	4,006	13
Fringe benefits and payroll tax	1,187	4
Pension plan contributions	203	1

(continued)

Table 5.24. Revenues and Expenses for Reporting Public Charities in International and Foreign Affairs, 2013 *(continued)*

	All Organizations	
	$ millions	%
Other employee benefits	706	2
Payroll taxes	278	1
Supplies	635	2
Communications (printing, phone, etc.)	1,638	5
Professional fees	1,489	5
Occupancy	592	2
Interest	83	0
Depreciation and depletion	251	1
Other	3,837	12
Total current operating expenses	15,932	52
Grants and benefits	14,773	48
Grants and allocations	14,076	46
Specific assistance to individuals	682	2
Benefits paid to members	16	0
Payments to affiliates	120	0
Total expenses	**30,826**	**100**
Net income (revenue – expenses)	1,595	
Total assets	**39,343**	
Total liabilities	9,016	
Net assets (assets – liabilities)	**30,328**	

Sources: Urban Institute, National Center for Charitable Statistics, Core Files (Public Charities, 2013), Core Full 990 Files (Public Charities, 2012–13) and Core Supplement Files (2013); and Internal Revenue Service, Statistics of Income Sample Files (Public Charities, 2007–12).

Notes: Authors' calculations are based on U.S. Internal Revenue Service Forms 990 and 990-EZ, classified according to the National Taxonomy of Exempt Entities—Core Codes, and adjusted by the National Center for Charitable Statistics based on available data. See the methodology section at the end of the chapter for more information on how the estimates were created. Reporting public charities include only organizations that both reported (filed IRS Forms 990) and were required to do so. The following were excluded: foreign organizations, government-associated organizations, organizations without state identifiers, and organizations excluded by the authors' discretion. Organizations not required to report include religious congregations and organizations with less than $25,000 in gross receipts. The table includes separate analyses for operating public charities and supporting organizations to clarify the distribution of funds and to avoid double-counting the financial information for supporting organizations (see the methodology section at the end of this chapter for a detailed description of the methodology). The sum of the dollar amounts may not equal due to rounding. Percentages for revenue items and net income are expressed as percentages of total revenue. Program service revenue figures may include sizable income via government contracts, which the data source is unable to differentiate from funds raised via the public (i.e., fees for services). Percentages for current operating expense items are expressed as percentages of total current operating expenses. Percentages for other expense items, assets, and liabilities are expressed as percentages of total expenses.

Figure 5.14. Sources of Revenue for International Reporting Public Charities, 2013

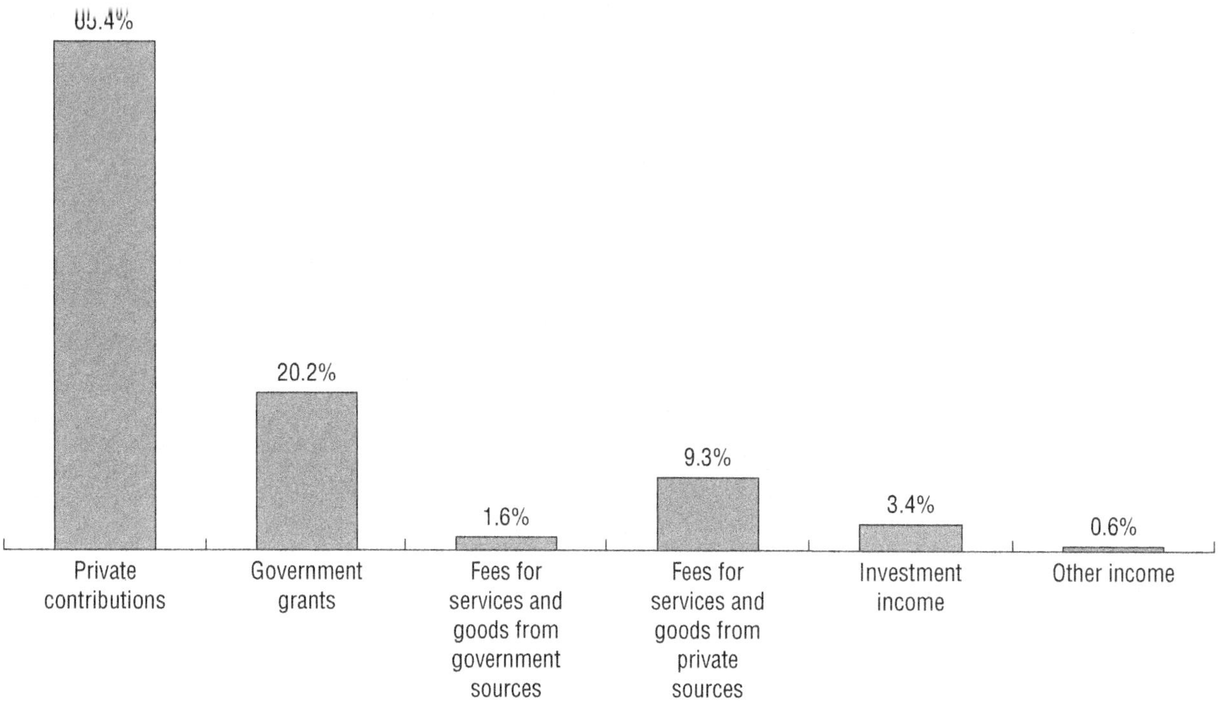

65.4%
Private contributions

20.2%
Government grants

1.6%
Fees for services and goods from government sources

9.3%
Fees for services and goods from private sources

3.4%
Investment income

0.6%
Other income

Sources: NCCS calculations of IRS Statistics of Income Division Exempt Organizations Sample (2009, 2011); Urban Institute, National Center for Charitable Statistics, Core Files (2013).

As in the other subsectors, operating expenses for international and foreign affairs organizations are divided between "other" expenses (12 percent) and wages, salaries, and personnel costs (24 percent). Grants and allocations account for 46 percent of total expenses, making international and foreign affairs first among sectors providing grants to individuals and other organizations (table 5.24).

The international and foreign affairs subsector reported net income of $1.6 billion. These organizations reported $39.3 billion in total assets and $30.3 billion in net assets.

Other Public Charities

The 52,379 reporting public charities classified as "other" include public and societal benefit organizations involved in civil rights and advocacy, community improvement, philanthropy and voluntarism, science and technology, telecommunications, veterans' affairs, insurance, cemeteries, and social science research. Religion-related organizations are also included in this category. As a group, these organizations account for 18 percent of public charities, 7 percent of total revenues, 6 percent of total expenses, and 11 percent of total assets.

In 2013, these organizations reported $115.6 billion in revenue and $96.3 billion in expenses (table 5.25). The public charities in this category generate revenue from a

Table 5.25. Revenues and Expenses for Reporting Public Charities for All Other Subsectors, 2013

	All Organizations	
	$ millions	%
Public support	70,187	61
Private contributions	50,570	44
Direct contributions	48,181	42
Indirect contributions	2,389	2
Government grants	19,617	17
Fee for service	32,327	28
Fees from government sources	5,044	4
Fees from private sources	26,228	23
Net income from sale of inventory	1,056	1
Investment income	11,359	10
Dividends, interest, and other similar amounts	4,498	4
Net gain on sale of assets or securities	6,590	6
Other investment income	271	0
Other income	1,854	2
Net income from special events	316	0
Other revenue	1,538	1
Total revenue	**115,600**	**100**
Paid personnel	33,144	34
Wages and salaries	27,192	28
Compensation of officers	7,229	8
Other wages and salaries	19,964	21
Fringe benefits and payroll tax	5,952	6
Pension plan contributions	1,208	1
Other employee benefits	3,119	3
Payroll taxes	1,625	2
Supplies	1,598	2
Communications (printing, phone, etc.)	4,242	4
Professional fees	8,014	8
Occupancy	2,749	3
Interest	1,265	1

(continued)

Table 5.25. Revenues and Expenses for Reporting Public Charities for All Other Subsectors, 2013 *(continued)*

	All Organizations	
	$ millions	%
Depreciation and depletion	2,303	2
Other	14,486	15
Total current operating expenses	67,802	70
Grants and benefits	28,134	29
Grants and allocations	25,461	26
Specific assistance to individuals	1,914	2
Benefits paid to members	759	1
Payments to affiliates	316	0
Total expenses	**96,251**	**100**
Net income (revenue – expenses)	19,349	
Total assets	**351,194**	
Total liabilities	100,640	
Net assets (assets – liabilities)	**250,557**	

Sources: Urban Institute, National Center for Charitable Statistics, Core Full 990 Files (Public Charities, 2012–13), and Internal Revenue Service, Statistics of Income Sample Files (Public Charities, 2007–12).
Notes: Authors' calculations are based on U.S. Internal Revenue Service Forms 990 and 990-EZ, classified according to the National Taxonomy of Exempt Entities—Core Codes, and adjusted by the National Center for Charitable Statistics based on available data. See the methodology section at the end of the chapter for more information on how the estimates were created. Reporting public charities include only organizations that both reported (filed IRS Forms 990) and were required to do so. The following were excluded: foreign organizations, government-associated organizations, organizations without state identifiers, and organizations excluded by the authors' discretion. Organizations not required to report include religious congregations and organizations with less than $25,000 in gross receipts. The table includes separate analyses for operating public charities and supporting organizations to clarify the distribution of funds and to avoid double-counting the financial information for supporting organizations (see the methodology section at the end of this chapter for a detailed description of the methodology). The sum of the dollar amounts may not equal due to rounding. Percentages for revenue items and net income are expressed as percentages of total revenue. Program service revenue figures may include sizable income via government contracts, which the data source is unable to differentiate from funds raised via the public (i.e., fees for services). Percentages for current operating expense items are expressed as percentages of total current operating expenses. Percentages for other expense items, assets, and liabilities are expressed as percentages of total expenses.

variety of sources. Private contributions account for 44 percent, followed by fees for goods and services at 27 percent, and government grants at 17 percent (figure 5.15). Grants and allocations account for 26 percent of total expenses, making this the second-largest group of organizations providing grants to individuals and other organizations behind international and foreign affairs organizations.

Other public charity organizations reported a net income of $19.3 billion. These organizations reported $351.2 billion in total assets and had net assets of $250.6 billion.

Figure 5.15. Sources of Revenue for Other Reporting Public Charities, 2013

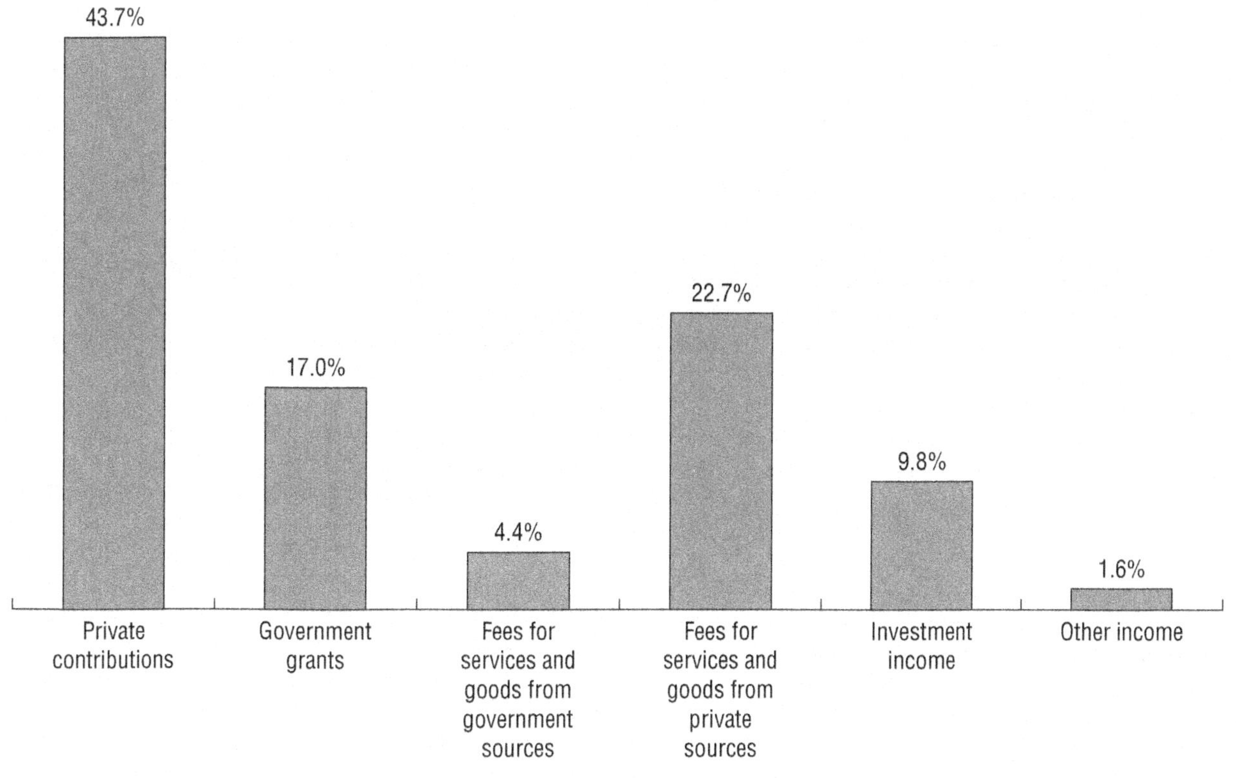

Sources: NCCS calculations of IRS Statistics of Income Division Exempt Organizations Sample (2009, 2011); Urban Institute, National Center for Charitable Statistics, Core Files (2013).

Figure 5.16 displays the number, assets, revenues, and expenses of reporting public charities in this category. Religion-related organizations account for just over one-third of organizations. Community improvement and philanthropy and voluntarism organizations each account for another quarter. Philanthropy and voluntarism organizations hold 50 percent of this group's assets and account for 37 percent of revenue and 30 percent of expenses.

Reporting Public Charities by State

The number of reporting public charities by state ranged from 866 in Wyoming to 34,068 in California in 2013 (table 5.26). Not surprisingly, the number of reporting public charities in a state correlates directly with the state's population. Highly populated states like California, New York, and Texas have the most charities, while less-populated states like Wyoming and North Dakota have fewer.

Public charities in New York, California, Pennsylvania, Massachusetts, and Oregon reported the highest revenue and expenses in 2013. When states are ranked by total assets, four of the same states reappear in the top five and Texas replaces Oregon.

Figure 5.16. Number, Assets, Revenue, and Expenses for Other Public Charities, 2013

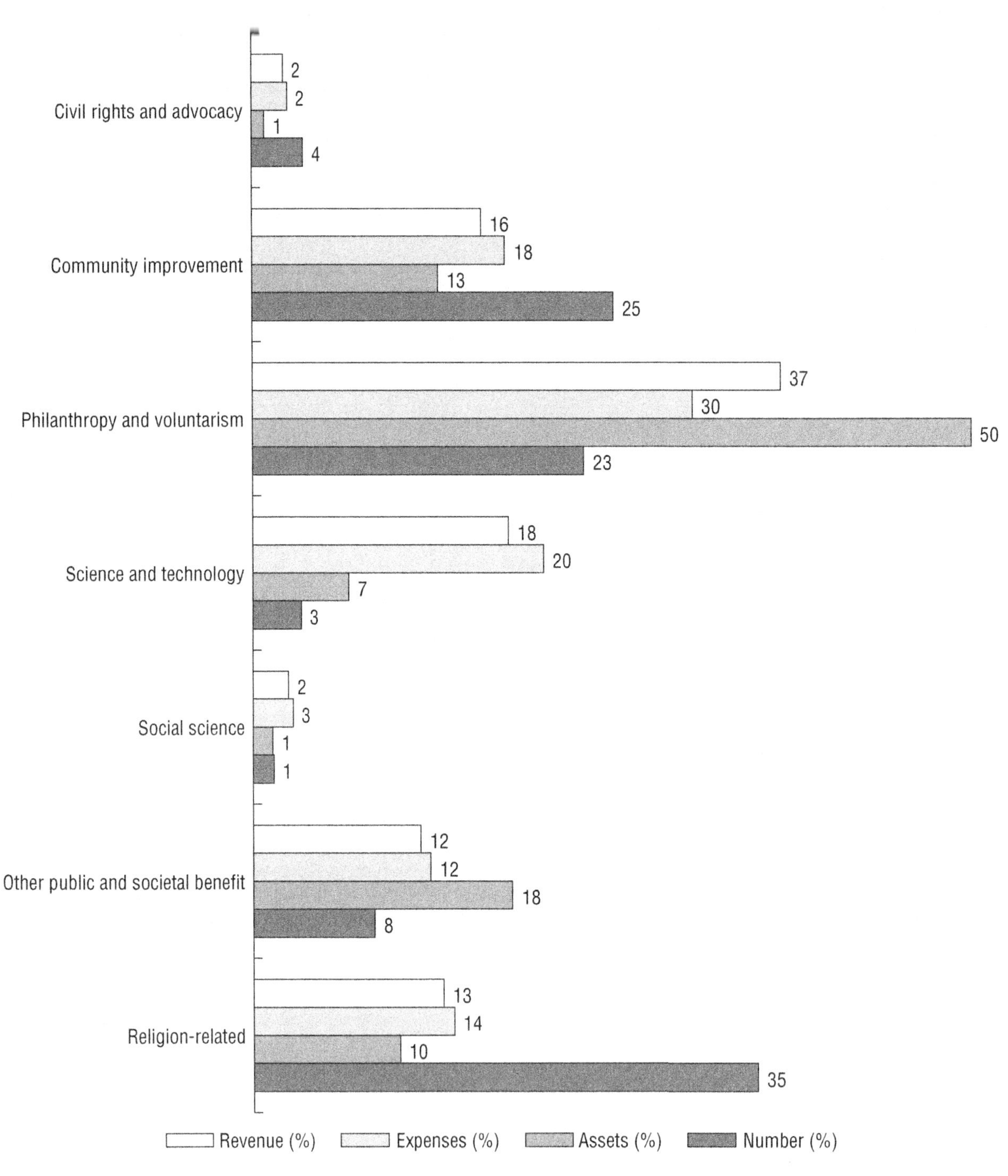

Source: Urban Institute, National Center for Charitable Statistics, Core Files (Public Charities, 2013).

Table 5.26. Number, Revenue, Expenses, and Assets of Reporting Public Charities, by State, 2013

		$, Millions						
	Number	Revenue	Expenses	Assets	Population	Organizations per 10,000 residents	Expenses per resident	Assets per resident
United States	**293,102**	**1,734,102**	**1,623,788**	**3,224,987**	**316,427,395**	**9.3**	**5,132**	**10,192**
Northeast	**65,174**	**475,331**	**445,844**	**964,796**	**56,019,353**	**11.6**	**7,959**	**17,223**
New England	**20,503**	**154,354**	**140,972**	**395,253**	**14,637,401**	**14.0**	**9,631**	**27,003**
Connecticut	4,621	28,479	26,666	74,723	3,597,168	12.8	7,413	20,773
Maine	2,070	10,750	10,230	16,372	1,328,778	15.6	7,699	12,321
Massachusetts	9,187	89,822	80,301	255,934	6,708,810	13.7	11,969	38,149
New Hampshire	1,806	9,959	9,161	22,253	1,322,660	13.7	6,926	16,824
Rhode Island	1,349	10,470	10,034	17,590	1,052,856	12.8	9,530	16,707
Vermont	1,470	4,873	4,580	8,382	627,129	23.4	7,303	13,365
Middle Atlantic	**44,671**	**320,977**	**304,872**	**569,543**	**41,381,952**	**10.8**	**7,367**	**13,763**
New Jersey	8,254	37,934	37,648	81,454	8,907,384	9.3	4,227	9,145
New York	22,352	188,004	178,867	301,053	19,691,032	11.4	9,084	15,289
Pennsylvania	14,065	95,039	88,357	187,036	12,783,536	11.0	6,912	14,631
Midwest	**66,256**	**409,964**	**383,086**	**740,820**	**67,565,788**	**9.8**	**5,670**	**10,964**
East North Central	**42,993**	**280,297**	**261,921**	**500,405**	**46,676,489**	**9.2**	**5,611**	**10,721**
Illinois	11,287	75,828	70,355	156,020	12,889,580	8.8	5,458	12,104
Indiana	5,985	34,911	32,107	70,039	6,570,518	9.1	4,887	10,660
Michigan	8,134	46,659	44,597	71,497	9,900,506	8.2	4,505	7,222
Ohio	11,351	84,952	79,329	138,152	11,572,232	9.8	6,855	11,938
Wisconsin	6,236	37,947	35,533	64,698	5,743,653	10.9	6,187	11,264

(continued)

Table 5.26. Number, Revenue, Expenses, and Assets of Reporting Public Charities, by State, 2013 *(continued)*

	Number	$, Millions			Population	Organizations per 10,000 residents	Expenses per resident	Assets per resident
		Revenue	Expenses	Assets				
West North Central	**23,263**	**129,667**	**121,165**	**240,415**	**20,889,299**	**11.1**	**5,800**	**11,509**
Iowa	3,608	13,073	12,339	29,099	3,092,224	11.7	3,990	9,411
Kansas	2,801	9,459	8,863	16,377	2,894,630	9.7	3,062	5,658
Minnesota	7,116	44,676	41,414	75,588	5,420,541	13.1	7,640	13,945
Missouri	5,435	38,851	36,659	78,517	6,043,708	9.0	6,066	12,992
Nebraska	2,192	11,569	10,420	22,566	1,869,300	11.7	5,574	12,072
North Dakota	1,010	7,154	6,933	8,445	723,626	14.0	9,581	11,671
South Dakota	1,101	4,886	4,536	9,821	845,270	13.0	5,366	11,619
South	**93,726**	**473,244**	**442,137**	**917,064**	**118,487,418**	**7.9**	**3,732**	**7,740**
South Atlantic	**53,439**	**296,379**	**278,124**	**575,061**	**61,831,752**	**8.6**	**4,498**	**9,300**
Delaware	1,009	3,224	3,030	7,277	925,353	10.9	3,275	7,864
District of Columbia	3,668	32,859	30,310	55,269	649,540	56.5	46,664	85,089
Florida	13,132	68,000	63,418	119,229	19,594,467	6.7	3,237	6,085
Georgia	7,203	41,809	39,408	84,092	9,991,562	7.2	3,944	8,416
Maryland	6,199	42,475	40,561	91,620	5,936,040	10.4	6,833	15,435
North Carolina	8,520	44,086	41,015	87,878	9,845,432	8.7	4,166	8,926
South Carolina	3,450	12,058	11,342	28,282	4,768,498	7.2	2,378	5,931
Virginia	8,544	43,584	41,119	89,497	8,267,875	10.3	4,973	10,825
West Virginia	1,714	8,284	7,922	11,916	1,852,985	9.2	4,275	6,431
East South Central	**13,698**	**63,605**	**60,687**	**114,723**	**18,716,139**	**7.3**	**3,243**	**6,130**
Alabama	3,376	9,844	9,357	18,366	4,830,533	7.0	1,937	3,802
Kentucky	3,339	19,769	19,198	29,876	4,398,500	7.6	4,365	6,792

Mississippi	1,762	6,026	5,767	11,179	2,990,976	5.9	1,928	3,737
Tennessee	5,221	27,967	26,366	55,303	6,496,130	8.0	4,059	8,513
West South Central	**26,589**	**113,260**	**103,326**	**227,280**	**37,939,527**	**7.0**	**2,723**	**5,991**
Arkansas	2,325	8,571	8,044	13,305	2,957,957	7.9	2,719	4,498
Louisiana	3,258	18,775	17,938	26,490	4,627,491	7.0	3,876	5,724
Oklahoma	3,059	9,831	8,704	26,078	3,853,405	7.9	2,259	6,767
Texas	17,947	76,083	68,640	161,408	26,500,674	6.8	2,590	6,091
West	**67,946**	**375,563**	**352,721**	**602,308**	**74,354,836**	**9.1**	**4,744**	**8,100**
Mountain	**19,270**	**75,893**	**71,579**	**126,789**	**22,893,190**	**8.4**	**3,127**	**5,538**
Arizona	4,306	24,197	22,906	32,342	6,630,799	6.5	3,454	4,878
Colorado	6,269	24,877	23,716	47,164	5,271,132	11.9	4,499	8,948
Idaho	1,269	4,273	4,163	6,124	1,612,785	7.9	2,582	3,797
Montana	1,704	4,805	4,562	7,806	1,014,402	16.8	4,497	7,695
Nevada	1,286	3,236	2,976	6,340	2,790,366	4.6	1,066	2,272
New Mexico	2,013	5,065	4,710	9,935	2,086,890	9.6	2,257	4,761
Utah	1,557	8,240	7,456	14,118	2,903,685	5.4	2,568	4,862
Wyoming	866	1,200	1,089	2,961	583,131	14.9	1,868	5,078
Pacific	**48,676**	**299,671**	**281,142**	**475,518**	**51,461,646**	**9.5**	**5,463**	**9,240**
Alaska	1,205	3,486	3,177	5,300	737,442	16.3	4,308	7,187
California	34,068	164,297	151,639	310,515	38,414,128	8.9	3,947	8,083
Hawaii	1,505	5,836	5,327	17,934	1,408,765	10.7	3,781	12,730
Oregon	4,811	87,535	84,117	84,664	3,928,030	12.2	21,415	21,554
Washington	7,087	38,517	36,882	57,104	6,973,281	10.2	5,289	8,189

Sources: Urban Institute, National Center for Charitable Statistics, Core Files (Public Charities, 2013); and United States Census Bureau, Population Division (December, 2015).
Note: Figures are not adjusted for inflation.

While these figures give some insight into the distribution of public charities nationwide, the density of public charities by state (as measured by the number of reporting public charities divided by the population) and the expenses, revenue, and assets per resident (as measured by the total expenses, revenue, or assets divided by the population) provide more meaningful information. The per capita rankings presented here exclude the District of Columbia, as many nonprofits in the District have a national or international scope and may not directly benefit local residents.

The density of reporting public charities ranges from 4.6 organizations per 10,000 residents in Nevada to 23.4 organizations per 10,000 residents in Vermont. Less populated states have more reporting public charities per person than more populated states. Vermont, Montana, Alaska, Maine, and Wyoming are the top five states in nonprofit density.

Nonprofit expenses per resident in 2013 ranged from $1,066 in Nevada to $21,415 in Oregon. Oregon, Massachusetts, North Dakota, Rhode Island, and New York report the highest expenditures per resident. Oregon, Massachusetts, and New York are in the top five for both expenses per resident and total expenses per state.

Assets per resident for reporting charities ranged from $2,272 in Nevada to $38,149 in Massachusetts. Massachusetts, Oregon, Connecticut, New Hampshire, and Rhode Island are the top five states in total assets per resident. Massachusetts is the only state that is in the top five in both assets per resident and total assets per state.

Trends in Reporting Public Charities by State

The number of reporting public charities grew from 237,524 in 2003 to 293,102 in 2013, an increase of 23 percent. Growth in public charities varied greatly among the states, ranging from a decline of 9 percent in Rhode Island (the only state to experience a decline) to growth of 37 percent in Georgia. Looking at growth across census regions, the South had the greatest growth at 28 percent, followed by the West at 27 percent. Within the West, the mountain states experienced growth of 30 percent (table 5.27).

Table 5.28 shows the top 10 states ranked by growth of public charities from 2003 to 2013. Six of these states were also in the top 10 in population growth, and all experienced above average population growth.

Total nonprofit revenue grew from $967.9 billion in 2003 to $1.73 trillion in 2013, an inflation-adjusted increase of 42 percent (table 5.29). Western states saw the greatest revenue increase over the period, growing 96 percent (55 percent after adjusting for inflation). Table 5.30 displays the top 10 states in public charity revenue growth. Oregon saw the greatest growth at 240 percent after adjusting for inflation. North Dakota and Idaho both doubled their revenue over the 10 years, even after adjusting for inflation. At the other end of the spectrum Arkansas showed a decline in revenue, but only after adjusting for inflation.

As table 5.31 shows, total public support from individual donations, foundations, corporations, and government grants grew 71 percent (an inflation-adjusted 35 percent) from 2003 to 2013. The West showed the largest increase in public support over the 10-year period, increasing by 79 percent (41 percent after adjusting for inflation).

Table 5.27. Change in the Number of Reporting Public Charities by State, 2003, 2008, and 2013

	Number of Organizations			Total Percentage Change	Average Annual Percentage Change		
	2003	2008	2013	2003–13	2003–13	2003–08	2008–13
United States	**237,524**	**286,500**	**293,102**	**23.4**	**2.1**	**3.8**	**0.5**
Northeast	**54,958**	**64,478**	**65,174**	**18.6**	**1.7**	**3.2**	**0.2**
New England	**17,751**	**20,746**	**20,503**	**15.5**	**1.5**	**3.2**	**–0.2**
Connecticut	3,938	4,626	4,621	17.3	1.6	3.3	0.0
Maine	1,801	2,109	2,070	14.9	1.4	3.2	–0.4
Massachusetts	7,740	9,032	9,187	18.7	1.7	3.1	0.3
New Hampshire	1,519	1,803	1,806	18.9	1.7	3.5	0.0
Rhode Island	1,486	1,685	1,349	–9.2	–1.0	2.5	–4.4
Vermont	1,267	1,491	1,470	16.0	1.5	3.3	–0.3
Middle Atlantic	**37,207**	**43,732**	**44,671**	**20.1**	**1.8**	**3.3**	**0.4**
New Jersey	6,871	8,127	8,254	20.1	1.9	3.4	0.3
New York	18,552	21,803	22,352	20.5	1.9	3.3	0.5
Pennsylvania	11,784	13,802	14,065	19.4	1.8	3.2	0.4
Midwest	**55,546**	**65,538**	**66,256**	**19.3**	**1.8**	**3.4**	**0.2**
East North Central	**36,567**	**42,864**	**42,993**	**17.6**	**1.6**	**3.2**	**0.1**
Illinois	9,468	11,035	11,287	19.2	1.8	3.1	0.5
Indiana	4,897	5,862	5,985	22.2	2.0	3.7	0.4
Michigan	6,968	7,966	8,134	16.7	1.6	2.7	0.4
Ohio	9,931	11,556	11,351	14.3	1.3	3.1	–0.4
Wisconsin	5,303	6,445	6,236	17.6	1.6	4.0	–0.7
West North Central	**18,979**	**22,674**	**23,263**	**22.6**	**2.1**	**3.6**	**0.5**
Iowa	2,880	3,402	3,608	25.3	2.3	3.4	1.2
Kansas	2,386	2,875	2,801	17.4	1.6	3.8	–0.5
Minnesota	5,684	6,854	7,116	25.2	2.3	3.8	0.8
Missouri	4,551	5,396	5,435	19.4	1.8	3.5	0.1
Nebraska	1,785	2,156	2,192	22.8	2.1	3.8	0.3
North Dakota	818	934	1,010	23.5	2.1	2.7	1.6
South Dakota	875	1,057	1,101	25.8	2.3	3.9	0.8

(continued)

Table 5.27. Change in the Number of Reporting Public Charities by State, 2003, 2008, and 2013 *(continued)*

	Number of Organizations			Total Percentage Change	Average Annual Percentage Change		
	2003	2008	2013	2003–13	2003–13	2003–08	2008–13
South	**73,539**	**90,699**	**93,726**	**27.5**	**2.5**	**4.3**	**0.7**
South Atlantic	**42,324**	**52,109**	**53,439**	**26.3**	**2.4**	**4.2**	**0.5**
Delaware	836	980	1,009	20.7	1.9	3.2	0.6
District of Columbia	3,314	3,725	3,668	10.7	1.0	2.4	–0.3
Florida	10,162	12,681	13,132	29.2	2.6	4.5	0.7
Georgia	5,245	6,820	7,203	37.3	3.2	5.4	1.1
Maryland	5,219	6,167	6,199	18.8	1.7	3.4	0.1
North Carolina	6,784	8,432	8,520	25.6	2.3	4.4	0.2
South Carolina	2,624	3,259	3,450	31.5	2.8	4.4	1.1
Virginia	6,660	8,360	8,544	28.3	2.5	4.7	0.4
West Virginia	1,480	1,685	1,714	15.8	1.5	2.6	0.3
East South Central	**10,994**	**13,446**	**13,698**	**24.6**	**2.2**	**4.1**	**0.4**
Alabama	2,713	3,381	3,376	24.4	2.2	4.5	0.0
Kentucky	2,814	3,349	3,339	18.7	1.7	3.5	–0.1
Mississippi	1,467	1,783	1,762	20.1	1.8	4.0	–0.2
Tennessee	4,000	4,933	5,221	30.5	2.7	4.3	1.1
West South Central	**20,221**	**25,144**	**26,589**	**31.5**	**2.8**	**4.5**	**1.1**
Arkansas	1,814	2,164	2,325	28.2	2.5	3.6	1.4
Louisiana	2,688	3,173	3,258	21.2	1.9	3.4	0.5
Oklahoma	2,467	3,032	3,059	24.0	2.2	4.2	0.2
Texas	13,252	16,775	17,947	35.4	3.1	4.8	1.4
West	**53,481**	**65,785**	**67,946**	**27.0**	**2.4**	**4.2**	**0.6**
Mountain	**14,781**	**18,634**	**19,270**	**30.4**	**2.7**	**4.7**	**0.7**
Arizona	3,348	4,284	4,306	28.6	2.5	5.1	0.1
Colorado	4,751	5,898	6,269	32.0	2.8	4.4	1.2
Idaho	934	1,245	1,269	35.9	3.1	5.9	0.4
Montana	1,275	1,602	1,704	33.6	2.9	4.7	1.2
Nevada	979	1,261	1,286	31.4	2.8	5.2	0.4

(continued)

Table 5.27. Change in the Number of Reporting Public Charities by State, 2003, 2008, and 2013 *(continued)*

	Number of Organizations			Total Percentage Change	Average Annual Percentage Change		
	2003	2008	2013	2003–13	2003–13	2003–08	2008–13
New Mexico	1,632	1,961	2,013	23.3	2.1	3.7	0.5
Utah	1,210	1,533	1,557	28.7	2.6	4.8	0.3
Wyoming	652	850	866	32.8	2.9	5.4	0.4
Pacific	**38,700**	**47,151**	**48,676**	**25.8**	**2.3**	**4.0**	**0.6**
Alaska	963	1,149	1,205	25.1	2.3	3.6	1.0
California	27,278	32,936	34,068	24.9	2.2	3.8	0.7
Hawaii	1,173	1,484	1,505	28.3	2.5	4.8	0.3
Oregon	3,703	4,647	4,811	29.9	2.7	4.6	0.7
Washington	5,583	6,935	7,087	26.9	2.4	4.4	0.4

Source: Urban Institute, National Center for Charitable Statistics, Core Files (Public Charities, 2003, 2008, and 2013).
Note: The subtotals may not sum to totals because of rounding.

Table 5.28. The 10 States with the Highest Growth in Number of Reporting Public Charities

	Reporting Public Charities			Percentage change in public charities, 2003–13	Percentage change in population, 2003–13	Rank change in population, 2003–13
Rank	State	2003	2013			
1	Georgia	5,245	7,203	37	14	11
2	Idaho	934	1,269	36	18	5
3	Texas	13,252	17,947	35	20	3
4	Montana	1,275	1,704	34	11	21
5	Wyoming	652	866	33	17	7
6	Colorado	4,751	6,269	32	16	8
7	South Carolina	2,624	3,450	31	15	10
8	Nevada	979	1,286	31	25	1
9	Tennessee	4,000	5,221	31	11	20
10	Oregon	3,703	4,811	30	11	22

Sources: Urban Institute, National Center for Charitable Statistics, Core Files (Public Charities, 2013); and the United States Census Bureau, Population Division (December, 2015).
Note: Figures are not adjusted for inflation.

Table 5.29. Change in Total Revenue for Reporting Public Charities by State, 2003, 2008, and 2013 ($ millions)

	Total Revenue			Total Percentage Change	Average Annual Percentage Change		
	2003	2008	2013	2003–13	2003–13	2003–08	2008–13
United States	**967,941**	**1,439,735**	**1,734,102**	**79.2**	**6.0**	**8.3**	**3.8**
Northeast	**277,014**	**422,834**	**475,331**	**71.6**	**5.5**	**8.8**	**2.4**
New England	**89,175**	**148,637**	**154,354**	**73.1**	**5.6**	**10.8**	**0.8**
Connecticut	18,053	26,963	28,479	57.8	4.7	8.4	1.1
Maine	6,131	8,769	10,750	75.3	5.8	7.4	4.2
Massachusetts	51,063	92,294	89,822	75.9	5.8	12.6	–0.5
New Hampshire	5,390	8,137	9,959	84.8	6.3	8.6	4.1
Rhode Island	6,015	8,844	10,470	74.1	5.7	8.0	3.4
Vermont	2,524	3,629	4,873	93.1	6.8	7.5	6.1
Middle Atlantic	**187,839**	**274,197**	**320,977**	**70.9**	**5.5**	**7.9**	**3.2**
New Jersey	28,420	36,728	37,934	33.5	2.9	5.3	0.6
New York	101,870	152,853	188,004	84.6	6.3	8.5	4.2
Pennsylvania	57,548	84,616	95,039	65.1	5.1	8.0	2.4
Midwest	**230,610**	**331,119**	**409,964**	**77.8**	**5.9**	**7.5**	**4.4**
East North Central	**160,861**	**228,093**	**280,297**	**74.2**	**5.7**	**7.2**	**4.2**
Illinois	44,690	64,674	75,828	69.7	5.4	7.7	3.2
Indiana	19,523	27,904	34,911	78.8	6.0	7.4	4.6
Michigan	31,930	40,983	46,659	46.1	3.9	5.1	2.6
Ohio	44,077	64,358	84,952	92.7	6.8	7.9	5.7
Wisconsin	20,640	30,173	37,947	83.9	6.3	7.9	4.7

West North Central	**69,749**	**103,026**	**129,667**	**85.9**	**6.4**	**8.1**	**4.7**
Iowa	8,375	10,768	13,073	56.1	4.6	5.2	4.0
Kansas	6,573	9,631	9,459	43.9	3.7	7.9	–0.4
Minnesota	21,456	33,818	44,676	108.2	7.6	9.5	5.7
Missouri	21,598	32,092	38,851	79.9	6.0	8.2	3.9
Nebraska	5,955	8,384	11,569	94.3	6.9	7.1	6.7
North Dakota	2,446	3,459	7,154	192.5	11.3	7.2	15.6
South Dakota	3,346	4,874	4,886	46.0	3.9	7.8	0.0
South	**269,091**	**391,956**	**473,244**	**75.9**	**5.8**	**7.8**	**3.8**
South Atlantic	**162,400**	**242,028**	**296,379**	**82.5**	**6.2**	**8.3**	**4.1**
Delaware	2,131	3,617	3,224	51.3	4.2	11.2	–2.3
District of Columbia	19,683	22,331	32,859	66.9	5.3	2.6	8.0
Florida	37,580	56,356	68,000	80.9	6.1	8.4	3.8
Georgia	22,618	32,883	41,809	84.9	6.3	7.8	4.9
Maryland	22,535	36,412	42,475	88.5	6.5	10.1	3.1
North Carolina	22,385	36,749	44,086	96.9	7.0	10.4	3.7
South Carolina	6,918	10,422	12,058	74.3	5.7	8.5	3.0
Virginia	23,553	36,491	43,584	85.0	6.3	9.2	3.6
West Virginia	4,997	6,768	8,284	65.8	5.2	6.3	4.1
East South Central	**39,023**	**57,749**	**63,605**	**63.0**	**5.0**	**8.2**	**2.0**
Alabama	7,015	8,535	9,844	40.3	3.4	4.0	2.9
Kentucky	11,566	21,413	19,769	70.9	5.5	13.1	–1.6
Mississippi	4,565	5,808	6,026	32.0	2.8	4.9	0.7
Tennessee	15,877	21,992	27,967	76.1	5.8	6.7	4.9
West South Central	**67,668**	**92,179**	**113,260**	**67.4**	**5.3**	**6.4**	**4.2**
Arkansas	7,829	9,438	8,571	9.5	0.9	3.8	–1.9

(continued)

Table 5.29. Change in Total Revenue for Reporting Public Charities by State, 2003, 2008, and 2013 ($ millions) *(continued)*

	Total Revenue			Total Percentage Change	Average Annual Percentage Change		
	2003	2008	2013	2003–13	2003–13	2003–08	2008–13
Louisiana	8,757	13,973	18,775	114.4	7.9	9.8	6.1
Oklahoma	7,351	9,892	9,831	33.7	3.0	6.1	–0.1
Texas	43,731	58,875	76,083	74.0	5.7	6.1	5.3
West	**191,226**	**293,826**	**375,563**	**96.4**	**7.0**	**9.0**	**5.0**
Mountain	**36,735**	**56,533**	**75,893**	**106.6**	**7.5**	**9.0**	**6.1**
Arizona	12,244	20,092	24,197	97.6	7.0	10.4	3.8
Colorado	10,620	16,544	24,877	134.2	8.9	9.3	8.5
Idaho	1,638	2,880	4,273	160.9	10.1	12.0	8.2
Montana	2,740	3,501	4,805	75.4	5.8	5.0	6.5
Nevada	1,742	2,842	3,236	85.7	6.4	10.3	2.6
New Mexico	3,102	4,442	5,065	63.2	5.0	7.4	2.7
Utah	4,051	5,165	8,240	103.4	7.4	5.0	9.8
Wyoming	597	1,068	1,200	100.9	7.2	12.3	2.4
Pacific	**154,491**	**237,293**	**299,671**	**94.0**	**6.8**	**9.0**	**4.8**
Alaska	2,051	2,632	3,486	69.9	5.4	5.1	5.8
California	108,538	135,938	164,297	51.4	4.2	4.6	3.9
Hawaii	3,967	5,079	5,836	47.1	3.9	5.1	2.8
Oregon	20,341	66,317	87,535	330.3	15.7	26.7	5.7
Washington	19,594	27,327	38,517	96.6	7.0	6.9	7.1

Source: Urban Institute, National Center for Charitable Statistics, Core Files (Public Charities, 2003, 2008, and 2013).
Notes: The subtotals may not sum to totals because of rounding. Total revenue figures are shown in current dollars and are not adjusted for inflation.

Table 5.30. The 10 States with the Highest Growth in Total Revenue Reported by Public Charities

Rank	State	Total revenue for reporting public charities, 2003 ($ millions)	Total revenue for reporting public charities, 2013 ($ millions)	Percentage change 2003–13	Percentage change 2003–13 (inflation adjusted)
1	Oregon	20,341	87,535	330	240
2	North Dakota	2,446	7,154	193	131
3	Idaho	1,638	4,273	161	106
4	Colorado	10,620	24,877	134	85
5	Louisiana	8,757	18,775	114	69
6	Minnesota	21,456	44,676	108	64
7	Utah	4,051	8,240	103	61
8	Wyoming	597	1,200	101	59
9	Arizona	12,244	24,197	98	56
10	North Carolina	22,385	44,086	97	56

Source: Urban Institute, National Center for Charitable Statistics, Core Files (Public Charities, 2003, 2013).
Note: Total revenue figures are shown in current dollars and are not adjusted for inflation.

Table 5.31. Change in the Public Support for Reporting Public Charities by State, 2003, 2008, and 2013 ($ millions)

	Public Support			Total Percentage Change	Average Annual Percentage Change		
	2003	2008	2013	2003–13	2003–13	2003–08	2008–13
United States	**215,905**	**326,841**	**368,324**	**70.6**	**5.5**	**8.6**	**2.4**
Northeast	**61,984**	**102,250**	**98,596**	**59.1**	**4.8**	**10.5**	**–0.7**
New England	**20,468**	**39,085**	**32,948**	**61.0**	**4.9**	**13.8**	**–3.4**
Connecticut	3,653	5,763	6,056	65.8	5.2	9.5	1.0
Maine	951	1,084	1,207	26.9	2.4	2.7	2.2
Massachusetts	13,121	28,461	21,570	64.4	5.1	16.8	–5.4
New Hampshire	883	1,178	1,213	37.5	3.2	5.9	0.6
Rhode Island	1,236	1,889	2,056	66.3	5.2	8.8	1.7
Vermont	624	709	846	35.5	3.1	2.6	3.6
Middle Atlantic	**41,516**	**63,166**	**65,648**	**58.1**	**4.7**	**8.8**	**0.8**
New Jersey	4,877	6,604	7,050	44.6	3.8	6.3	1.3

(continued)

Table 5.31. Change in the Public Support for Reporting Public Charities by State, 2003, 2008, and 2013 ($ millions) *(continued)*

	Public Support			Total Percentage Change	Average Annual Percentage Change		
	2003	2008	2013	2003–13	2003–13	2003–08	2008–13
New York	26,238	40,249	43,289	65.0	5.1	8.9	1.5
Pennsylvania	10,402	16,313	15,309	47.2	3.9	9.4	–1.3
Midwest	**40,851**	**55,025**	**68,378**	**67.4**	**5.3**	**6.1**	**4.4**
East North Central	**28,737**	**38,286**	**47,797**	**66.3**	**5.2**	**5.9**	**4.5**
Illinois	9,180	11,943	16,296	77.5	5.9	5.4	6.4
Indiana	3,494	4,143	5,160	47.7	4.0	3.5	4.5
Michigan	4,633	5,367	6,744	45.5	3.8	3.0	4.7
Ohio	8,708	13,214	15,111	73.5	5.7	8.7	2.7
Wisconsin	2,722	3,619	4,487	64.8	5.1	5.9	4.4
West North Central	**12,114**	**16,740**	**20,581**	**69.9**	**5.4**	**6.7**	**4.2**
Iowa	1,304	1,937	2,080	59.5	4.8	8.2	1.4
Kansas	1,317	1,671	1,842	39.9	3.4	4.9	2.0
Minnesota	3,834	5,448	6,825	78.0	5.9	7.3	4.6
Missouri	3,890	4,967	6,067	56.0	4.5	5.0	4.1
Nebraska	1,011	1,686	2,337	131.2	8.7	10.8	6.7
North Dakota	309	375	619	100.2	7.2	3.9	10.5
South Dakota	450	655	812	80.4	6.1	7.8	4.4
South	**69,702**	**102,903**	**123,671**	**77.4**	**5.9**	**8.1**	**3.7**
South Atlantic	**46,816**	**69,478**	**82,517**	**76.3**	**5.8**	**8.2**	**3.5**
Delaware	522	688	1,070	104.9	7.4	5.7	9.2
District of Columbia	9,079	12,761	17,757	95.6	6.9	7.0	6.8
Florida	9,750	15,441	17,353	78.0	5.9	9.6	2.4
Georgia	6,592	9,478	11,406	73.0	5.6	7.5	3.8
Maryland	4,822	6,738	9,269	92.2	6.8	6.9	6.6
North Carolina	5,962	9,873	10,011	67.9	5.3	10.6	0.3
South Carolina	1,619	2,245	2,620	61.8	4.9	6.8	3.1
Virginia	7,669	11,350	11,964	56.0	4.5	8.2	1.1
West Virginia	802	904	1,066	32.9	2.9	2.4	3.4

(continued)

Table 5.31. Change in the Public Support for Reporting Public Charities by State, 2003, 2008, and 2013 ($ millions) *(continued)*

	Public Support			Total Percentage Change	Average Annual Percentage Change		
	2003	2008	2013	2003–13	2003–13	2003–08	2008–13
East South Central	**8,181**	**11,607**	**12,704**	**55.3**	**4.5**	**7.2**	**1.8**
Alabama	1,598	2,345	2,600	62.7	5.0	8.0	2.1
Kentucky	1,792	2,593	2,580	44.0	3.7	7.7	–0.1
Mississippi	1,097	1,414	1,313	19.7	1.8	5.2	–1.5
Tennessee	3,695	5,255	6,211	68.1	5.3	7.3	3.4
West South Central	**14,705**	**21,818**	**28,450**	**93.5**	**6.8**	**8.2**	**5.5**
Arkansas	1,388	1,634	2,074	49.4	4.1	3.3	4.9
Louisiana	1,577	2,443	2,793	77.1	5.9	9.1	2.7
Oklahoma	2,319	3,926	3,237	39.6	3.4	11.1	–3.8
Texas	9,421	13,815	20,346	116.0	8.0	8.0	8.0
West	**43,367**	**66,662**	**77,678**	**79.1**	**6.0**	**9.0**	**3.1**
Mountain	**9,228**	**14,193**	**17,008**	**84.3**	**6.3**	**9.0**	**3.7**
Arizona	2,883	4,264	4,701	63.1	5.0	8.1	2.0
Colorado	3,072	4,970	6,249	103.4	7.4	10.1	4.7
Idaho	308	642	654	112.7	7.8	15.9	0.4
Montana	554	753	903	62.9	5.0	6.3	3.7
Nevada	525	794	1,205	129.7	8.7	8.6	8.7
New Mexico	895	1,303	1,360	51.9	4.3	7.8	0.9
Utah	700	1,036	1,419	102.8	7.3	8.2	6.5
Wyoming	292	431	518	77.3	5.9	8.1	3.7
Pacific	**34,140**	**52,469**	**60,670**	**77.7**	**5.9**	**9.0**	**2.9**
Alaska	1,224	1,472	1,824	49.0	4.1	3.8	4.4
California	25,732	39,841	46,498	80.7	6.1	9.1	3.1
Hawaii	796	1,096	1,191	49.6	4.1	6.6	1.7
Oregon	2,103	3,346	3,898	85.4	6.4	9.7	3.1
Washington	4,285	6,714	7,258	69.4	5.4	9.4	1.6

Source: Urban Institute, National Center for Charitable Statistics, Core Files (Public Charities, 2003, 2008, and 2013).
Notes: The subtotals may not sum to totals because of rounding. Public support figures are shown in current dollars and are not adjusted for inflation.

Table 5.32. The 10 States with the Highest Growth in Public Support Reported by Public Charities

Rank	State	Public support for reporting public charities, 2003 ($ millions)	Public support for reporting public charities, 2013 ($ millions)	Percentage change 2003–13	Percentage change 2003–13 (inflation adjusted)
1	Nebraska	1,011	2,337	131	83
2	Nevada	525	1,205	130	81
3	Texas	9,421	20,346	116	71
4	Idaho	308	654	113	68
5	Delaware	522	1,070	105	62
6	Colorado	3,072	6,249	103	61
7	Utah	700	1,419	103	60
8	North Dakota	309	619	100	58
9	District of Columbia	9,079	17,757	96	54
10	Maryland	4,822	9,269	92	52

Source: Urban Institute, National Center for Charitable Statistics, Core Files (2003, 2013).
Note: Public support figures are shown in current dollars and are not adjusted for inflation.

Table 5.32 shows the top 10 states by public support growth. Nebraska reported the highest growth (83 percent after adjusting for inflation) followed by Nevada, Texas, Idaho, and Delaware. Mississippi showed the least growth among the states: 20 percent (−5.5 percent after adjusting for inflation).

The expenses of public charities grew from $938.0 billion in 2003 to $1.62 trillion in 2013, a 37 percent increase after adjusting for inflation (table 5.33). The Western region saw the largest increase in expenses over the 10 years, growing by 91 percent (51 percent after adjusting for inflation). Oregon (236 percent), North Dakota (131 percent), Idaho (107 percent), Colorado (87 percent), and Wyoming (71 percent) saw the greatest increases in expenses after adjusting for inflation (table 5.34). Arkansas showed the slowest growth over the 10 years at 7 percent (−16 percent after adjusting for inflation, the only state to show a decline).

Total assets for reporting public charities increased from $1.74 trillion in 2003 to $3.22 trillion in 2013 (table 5.35), an inflation-adjusted 46 percent increase. The West saw the greatest increase in assets, growing 112 percent (68 percent after adjusting for inflation). The top five states in asset growth (table 5.36; inflation-adjusted growth rates in parentheses) are Oregon (163 percent), Utah (129 percent), North Dakota (110 percent), Colorado (98 percent), and Idaho (80 percent). Delaware was the only state to show a decline, with assets decreasing 16 percent between 2003 and 2013 (a decline of 34 percent after adjusting for inflation).

Net assets (assets minus liabilities) of public charities grew by 87 percent (48 percent after adjusting for inflation) from 2003 to 2013 (table 5.37). The West saw the

Table 5.33. Change in Total Expenses for Reporting Public Charities, by State, Circa 2003, 2008, and 2013 ($ millions)

	Total Expenses			Total Percentage Change	Average Annual Percentage Change		
	2003	2008	2013	2003–13	2003–13	2003–08	2008–13
United States	**938,014**	**1,340,254**	**1,623,788**	**73.1**	**5.6**	**7.4**	**3.9**
Northeast	**269,513**	**385,126**	**445,844**	**65.4**	**5.2**	**7.4**	**3.0**
New England	**84,465**	**127,064**	**140,972**	**66.9**	**5.3**	**8.5**	**2.1**
Connecticut	16,970	23,464	26,666	57.1	4.6	6.7	2.6
Maine	5,918	8,366	10,230	72.9	5.6	7.2	4.1
Massachusetts	48,034	76,105	80,301	67.2	5.3	9.6	1.1
New Hampshire	5,334	7,733	9,161	71.7	5.6	7.7	3.4
Rhode Island	5,843	7,978	10,034	71.7	5.6	6.4	4.7
Vermont	2,366	3,418	4,580	93.6	6.8	7.6	6.0
Middle Atlantic	**185,048**	**258,062**	**304,872**	**64.8**	**5.1**	**6.9**	**3.4**
New Jersey	27,553	33,693	37,648	36.6	3.2	4.1	2.2
New York	101,192	144,745	178,867	76.8	5.9	7.4	4.3
Pennsylvania	56,303	79,624	88,357	56.9	4.6	7.2	2.1
Midwest	**223,796**	**313,584**	**383,086**	**71.2**	**5.5**	**7.0**	**4.1**
East North Central	**156,672**	**215,487**	**261,921**	**67.2**	**5.3**	**6.6**	**4.0**
Illinois	43,705	59,654	70,355	61.0	4.9	6.4	3.4
Indiana	18,815	25,706	32,107	70.6	5.5	6.4	4.5
Michigan	31,441	39,678	44,597	41.8	3.6	4.8	2.4
Ohio	43,089	61,712	79,329	84.1	6.3	7.4	5.2
Wisconsin	19,623	28,737	35,533	81.1	6.1	7.9	4.3
West North Central	**67,124**	**98,097**	**121,165**	**80.5**	**6.1**	**7.9**	**4.3**
Iowa	7,871	10,074	12,339	56.8	4.6	5.1	4.1
Kansas	6,353	9,011	8,863	39.5	3.4	7.2	–0.3
Minnesota	21,014	33,022	41,414	97.1	7.0	9.5	4.6
Missouri	20,626	30,376	36,659	77.7	5.9	8.0	3.8
Nebraska	5,726	7,629	10,420	82.0	6.2	5.9	6.4
North Dakota	2,367	3,398	6,933	192.9	11.3	7.5	15.3
South Dakota	3,166	4,587	4,536	43.3	3.7	7.7	–0.2

(continued)

Table 5.33. Change in Total Expenses for Reporting Public Charities, by State, Circa 2003, 2008, and 2013 ($ millions) *(continued)*

	Total Expenses			Total Percentage Change	Average Annual Percentage Change		
	2003	2008	2013	2003–13	2003–13	2003–08	2008–13
South	**260,387**	**368,105**	**442,137**	**69.8**	**5.4**	**7.2**	**3.7**
South Atlantic	**157,403**	**227,417**	**278,124**	**76.7**	**5.9**	**7.6**	**4.1**
Delaware	2,074	3,486	3,030	46.1	3.9	10.9	–2.8
District of Columbia	19,775	21,670	30,310	53.3	4.4	1.8	6.9
Florida	36,265	54,452	63,418	74.9	5.7	8.5	3.1
Georgia	21,902	31,048	39,408	79.9	6.0	7.2	4.9
Maryland	22,371	33,557	40,561	81.3	6.1	8.4	3.9
North Carolina	21,293	33,025	41,015	92.6	6.8	9.2	4.4
South Carolina	6,533	9,706	11,342	73.6	5.7	8.2	3.2
Virginia	22,321	33,862	41,119	84.2	6.3	8.7	4.0
West Virginia	4,868	6,612	7,922	62.7	5.0	6.3	3.7
East South Central	**37,854**	**55,196**	**60,687**	**60.3**	**4.8**	**7.8**	**1.9**
Alabama	7,000	8,230	9,357	33.7	2.9	3.3	2.6
Kentucky	11,263	20,304	19,198	70.5	5.5	12.5	–1.1
Mississippi	4,253	5,597	5,767	35.6	3.1	5.6	0.6
Tennessee	15,338	21,064	26,366	71.9	5.6	6.6	4.6
West South Central	**65,129**	**85,492**	**103,326**	**58.6**	**4.7**	**5.6**	**3.9**
Arkansas	7,532	9,181	8,044	6.8	0.7	4.0	–2.6
Louisiana	8,712	13,311	17,938	105.9	7.5	8.8	6.1
Oklahoma	6,806	8,334	8,704	27.9	2.5	4.1	0.9
Texas	42,080	54,667	68,640	63.1	5.0	5.4	4.7
West	**184,318**	**273,439**	**352,721**	**91.4**	**6.7**	**8.2**	**5.2**
Mountain	**34,942**	**53,388**	**71,579**	**104.8**	**7.4**	**8.8**	**6.0**
Arizona	11,694	19,043	22,906	95.9	7.0	10.2	3.8
Colorado	10,024	15,508	23,716	136.6	9.0	9.1	8.9
Idaho	1,591	2,582	4,163	161.7	10.1	10.2	10.0
Montana	2,605	3,300	4,562	75.1	5.8	4.8	6.7
Nevada	1,619	2,721	2,976	83.7	6.3	10.9	1.8

(continued)

Table 5.33. Change in Total Expenses for Reporting Public Charities, by State, Circa 2003, 2008, and 2013 ($ millions) *(continued)*

	Total Expenses			Total Percentage Change	Average Annual Percentage Change		
	2003	2008	2013	2003–13	2003–13	2003–08	2008–13
New Mexico	2,944	4,224	4,710	60.0	4.8	7.5	2.2
Utah	3,963	5,056	7,456	88.1	6.5	5.0	8.1
Wyoming	502	955	1,089	117.1	8.1	13.7	2.7
Pacific	**149,376**	**220,051**	**281,142**	**88.2**	**6.5**	**8.1**	**5.0**
Alaska	1,928	2,414	3,177	64.8	5.1	4.6	5.7
California	105,540	123,963	151,639	43.7	3.7	3.3	4.1
Hawaii	3,481	4,347	5,327	53.0	4.3	4.5	4.1
Oregon	19,788	63,846	84,117	325.1	15.6	26.4	5.7
Washington	18,638	25,481	36,882	97.9	7.1	6.5	7.7

Source: Urban Institute, National Center for Charitable Statistics, Core Files (Public Charities, 2003, 2008, and 2013).
Notes: The subtotals may not sum to totals because of rounding. Total expenses are shown in current dollars and are not adjusted for inflation.

Table 5.34. The 10 States with the Highest Growth in Expenses Reported by Public Charities, 2003–13

Rank	State	Total revenue for reporting public charities, 2003 ($ millions)	Total revenue for reporting public charities, 2013 ($ millions)	Percentage change 2003–13	Percentage change 2003–13 (inflation adjusted)
1	Oregon	19,788	84,117	325	236
2	North Dakota	2,367	6,933	193	131
3	Idaho	1,591	4,163	162	107
4	Colorado	10,024	23,716	137	87
5	Wyoming	502	1,089	117	71
6	Louisiana	8,712	17,938	106	63
7	Washington	18,638	36,882	98	56
8	Minnesota	21,014	41,414	97	56
9	Arizona	11,694	22,906	96	55
10	Vermont	2,366	4,580	94	53

Source: Urban Institute, National Center for Charitable Statistics, Core Files (2003, 2013).
Note: Total expenses are shown in current dollars and are not adjusted for inflation.

Table 5.35. Change in Total Assets for Reporting Public Charities, by State, Circa 2003, 2008, and 2013 ($ millions)

	Total Assets			Total Percentage Change	Average Annual Percentage Change		
	2003	2008	2013	2003–13	2003–13	2003–08	2008–13
United States	**1,743,501**	**2,590,879**	**3,224,987**	**85.0**	**6.3**	**8.2**	**4.5**
Northeast	**559,062**	**811,604**	**964,796**	**72.6**	**5.6**	**7.7**	**3.5**
New England	**246,826**	**355,846**	**395,253**	**60.1**	**4.8**	**7.6**	**2.1**
Connecticut	58,485	76,779	74,723	27.8	2.5	5.6	–0.5
Maine	8,417	12,637	16,372	94.5	6.9	8.5	5.3
Massachusetts	153,108	225,854	255,934	67.2	5.3	8.1	2.5
New Hampshire	12,295	18,532	22,253	81.0	6.1	8.6	3.7
Rhode Island	10,262	15,887	17,590	71.4	5.5	9.1	2.1
Vermont	4,259	6,158	8,382	96.8	7.0	7.7	6.4
Middle Atlantic	**312,236**	**455,758**	**569,543**	**82.4**	**6.2**	**7.9**	**4.6**
New Jersey	45,794	64,288	81,454	77.9	5.9	7.0	4.8
New York	165,878	245,308	301,053	81.5	6.1	8.1	4.2
Pennsylvania	100,564	146,163	187,036	86.0	6.4	7.8	5.1
Midwest	**407,694**	**595,071**	**740,820**	**81.7**	**6.2**	**7.9**	**4.5**
East North Central	**276,909**	**401,769**	**500,405**	**80.7**	**6.1**	**7.7**	**4.5**
Illinois	86,170	124,348	156,020	81.1	6.1	7.6	4.6
Indiana	37,377	55,313	70,039	87.4	6.5	8.2	4.8
Michigan	45,989	63,759	71,497	55.5	4.5	6.8	2.3
Ohio	75,830	110,053	138,152	82.2	6.2	7.7	4.7
Wisconsin	31,544	48,295	64,698	105.1	7.4	8.9	6.0
West North Central	**130,784**	**193,302**	**240,415**	**83.8**	**6.3**	**8.1**	**4.5**
Iowa	18,902	24,971	29,099	54.0	4.4	5.7	3.1
Kansas	10,794	15,780	16,377	51.7	4.3	7.9	0.7
Minnesota	38,280	63,637	75,588	97.5	7.0	10.7	3.5
Missouri	43,435	61,019	78,517	80.8	6.1	7.0	5.2
Nebraska	11,255	15,452	22,566	100.5	7.2	6.5	7.9
North Dakota	3,182	4,449	8,445	165.5	10.3	6.9	13.7
South Dakota	4,937	7,994	9,821	98.9	7.1	10.1	4.2

(continued)

Table 5.35. Change in Total Assets for Reporting Public Charities, by State, Circa 2003, 2008, and 2013 ($ millions) *(continued)*

	Total Assets			Total Percentage Change	Average Annual Percentage Change		
	2003	2008	2013	2003–13	2003–13	2003–08	2008–13
South	**493,202**	**748,859**	**917,064**	**85.9**	**6.4**	**8.7**	**4.1**
South Atlantic	**307,223**	**472,581**	**575,061**	**87.2**	**6.5**	**9.0**	**4.0**
Delaware	8,688	17,632	7,277	–16.2	–1.8	15.2	–16.2
District of Columbia	30,811	37,488	55,269	79.4	6.0	4.0	8.1
Florida	62,655	91,629	119,229	90.3	6.6	7.9	5.4
Georgia	42,239	67,036	84,092	99.1	7.1	9.7	4.6
Maryland	50,094	78,533	91,620	82.9	6.2	9.4	3.1
North Carolina	45,359	73,717	87,878	93.7	6.8	10.2	3.6
South Carolina	15,067	21,885	28,282	87.7	6.5	7.8	5.3
Virginia	45,711	75,644	89,497	95.8	6.9	10.6	3.4
West Virginia	6,599	9,017	11,916	80.6	6.1	6.4	5.7
East South Central	**68,022**	**101,921**	**114,723**	**68.7**	**5.4**	**8.4**	**2.4**
Alabama	11,881	15,288	18,366	54.6	4.5	5.2	3.7
Kentucky	18,215	30,503	29,876	64.0	5.1	10.9	–0.4
Mississippi	7,382	10,342	11,179	51.4	4.2	7.0	1.6
Tennessee	30,545	45,788	55,303	81.1	6.1	8.4	3.8
West South Central	**117,958**	**174,358**	**227,280**	**92.7**	**6.8**	**8.1**	**5.4**
Arkansas	7,703	9,550	13,305	72.7	5.6	4.4	6.9
Louisiana	13,755	18,759	26,490	92.6	6.8	6.4	7.1
Oklahoma	14,175	23,037	26,078	84.0	6.3	10.2	2.5
Texas	82,324	123,012	161,408	96.1	7.0	8.4	5.6
West	**283,543**	**435,344**	**602,308**	**112.4**	**7.8**	**9.0**	**6.7**
Mountain	**58,634**	**85,705**	**126,789**	**116.2**	**8.0**	**7.9**	**8.1**
Arizona	18,101	24,018	32,342	78.7	6.0	5.8	6.1
Colorado	18,800	28,068	47,164	150.9	9.6	8.3	10.9
Idaho	2,681	4,256	6,124	128.4	8.6	9.7	7.5
Montana	4,451	6,778	7,806	75.4	5.8	8.8	2.9
Nevada	3,304	5,105	6,340	91.9	6.7	9.1	4.4

(continued)

Table 5.35. Change in Total Assets for Reporting Public Charities, by State, Circa 2003, 2008, and 2013 ($ millions) *(continued)*

	Total Assets			Total Percentage Change	Average Annual Percentage Change		
	2003	2008	2013	2003–13	2003–13	2003–08	2008–13
New Mexico	4,992	7,494	9,935	99.0	7.1	8.5	5.8
Utah	4,864	7,558	14,118	190.2	11.2	9.2	13.3
Wyoming	1,442	2,428	2,961	105.4	7.5	11.0	4.0
Pacific	**224,909**	**349,639**	**475,518**	**111.4**	**7.8**	**9.2**	**6.3**
Alaska	2,522	3,509	5,300	110.1	7.7	6.8	8.6
California	159,088	237,226	310,515	95.2	6.9	8.3	5.5
Hawaii	10,321	15,953	17,934	73.8	5.7	9.1	2.4
Oregon	25,384	52,431	84,664	233.5	12.8	15.6	10.1
Washington	27,594	40,520	57,104	106.9	7.5	8.0	7.1

Source: Urban Institute, National Center for Charitable Statistics, Core Files (Public Charities, 2003, 2008, and 2013).
Notes: The subtotals may not sum to the total because of rounding. Total assets are shown in current dollars and are not adjusted for inflation.

Table 5.36. The 10 States with the Highest Growth in Assets Reported by Public Charities, 2003–13

Rank	State	Total assets for reporting public charities, 2003 ($ millions)	Total assets for reporting public charities, 2013 ($ millions)	Percentage change 2003–13	Percentage change 2003–13 (inflation adjusted)
1	Oregon	25,384	84,664	234	163
2	Utah	4,864	14,118	190	129
3	North Dakota	3,182	8,445	165	110
4	Colorado	18,800	47,164	151	98
5	Idaho	2,681	6,124	128	80
6	Alaska	2,522	5,300	110	66
7	Washington	27,594	57,104	107	63
8	Wyoming	1,442	2,961	105	62
9	Wisconsin	31,544	64,698	105	62
10	Nebraska	11,255	22,566	101	58

Source: Urban Institute, National Center for Charitable Statistics, Core Files (Public Charities, 2003 and 2013).
Note: Total assets are shown in current dollars and are not adjusted for inflation.

Table 5.37. Change in Net Assets for Reporting Public Charities, by State, Circa 2003, 2008, and 2013 ($ millions)

				Total Percentage Change	Average Annual Percent Change		
	2003	2008	2013	2003–13	2003–13	2003–08	2008–13
United States	**1,058,139**	**1,585,900**	**1,979,134**	**87.0**	**6.5**	**8.4**	**4.5**
Northeast	**340,561**	**522,714**	**600,512**	**76.3**	**5.8**	**8.9**	**2.8**
New England	**154,114**	**254,405**	**264,085**	**71.4**	**5.5**	**10.5**	**0.7**
Connecticut	46,659	57,218	52,792	13.1	1.2	4.2	–1.6
Maine	5,613	8,631	10,758	91.7	6.7	9.0	4.5
Massachusetts	83,912	161,689	168,996	101.4	7.3	14.0	0.9
New Hampshire	7,707	11,321	14,050	82.3	6.2	8.0	4.4
Rhode Island	7,385	11,426	12,317	66.8	5.2	9.1	1.5
Vermont	2,837	4,121	5,172	82.3	6.2	7.8	4.6
Middle Atlantic	**186,447**	**268,309**	**336,428**	**80.4**	**6.1**	**7.6**	**4.6**
New Jersey	27,808	39,234	50,469	81.5	6.1	7.1	5.2
New York	99,371	140,747	174,802	75.9	5.8	7.2	4.4
Pennsylvania	59,268	88,328	111,156	87.5	6.5	8.3	4.7
Midwest	**248,658**	**352,851**	**454,065**	**82.6**	**6.2**	**7.3**	**5.2**
East North Central	**172,286**	**245,985**	**310,233**	**80.1**	**6.1**	**7.4**	**4.8**
Illinois	54,235	76,292	96,079	77.2	5.9	7.1	4.7
Indiana	25,790	36,104	48,292	87.3	6.5	7.0	6.0
Michigan	25,976	37,045	41,897	61.3	4.9	7.4	2.5
Ohio	47,008	67,020	84,603	80.0	6.1	7.4	4.8
Wisconsin	19,278	29,524	39,363	104.2	7.4	8.9	5.9
West North Central	**76,372**	**106,866**	**143,832**	**88.3**	**6.5**	**7.0**	**6.1**
Iowa	10,271	13,831	18,195	77.2	5.9	6.1	5.6
Kansas	6,616	10,377	11,080	67.5	5.3	9.4	1.3
Minnesota	20,362	27,447	40,619	99.5	7.1	6.2	8.2
Missouri	26,004	36,663	46,382	78.4	6.0	7.1	4.8
Nebraska	8,138	11,131	17,009	109.0	7.6	6.5	8.9
North Dakota	1,859	2,509	4,416	137.6	9.0	6.2	12.0
South Dakota	3,122	4,909	6,130	96.4	7.0	9.5	4.5

(continued)

Table 5.37. Change in Net Assets for Reporting Public Charities, by State, Circa 2003, 2008, and 2013 ($ millions) *(continued)*

				Total Percentage Change	Average Annual Percent Change		
	2003	2008	2013	2003–13	2003–13	2003–08	2008–13
South	**304,839**	**447,119**	**564,151**	**85.1**	**6.3**	**8.0**	**4.8**
South Atlantic	**192,239**	**279,368**	**348,982**	**81.5**	**6.1**	**7.8**	**4.6**
Delaware	3,662	4,963	5,097	39.2	3.4	6.3	0.5
District of Columbia	20,776	24,741	36,922	77.7	5.9	3.6	8.3
Florida	37,203	51,485	68,466	84.0	6.3	6.7	5.9
Georgia	26,666	40,425	49,620	86.1	6.4	8.7	4.2
Maryland	30,962	45,522	53,384	72.4	5.6	8.0	3.2
North Carolina	29,887	50,567	59,316	98.5	7.1	11.1	3.2
South Carolina	8,341	11,574	14,628	75.4	5.8	6.8	4.8
Virginia	30,518	45,018	54,591	78.9	6.0	8.1	3.9
West Virginia	4,224	5,072	6,958	64.7	5.1	3.7	6.5
East South Central	**38,432**	**57,392**	**67,942**	**76.8**	**5.9**	**8.4**	**3.4**
Alabama	6,900	9,305	11,106	61.0	4.9	6.2	3.6
Kentucky	9,513	16,558	17,099	79.7	6.0	11.7	0.6
Mississippi	4,429	6,128	7,561	70.7	5.5	6.7	4.3
Tennessee	17,591	25,401	32,175	82.9	6.2	7.6	4.8
West South Central	**74,168**	**110,358**	**147,226**	**98.5**	**7.1**	**8.3**	**5.9**
Arkansas	5,569	6,911	10,026	80.0	6.1	4.4	7.7
Louisiana	8,255	11,364	14,688	77.9	5.9	6.6	5.3
Oklahoma	9,992	18,018	20,229	102.5	7.3	12.5	2.3
Texas	50,352	74,065	102,284	103.1	7.3	8.0	6.7
West	**164,081**	**263,216**	**360,406**	**119.7**	**8.2**	**9.9**	**6.5**
Mountain	**34,444**	**50,535**	**74,593**	**116.6**	**8.0**	**8.0**	**8.1**
Arizona	8,214	13,666	18,706	127.7	8.6	10.7	6.5
Colorado	12,735	18,559	26,723	109.8	7.7	7.8	7.6
Idaho	1,747	2,615	3,606	106.4	7.5	8.4	6.6
Montana	2,526	3,123	4,408	74.5	5.7	4.3	7.1
Nevada	2,430	3,080	4,273	75.8	5.8	4.9	6.8

(continued)

Table 5.37. Change in Net Assets for Reporting Public Charities, by State, Circa 2003, 2008, and 2013 ($ millions) *(continued)*

	2003	2008	2013	Total Percentage Change 2003–13	Average Annual Percent Change 2003–13	2003–08	2008–13
New Mexico	2,955	4,190	6,209	110.1	7.7	7.2	8.2
Utah	2,906	3,649	8,505	192.6	11.3	4.7	18.4
Wyoming	930	1,652	2,163	132.5	8.8	12.2	5.5
Pacific	**129,637**	**212,680**	**285,813**	**120.5**	**8.2**	**10.4**	**6.1**
Alaska	1,773	2,494	3,965	123.6	8.4	7.1	9.7
California	90,210	150,428	196,497	117.8	8.1	10.8	5.5
Hawaii	8,032	12,727	13,982	74.1	5.7	9.6	1.9
Oregon	13,894	23,602	37,451	169.5	10.4	11.2	9.7
Washington	15,727	23,429	33,919	115.7	8.0	8.3	7.7

Source: Urban Institute, National Center for Charitable Statistics, Core Files (Public Charities, 2003, 2008, and 2013).
Notes: The subtotals may not sum to totals because of rounding. Net assets are shown in current dollars and are not adjusted for inflation.

greatest increase by far at 120 percent (73 percent after adjusting for inflation). Utah (131 percent), Oregon (113 percent), North Dakota (88 percent), Wyoming (84 percent), and Arizona (80 percent) saw the greatest growth in net assets among the states (table 5.38; all growth rates adjusted for inflation). Connecticut showed the lowest growth in net assets at 13 percent (−11 percent after adjusting for inflation).

Reporting Public Charities by Metropolitan Area

This section reports information for public charities by the 50 largest United States metropolitan areas, according to number of residents. The number of reporting public charities ranges from 677 in the Las Vegas-Henderson-Paradise, Nevada metropolitan area to 20,805 in the New York-Newark-Jersey City metropolitan area (which includes parts of New Jersey, Pennsylvania, and New York State) (table 5.39). The number of reporting public charities in a metropolitan area is highly correlated with the population of the metropolitan area. In order, the New York-Newark-Jersey City, Los

Table 5.38. The 10 States with the Highest Growth in Net Assets Reported by Public Charities, 2003–13

Rank	State	Total net assets for reporting public charities, 2003 ($ millions)	Total net assets for reporting public charities, 2013 ($ millions)	Percentage change 2003–13	Percentage change 2003–13 (inflation adjusted)
1	Utah	2,906	8,505	193	131
2	Oregon	13,894	37,451	170	113
3	North Dakota	1,859	4,416	138	88
4	Wyoming	930	2,163	133	84
5	Arizona	8,214	18,706	128	80
6	Alaska	1,773	3,965	124	77
7	California	90,210	196,497	118	72
8	Washington	15,727	33,919	116	70
9	New Mexico	2,955	6,209	110	66
10	Colorado	12,735	26,723	110	66

Source: Urban Institute, National Center for Charitable Statistics, Core Files (Public Charities, 2003, 2013).
Note: Net assets are shown in current dollars and are not adjusted for inflation.

Angeles-Long Beach-Anaheim (California), Washington, DC-Arlington-Alexandria, Chicago-Naperville-Elgin, and Boston-Cambridge-Newton metropolitan areas had the most reporting public charities, and all five areas are among the 10 largest metropolitan areas by population. Less populated metropolitan areas, such as Salt Lake City and Birmingham-Hoover, tended to have fewer reporting public charities. The Columbus, Ohio, metropolitan area is notable for having more reporting public charities than would be predicted based on its size (ranked 22 out of 50 by number of public charities, 32 out of 50 by population), while the Las Vegas-Henderson-Paradise metropolitan area had fewer reporting public charities than its population size would suggest (ranked 50 out of 50 by number of public charities, 31 out of 50 by population).

Public charities in the New York-Newark-Jersey City, Portland-Vancouver-Hillsboro, Boston-Cambridge-Newton, Washington-Arlington-Alexandria, and Chicago-Naperville-Elgin metropolitan areas reported the highest revenue and expenses in 2013. The Los Angeles-Long Beach-Anaheim metropolitan area replaces Portland-Vancouver-Hillsboro in the top five when ranking by assets.

The total number and total finances of reporting public charities within a metropolitan area is very positively linked with the population of that metropolitan area. However, ranking the metropolitan areas solely by these totals runs the risk of obscuring

Table 5.39. Number, Revenue, Expenses, and Assets of Reporting Public Charities for 50 Largest Metropolitan Areas, 2013

	Number of public charities	$, Millions			Population	Public charities per 10,000 residents	Expenses per resident	Assets per resident
		Revenue	Expenses	Assets				
New York-Newark-Jersey City, NY-NJ-PA	20,805	171,824.6	162,971.3	267,854.2	20,002,086	10.4	8,148	13,391
Los Angeles-Long Beach-Anaheim, CA	10,994	56,587.2	52,805.9	108,731.3	13,175,849	8.3	4,008	8,252
Chicago-Naperville-Elgin, IL-IN-WI	8,406	61,701.7	57,226.8	132,556.7	9,544,796	8.8	5,996	13,888
Dallas-Fort Worth-Arlington, TX	4,884	24,037.9	21,604.2	54,161.2	6,823,113	7.2	3,166	7,938
Houston-The Woodlands-Sugar Land, TX	4,027	22,011.4	19,042.2	49,681.7	6,333,809	6.4	3,006	7,844
Philadelphia-Camden-Wilmington, PA-NJ-DE-MD	6,518	44,763.8	41,566.5	93,052.0	6,036,228	10.8	6,886	15,416
Washington-Arlington-Alexandria, DC-VA-MD-WV	9,851	63,122.8	58,566.9	130,095.1	5,967,176	16.5	9,815	21,802
Miami-Fort Lauderdale-West Palm Beach, FL	3,703	19,753.5	18,796.0	26,273.9	5,863,458	6.3	3,206	4,481
Atlanta-Sandy Springs-Roswell, GA	4,528	28,240.9	26,409.8	59,725.6	5,525,432	8.2	4,780	10,809
Boston-Cambridge-Newton, MA-NH	6,808	70,951.4	62,045.9	223,090.7	4,698,049	14.5	13,207	47,486
San Francisco-Oakland-Hayward, CA	6,619	38,473.4	35,569.1	68,273.9	4,529,654	14.6	7,852	15,073
Phoenix-Mesa-Scottsdale, AZ	2,698	16,941.4	15,861.7	23,274.8	4,404,129	6.1	3,602	5,285
Riverside-San Bernardino-Ontario, CA	2,032	6,610.2	6,351.9	10,359.1	4,390,262	4.6	1,447	2,360
Detroit-Warren-Dearborn, MI	2,984	21,123.6	20,406.3	30,809.4	4,295,394	6.9	4,751	7,173
Seattle-Tacoma-Bellevue, WA	3,991	29,794.6	28,691.1	41,890.2	3,613,621	11.0	7,940	11,592
Minneapolis-St. Paul-Bloomington, MN-WI	4,576	28,528.8	26,502.2	47,706.3	3,461,434	13.2	7,656	13,782
San Diego-Carlsbad, CA	2,836	14,836.8	13,647.7	23,304.6	3,222,558	8.8	4,235	7,232
Tampa-St. Petersburg-Clearwater, FL	1,924	12,735.9	11,303.3	29,376.2	2,874,154	6.7	3,933	10,221
St. Louis, MO-IL	2,509	26,171.6	24,967.7	54,590.4	2,801,587	9.0	8,912	19,486

(continued)

Table 5.39. Number, Revenue, Expenses, and Assets of Reporting Public Charities for 50 Largest Metropolitan Areas, 2013 *(continued)*

	Number of public charities	$, Millions			Population	Public charities per 10,000 residents	Expenses per resident	Assets per resident
		Revenue	Expenses	Assets				
Baltimore-Columbia-Towson, MD	2,869	27,797.5	26,970.9	49,263.8	2,774,050	10.3	9,723	17,759
Denver-Aurora-Lakewood, CO	2,949	16,097.5	15,529.7	32,763.5	2,699,750	10.9	5,752	12,136
Pittsburgh, PA	2,736	22,993.3	21,363.8	34,399.8	2,360,565	11.6	9,050	14,573
Charlotte-Concord-Gastonia, NC-SC	1,751	5,456.6	4,951.7	11,501.7	2,337,339	7.5	2,119	4,921
Portland-Vancouver-Hillsboro, OR-WA	2,714	83,287.6	80,110.0	77,777.2	2,314,747	11.7	34,609	33,601
San Antonio-New Braunfels, TX	1,477	4,960.5	4,408.4	11,242.6	2,282,201	6.5	1,932	4,926
Orlando-Kissimmee-Sanford, FL	1,478	10,613.9	10,012.4	23,155.1	2,271,083	6.5	4,409	10,196
Sacramento—Roseville—Arden-Arcade, CA	2,055	8,394.2	8,077.7	14,968.0	2,217,515	9.3	3,643	6,750
Cincinnati, OH-KY-IN	1,990	14,594.5	13,512.1	27,053.3	2,138,536	9.3	6,318	12,650
Cleveland-Elyria, OH	2,080	23,210.3	21,607.7	46,084.7	2,065,328	10.1	10,462	22,313
Kansas City, MO-KS	1,921	9,301.0	8,742.3	18,248.8	2,055,351	9.3	4,253	8,879
Las Vegas-Henderson-Paradise, NV	677	1,314.9	1,146.4	2,759.4	2,029,316	3.3	565	1,360
Columbus, OH	2,258	18,174.4	17,108.0	23,478.6	1,969,032	11.5	8,689	11,924
Indianapolis-Carmel-Anderson, IN	2,027	15,041.0	13,952.0	25,002.0	1,953,146	10.4	7,143	12,801

San Jose-Sunnyvale-Santa Clara, CA	1,947	17,280.7	14,455.2	53,216.8	1,928,701	10.1	7,495	27,592
Austin-Round Rock, TX	1,880	5,671.5	5,475.0	9,884.3	1,885,803	10.0	2,903	5,241
Nashville-Davidson—Murfreesboro—Franklin, TN	1,777	10,277.5	9,585.5	19,139.2	1,758,577	10.1	5,451	10,883
Virginia Beach-Norfolk-Newport News, VA-NC	1,126	9,672.4	9,095.7	14,604.3	1,707,385	6.6	5,327	8,554
Providence-Warwick, RI-MA	1,779	12,718.9	12,213.9	20,870.8	1,605,521	11.1	7,607	12,999
Milwaukee-Waukesha-West Allis, WI	1,839	16,535.2	15,770.6	27,743.6	1,570,167	11.7	10,044	17,669
Jacksonville, FL	997	7,176.3	6,604.2	10,865.1	1,396,046	7.1	4,731	7,783
Memphis, TN-MS-AR	990	8,316.3	7,831.2	16,606.8	1,341,710	7.4	5,837	12,377
Oklahoma City, OK	1,141	4,356.1	3,922.2	9,379.1	1,320,585	8.6	2,970	7,102
Louisville/Jefferson County, KY-IN	1,062	8,596.5	8,408.4	13,950.1	1,262,244	8.4	6,661	11,052
Richmond, VA	1,199	4,896.9	4,510.7	8,368.9	1,246,867	9.6	3,618	6,712
New Orleans-Metairie, LA	1,087	11,257.8	10,723.5	12,723.0	1,241,949	8.8	8,634	10,244
Hartford-West Hartford-East Hartford, CT	1,450	8,277.3	7,887.2	14,869.0	1,215,943	11.9	6,486	12,228
Raleigh, NC	1,240	4,270.7	4,043.7	6,628.0	1,215,299	10.2	3,327	5,454
Salt Lake City, UT	799	7,089.3	6,355.8	12,183.2	1,141,584	7.0	5,568	10,672
Birmingham-Hoover, AL	985	4,892.8	4,655.9	7,603.3	1,139,556	8.6	4,086	6,672
Buffalo-Cheektowaga-Niagara Falls, NY	1,258	6,201.9	6,007.9	8,482.1	1,136,153	11.1	5,288	7,466

Sources: Urban Institute, National Center for Charitable Statistics, Core Files (Public Charities 2013); and United States Census Bureau, 2010 Census.

other potentially meaningful information. Examining the density of public charities by metropolitan area (as measured by the number of reporting public charities divided by total population) and the revenue, expenses, and assets per resident (as measured by the revenue, expenses, or assets divided by the population) can grant additional understanding of the nonprofit sector's presence within the given metropolitan area.

The density of reporting public charities ranges from 3.3 organizations per 10,000 residents in the Las Vegas-Henderson-Paradise metropolitan area to 16.5 organizations per 10,000 residents in the Washington-Arlington-Alexandria metropolitan area. However, it is worth noting that many organizations in the Washington, D.C., area have a mission related to national or international aims, and may not directly serve the local community. Behind the Washington-Arlington-Alexandria area, the metropolitan area with the next-highest density is the San Francisco-Oakland-Hayward metropolitan area of California.

Nonprofit expenses per resident ranged from $565 in the Las Vegas-Henderson-Paradise metropolitan area to $34,609 in the Portland-Vancouver-Hillsboro metropolitan area. The Portland-Vancouver-Hillsboro area boasts far more expenses per resident than any other metropolitan area; the next-highest amount of expenditures per resident is $13,207 for the Boston-Cambridge-Newton metropolitan area. The total number of expenditures for the Portland-Vancouver-Hillsboro metropolitan area ranks it second overall (out of the 50 largest metropolitan areas), despite its rank of 24th in size.

Assets per resident ranged from $1,360 in the Las Vegas-Henderson-Paradise metropolitan area to $47,486 in the Boston-Cambridge-Newton metropolitan area. The Portland-Vancouver-Hillsboro metropolitan area is next-highest in assets per resident behind Boston-Cambridge-Newton, with $33,601.

Trends in Reporting Public Charities by Metropolitan Area

The total number of reporting charities in the United States grew from 237,524 in 2003 to 293,102 in 2013, a growth of 23 percent. The change in the number of reporting charities varied greatly by metropolitan area, however. Among the 50 largest metropolitan areas, only one reported a decline in the number of reporting public charities over the 10 years: the Providence-Warwick area saw a decline of 3 percent (table 5.40). All 49 other metropolitan areas reported some degree of growth, with Austin-Round Rock seeing the most growth at almost 50 percent. Table 5.41 displays the top 10 metropolitan areas ranked by growth in number of public charities from 2003 to 2013.

The total revenue for reporting charities grew 79 percent between 2003 and 2013, increasing from $968 billion to $1.73 trillion. For the 50 largest metropolitan areas, revenue growth ranged from 8 percent for the San Francisco-Oakland-Hayward area (a decline of 15 percent after adjusting for inflation) to 385 percent

Table 5.40. Change in the Number of Reporting Public Charities for 50 Largest Metropolitan Areas, 2003, 2008, and 2013

	Total Number of Organizations			Total Percentage Change	Average Annual Percentage Change		
	2003	2008	2013	2003–13	2003–13	2003–08	2008–13
New York-Newark-Jersey City, NY-NJ-PA	17,081	20,221	20,805	21.8	2.0	3.4	0.6
Los Angeles-Long Beach-Anaheim, CA	8,714	10,713	10,994	26.2	2.4	4.2	0.5
Chicago-Naperville-Elgin, IL-IN-WI	6,961	8,107	8,406	20.8	1.9	3.1	0.7
Dallas-Fort Worth-Arlington, TX	3,565	4,498	4,884	37.0	3.2	4.8	1.7
Houston-The Woodlands-Sugar Land, TX	2,934	3,781	4,027	37.3	3.2	5.2	1.3
Philadelphia-Camden-Wilmington, PA-NJ-DE-MD	5,462	6,409	6,518	19.3	1.8	3.2	0.3
Washington-Arlington-Alexandria, DC-VA-MD-WV	8,096	9,673	9,851	21.7	2.0	3.6	0.4
Miami-Fort Lauderdale-West Palm Beach, FL	2,904	3,585	3,703	27.5	2.5	4.3	0.6
Atlanta-Sandy Springs-Roswell, GA	3,115	4,197	4,528	45.4	3.8	6.1	1.5
Boston-Cambridge-Newton, MA-NH	5,701	6,662	6,808	19.4	1.8	3.2	0.4
San Francisco-Oakland-Hayward, CA	5,699	6,503	6,619	16.1	1.5	2.7	0.4
Phoenix-Mesa-Scottsdale, AZ	1,973	2,618	2,698	36.7	3.2	5.8	0.6
Riverside-San Bernardino-Ontario, CA	1,615	2,021	2,032	25.8	2.3	4.6	0.1
Detroit-Warren-Dearborn, MI	2,556	2,950	2,984	16.7	1.6	2.9	0.2
Seattle-Tacoma-Bellevue, WA	3,267	3,978	3,991	22.2	2.0	4.0	0.1
Minneapolis-St. Paul-Bloomington, MN-WI	3,635	4,378	4,576	25.9	2.3	3.8	0.9
San Diego-Carlsbad, CA	2,163	2,654	2,836	31.1	2.7	4.2	1.3

(continued)

Table 5.40. Change in the Number of Reporting Public Charities for 50 Largest Metropolitan Areas, 2003, 2008, and 2013 *(continued)*

	Total Number of Organizations			Total Percentage Change	Average Annual Percentage Change		
	2003	2008	2013	2003–13	2003–13	2003–08	2008–13
Tampa-St. Petersburg-Clearwater, FL	1,510	1,870	1,924	27.4	2.5	4.4	0.6
St. Louis, MO-IL	2,093	2,456	2,509	19.9	1.8	3.3	0.4
Baltimore-Columbia-Towson, MD	2,471	2,876	2,869	16.1	1.5	3.1	0.0
Denver-Aurora-Lakewood, CO	2,292	2,806	2,949	28.7	2.6	4.1	1.0
Pittsburgh, PA	2,410	2,796	2,736	13.5	1.3	3.0	–0.4
Charlotte-Concord-Gastonia, NC-SC	1,527	1,617	1,751	14.7	1.4	1.2	1.6
Portland-Vancouver-Hillsboro, OR-WA	2,007	2,549	2,714	35.2	3.1	4.9	1.3
San Antonio-New Braunfels, TX	1,092	1,358	1,477	35.3	3.1	4.5	1.7
Orlando-Kissimmee-Sanford, FL	1,105	1,434	1,478	33.8	3.0	5.4	0.6
Sacramento—Roseville—Arden-Arcade, CA	1,596	1,968	2,055	28.8	2.6	4.3	0.9
Cincinnati, OH-KY-IN	1,740	2,054	1,990	14.4	1.4	3.4	–0.6
Cleveland-Elyria, OH	2,034	2,356	2,080	2.3	0.2	3.0	–2.5
Kansas City, MO-KS	1,590	1,946	1,921	20.8	1.9	4.1	–0.3
Las Vegas-Henderson-Paradise, NV	500	647	677	35.4	3.1	5.3	0.9
Columbus, OH	1,759	2,127	2,258	28.4	2.5	3.9	1.2
Indianapolis-Carmel-Anderson, IN	1,621	1,931	2,027	25.0	2.3	3.6	1.0

San Jose-Sunnyvale-Santa Clara, CA	1,521	1,805	1,947	28.0	2.5	3.5	1.5
Austin-Round Rock, TX	1,257	1,661	1,880	49.6	4.1	5.7	2.5
Nashville-Davidson—Murfreesboro—Franklin, TN	1,247	1,657	1,777	42.5	3.6	5.9	1.4
Virginia Beach-Norfolk-Newport News, VA-NC	972	1,188	1,126	15.8	1.5	4.1	–1.1
Providence-Warwick, RI-MA	1,828	2,093	1,779	–2.7	–0.3	2.7	–3.2
Milwaukee-Waukesha-West Allis, WI	1,808	2,244	1,839	1.7	0.2	4.4	–3.9
Jacksonville, FL	769	967	997	29.6	2.6	4.7	0.6
Memphis, TN-MS-AR	826	959	990	19.9	1.8	3.0	0.6
Oklahoma City, OK	899	1,101	1,141	26.9	2.4	4.1	0.7
Louisville/Jefferson County, KY-IN	917	1,055	1,062	15.8	1.5	2.8	0.1
Richmond, VA	948	1,192	1,199	26.5	2.4	4.7	0.1
New Orleans-Metairie, LA	941	1,033	1,087	15.5	1.5	1.9	1.0
Hartford-West Hartford-East Hartford, CT	1,268	1,499	1,450	14.4	1.4	3.4	–0.7
Raleigh, NC	864	1,147	1,240	43.5	3.7	5.8	1.6
Salt Lake City, UT	664	804	799	20.3	1.9	3.9	–0.1
Birmingham-Hoover, AL	844	1,023	985	16.7	1.6	3.9	–0.8
Buffalo-Cheektowaga-Niagara Falls, NY	1,084	1,171	1,258	16.1	1.5	1.6	1.4

Sources: Urban Institute, National Center for Charitable Statistics, Core Files (Public Charities 2003, 2008, 2013); and United States Census Bureau, 2010 Census.

Table 5.41. The 10 Metropolitan Areas with the Highest Growth in Number of Reporting Public Charities, of 50 Largest Metropolitan Areas, 2003–13

Rank	Metropolitan area	Total number for reporting public charities, 2003	Total number of reporting public charities, 2013	Percentage change, 2003–13
1	Austin-Round Rock, TX	1,257	1,880	50
2	Atlanta-Sandy Springs-Roswell, GA	3,115	4,528	45
3	Raleigh, NC	864	1,240	44
4	Nashville-Davidson—Murfreesboro—Franklin, TN	1,247	1,777	43
5	Houston-The Woodlands-Sugar Land, TX	2,934	4,027	37
6	Dallas-Fort Worth-Arlington, TX	3,565	4,884	37
7	Phoenix-Mesa-Scottsdale, AZ	1,973	2,698	37
8	Las Vegas-Henderson-Paradise, NV	500	677	35
9	San Antonio-New Braunfels, TX	1,092	1,477	35
10	Portland-Vancouver-Hillsboro, OR-WA	2,007	2,714	35

Sources: Urban Institute, National Center for Charitable Statistics, Core Files (Public Charities, 2003, 2013); and United States Census Bureau, 2010 Census.

for the Portland-Vancouver-Hillsboro area (283 percent after adjusting for inflation) (table 5.42). Table 5.43 shows the top 10 metropolitan areas (of the 50 largest metropolitan areas) ranked by revenue growth. In addition to the growth in the Portland-Vancouver-Hillsboro area, the Denver-Aurora-Lakewood and New Orleans-Metairie metropolitan areas also more than doubled their revenue over the time period, even after adjusting for inflation.

As shown in table 5.11, total public support for reporting public charities grew from $215.9 billion in 2003 to $368.3 billion in 2013, an increase of 71 percent (35 percent after adjusting for inflation). When considering the top 50 largest metropolitan areas, the growth in public support for public charities ranged from 22 percent in the Hartford-West Hartford-East Hartford metropolitan area (a decline of 4 percent after adjusting for inflation) to 160 percent in the Houston-The Woodlands-Sugar Land metropolitan area (106 percent after adjusting for inflation) (table 5.44). The top 10 metropolitan areas as ranked by growth in public support from 2003 to 2013 can be seen in table 5.45. The Las Vegas-Henderson-Paradise metropolitan area, despite evincing the lowest total public support of any of the 50 largest metropolitan areas in both 2003 and 2013, almost doubled in public support between the two years, after adjusting for inflation, and was second in growth rate only behind the Houston-The Woodlands-Sugar Land metropolitan area.

Table 5.42. Change in the Revenue of Reporting Public Charities for 50 Largest Metropolitan Areas, 2003, 2008, and 2013

	Total Revenue ($ millions)			Total Percentage Change	Average Annual Percentage Change		
	2003	2008	2013	2003–13	2003–13	2003–08	2008–13
New York-Newark-Jersey City, NY-NJ-PA	94,619	134,244	171,825	81.6	6.1	7.2	5.1
Los Angeles-Long Beach-Anaheim, CA	34,100	46,820	56,587	65.9	5.2	6.5	3.9
Chicago-Naperville-Elgin, IL-IN-WI	36,683	52,956	61,702	68.2	5.3	7.6	3.1
Dallas-Fort Worth-Arlington, TX	12,866	16,766	24,038	86.8	6.5	5.4	7.5
Houston-The Woodlands-Sugar Land, TX	11,522	15,564	22,011	91.0	6.7	6.2	7.2
Philadelphia-Camden-Wilmington, PA-NJ-DE-MD	31,977	42,746	44,764	40.0	3.4	6.0	0.9
Washington-Arlington-Alexandria, DC-VA-MD-WV	36,079	50,323	63,123	75.0	5.8	6.9	4.6
Miami-Fort Lauderdale-West Palm Beach, FL	10,201	16,828	19,753	93.6	6.8	10.5	3.3
Atlanta-Sandy Springs-Roswell, GA	14,069	21,886	28,241	100.7	7.2	9.2	5.2
Boston-Cambridge-Newton, MA-NH	40,693	76,982	70,951	74.4	5.7	13.6	–1.6
San Francisco-Oakland-Hayward, CA	35,709	32,848	38,473	7.7	0.7	–1.7	3.2
Phoenix-Mesa-Scottsdale, AZ	8,276	13,519	16,941	104.7	7.4	10.3	4.6
Riverside-San Bernardino-Ontario, CA	4,097	5,809	6,610	61.3	4.9	7.2	2.6
Detroit-Warren-Dearborn, MI	17,911	21,420	21,124	17.9	1.7	3.6	–0.3
Seattle-Tacoma-Bellevue, WA	14,314	21,350	29,795	108.2	7.6	8.3	6.9
Minneapolis-St. Paul-Bloomington, MN-WI	13,914	21,177	28,529	105.0	7.4	8.8	6.1
San Diego-Carlsbad, CA	7,793	11,522	14,837	90.4	6.7	8.1	5.2

(continued)

Table 5.42. Change in the Revenue of Reporting Public Charities for 50 Largest Metropolitan Areas, 2003, 2008, and 2013 *(continued)*

	Total Revenue ($ millions)			Total Percentage Change	Average Annual Percentage Change		
	2003	2008	2013	2003–13	2003–13	2003–08	2008–13
Tampa-St. Petersburg-Clearwater, FL	7,023	9,805	12,736	81.3	6.1	6.9	5.4
St. Louis, MO-IL	13,142	20,089	26,172	99.1	7.1	8.9	5.4
Baltimore-Columbia-Towson, MD	14,492	22,895	27,797	91.8	6.7	9.6	4.0
Denver-Aurora-Lakewood, CO	6,025	9,514	16,097	167.2	10.3	9.6	11.1
Pittsburgh, PA	11,817	19,613	22,993	94.6	6.9	10.7	3.2
Charlotte-Concord-Gastonia, NC-SC	2,847	3,962	5,457	91.6	6.7	6.8	6.6
Portland-Vancouver-Hillsboro, OR-WA	17,170	61,916	83,288	385.1	17.1	29.2	6.1
San Antonio-New Braunfels, TX	2,934	3,941	4,961	69.1	5.4	6.1	4.7
Orlando-Kissimmee-Sanford, FL	5,583	8,397	10,614	90.1	6.6	8.5	4.8
Sacramento—Roseville—Arden-Arcade, CA	5,426	6,788	8,394	54.7	4.5	4.6	4.3
Cincinnati, OH-KY-IN	7,559	15,098	14,594	93.1	6.8	14.8	–0.7
Cleveland-Elyria, OH	11,971	17,391	23,210	93.9	6.8	7.8	5.9
Kansas City, MO-KS	5,887	9,641	9,301	58.0	4.7	10.4	–0.7
Las Vegas-Henderson-Paradise, NV	534	987	1,315	146.4	9.4	13.1	5.9
Columbus, OH	8,680	13,784	18,174	109.4	7.7	9.7	5.7
Indianapolis-Carmel-Anderson, IN	6,659	10,466	15,041	125.9	8.5	9.5	7.5

San Jose-Sunnyvale-Santa Clara, CA	7,461	13,606	17,281	131.6	8.8	12.8	4.9
Austin-Round Rock, TX	2,636	3,971	5,672	115.2	8.0	8.5	7.4
Nashville-Davidson—Murfreesboro—Franklin, TN	5,445	7,933	10,277	88.8	6.6	7.8	5.3
Virginia Beach-Norfolk-Newport News, VA-NC	5,099	7,303	9,672	89.7	6.6	7.4	5.8
Providence-Warwick, RI-MA	7,661	10,945	12,719	66.0	5.2	7.4	3.0
Milwaukee-Waukesha-West Allis, WI	9,185	12,182	16,535	80.0	6.1	5.8	6.3
Jacksonville, FL	3,538	5,310	7,176	102.8	7.3	8.5	6.2
Memphis, TN-MS-AR	4,764	6,278	8,316	74.6	5.7	5.7	5.8
Oklahoma City, OK	3,287	4,322	4,356	32.5	2.9	5.6	0.2
Louisville/Jefferson County, KY-IN	4,763	7,303	8,596	80.5	6.1	8.9	3.3
Richmond, VA	2,418	3,749	4,897	102.5	7.3	9.2	5.5
New Orleans-Metairie, LA	4,386	7,888	11,258	156.7	9.9	12.5	7.4
Hartford-West Hartford-East Hartford, CT	5,535	8,214	8,277	49.5	4.1	8.2	0.2
Raleigh, NC	1,964	3,305	4,271	117.5	8.1	11.0	5.3
Salt Lake City, UT	3,410	4,287	7,089	107.9	7.6	4.7	10.6
Birmingham-Hoover, AL	3,328	4,020	4,893	47.0	3.9	3.9	4.0
Buffalo-Cheektowaga-Niagara Falls, NY	2,937	8,251	6,202	111.2	7.8	22.9	–5.6

Sources: Urban Institute, National Center for Charitable Statistics, Core Files (Public Charities 2003, 2008, 2013); and United States Census Bureau, 2010 Census.

Table 5.43. The 10 Metropolitan Areas with the Highest Growth in Revenue Reported by Public Charities, of 50 Largest Metropolitan Areas, 2003–13

Rank	Metropolitan area	Total revenue for reporting public charities, 2003 ($ millions)	Total revenue for reporting public charities, 2013 ($ millions)	Percentage change, 2003–13	Percentage change, 2003–13 (inflation adjusted)
1	Portland-Vancouver-Hillsboro, OR-WA	17,170	83,288	385	283
2	Denver-Aurora-Lakewood, CO	6,025	16,097	167	111
3	New Orleans-Metairie, LA	4,386	11,258	157	103
4	Las Vegas-Henderson-Paradise, NV	534	1,315	146	95
5	San Jose-Sunnyvale-Santa Clara, CA	7,461	17,281	132	83
6	Indianapolis-Carmel-Anderson, IN	6,659	15,041	126	78
7	Raleigh, NC	1,964	4,271	117	72
8	Austin-Round Rock, TX	2,636	5,672	115	70
9	Buffalo-Cheektowaga-Niagara Falls, NY	2,937	6,202	111	67
10	Columbus, OH	8,680	18,174	109	65

Sources: Urban Institute, National Center for Charitable Statistics, Core Files (Public Charities, 2003, 2013); and United States Census Bureau, 2010 Census.
Note: Total revenue figures are shown in current dollars and are not adjusted for inflation.

Total expenses reported by public charities grew from $938.0 billion in 2003 to $1,623.8 billion in 2013, an increase of 73 percent (37 percent after adjusting for inflation). Change in expenses for the 50 largest metropolitan areas over the same period ranged from a decline of less than 1 percent in the San Francisco-Oakland-Hayward metropolitan area (an inflation-adjusted decline of 21 percent) to an increase of 377 percent for the Portland-Vancouver-Hillsboro metropolitan area (276 percent after adjusting for inflation). Three metropolitan areas saw declines in expenses over the 10-year period after adjusting for inflation: San Francisco-Oakland-Heyward (21 percent decline), Detroit-Warren-Dearborn (9 percent decline), and Oklahoma City (1 percent decline)(table 5.46). Table 5.47 shows the top 10 metropolitan areas as ranked by percent increase in inflation-adjusted expenses between 2003 and 2013: the Portland-Vancouver-Hillsboro (276 percent), Denver-Aurora-Lakewood (118 percent), New Orleans-Metairie (92 percent), Las Vegas-Henderson-Paradise (87 percent), and Austin-Round Rock (75 percent) metropolitan areas saw the largest increases in expenses, after adjusting for inflation.

Public charities reported that total assets grew from $1.74 trillion in 2003 to $3.22 trillion in 2013, a growth of 85 percent (46 percent after adjusting for inflation).

Table 5.44. Change in the Public Support of Reporting Public Charities for 50 Largest Metropolitan Areas, 2003, 2008, and 2013

	Total Public Support ($ millions)			Total Percentage Change	Average Annual Percentage Change		
	2003	2008	2013	2003–13	2003–13	2003–08	2008–13
New York-Newark-Jersey City, NY-NJ-PA	23,396	35,758	40,585	73.5	5.7	8.9	2.6
Los Angeles-Long Beach-Anaheim, CA	9,983	14,781	15,761	57.9	4.7	8.2	1.3
Chicago-Naperville-Elgin, IL-IN-WI	7,869	10,143	14,213	80.6	6.1	5.2	7.0
Dallas-Fort Worth-Arlington, TX	2,575	4,361	5,813	125.7	8.5	11.1	5.9
Houston-The Woodlands-Sugar Land, TX	2,480	3,719	6,454	160.3	10.0	8.4	11.7
Philadelphia-Camden-Wilmington, PA-NJ-DE-MD	6,292	9,810	9,086	44.4	3.7	9.3	–1.5
Washington-Arlington-Alexandria, DC-VA-MD-WV	15,422	23,417	28,644	85.7	6.4	8.7	4.1
Miami-Fort Lauderdale-West Palm Beach, FL	3,560	6,493	6,697	88.1	6.5	12.8	0.6
Atlanta-Sandy Springs-Roswell, GA	5,128	7,472	8,936	74.3	5.7	7.8	3.6
Boston-Cambridge-Newton, MA-NH	11,680	26,422	18,959	62.3	5.0	17.7	–6.4
San Francisco-Oakland-Hayward, CA	5,129	9,552	11,638	126.9	8.5	13.2	4.0
Phoenix-Mesa-Scottsdale, AZ	1,628	2,454	2,937	80.4	6.1	8.6	3.7
Riverside-San Bernardino-Ontario, CA	955	1,476	1,608	68.3	5.3	9.1	1.7
Detroit-Warren-Dearborn, MI	2,114	2,236	2,876	36.0	3.1	1.1	5.2
Seattle-Tacoma-Bellevue, WA	3,244	5,249	5,531	70.5	5.5	10.1	1.1
Minneapolis-St. Paul-Bloomington, MN-WI	2,655	3,456	4,517	70.1	5.5	5.4	5.5
San Diego-Carlsbad, CA	2,293	3,376	3,938	71.8	5.6	8.0	3.1

(continued)

Table 5.44. Change in the Public Support of Reporting Public Charities for 50 Largest Metropolitan Areas, 2003, 2008, and 2013 *(continued)*

	Total Public Support ($ millions)			Total Percentage Change	Average Annual Percentage Change		
	2003	2008	2013	2003–13	2003–13	2003–08	2008–13
Tampa-St. Petersburg-Clearwater, FL	1,476	2,279	2,821	91.0	6.7	9.1	4.4
St. Louis, MO-IL	1,994	2,375	3,071	54.0	4.4	3.6	5.3
Baltimore-Columbia-Towson, MD	2,505	3,111	5,271	110.4	7.7	4.4	11.1
Denver-Aurora-Lakewood, CO	1,353	2,288	2,932	116.6	8.0	11.1	5.1
Pittsburgh, PA	2,013	3,505	3,666	82.1	6.2	11.7	0.9
Charlotte-Concord-Gastonia, NC-SC	944	1,450	1,710	81.2	6.1	9.0	3.4
Portland-Vancouver-Hillsboro, OR-WA	1,439	2,282	2,708	88.2	6.5	9.7	3.5
San Antonio-New Braunfels, TX	890	1,105	1,734	94.9	6.9	4.4	9.4
Orlando-Kissimmee-Sanford, FL	1,079	1,531	1,566	45.2	3.8	7.3	0.4
Sacramento—Roseville—Arden-Arcade, CA	1,253	1,592	2,183	74.3	5.7	4.9	6.5
Cincinnati, OH-KY-IN	1,412	1,950	2,251	59.4	4.8	6.7	2.9
Cleveland-Elyria, OH	1,959	2,721	2,967	51.5	4.2	6.8	1.7
Kansas City, MO-KS	1,614	2,215	2,346	45.4	3.8	6.5	1.2
Las Vegas-Henderson-Paradise, NV	299	478	748	150.2	9.6	9.8	9.4
Columbus, OH	2,814	5,275	6,110	117.1	8.1	13.4	3.0
Indianapolis-Carmel-Anderson, IN	1,237	1,378	2,115	71.1	5.5	2.2	9.0

San Jose-Sunnyvale-Santa Clara, CA	2,483	4,408	5,290	113.1	7.9	12.2	3.7
Austin-Round Rock, TX	712	1,242	1,687	136.8	9.0	11.8	6.3
Nashville-Davidson—Murfreesboro—Franklin, TN	1,201	1,620	1,702	41.6	3.5	6.2	1.0
Virginia Beach-Norfolk-Newport News, VA-NC	1,073	1,311	1,423	32.7	2.9	4.1	1.7
Providence-Warwick, RI-MA	1,427	2,125	2,372	66.2	5.2	8.3	2.2
Milwaukee-Waukesha-West Allis, WI	1,194	1,656	1,877	57.2	4.6	6.8	2.5
Jacksonville, FL	658	1,076	1,568	138.1	9.1	10.3	7.8
Memphis, TN-MS-AR	1,457	2,110	2,581	77.1	5.9	7.7	4.1
Oklahoma City, OK	1,146	2,057	1,591	38.9	3.3	12.4	−5.0
Louisville/Jefferson County, KY-IN	742	1,001	1,060	43.0	3.6	6.2	1.2
Richmond, VA	720	1,019	1,261	75.0	5.8	7.2	4.4
New Orleans-Metairie, LA	814	1,306	1,556	91.1	6.7	9.9	3.6
Hartford-West Hartford-East Hartford, CT	1,129	1,424	1,376	21.9	2.0	4.8	−0.7
Raleigh, NC	764	1,348	1,268	66.0	5.2	12.0	−1.2
Salt Lake City, UT	460	553	828	80.0	6.1	3.8	8.4
Birmingham-Hoover, AL	521	1,001	1,104	111.9	7.8	14.0	2.0
Buffalo-Cheektowaga-Niagara Falls, NY	689	1,615	928	34.8	3.0	18.6	−10.5

Sources: Urban Institute, National Center for Charitable Statistics, Core Files (Public Charities 2003, 2008, 2013); and United States Census Bureau, 2010 Census.

Table 5.45. The 10 Metropolitan Areas with the Highest Growth in Public Support Reported by Public Charities, of 50 Largest Metropolitan Areas, 2003–13

Rank	Metropolitan area	Total public support for reporting public charities, 2003 ($ millions)	Total public support for reporting public charities, 2013 ($ millions)	Percentage change, 2003–13	Percentage change, 2003–13 (inflation adjusted)
1	Houston-The Woodlands-Sugar Land, TX	2,480	6,454	160	106
2	Las Vegas-Henderson-Paradise, NV	299	748	150	98
3	Jacksonville, FL	658	1,568	138	88
4	Austin-Round Rock, TX	712	1,687	137	87
5	San Francisco-Oakland-Hayward, CA	5,129	11,638	127	79
6	Dallas-Fort Worth-Arlington, TX	2,575	5,813	126	78
7	Columbus, OH	2,814	6,110	117	72
8	Denver-Aurora-Lakewood, CO	1,353	2,932	117	71
9	San Jose-Sunnyvale-Santa Clara, CA	2,483	5,290	113	68
10	Birmingham-Hoover, AL	521	1,104	112	67

Sources: Urban Institute, National Center for Charitable Statistics, Core Files (Public Charities, 2003, 2013); and United States Census Bureau, 2010 Census.
Note: Total public support figures are shown in current dollars and are not adjusted for inflation.

For the top 50 most populated metropolitan areas, asset growth ranged from 26 percent in Detroit-Warren-Dearborn (a decline of less than 1 percent, after adjusting for inflation) to 277 percent (198 percent after adjusting for inflation) in Portland-Vancouver-Hillsboro (table 5.48). Table 5.49 lists the 10 top metropolitan areas as ranked by growth in total assets. Portland-Vancouver-Hillsboro, Denver-Aurora-Lakewood, Las Vegas-Henderson-Paradise, Salt Lake City, Sacramento-Roseville-Arden-Arcade, and Orlando-Kissimmee-Sanford all more than doubled in total assets between 2003 and 2013 after adjusting for inflation.

The total net assets (assets minus liabilities) of public charities rose from $1.06 trillion in 2003 to $1.98 trillion in 2013, a growth of 87 percent (48 percent after adjusting for inflation). The growth in net assets for the 50 most-populated metropolitan areas ranged from 27 percent for Detroit-Warren-Dearborn (essentially no change after adjusting for inflation) to 276 percent for the Sacramento-Roseville-Arden-Arcade metropolitan area (197 percent after adjusting for inflation) (table 5.50). Table 5.51 shows the 10 metropolitan areas with the largest growth in net assets: the top six more than doubled in net assets reported by public charities between 2003 and 2013.

Table 5.46. Change in the Expenses of Reporting Public Charities for 50 Largest Metropolitan Areas, 2003, 2008, and 2013

	Total Expenses ($ millions) Expenses of Organizations			Total Percentage Change	Average Annual Percentage Change		
	2003	2008	2013	2003–13	2003–13	2003–08	2008–13
New York-Newark-Jersey City, NY-NJ-PA	93,607	127,282	162,971	74.1	5.7	6.3	5.1
Los Angeles-Long Beach-Anaheim, CA	32,693	43,491	52,806	61.5	4.9	5.9	4.0
Chicago-Naperville-Elgin, IL-IN-WI	35,835	48,444	57,227	59.7	4.8	6.2	3.4
Dallas-Fort Worth-Arlington, TX	12,453	15,451	21,604	73.5	5.7	4.4	6.9
Houston-The Woodlands-Sugar Land, TX	11,161	14,194	19,042	70.6	5.5	4.9	6.1
Philadelphia-Camden-Wilmington, PA-NJ-DE-MD	30,883	39,896	41,566	34.6	3.0	5.3	0.8
Washington-Arlington-Alexandria, DC-VA-MD-WV	35,841	46,441	58,567	63.4	5.0	5.3	4.7
Miami-Fort Lauderdale-West Palm Beach, FL	9,890	16,114	18,796	90.1	6.6	10.3	3.1
Atlanta-Sandy Springs-Roswell, GA	13,573	20,489	26,410	94.6	6.9	8.6	5.2
Boston-Cambridge-Newton, MA-NH	37,926	61,911	62,046	63.6	5.0	10.3	0.0
San Francisco-Oakland-Hayward, CA	35,686	29,385	35,569	–0.3	0.0	–3.8	3.9
Phoenix-Mesa-Scottsdale, AZ	7,924	12,797	15,862	100.2	7.2	10.1	4.4
Riverside-San Bernardino-Ontario, CA	3,911	5,517	6,352	62.4	5.0	7.1	2.9
Detroit-Warren-Dearborn, MI	17,794	21,092	20,406	14.7	1.4	3.5	–0.7
Seattle-Tacoma-Bellevue, WA	13,605	19,953	28,691	110.9	7.7	8.0	7.5
Minneapolis-St. Paul-Bloomington, MN-WI	13,467	20,600	26,502	96.8	7.0	8.9	5.2
San Diego-Carlsbad, CA	7,567	10,447	13,648	80.4	6.1	6.7	5.5

(continued)

Table 5.46. Change in the Expenses of Reporting Public Charities for 50 Largest Metropolitan Areas, 2003, 2008, and 2013 *(continued)*

	Total Expenses ($ millions) Expenses of Organizations			Total Percentage Change	Average Annual Percentage Change		
	2003	2008	2013	2003–13	2003–13	2003–08	2008–13
Tampa-St. Petersburg-Clearwater, FL	6,791	9,858	11,303	66.5	5.2	7.7	2.8
St. Louis, MO-IL	12,571	19,086	24,968	98.6	7.1	8.7	5.5
Baltimore-Columbia-Towson, MD	14,179	21,812	26,971	90.2	6.6	9.0	4.3
Denver-Aurora-Lakewood, CO	5,637	8,971	15,530	175.5	10.7	9.7	11.6
Pittsburgh, PA	11,716	18,934	21,364	82.3	6.2	10.1	2.4
Charlotte-Concord-Gastonia, NC-SC	2,634	3,646	4,952	88.0	6.5	6.7	6.3
Portland-Vancouver-Hillsboro, OR-WA	16,808	59,648	80,110	376.6	16.9	28.8	6.1
San Antonio-New Braunfels, TX	2,720	3,595	4,408	62.1	4.9	5.7	4.2
Orlando-Kissimmee-Sanford, FL	5,332	8,084	10,012	87.8	6.5	8.7	4.4
Sacramento—Roseville—Arden-Arcade, CA	5,227	6,355	8,078	54.5	4.4	4.0	4.9
Cincinnati, OH-KY-IN	7,433	14,396	13,512	81.8	6.2	14.1	−1.3
Cleveland-Elyria, OH	11,807	16,535	21,608	83.0	6.2	7.0	5.5
Kansas City, MO-KS	5,611	9,085	8,742	55.8	4.5	10.1	−0.8
Las Vegas-Henderson-Paradise, NV	485	929	1,146	136.3	9.0	13.9	4.3
Columbus, OH	8,349	13,159	17,108	104.9	7.4	9.5	5.4
Indianapolis-Carmel-Anderson, IN	6,390	9,824	13,952	118.3	8.1	9.0	7.3

San Jose-Sunnyvale-Santa Clara, CA	7,153	11,228	14,455	102.1	7.3	9.4	5.2
Austin-Round Rock, TX	2,469	3,662	5,475	121.7	8.3	8.2	8.4
Nashville-Davidson—Murfreesboro—Franklin, TN	5,388	7,601	9,586	77.9	5.9	7.1	4.7
Virginia Beach-Norfolk-Newport News, VA-NC	4,816	7,111	9,096	88.9	6.6	8.1	5.0
Providence-Warwick, RI-MA	7,429	9,980	12,214	64.4	5.1	6.1	4.1
Milwaukee-Waukesha-West Allis, WI	8,849	11,587	15,771	78.2	5.9	5.5	6.4
Jacksonville, FL	3,334	5,110	6,604	98.1	7.1	8.9	5.3
Memphis, TN-MS-AR	4,516	5,975	7,831	73.4	5.7	5.8	5.6
Oklahoma City, OK	3,143	3,930	3,922	24.8	2.2	4.6	0.0
Louisville/Jefferson County, KY-IN	4,669	6,945	8,408	80.1	6.1	8.3	3.9
Richmond, VA	2,297	3,395	4,511	96.4	7.0	8.1	5.8
New Orleans-Metairie, LA	4,422	7,539	10,724	142.5	9.3	11.3	7.3
Hartford-West Hartford-East Hartford, CT	5,508	7,989	7,887	43.2	3.7	7.7	–0.3
Raleigh, NC	1,850	2,911	4,044	118.6	8.1	9.5	6.8
Salt Lake City, UT	3,350	4,271	6,356	89.7	6.6	5.0	8.3
Birmingham-Hoover, AL	3,356	3,912	4,656	38.7	3.3	3.1	3.5
Buffalo-Cheektowaga-Niagara Falls, NY	2,922	8,554	6,008	105.6	7.5	24.0	–6.8

Sources: Urban Institute, National Center for Charitable Statistics, Core Files (Public Charities 2003, 2008, 2013); and United States Census Bureau, 2010 Census.

Table 5.47. The 10 Metropolitan Areas with the Highest Growth in Expenses Reported by Public Charities, of 50 Largest Metropolitan Areas, 2003–13

Rank	Metropolitan area	Total expenses for reporting public charities, 2003 ($ millions)	Total expenses for reporting public charities, 2013 ($ millions)	Percentage change, 2003–13	Percentage change, 2003–13 (inflation adjusted)
1	Portland-Vancouver-Hillsboro, OR-WA	16,808	80,110	377	276
2	Denver-Aurora-Lakewood, CO	5,637	15,530	175	118
3	New Orleans-Metairie, LA	4,422	10,724	142	92
4	Las Vegas-Henderson-Paradise, NV	485	1,146	136	87
5	Austin-Round Rock, TX	2,469	5,475	122	75
6	Raleigh, NC	1,850	4,044	119	73
7	Indianapolis-Carmel-Anderson, IN	6,390	13,952	118	72
8	Seattle-Tacoma-Bellevue, WA	13,605	28,691	111	67
9	Buffalo-Cheektowaga-Niagara Falls, NY	2,922	6,008	106	62
10	Columbus, OH	8,349	17,108	105	62

Sources: Urban Institute, National Center for Charitable Statistics, Core Files (Public Charities, 2003, 2013); and United States Census Bureau, 2010 Census.
Note: Total expenses figures are shown in current dollars and are not adjusted for inflation.

Conclusion

Whereas other chapters in this book have discussed the size of the nonprofit sector, this chapter focused on the size and scope of public charities. In 2013, public charities accounted for over two-thirds of all registered nonprofit organizations and over three-quarters of the revenue and expenses of the nonprofit sector in the United States. Many organizations saw slower growth in the years after the recession than in the years before the recession. Overall, however, revenue for reporting public charities grew by 42 percent, expenses grew by 37 percent, and assets increased by 46 percent, after adjusting for inflation, between 2003 and 2013.

Table 5.48. Change in the Assets of Reporting Public Charities for 50 Largest Metropolitan Areas, 2003, 2008, and 2013

	Total Assets ($ millions)			Total Percentage Change	Average Annual Percentage Change		
	2003	2008	2013	2003–13	2003–13	2003–08	2008–13
New York-Newark-Jersey City, NY-NJ-PA	148,073	209,706	267,854	80.9	6.1	7.2	5.0
Los Angeles-Long Beach-Anaheim, CA	56,381	84,560	108,731	92.9	6.8	8.4	5.2
Chicago-Naperville-Elgin, IL-IN-WI	73,225	105,308	132,557	81.0	6.1	7.5	4.7
Dallas-Fort Worth-Arlington, TX	24,363	34,933	54,161	122.3	8.3	7.5	9.2
Houston-The Woodlands-Sugar Land, TX	25,141	39,547	49,682	97.6	7.0	9.5	4.7
Philadelphia-Camden-Wilmington, PA-NJ-DE-MD	54,751	85,351	93,052	70.0	5.4	9.3	1.7
Washington-Arlington-Alexandria, DC-VA-MD-WV	71,757	102,613	130,095	81.3	6.1	7.4	4.9
Miami-Fort Lauderdale-West Palm Beach, FL	14,279	21,059	26,274	84.0	6.3	8.1	4.5
Atlanta-Sandy Springs-Roswell, GA	29,170	48,553	59,726	104.7	7.4	10.7	4.2
Boston-Cambridge-Newton, MA-NH	135,039	199,844	223,091	65.2	5.1	8.2	2.2
San Francisco-Oakland-Hayward, CA	44,100	52,718	68,274	54.8	4.5	3.6	5.3
Phoenix-Mesa-Scottsdale, AZ	13,635	16,920	23,275	70.7	5.5	4.4	6.6
Riverside-San Bernardino-Ontario, CA	4,889	8,892	10,359	111.9	7.8	12.7	3.1
Detroit-Warren-Dearborn, MI	24,556	31,912	30,809	25.5	2.3	5.4	–0.7
Seattle-Tacoma-Bellevue, WA	18,389	29,961	41,890	127.8	8.6	10.3	6.9
Minneapolis-St. Paul-Bloomington, MN-WI	24,052	40,331	47,706	98.3	7.1	10.9	3.4
San Diego-Carlsbad, CA	9,452	15,366	23,305	146.6	9.4	10.2	8.7
Tampa-St. Petersburg-Clearwater, FL	18,061	21,614	29,376	62.7	5.0	3.7	6.3
St. Louis, MO-IL	29,256	41,926	54,590	86.6	6.4	7.5	5.4

(continued)

Table 5.48. Change in the Assets of Reporting Public Charities for 50 Largest Metropolitan Areas, 2003, 2008, and 2013 *(continued)*

	Total Assets ($ millions)			Total Percentage Change	Average Annual Percentage Change		
	2003	2008	2013	2003–13	2003–13	2003–08	2008–13
Baltimore-Columbia-Towson, MD	25,159	39,428	49,264	95.8	7.0	9.4	4.6
Denver-Aurora-Lakewood, CO	10,318	16,054	32,763	217.5	12.2	9.2	15.3
Pittsburgh, PA	20,482	30,305	34,400	68.0	5.3	8.2	2.6
Charlotte-Concord-Gastonia, NC-SC	6,946	8,288	11,502	65.6	5.2	3.6	6.8
Portland-Vancouver-Hillsboro, OR-WA	20,634	46,310	77,777	276.9	14.2	17.5	10.9
San Antonio-New Braunfels, TX	5,559	7,943	11,243	102.3	7.3	7.4	7.2
Orlando-Kissimmee-Sanford, FL	8,641	17,471	23,155	168.0	10.4	15.1	5.8
Sacramento—Roseville—Arden-Arcade, CA	5,566	9,123	14,968	168.9	10.4	10.4	10.4
Cincinnati, OH-KY-IN	18,514	31,342	27,053	46.1	3.9	11.1	–2.9
Cleveland-Elyria, OH	23,121	36,212	46,085	99.3	7.1	9.4	4.9
Kansas City, MO-KS	11,281	17,234	18,249	61.8	4.9	8.8	1.2
Las Vegas-Henderson-Paradise, NV	894	2,010	2,759	208.8	11.9	17.6	6.5
Columbus, OH	11,188	15,842	23,479	109.8	7.7	7.2	8.2
Indianapolis-Carmel-Anderson, IN	12,657	19,869	25,002	97.5	7.0	9.4	4.7
San Jose-Sunnyvale-Santa Clara, CA	22,292	41,291	53,217	138.7	9.1	13.1	5.2

Austin-Round Rock, TX	4,347	7,284	9,884	127.4	8.6	10.9	6.3
Nashville-Davidson—Murfreesboro—Franklin, TN	10,080	14,913	19,139	89.9	6.6	8.1	5.1
Virginia Beach-Norfolk-Newport News, VA-NC	8,344	11,305	14,604	75.0	5.8	6.3	5.3
Providence-Warwick, RI-MA	12,115	18,532	20,871	72.3	5.6	8.9	2.4
Milwaukee-Waukesha-West Allis, WI	13,781	20,158	27,744	101.3	7.2	7.9	6.6
Jacksonville, FL	5,103	7,669	10,865	112.9	7.9	8.5	7.2
Memphis, TN-MS-AR	8,551	12,105	16,607	94.2	6.9	7.2	6.5
Oklahoma City, OK	4,897	7,891	9,379	91.5	6.7	10.0	3.5
Louisville/Jefferson County, KY-IN	7,181	10,534	13,950	94.3	6.9	8.0	5.8
Richmond, VA	6,128	9,196	8,369	36.6	3.2	8.5	–1.9
New Orleans-Metairie, LA	6,508	8,544	12,723	95.5	6.9	5.6	8.3
Hartford-West Hartford-East Hartford, CT	9,492	12,598	14,869	56.6	4.6	5.8	3.4
Raleigh, NC	3,277	4,895	6,628	102.2	7.3	8.4	6.2
Salt Lake City, UT	4,121	6,240	12,183	195.6	11.4	8.6	14.3
Birmingham-Hoover, AL	5,372	6,232	7,603	41.5	3.5	3.0	4.1
Buffalo-Cheektowaga-Niagara Falls, NY	3,816	10,060	8,482	122.3	8.3	21.4	–3.4

Sources: Urban Institute, National Center for Charitable Statistics, Core Files (Public Charities 2003, 2008, 2013); and United States Census Bureau, 2010 Census.

Table 5.49. The 10 Metropolitan Areas with the Highest Growth in Assets Reported by Public Charities, of 50 Largest Metropolitan Areas, 2003–13

Rank	Metropolitan area	Total assets for reporting public charities, 2003 ($ millions)	Total assets for reporting public charities, 2013 ($ millions)	Percentage change, 2003–13	Percentage change, 2003–13 (inflation adjusted)
1	Portland-Vancouver-Hillsboro, OR-WA	20,634	77,777	277	198
2	Denver-Aurora-Lakewood, CO	10,318	32,763	218	151
3	Las Vegas-Henderson-Paradise, NV	894	2,759	209	144
4	Salt Lake City, UT	4,121	12,183	196	133
5	Sacramento—Roseville—Arden-Arcade, CA	5,566	14,968	169	112
6	Orlando-Kissimmee-Sanford, FL	8,641	23,155	168	112
7	San Diego-Carlsbad, CA	9,452	23,305	147	95
8	San Jose-Sunnyvale-Santa Clara, CA	22,292	53,217	139	89
9	Seattle-Tacoma-Bellevue, WA	18,389	41,890	128	80
10	Austin-Round Rock, TX	4,347	9,884	127	80

Sources: Urban Institute, National Center for Charitable Statistics, Core Files (Public Charities, 2003, 2013); and United States Census Bureau, 2010 Census.
Note: Total expenses figures are shown in current dollars and are not adjusted for inflation.

Table 5.50. Change in the Net Assets of Reporting Public Charities for 50 Largest Metropolitan Areas, 2003, 2008, and 2013

	Total Net Assets ($ millions)			Total Percentage Change	Average Annual Percentage Change		
	2003	2008	2013	2003–13	2003–13	2003–08	2008–13
New York-Newark-Jersey City, NY-NJ-PA	86,480	115,951	153,181	77.1	5.9	6.0	5.7
Los Angeles-Long Beach-Anaheim, CA	34,921	52,637	65,804	88.4	6.5	8.6	4.6
Chicago-Naperville-Elgin, IL-IN-WI	46,028	64,515	81,053	76.1	5.8	7.0	4.7
Dallas-Fort Worth-Arlington, TX	14,774	22,527	32,203	118.0	8.1	8.8	7.4
Houston-The Woodlands-Sugar Land, TX	17,151	24,696	33,786	97.0	7.0	7.6	6.5
Philadelphia-Camden-Wilmington, PA-NJ-DE-MD	30,055	46,605	54,005	79.7	6.0	9.2	3.0
Washington-Arlington-Alexandria, DC-VA-MD-WV	48,645	68,322	87,805	80.5	6.1	7.0	5.1
Miami-Fort Lauderdale-West Palm Beach, FL	7,957	11,909	14,668	84.4	6.3	8.4	4.3
Atlanta-Sandy Springs-Roswell, GA	18,341	29,734	35,259	92.2	6.8	10.1	3.5
Boston-Cambridge-Newton, MA-NH	72,431	144,700	148,648	105.2	7.5	14.8	0.5
San Francisco-Oakland-Hayward, CA	18,973	31,506	41,500	118.7	8.1	10.7	5.7
Phoenix-Mesa-Scottsdale, AZ	5,355	9,251	13,165	145.9	9.4	11.6	7.3
Riverside-San Bernardino-Ontario, CA	2,765	4,539	5,621	103.3	7.4	10.4	4.4
Detroit-Warren-Dearborn, MI	12,095	17,313	15,313	26.6	2.4	7.4	–2.4
Seattle-Tacoma-Bellevue, WA	9,738	15,739	23,457	140.9	9.2	10.1	8.3
Minneapolis-St. Paul-Bloomington, MN-WI	12,847	19,471	27,718	115.8	8.0	8.7	7.3
San Diego-Carlsbad, CA	5,784	9,822	14,907	157.7	9.9	11.2	8.7
Tampa-St. Petersburg-Clearwater, FL	13,086	14,255	20,568	57.2	4.6	1.7	7.6
St. Louis, MO-IL	16,808	23,909	29,779	77.2	5.9	7.3	4.5

(continued)

Table 5.50. Change in the Net Assets of Reporting Public Charities for 50 Largest Metropolitan Areas, 2003, 2008, and 2013 *(continued)*

	Total Net Assets ($ millions)			Total Percentage Change	Average Annual Percentage Change		
	2003	2008	2013	2003–13	2003–13	2003–08	2008–13
Baltimore-Columbia-Towson, MD	13,123	18,737	23,228	77.0	5.9	7.4	4.4
Denver-Aurora-Lakewood, CO	6,977	10,656	16,814	141.0	9.2	8.8	9.6
Pittsburgh, PA	10,993	15,996	20,381	85.4	6.4	7.8	5.0
Charlotte-Concord-Gastonia, NC-SC	4,821	5,388	7,843	62.7	5.0	2.3	7.8
Portland-Vancouver-Hillsboro, OR-WA	10,740	19,758	32,832	205.7	11.8	13.0	10.7
San Antonio-New Braunfels, TX	3,671	5,245	7,564	106.0	7.5	7.4	7.6
Orlando-Kissimmee-Sanford, FL	4,277	7,121	9,000	110.4	7.7	10.7	4.8
Sacramento—Roseville—Arden-Arcade, CA	2,177	4,582	8,177	275.6	14.2	16.1	12.3
Cincinnati, OH-KY-IN	9,118	16,061	15,199	66.7	5.2	12.0	–1.1
Cleveland-Elyria, OH	14,024	22,293	27,092	93.2	6.8	9.7	4.0
Kansas City, MO-KS	6,707	11,021	12,287	83.2	6.2	10.4	2.2
Las Vegas-Henderson-Paradise, NV	661	1,247	2,163	227.3	12.6	13.5	11.7
Columbus, OH	7,017	9,763	14,334	104.3	7.4	6.8	8.0
Indianapolis-Carmel-Anderson, IN	8,451	11,137	16,449	94.6	6.9	5.7	8.1
San Jose-Sunnyvale-Santa Clara, CA	15,867	31,998	40,321	154.1	9.8	15.1	4.7

Austin-Round Rock, TX	2,810	4,673	6,491	131.0	8.7	10.7	6.8
Nashville-Davidson—Murfreesboro—Franklin, TN	6,290	9,536	11,343	80.3	6.1	8.7	3.5
Virginia Beach-Norfolk-Newport News, VA-NC	5,511	6,778	9,360	69.8	5.4	4.2	6.7
Providence-Warwick, RI-MA	8,584	13,217	14,580	69.9	5.4	9.0	2.0
Milwaukee-Waukesha-West Allis, WI	7,882	11,355	14,507	84.0	6.3	7.6	5.0
Jacksonville, FL	2,844	4,376	6,250	119.8	8.2	9.0	7.4
Memphis, TN-MS-AR	6,094	8,884	11,688	91.8	6.7	7.8	5.6
Oklahoma City, OK	3,514	6,136	6,880	95.8	7.0	11.8	2.3
Louisville/Jefferson County, KY-IN	4,220	6,122	7,747	83.6	6.3	7.7	4.8
Richmond, VA	4,541	6,673	5,878	29.4	2.6	8.0	–2.5
New Orleans-Metairie, LA	3,984	5,274	7,338	84.2	6.3	5.8	6.8
Hartford-West Hartford-East Hartford, CT	6,177	7,531	9,529	54.3	4.4	4.0	4.8
Raleigh, NC	2,192	3,403	4,685	113.8	7.9	9.2	6.6
Salt Lake City, UT	2,338	2,689	7,268	210.8	12.0	2.8	22.0
Birmingham-Hoover, AL	3,154	3,914	4,590	45.5	3.8	4.4	3.2
Buffalo-Cheektowaga-Niagara Falls, NY	1,922	5,444	4,323	124.9	8.4	23.1	–4.5

Sources: Urban Institute, National Center for Charitable Statistics, Core Files (Public Charities 2003, 2008, 2013); United States Census Bureau, 2010 Census.

Table 5.51. The 10 Metropolitan Areas with the Highest Growth in Net Assets Reported by Public Charities, of 50 Largest Metropolitan Areas, 2003–13

Rank	Metropolitan area	Total net assets for reporting public charities, 2003 ($ millions)	Total net assets for reporting public charities, 2013 ($ millions)	Percentage change, 2003–13	Percentage change, 2003–13 (inflation adjusted)
1	Sacramento—Roseville—Arden-Arcade, CA	2,177	8,177	276	197
2	Las Vegas-Henderson-Paradise, NV	661	2,163	227	159
3	Salt Lake City, UT	2,338	7,268	211	145
4	Portland-Vancouver-Hillsboro, OR-WA	10,740	32,832	206	141
5	San Diego-Carlsbad, CA	5,784	14,907	158	104
6	San Jose-Sunnyvale-Santa Clara, CA	15,867	40,321	154	101
7	Phoenix-Mesa-Scottsdale, AZ	5,355	13,165	146	94
8	Denver-Aurora-Lakewood, CO	6,977	16,814	141	90
9	Seattle-Tacoma-Bellevue, WA	9,738	23,457	141	90
10	Austin-Round Rock, TX	2,810	6,491	131	82

Sources: Urban Institute, National Center for Charitable Statistics, Core Files (Public Charities, 2003, 2013); and United States Census Bureau, 2010 Census.
Note: Total expenses figures are shown in current dollars and are not adjusted for inflation.

Technical Notes

This chapter used two primary datasets: the IRS Business Master Files of Tax-Exempt Organizations, and a special research version of the National Center for Charitable Statistics (NCCS) Core Files that excludes organizations marked as "out of scope" by the author. Below are the descriptions of the datasets, methodology for estimated detailed revenue and expense breakdowns, and a description of the organizational classification system used throughout the chapter.

IRS Business Master Files of Tax-Exempt Organizations, 1998–2015

The IRS Business Master Files (BMF) are cumulative files containing descriptive information on all active tax-exempt organizations. Data contained in the BMF are derived mostly from IRS Forms 1023 and 1024 (the applications for IRS recognition of tax-exempt status). NCCS downloads these files monthly. An organization must apply for recognition with the IRS to be included in the BMF unless it is a religious congregation or has less than $5,000 in annual gross receipts.

Business Master Files were used for information on the number of nonprofits, filers and non-filers, contained in table 5.1. For each year reported, the author used the BMF from the first available month of the next year to ensure that organizations registering in December were included for the yearly counts. For example, for the 2013 total nonprofit number, we used the February 2014 BMF.

NCCS Core Files

The NCCS Core Files are based on the Internal Revenue Service's annual Return Transaction Files (RTF), which contain data on all organizations that were required to file a Form 990 or Form 990-EZ and complied. It is important to note that the IRS does not keypunch financial data for approximately 80,000 organizations that filed a Form 990 but were not required to do so, either because it is a religious congregation or because it received less than $50,000 in annual gross receipts. In addition, NCCS also excludes a small number of other organizations, such as foreign organizations or those that are generally considered part of government. These organizations are deemed out of scope.

The NCCS Core Files (1998–2013) contain a number of key financial variables from Form 990, including contributions, program revenue, total revenue, total expenses, and assets.

Estimates Methodology

Data from the Core Full 990 Files, Core Supplement Files, and the IRS Statistics of Income Samples Files, were used to produce the detailed revenue and expense breakdowns shown in chapter 5. While the NCCS Core Files served as the basis for these tables, these additional variables available in the Core Full 990, Core Supplement, and SOI files allow for more detailed financial analysis than the NCCS Core Files.

Core Full 990

The NCCS Core Full 990 Files are based on information released by the Internal Revenue Service on all organizations filing a Form 990 (but not a 990-EZ or 990-N). These datasets act as companion sets to the corresponding NCCS Core File for the given year. Starting with the 2012 IRS Return Transaction File, the IRS began releasing information for a larger variety of fields on the Form 990, beyond those fields typically covered by the NCCS Core File. The NCCS Core Full 990 Files contain almost 300 fields for over 200,000 organizations, comprising the majority of information available on Forms 990 for the covered organizations for Core File years 2012 and 2013.

Core Supplement

The Core Supplement Files include select Forms 990 and Forms 990-EZ filed by 501(c)(3) organizations. To produce the Core Supplement Files, IRS Form 990s and Form 990-EZs that are received by the IRS are manually entered into a database. Most variables from the forms, schedules, and attachments are keyed by hand, and NCCS checks the financial variables for accuracy. The Core Supplement database contains over 100 variables from the balance sheet, statement of revenue, and functional expenses sections of Form 990. The Core Supplement data include over 340,000 records covering tax years 2006 to 2013.

Statistics of Income

The Statistics of Income (SOI) Division of the IRS annually creates sample files of 501(c) organizations. These files, which are available from IRS and NCCS, have included over 15,000 501(c)(3) filing organizations since 2000. Since 2003, SOI files for 501(c)(3) entities have included all organizations with $50 million or more in total assets ($30 million for years 1997–2002; $10 million for years prior to 1997), plus a random sample of smaller organizations stratified and weighted by asset level. Thus, all organizations with total assets (end-of-year) of more than $50 million (since 2003) or the relevant threshold for prior years are included with a weight of 1. Weights for other organizations are designed to match populations of six other asset classes. The SOI file includes more than 300 financial and programmatic variables from Form 990.

The detailed estimates were created as follows. Data from the Core Full 990 were used when the organization filed a full Form 990 and the information was available. If that data were unavailable, Core Supplement database was used when the fiscal year was the same as the fiscal year in the Core File. Next, data from the Statistics of Income Samples Files were used when the fiscal year was the same as the fiscal year in the Core File. When the fiscal year information was not available, we assumed that the overall distribution of sources of revenue and types of expenses were similar in the prior or following fiscal year and used revenue and expense ratios from the datasets to estimate current figures. For any remaining organizations missing detailed information, estimates were made by comparing total revenue and expenses against average ratios for sources of revenue and types of expenses for similar organizations based on NTEE code and size.

Classification of Organizations

Tables that group organizations into subsectors based on their primary activities use the National Taxonomy of Exempt Entities–Core Codes (NTEE-CC). Both summary and detailed information on this classification system is available on the NCCS web site at www.nccs.urban.org. Also, a complete listing of the NTEE Core Codes used for each subsector breakout is available below.

While the vast majority of organizations are coded with a specific NTEE-CC code, a few organizations are coded as unknown. This code is normally temporary but may be permanent if no detailed information on the organization—a Form 990 with its program descriptions or a web site—is available.

Arts, Culture, and Humanities

Performing Arts Organizations

A60—Performing Arts
A61—Performing Arts Centers
A62—Dance
A63—Ballet
A65—Theater
A68—Music
A69—Symphony Orchestra
A6A—Opera
A6B—Singing and Choral Groups
A6C—Bands and Ensembles
A6E—Performing Arts Schools

Historical Societies and Related Organizations

A80—Historical Societies and Related Historical Activities
A84—Commemorative Events

Museums and Museum Activities

A50—Museums and Museum Activities
A51—Art Museums
A52—Children's Museums
A54—History Museums
A56—Natural History and Natural Science Museums
A57—Science and Technology Museums

Other Arts, Culture, and Humanities

A01—Alliances and Advocacy
A02—Management and Technical Assistance

A03—Professional Societies and Associations
A05—Research Institutes and Public Policy Analysis
A11—Single-Organization Support
A12—Fund Raising and Fund Distribution
A19—Support NEC
A20—Arts and Culture
A23—Cultural and Ethnic Awareness
A25—Arts Education
A26—Arts Councils and Agencies
A30—Media and Communications
A31—Film and Video
A32—Television
A33—Printing and Publishing
A34—Radio
A40—Visual Arts
A70—Humanities
A90—Arts Services
A99—Arts, Culture, and Humanities NEC

Education

Higher Education

B40—Higher Education
B41—Two-Year Colleges
B42—Undergraduate Colleges
B43—Universities
B50—Graduate and Professional Schools

Student Services

B80—Student Services
B82—Scholarships and Student Financial Aid
B83—Student Sororities and Fraternities
B84—Alumni Associations

Elementary and Secondary Education

B20—Elementary and Secondary Schools
B21—Preschools
B24—Primary and Elementary Schools
B25—Secondary and High Schools
B28—Special Education
B29—Charter Schools

Other Education

B01—Alliances and Advocacy
B02—Management and Technical Assistance
B03—Professional Societies and Associations
B05—Research Institutes and Public Policy Analysis
B11—Single-Organization Support
B12—Fundraising and Fund Distribution
B19—Support NEC
B30—Vocational and Technical Schools
B60—Adult Education
B70—Libraries
B90—Educational Support
B92—Remedial Reading and Encouragement
B94—Parent and Teacher Groups
B99—Education NEC

Environment and Animals

Environment

C01—Alliances and Advocacy
C02—Management and Technical Assistance
C03—Professional Societies and Associations
C05—Research Institutes and Public Policy Analysis
C11—Single-Organization Support
C12—Fundraising and Fund Distribution
C19—Support NEC
C20—Pollution Abatement and Control
C27—Recycling
C30—Natural Resources Conservation and Protection
C32—Water Resources, Wetlands Conservation and Management
C34—Land Resources and Conservation
C35—Energy Resources Conservation and Development
C36—Forest Conservation
C40—Botanical, Horticultural, and Landscape Services
C41—Botanical Gardens and Arboreta
C42—Garden Clubs
C50—Environmental Beautification
C60—Environmental Education
C99—Environment NEC

Animals

D01—Alliances and Advocacy
D02—Management and Technical Assistance
D03—Professional Societies and Associations
D05—Research Institutes and Public Policy Analysis
D11—Single-Organization Support

D12—Fundraising and Fund Distribution
D19—Support NEC
D20—Animal Protection and Welfare
D30—Wildlife Preservation and Protection
D31—Protection of Endangered Species
D32—Bird Sanctuaries
D33—Fisheries Resources
D34—Wildlife Sanctuaries
D40—Veterinary Services
D50—Zoos and Aquariums
D60—Animal Services NEC
D61—Animal Training
D99—Animal-Related NEC

Health

Nursing Services
E90—Nursing
E91—Nursing Facilities
E92—Home Health Care

Hospitals and Primary Treatment Facilities
E20—Hospitals
E21—Community Health Systems
E22—General Hospitals
E24—Specialty Hospitals

Outpatient Facilities
E30—Ambulatory and Primary Health Care
E31—Group Health Practices
E32—Community Clinics

Mental Health
F01—Alliances and Advocacy
F02—Management and Technical Assistance
F03—Professional Societies and Associations
F05—Research Institutes and Public Policy Analysis
F11—Single-Organization Support
F12—Fundraising and Fund Distribution
F19—Support NEC
F20—Substance Abuse Dependency, Prevention, and Treatment
F21—Substance Abuse Prevention
F22—Substance Abuse Treatment
F30—Mental Health Treatment
F31—Psychiatric Hospitals
F32—Community Mental Health Centers
F33—Residential Mental Health Treatment
F40—Hotlines and Crisis Intervention
F42—Sexual Assault Services
F50—Addictive Disorders
F52—Smoking Addiction
F53—Eating Disorders
F54—Gambling Addiction
F60—Counseling
F70—Mental Health Disorders
F80—Mental Health Associations
F99—Mental Health NEC

Disease-Specific
G01—Alliances and Advocacy
G02—Management and Technical Assistance
G03—Professional Societies and Associations
G05—Research Institutes and Public Policy Analysis
G11—Single-Organization Support
G12—Fundraising and Fund Distribution
G19—Support NEC
G20—Birth Defects and Genetic Diseases
G25—Down Syndrome
G30—Cancer
G32—Breast Cancer
G40—Diseases of Specific Organs
G41—Eye Diseases, Blindness, and Vision Impairments
G42—Ear and Throat Diseases
G43—Heart and Circulatory System Diseases and Disorders
G44—Kidney Diseases
G45—Lung Diseases
G48—Brain Disorders
G50—Nerve, Muscle, and Bone Diseases
G51—Arthritis
G54—Epilepsy
G60—Allergy-Related Diseases
G61—Asthma
G70—Digestive Diseases and Disorders
G80—Specifically Named Diseases
G81—AIDS
G82—Alzheimer's Disease
G84—Autism
G90—Medical Disciplines
G92—Biomedicine and Bioengineering
G94—Geriatrics
G96—Neurology and Neuroscience
G98—Pediatrics
G9B—Surgical Specialties
G99—Diseases, Disorders, and Medical Disciplines NEC

Medical Research

H01—Alliances and Advocacy
H02—Management and Technical Assistance
H03—Professional Societies and Associations
H05—Research Institutes and Public Policy Analysis
H11—Single-Organization Support
H12—Fundraising and Fund Distribution
H19—Support NEC
H20—Birth Defects and Genetic Diseases Research
H25—Down Syndrome Research
H30—Cancer Research
H32—Breast Cancer Research
H40—Disease-Specific Research
H41—Eye Diseases, Blindness, and Vision Impairments Research
H42—Ear and Throat Diseases Research
H43—Heart and Circulatory System Diseases and Disorders Research
H44—Kidney Diseases Research
H45—Lung Diseases Research
H48—Brain Disorders Research
H50—Nerve, Muscle, and Bone Diseases Research
H51—Arthritis Research
H54—Epilepsy Research
H60—Allergy-Related Diseases Research
H61—Asthma Research
H70—Digestive Diseases and Disorders Research
H80—Specifically Named Diseases Research
H81—AIDS Research
H83—Alzheimer's Disease Research
H84—Autism Research
H90—Medical Discipline Research
H92—Biomedicine and Bioengineering Research
H94—Geriatrics Research
H96—Neurology and Neuroscience Research
H98—Pediatrics Research
H9B—Surgical Specialties Research
H99—Medical Research NEC

Other Health

E01—Alliances and Advocacy
E02—Management and Technical Assistance
E03—Professional Societies and Associations
E05—Research Institutes and Public Policy Analysis
E11—Single-Organization Support
E12—Fundraising and Fund Distribution
E19—Support NEC
E40—Reproductive Health Care
E42—Family Planning
E50—Rehabilitative Care
E60—Health Support
E61—Blood Banks
E62—Emergency Medical Transport
E65—Organ and Tissue Banks
E70—Public Health
E80—Health (General and Financing)
E86—Patient and Family Support
E99—Health Care NEC

Human Services

Crime and Legal-Related

I01—Alliances and Advocacy
I02—Management and Technical Assistance
I03—Professional Societies and Associations
I05—Research Institutes and Public Policy Analysis
I11—Single-Organization Support
I12—Fundraising and Fund Distribution
I19—Support NEC
I20—Crime Prevention
I21—Youth Violence Prevention
I23—Drunk Driving–Related
I30—Correctional Facilities
I31—Halfway Houses for Offenders and Ex-Offenders
I40—Rehabilitation Services for Offenders
I43—Inmate Support
I44—Prison Alternatives
I50—Administration of Justice
I51—Dispute Resolution and Mediation
I60—Law Enforcement
I70—Protection Against Abuse
I71—Spouse Abuse Prevention
I72—Child Abuse Prevention
I73—Sexual Abuse Prevention
I80—Legal Services
I83—Public Interest Law
I99—Crime and Legal-Related NEC

Employment and Job-Related

J01—Alliances and Advocacy
J02—Management and Technical Assistance
J03—Professional Societies and Associations

J05—Research Institutes and Public Policy Analysis
J11—Single-Organization Support
J12—Fundraising and Fund Distribution
J19—Support NEC
J20—Employment Preparation and Procurement
J21—Vocational Counseling
J22—Job Training
J30—Vocational Rehabilitation
J32—Goodwill Industries
J33—Sheltered Employment
J40—Labor Unions
J99—Employment NEC

Food, Agriculture, and Nutrition

K01—Alliances and Advocacy
K02—Management and Technical Assistance
K03—Professional Societies and Associations
K05—Research Institutes and Public Policy Analysis
K11—Single-Organization Support
K12—Fundraising and Fund Distribution
K19—Support NEC
K20—Agricultural Programs
K25—Farmland Preservation
K26—Animal Husbandry
K28—Farm Bureaus and Granges
K30—Food Programs
K31—Food Banks and Pantries
K34—Congregate Meals
K35—Soup Kitchens
K36—Meals on Wheels
K40—Nutrition
K50—Home Economics
K99—Food, Agriculture, and Nutrition NEC

Housing and Shelter

L01—Alliances and Advocacy
L02—Management and Technical Assistance
L03—Professional Societies and Associations
L05—Research Institutes and Public Policy Analysis
L11—Single-Organization Support
L12—Fundraising and Fund Distribution
L19—Support NEC
L20—Housing Development, Construction, and Management
L21—Public Housing
L22—Senior Citizens' Housing and Retirement Communities
L25—Housing Rehabilitation
L30—Housing Search Assistance
L40—Temporary Housing
L41—Homeless Shelters
L50—Homeowners' and Tenants' Associations
L80—Housing Support
L81—Home Improvement and Repairs
L82—Housing Expense Reduction
L99—Housing and Shelter NEC

Public Safety and Disaster Preparedness

M01—Alliances and Advocacy
M02—Management and Technical Assistance
M03—Professional Societies and Associations
M05—Research Institutes and Public Policy Analysis
M11—Single-Organization Support
M12—Fundraising and Fund Distribution
M19—Support NEC
M20—Disaster Preparedness and Relief Services
M23—Search and Rescue Squads
M24—Fire Prevention
M40—Safety Education
M41—First Aid
M42—Automotive Safety
M99—Public Safety, Disaster Preparedness, and Relief NEC

Recreation and Sports

N01—Alliances and Advocacy
N02—Management and Technical Assistance
N03—Professional Societies and Associations
N05—Research Institutes and Public Policy Analysis
N11—Single-Organization Support
N12—Fundraising and Fund Distribution
N19—Support NEC
N20—Camps
N30—Physical Fitness and Community Recreational Facilities
N31—Community Recreational Centers
N32—Parks and Playgrounds
N40—Sports Training Facilities

N50—Recreational Clubs
N52—Fairs
N60—Amateur Sports
N61—Fishing and Hunting
N62—Basketball
N63—Baseball and Softball
N64—Soccer
N65—Football
N66—Racquet Sports
N67—Swimming and Other Water Recreation
N68—Winter Sports
N69—Equestrian
N6A—Golf
N70—Amateur Sports Competitions
N71—Olympics
N72—Special Olympics
N80—Professional Athletic Leagues
N99—Recreation and Sports NEC

Youth Development
O01—Alliances and Advocacy
O02—Management and Technical Assistance
O03—Professional Societies and Associations
O05—Research Institutes and Public Policy Analysis
O11—Single-Organization Support
O12—Fundraising and Fund Distribution
O19—Support NEC
O20—Youth Centers and Clubs
O21—Boys Clubs
O22—Girls Clubs
O23—Boys and Girls Clubs
O30—Adult and Child Matching Programs
O31—Big Brothers and Big Sisters
O40—Scouting
O41—Boy Scouts of America
O42—Girls Scouts of the USA
O43—Camp Fire
O50—Youth Development Programs
O51—Youth Community Service Clubs
O52—Youth Development, Agriculture
O53—Youth Development, Business
O54—Youth Development, Citizenship
O55—Youth Development, Religious Leadership
O99—Youth Development NEC

Children and Youth Services
P30—Children and Youth Services
P31—Adoption
P32—Foster Care
P33—Child Day Care

Family Services
P40—Family Services
P42—Single-Parent Agencies
P43—Family Violence Agencies
P44—In-Home Assistance
P45—Family Services for Adolescent Parents
P46—Family Counseling

Residential and Custodial Care
P70—Residential Care
P73—Group Homes
P74—Hospice
P75—Senior Continuing Care Communities

Services Promoting Independence
P80—Centers to Support the Independence of Specific Populations
P81—Senior Centers
P82—Developmentally Disabled Centers
P84—Ethnic and Immigrant Centers
P85—Homeless Centers
P86—Blind and Visually Impaired Centers
P87—Deaf and Hearing-Impaired Centers

Other Human Services
P01—Alliances and Advocacy
P02—Management and Technical Assistance
P03—Professional Societies and Associations
P05—Research Institutes and Public Policy Analysis
P11—Single-Organization Support
P12—Fundraising and Fund Distribution
P19—Support NEC
P20—Human Services
P21—American Red Cross
P22—Urban League
P24—Salvation Army
P26—Volunteers of America
P27—Young Men's or Women's Associations
P28—Neighborhood Centers
P29—Thrift Shops
P50—Personal Social Services
P51—Financial Counseling
P52—Transportation Assistance

P58—Gift Distribution
P60—Emergency Assistance
P61—Travelers' Aid
P62—Victim's Services
P99—Human Service NEC

International and Foreign Affairs
Q01—Alliances and Advocacy
Q02—Management and Technical Assistance
Q03—Professional Societies and Associations
Q05—Research Institutes and Public Policy Analysis
Q11—Single-Organization Support
Q12—Fundraising and Fund Distribution
Q19—Support NEC
Q20—Promotion of International Understanding
Q21—International Cultural Exchanges
Q22—International Student Exchanges
Q23—International Exchanges
Q30—International Development
Q31—International Agricultural Development
Q32—International Economic Development
Q33—International Relief
Q40—International Peace and Security
Q41—Arms Control and Peace
Q42—United Nations Associations
Q43—National Security
Q70—International Human Rights
Q71—International Migration and Refugee Issues
Q99—International, Foreign Affairs, and National Security NEC

Other

Civil Rights and Advocacy
R01—Alliances and Advocacy
R02—Management and Technical Assistance
R03—Professional Societies and Associations
R05—Research Institutes and Public Policy Analysis
R11—Single-Organization Support
R12—Fundraising and Fund Distribution
R19—Support NEC
R20—Civil Rights
R22—Minority Rights
R23—Disabled Persons' Rights
R24—Women's Rights
R25—Senior's Rights
R26—Lesbian and Gay Rights
R30—Intergroup and Race Relations
R40—Voter Education and Registration
R60—Civil Liberties
R61—Reproductive Rights
R62—Right to Life
R63—Censorship, Freedom of Speech and Press
R67—Right to Die and Euthanasia
R99—Civil Rights, Social Action, and Advocacy NEC

Community Improvement
S01—Alliances and Advocacy
S02—Management and Technical Assistance
S03—Professional Societies and Associations
S05—Research Institutes and Public Policy Analysis
S11—Single-Organization Support
S12—Fundraising and Fund Distribution
S19—Support NEC
S20—Community and Neighborhood Development
S21—Community Coalitions
S22—Neighborhood and Block Associations
S30—Economic Development
S31—Urban and Community Economic Development
S32—Rural Economic Development
S40—Business and Industry
S41—Chambers of Commerce and Business Leagues
S43—Small Business Development
S46—Boards of Trade
S47—Real Estate Associations
S50—Nonprofit Management
S80—Community Service Clubs
S81—Women's Service Clubs
S82—Men's Service Clubs
S99—Community Improvement and Capacity Building NEC

Philanthropy and Voluntarism
T01—Alliances and Advocacy
T02—Management and Technical Assistance
T03—Professional Societies and Associations
T05—Research Institutes and Public Policy Analysis

T11—Single-Organization Support
T12—Fundraising and Fund Distribution
T19—Support NEC
T20—Private Grantmaking Foundations
T21—Corporate Foundations
T22—Private Independent Foundations
T23—Private Operating Foundations
T30—Public Foundations
T31—Community Foundations
T40—Voluntarism Promotion
T50—Philanthropy, Charity, and Voluntarism Promotion
T70—Federated Giving Programs
T90—Named Trusts and Foundations NEC
T99—Philanthropy, Voluntarism, and Grantmaking NEC

Science and Technology

U01—Alliances and Advocacy
U02—Management and Technical Assistance
U03—Professional Societies and Associations
U05—Research Institutes and Public Policy Analysis
U11—Single-Organization Support
U12—Fundraising and Fund Distribution
U19—Support NEC
U20—General Science
U21—Marine Science and Oceanography
U30—Physical and Earth Sciences
U31—Astronomy
U33—Chemistry and Chemical Engineering
U34—Mathematics
U36—Geology
U40—Engineering and Technology Research
U41—Computer Science
U42—Engineering
U50—Biological and Life Sciences
U99—Science and Technology NEC

Social Science

V01—Alliances and Advocacy
V02—Management and Technical Assistance
V03—Professional Societies and Associations
V05—Research Institutes and Public Policy Analysis
V11—Single-Organization Support
V12—Fundraising and Fund Distribution
V19—Support NEC
V20—Social Science
V21—Anthropology and Sociology
V22—Economics
V23—Behavioral Science
V24—Political Science
V25—Population Studies
V26—Law and Jurisprudence
V30—Interdisciplinary Research
V31—Black Studies
V32—Women's Studies
V33—Ethnic Studies
V34—Urban Studies
V35—International Studies
V36—Gerontology
V37—Labor Studies
V99—Social Science NEC

Other Public and Societal Benefit

W01—Alliances and Advocacy
W02—Management and Technical Assistance
W03—Professional Societies and Associations
W05—Research Institutes and Public Policy Analysis
W11—Single-Organization Support
W12—Fundraising and Fund Distribution
W19—Support NEC
W20—Government and Public Administration
W22—Public Finance, Taxation, and Monetary Policy
W24—Citizen Participation
W30—Military and Veterans' Organizations
W40—Public Transportation Systems
W50—Telecommunications
W60—Financial Institutions
W61—Credit Unions
W70—Leadership Development
W80—Public Utilities
W90—Consumer Protection
W99—Public and Societal Benefit NEC

Religion-Related

X01—Alliances and Advocacy
X02—Management and Technical Assistance

X03—Professional Societies and Associations
X05—Research Institutes and Public Policy Analysis
X11—Single-Organization Support
X12—Fundraising and Fund Distribution
X19—Support NEC
X20—Christian
X21—Protestant
X22—Roman Catholic
X30—Jewish
X40—Buddhist
X70—Hindu
X80—Religious Media and Communications
X81—Religious Film and Video
X82—Religious Television
X83—Religious Printing and Publishing
X84—Religious Radio
X90—Interfaith Coalitions
X99—Religion-Related NEC
Z99—Unknown

NEC = not elsewhere classified

Glossary

Some definitions have been taken from other publications, including the "Glossary of Philanthropic Terms" in Council on Foundations, *Corporate Philanthropy: Philosophy, Management, Trends, Future, Background* (Washington, DC: Council on Foundations, 1982); U.S. Census Bureau, *Statistical Abstract of the United States* (Washington, DC: U.S. Government Printing Office, 1985); and U.S. Census Bureau, *Social Indicators III* (Washington, DC: U.S. Government Printing Office, various years). We have revised many definitions from these publications to reflect their specific relationship to the non-profit (or independent) sector. Other definitions of particular terms used to describe the functions of activities of this sector, such as *assigned value for volunteer time,* have been written by the author.

Adjusted gross income (AGI). Total income as defined by the tax code, less statutory adjustments (primarily business, investment, or certain other deductions, such as payments to a Keogh retirement plan or an individual retirement account).

Assets. An organization's financial holdings, such as property or resources, cash, accounts receivable, equipment, and so on, and balances against liabilities.

Assigned value for volunteer time. The total number of hours formally volunteered to organizations in a year, multiplied by the average hourly wage for nonagricultural workers for that year.

Average. A single number of values often used to represent the typical value of a group of numbers. It is regarded as a measure of the "location" or "central tendency" of a group of numbers. The *arithmetic mean* is the type of average used most frequently. It is derived by totaling the values of individual items in a particular group and dividing that total by the number of items. The arithmetic mean is often referred to as simply the "mean" or "average." The *median* of a group of numbers is the number or value that falls in the middle of a group when each item in the group is ranked according to size (from lowest to highest or vice versa); the median generally has the same number of items above it as below it. If there is an even number of items in the group, the median is the average of the two middle items.

Average annual percentage change. A figure computed by using a compound interest formula. This formula assumes that the rate of change is constant throughout a specified compounding period (one year for average annual rates of change). The formula is similar to the one used to compute the balance of a savings account that earns compound interest. According to this formula, at the end of a compounding period, the amount of accrued change (for example, employment or bank interest) is added to the amount that existed at the beginning of one period. As a result, over time (for example, with each year or quarter), the same rate of change is applied to an ever larger figure.

Charitable contribution. A gift to a charitable cause that is allowed by the IRS as a deduction from taxable income. Both individual taxpayers and corporations can deduct contributions for charitable causes from their taxable incomes.

Community foundation. A public charity supported by combined funds contributed by individuals, foundations, nonprofit institutions, and corporations. A community foundation's giving is limited almost exclusively to a specific locale, such as a city, a county or counties, or a state.

Constant-dollar estimate. A computation that removes the effects of price changes from a statistical series reported in dollar terms. Constant-dollar series are derived by dividing current-dollar estimates by appropriate price indexes, such as the consumer price index, or by the various implicit price deflators for gross national product. The result is a series as it would presumably exist if prices remained the same throughout the period as they were in the base year—in other words, if the dollar had constant purchasing power. Changes in such a series would reflect only changes in the real (physical) volume of output. *See also* **Current dollars** *and* **Gross national product (GNP).**

Consumption expenditure. Expenditures for goods and services purchased by individuals; operating expenses of nonprofit institutions; the value of food, fuel, clothing, and rental of dwellings; financial services received in kind by individuals; and net purchases of used goods. All private purchases of dwellings are classified as gross private domestic investment. Per capita personal consumption expenditures are total personal consumption expenditures divided by the appropriate population base. Per capita components of personal consumption expenditures are derived in the same way. *See also* **Per capita.**

Contributions deduction. Taxpayers can deduct from their taxable income contributions made to certain religious, charitable, educational, scientific, or literary 501(c)(3) organizations. These could be in the form of cash, property, or out-of-pocket expenses incurred while performing volunteer work.

Corporate contribution. A general term referring to charitable contributions by a corporation. The term usually describes cash contributions only but may also include other items, such as the value of loaned executives, products, and services.

Corporate foundation. A private philanthropic organization set up and funded by a corporation. A corporate foundation is governed by a board that may include members of the corporation board and contributions committee, other staff members, and representatives of the community.

Corporate social responsibility program. A philanthropic program operated within a corporation. The program may be managed through a department of its own or through a community affairs (or similar) department.

Current dollars. The dollar amount that reflects the value of the dollar at the time of its use. *See also* **Constant-dollar estimate.**

Current operating expenditures. All expenses included in the Statement of Revenue, Expenses, and Changes in Net Assets on Form 990, except grants and allocations, specific assistance to individuals, and benefits paid to or for members. Among current operating expenditures are such components as wages and salaries, fringe benefits, supplies, communication charges, professional fees, and depreciation and depletion charges. *See also* **Form 990** *and* **Total expenses.**

Earnings. All cash income of $1 or more from wages and salaries and net cash income of $1 or more from farm and nonfarm self-employment.

Employment. See **Labor force.**

Endowment. Stocks, bonds, property, and funds given permanently to nonprofit entities, primarily to foundations, hospitals, or schools, so nonprofit entities may produce their own income for grantmaking or operating purposes.

Form 990. The annual tax return that tax-exempt organizations with gross revenues of more than $50,000 must file with the IRS. The Form 990 is also required by many state charity offices. This tax return includes information about the organization's assets, income, operating expenses, contributions, paid staff and salaries, names and addresses of persons to contact, and program areas. *See also* **Form 990-PF** *and* **Form 990-N.**

Form 990-N. The annual informational return that tax-exempt organizations with gross revenues of less than $50,000 must file with the IRS. The Form 990-N is also known as the e-postcard and contains basic information about an organization, such as name, address, and officer names.

Form 990-PF. The annual information return that must be filed with the IRS by private foundations and nonexempt charitable trusts that are treated as private foundations by the IRS. This form replaced Form 990-AR circa 1981.

Foundation. A nongovernmental nonprofit organization with funds and a program managed by its own trustees and directors, established to further social, educational, religious, or charitable activities by making grants. A private foundation receives its funds from, and is subject to control by, an individual, family, corporation, or other group consisting of a limited number of members. In contrast, a community foundation receives its funds from multiple public sources and is classified by the IRS as a public charity. *See also* **Community foundation** *and* **Public charity.**

Full-time employment. Full-time workers are those who usually work 35 hours or more in a given week, regardless of the number of hours worked in the reference week.

Full-time-equivalent volunteer. A figure derived from an estimation procedure used to transform total hours formally volunteered to an organization into a figure equivalent to the value of full-time paid employment. The total annual volunteer hours are divided by 1,700 (which is a reasonable approximation of actual hours worked by a full-time worker during a year).

Gross national product (GNP). GNP is the total national output of final goods and services valued at market prices. *See also* **National income.**

In-kind contribution. See **Noncash (in-kind) contribution.**

Independent sector. The portion of the economy that includes all 501(c)(3) and 501(c)(4) tax-exempt organizations as defined by the IRS, including all religious institutions (such as churches and synagogues) and all persons who give time and money to serve charitable purposes. The independent sector is also referred to as the voluntary sector, the nonprofit sector, and the third sector. *See also* **Section 501(c)(3)** *and* **Section 501(c)(4).**

Labor force. The civilian labor force is the sum of employed and unemployed civilian workers. The total labor force is the sum of the civilian labor force and the armed forces. "Employed" persons are all people age 16 and older in the civilian noninstitutional population who, during the reference week, worked at all (as paid employees, in their own business or profession, or on their own farm) or who worked 15 hours or more as unpaid workers in an enterprise operated by a family member. For purposes of this profile, the full-time-equivalent employment of volunteers has been added to the traditional definition of the labor force. Also included are workers who were not working but who had jobs or businesses from which they were temporarily absent because of illness, vacation, bad weather, labor-management dispute, or personal reasons, whether or not they were paid for the time off or were seeking other jobs. Each employed person is counted only once. Workers holding more than one job are counted in the job at which they worked the most hours during the reference week. *See also* **Full-time-equivalent volunteer.**

National income. The earnings of the private sector plus compensation (wages, salaries, and fringe benefits) earned by government employees during a specified period.

Earnings are recorded in the forms in which they are received, and they include taxes on those earnings. Earnings in the private sector consist of compensation of employees, profits of corporate and incorporated enterprises, net interest, and rental income of persons. National income is a component of gross national product and is less than gross national product, mainly because it does not include capital consumption (depreciation) allowances and indirect business taxes. *See also* **Gross national product (GNP).**

National Taxonomy of Exempt Entities–Core Codes (NTEE-CC). A classification system for tax-exempt nonprofit organizations, consisting of 26 major groups under 10 broad categories. (See the NCCS web site, http://nccs.urban.org/, for further details.)

Noncash (in-kind) contribution. An individual or corporate contribution of goods or commodities as distinguished from cash. Noncash contributions from individuals can include such items as clothing, works of art, food, furniture, and appliances. Noncash contributions from corporations may also take various forms, such as donation of used office furniture or equipment, office space, or the professional services of employees. Although noncash contributions from individuals are tax deductible, noncash contributions from corporations generally are not. *See also* **Corporate contribution.**

Nonprofit. A term describing the IRS designation of an organization whose income is not used for the benefit or private gain of stockholders, directors, or any other persons with an interest in the company. A nonprofit organization's income is used to support its operations. Such organizations are defined under section 501(c) of the Internal Revenue Code. Nonprofit organizations that are included in the definition of the independent sector are nonprofit, tax-exempt organizations that are included in sections 501(c)(3) and 501(c)(4) of the code. *See also* **Section 501(c)(3)** *and* **Section 501(c)(4).**

Nonprofit institutions serving households (NPISH). The nonprofit sector as defined by the Bureau of Economic Analysis. This definition includes tax-exempt organizations providing services in religion and welfare, medical care, education and research, recreation, and personal business, such as labor unions, legal aid, and professional associations. The category excludes nonprofits—such as chambers of commerce, trade associations, and homeowners' associations—that serve businesses rather than households; it also excludes nonprofits that sell goods and services in the same way as for-profit businesses, such as tax-exempt cooperatives, credit unions, mutual financial institutions, and tax-exempt manufacturers, such as university presses.

North American Industry Classification System (NAICS). NAICS was the system used by the 1997 Economic Census. Earlier censuses had used the SIC system. Although many individual NAICS industries correspond directly to industries in the SIC system, most higher-level groupings do not. As such, data comparison between the two systems should be done carefully. *See also* **Standard Industrial Classification (SIC).**

Operating foundation. A private foundation that devotes most of its earnings and assets directly to the conduct of its tax-exempt purposes (for example, operating a museum or home for the elderly) rather than making grants to other organizations for these purposes.

Operating organization. An operating organization engages in various activities, such as producing information or delivering services and products to its members and the public, in contrast to other entities that function as sources of financial support by raising funds and delivering them. Examples of operating organizations are museums, colleges, universities, and social services agencies.

Out-of-scope organization. An organization identified as either foreign in origin or a governmental or supporting government entity (such as a public or state college); it has been excluded from the IRS file of tax-exempt organizations for purposes of the *Almanac.*

Outlay. How a nonprofit organization uses its funds: whether it spends them, gives them away, or invests them.

Part-time employment. Part-time workers usually work less than 35 hours a week (at all jobs), regardless of the number of hours worked in the reference week.

Per capita. A per capita figure represents an average computed for every person in a specific group (or "population"). It is derived by taking the total of an item (such as income, taxes, or retail sales) and dividing it by the number of people in the specified population.

Personal income. Income received by persons from all sources. Personal income is the sum (less personal contributions for social insurance) of wage and salary disbursements, other labor income, proprietors' income, rental income, dividends, personal interest income, and transfer payments. Per capita personal income is total personal income divided by the appropriate population base. *See also* **Per capita.**

Pretax income. A corporation's annual income before it has paid taxes. The IRS allows corporations to deduct up to 10 percent of their taxable income as contributions to charitable organizations and to carry forward such contributions in excess of 10 percent over a five-year period. Corporations do not usually release information on their taxable income, however, and data collected by groups such as the Conference Board are based on income before calculation of income taxes. Taxable income and income before taxes may be similar or very different, depending on the industry and the corporation's tax structure.

Public charity. The largest category of 501(c)(3) organizations, which serve broad purposes, including assisting the poor and the underprivileged; advancing religion, education, health, science, art, and culture; and protecting the environment, among others. A public charity that is identified by the IRS as "not a private foundation" [as defined in section 509(a) of the Internal Revenue Code] normally receives a substantial part of its income, directly or indirectly, from the general public or from government sources, which a private foundation does not. The public support must be fairly broad and not limited to a few individuals or families. Only public charities and religious organizations can receive tax-deductible contributions.

Reporting public charity. Public charities that report to the IRS on Form 990. Charities that do not have to file Forms 990 are religious organizations and congregations and charities with less than $50,000 in annual gross receipts.

Section 501(c)(3). The Internal Revenue Code section that defines tax-exempt organizations organized and operated exclusively for religious, charitable, scientific, literary, educational, or similar purposes. Contributions to 501(c)(3) organizations are deductible as charitable donations for federal income tax purposes.

Section 501(c)(4). The Internal Revenue Code section that defines tax-exempt organizations organized to operate as civic leagues, social welfare organizations, and local associations of employees. These organizations are included in the independent sector.

Standard Industrial Classification (SIC). The classification system and definition of industries in accordance with the composition of the economy. Although this classification is designed to cover all economic activity in the United States, government statistical collections emanating from this classification system do not distinguish between private nonprofit organizations and private for-profit organizations. This system was replaced by the NAICS starting in 1999.

Support organization. Support organizations collect funds and distribute them primarily to operating organizations. Support organizations usually do not operate service delivery programs. Examples include federated fundraising organizations such as United Way or Catholic Charities. *See also* **Operating organization.**

Tax exempt. A classification granted by the IRS to qualified nonprofit organizations that frees them from the requirement to pay taxes on their income. Private foundations, including endowed company foundations, are tax exempt; however, they must pay a 1 or 2 percent excise tax on net investment income. All 501(c)(3) and 501(c)(4) organizations are tax exempt.

Total expenses. All current operating expenditures plus grants and allocations, specific assistance to individuals, benefits paid to or for members, and payments to affiliates. *See also* **Current operating expenditures.**

Transfer payments. Funds transferred from nonprofit institutions serving households to households. *See also* **Nonprofit institutions serving households (NPISH).**

Transfer receipts. Funds that nonprofit institutions serving households receive from private and public sources, such as donations and grants. *See also* **Nonprofit institutions serving households (NPISH).**

Volunteer. A person who gives time to help others for no monetary pay. *Formal volunteering* is defined as giving a specified amount of time to organizations such as hospitals, churches, or schools. *Informal volunteering* is ad hoc and involves helping organizations as well as individuals, including neighbors, family, and friends.

Index

Tables and figures are referred to by "*t*" and "*f*" after the page number.

CPSIA information can be obtained at www.ICGtesting.com
Printed in the USA
BVOW04s1447041016

464055BV00004B/7/P

9 781442 275935